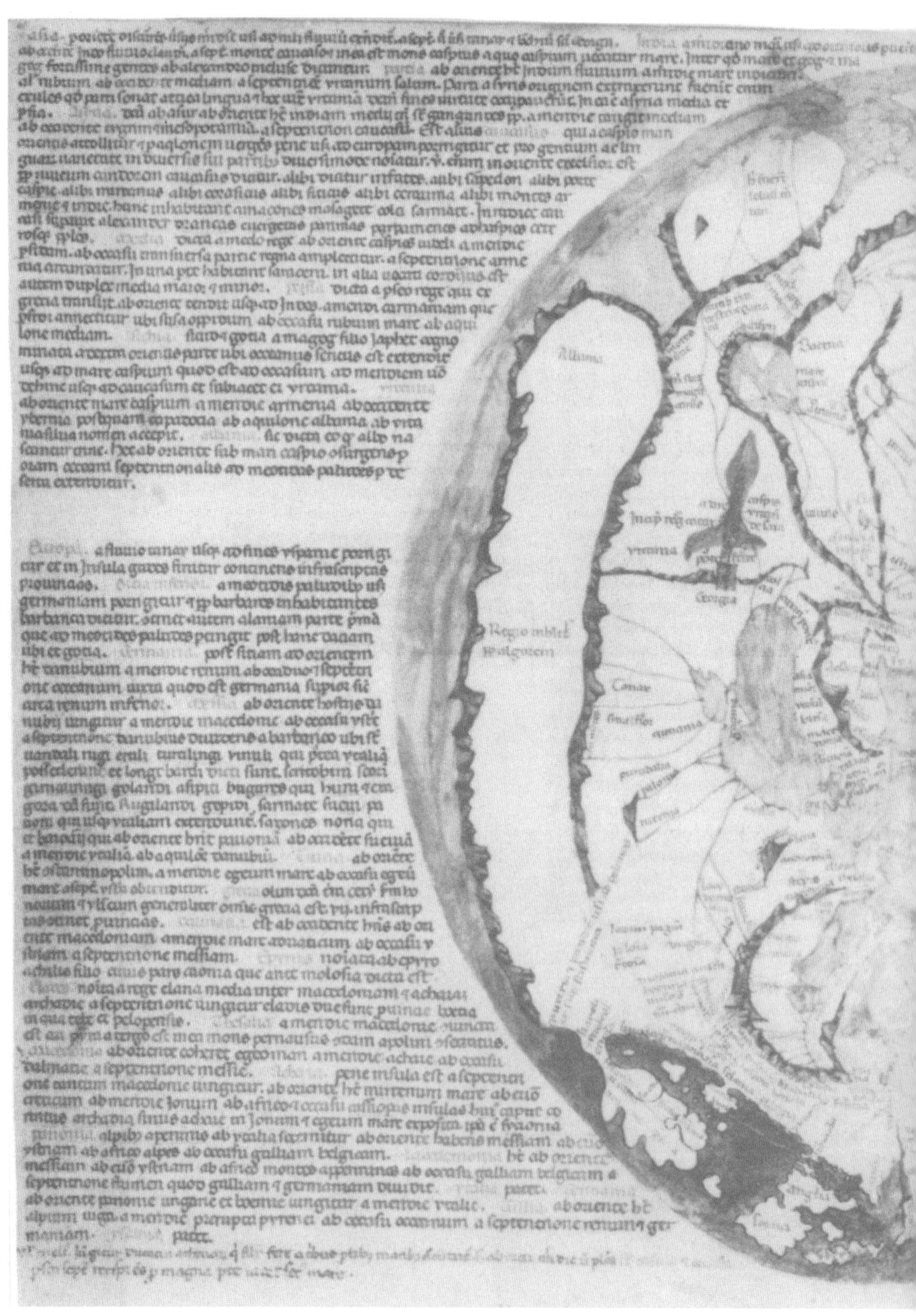

A twelfth-century world map with a detailed description: as was usual, Europe is at the foot, and Jerusalem in the centre.

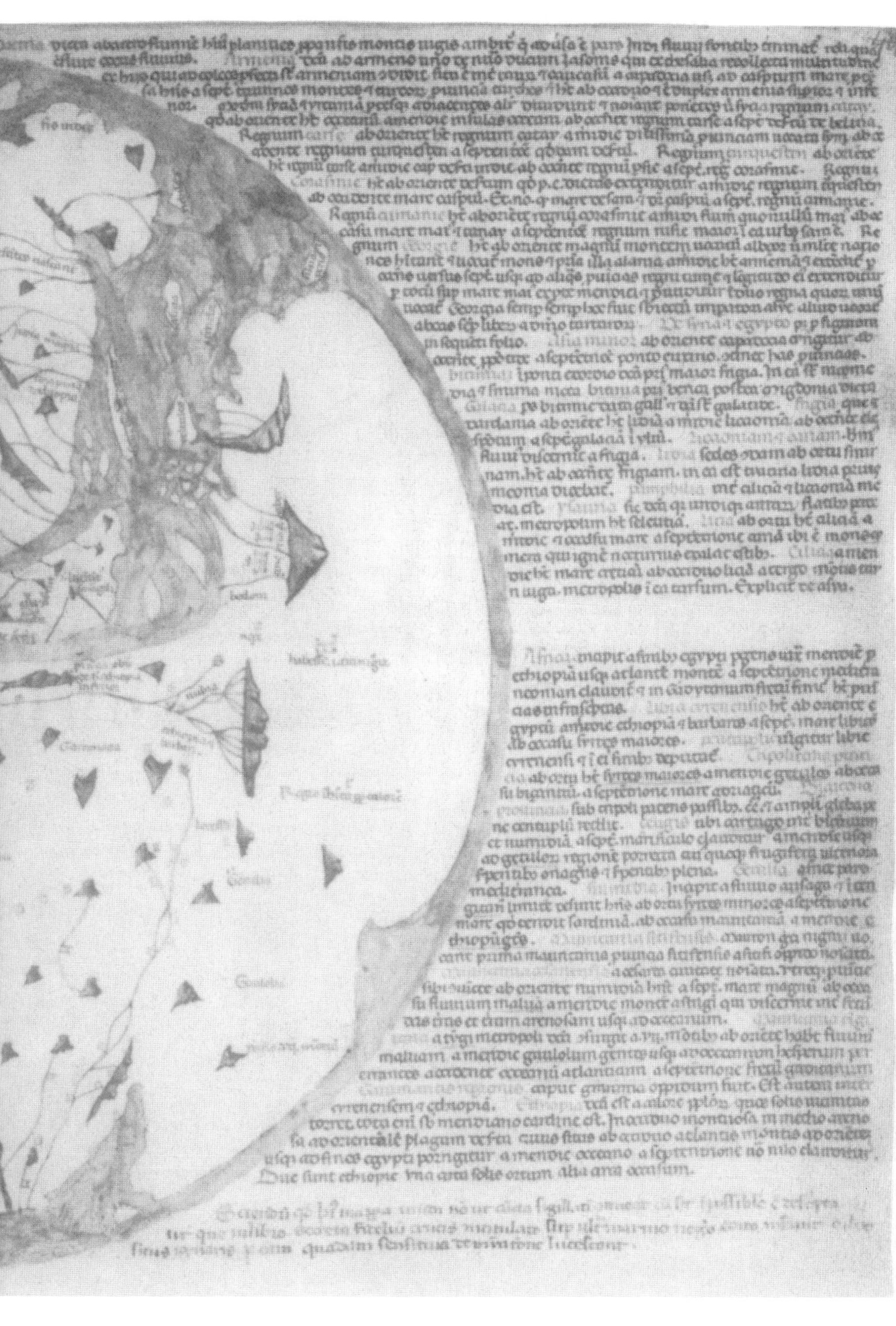

THE MEDIEVAL TRAVELLER

Frontispiece: A thirteenth-century travelling carriage. (Zentralbibliothek, Zurich, MS Rheinan 15 f. 54r)

THE MEDIEVAL TRAVELLER

NORBERT OHLER

translated by
CAROLINE HILLIER

THE BOYDELL PRESS

Translated from Norbert Ohler, *Reisen im Mittelalter*
First published in 1986 by Artemis Verlag

English translation first published 1989
The Boydell Press, Woodbridge
Reprinted in hardback 1995, 1998
Reprinted in paperback 1995, 1996, 2000
New edition 2010

ISBN 978 1 84383 507 3

The Boydell Press is an imprint of Boydell & Brewer Ltd
PO Box 9, Woodbridge, Suffolk IP12 3DF, UK
and of Boydell & Brewer Inc.
668 Mt Hope Avenue, Rochester, NY 14620, USA
website: www.boydellandbrewer.com

A CIP catalogue record for this book is available
from the British Library

Papers used by Boydell & Brewer Ltd are natural, recyclable products
made from wood grown in sustainable forests

Printed in Great Britain by
CPI Antony Rowe, Chippenham and Eastbourne

CONTENTS

FOREWORD

This book is intended for the general reader who would like to know what travel was really like in the past, and who has perhaps wondered if the 'mobility' of our own time is quite as unique as has sometimes been suggested. My aim has been to show not only the means by which people travelled, but also to examine how they saw foreign customs and people, how being abroad affected them and how they reacted. Travel and travellers are therefore not shown in isolation, but in the context of the broader historical framework.

I have taken pains to make the picture as vivid and authentic as possible. Much of the source material is included only indirectly; conclusions are often based on source references which could not be individually included or listed. Where possible, I have sought to link the material to the known facts; flashbacks to antiquity and glances forward to the present day seemed appropriate, since the traditional limits of the Middle Ages do not correspond with specific turning-points in the history of travel.

The book is divided into two parts. The first part deals with what the traveller had to contend with and take into consideration before undertaking his journey. This first section is set out as a cross-section of history, under subject-related matter; here a certain arbitrariness in the choice of sources was unavoidable. In the second part, which falls into a more chronological order, I have given an account of well documented journeys and travellers. The two parts are less strictly divided than might appear from the format: even in the first part I have frequently given in to the temptation to let the sources speak for themselves in telling their story, rather than dwelling on abstract ideas; this I hope also leads to greater readability.

The focal point of the book geographically is the West, although Byzantium, the Far East, the West Indies and the Islamic world are also included. A historical focal point is provided by the Frankish kingdom, because it was there that firm foundations for the future of Europe were laid.

I have not set out to shape the material into a treatise or a textbook; the content of the second part follows individual sources, and many points are mentioned at one time or another before being discussed (where possible) in their wider context. Sources are frequently quoted in the text, without being extensively examined in depth. The intention was to give the reader a clearer insight, not to limit the discussion within narrow confines.

Freiburg i.B., 1986 — Norbert Ohler

INTRODUCTION

'More overworked than they, scourged more severely, more often imprisoned, many a time face to face with death. Five times the Jews have given me the thirty-nine strokes; three times I have been beaten with rods; once I was stoned; three times I have been shipwrecked, and for twenty-four hours I was adrift on the open sea. I have been constantly on the road; I have met dangers from rivers, dangers from robbers, dangers from my fellow-countrymen, dangers from foreigners, dangers in towns, dangers in the country, dangers at sea, dangers from false friends. I have toiled and drudged, I have often gone without sleep; hungry and thirsty, I have often gone fasting; and I have suffered from cold and exposure.'

Paul, the people's apostle, travelled more than most of his contemporaries; yet what he underwent during his many years spreading the gospel, and so graphically describes (2. Corinthians II), was known to more people in medieval times than today. True, all the troubles he experienced both from men and nature, were less likely in general to rain down upon a single traveller, but many had even worse things to contend with on their way.

Accounts such as that of St Paul meant that those who wanted or needed to make a journey were under no illusions. Those who did not know the facts could learn them from people who had been abroad. Nevertheless, in spite of – or in many cases perhaps precisely because of – this, millions of people were on the road: pilgrims and messengers, churchmen and students, wanderers and vagabonds, beggars and the sick, merchants, kings and popes – not to mention the Germanic peoples during the barbarian invasions, Huns, Arabs, Avars and Normans, Hungarians and Mongols. Consciously or unconsciously, individuals, groups or peoples spread ideas and techniques, goods and diseases; with the result that Europe became more than a geographical location, growing into a cohesive whole with a community of shared interests which have lasted until the present day and which differentiate it from other cultural regions.

What does the word 'travel' encompass? 'Travel . . . [orig. the same word as TRAVAIL . . .] . . . To make a journey; to go from one place to another; to journey M.E. . . . To journey through . . . Traveller late M.E. . . . One who is travelling from place to place, or along a road or path; . . . a wayfarer; . . . One who travels abroad; one who journeys or has journeyed through foreign countries or strange places . . . .'

If we consider other languages, French has *voyager*, German *reisen* and *wandern*. The derivation of these words points to the nature of travel in earlier times. *Voyager*, like our 'journey' has a Latin root: *viaticum* describes that which was needed on the way (Lat. *via*); 'journey' goes back to the Latin *diurnum* – the space one could cover in a day. 'Travel' is derived from the French *travail*: toil, labour; the German *reisen* from the Old High German *rīsan*: to get up, rise, rise up in warfare. The words show all too clearly that (as the German *Brockhaus Encyclopedia* neatly puts it) until the eighteenth century travel was 'hard, expensive and dangerous'.

In early times the words travel and journey were used for a day's labour or travail, for a military campaign or knightly errand. In such instances there was clearly one thing noticeably absent: freedom of choice. We too have to travel on business, but we more often think of 'travel' as being associated with pleasant things such as holidays or excursions. If it is a question of a tiresome journey, we usually talk about having to 'go' there; during the war soldiers 'went' to the front, they didn't 'travel' there. Travel, for many centuries, certainly meant leaving a safe homeland, and setting out on a long and possibly hazardous journey abroad. It is no coincidence that the words and music of so many songs tell of the pain of parting and the uncertainty of a safe return.

By Middle Ages we mean here the time from about AD 500 to 1500, a thousand years of western European history, with glimpses into the world beyond. The dates correspond to a generally accepted definition of the period. The first date represents what was in fact a centuries-long process, the dissolution of the Roman Empire, the barbarian invasions and the resulting foundation of the Germanic empire in the place of Imperial Rome, and finally the expansion of Islam, which radically altered the Mediterranean world. The second date marks the time when the mighty powers of Europe were reaching out to conquer the world.

Medieval people were at the mercy of nature in a way which we can hardly imagine today. They travelled for the most part on foot, only a few having access to a mount; covered vehicles, such as those which had been known in the ancient world, were occasionally used in Byzantium; in the later Middle Ages they were again used in Europe, but initially only for women, children, the old and sick – and criminals.

More significant than natural dangers, to which people were also exposed at home, was the basic experience of going abroad. Most communities saw the world as being strictly divided into two camps: 'we' are here, out there are 'the others': Greeks – barbarians; Russians – Nemjetzki (strangers, literally: stutterers); Roman citizens (*civis Romanus*) – aliens (*peregrinus*, a foreigner who comes from outside the Roman state); Arabs – non-Arabs; the circumcised – the uncircumcised; Christians – heathens; Moslems – unbelievers; Germans – non-Germans, and so on. It was painfully borne in on the traveller that he was no longer among 'his' people but 'the others', and so had possibly no right to be alive, or to go in peace or receive help in an emergency. So he sought like-minded companions or 'brothers' on his way, who spoke the same language as himself, or spent the night with hosts who had come from his own homeland and settled in the foreign country.

As the lone traveller had little protection from all the natural or man-made dangers to which he was exposed, he joined up with others in a group. Even robbers and pirates formed their own bands to break any resistance they encountered in making off with their booty. Merchants and pilgrims formed temporary confederations or associations, to cope with any hazards they might encounter when stopping for the night or paying tolls, at inns or at ferries.

The traveller who set out on a journey of several months, following a barely known, let alone mapped, route day after day, through forests, across streams and rushing torrents, along narrow tracks which might be bombarded by boulders or avalanches, who was hounded by men, wild beasts and the weather, without any hope of a welcoming table or warm bed at night, had in general no eyes for the beauties of nature and saw it as a hostile force: heat and cold, floods, mist and snow, drought and pestilence, storms and calms at sea, had to be braved. If he wanted to survive, he had to learn to scent danger instinctively – to avoid enemies and natural hazards, or face up to them. This feeling of threat is vividly conjured up by tales which include descriptions of storm and shipwreck, and by fairy-tales and legends, in which fearsome animals such as wolves, bears or lions are only occasionally shown to be friendly or helpful to humans, as in the legend of St Jerome.

Although travel often brought with it quite unbelievable hardship, people had journeyed forth since the earliest times. In their quest for a means of existence they had colonised ever more distant tracts of land; as groups or tribes they often infiltrated unoccupied territory unnoticed by those who might have chronicled their existence. The wish to survive or hopes of a better life had forced them to leave their previous home – just as millions of people left their homeland to set out for the New World in the nineteenth and twentieth centuries. They took all the known disadvantages of the journey into account, but hoped to find better long-term conditions for survival elsewhere. Others set out for some far-off land in the hope of finding riches, health or adventure, but with the intention of returning home again later. Then there were those who had always roamed abroad, singly or in bands: nomads, who moved with their tribes and flocks following the seasonal vegetation, and wandering shepherds who left their families in spring, to herd their flocks up into the high mountain pastures, returning home in the autumn with the first snows. There were those who wandered ceaselessly abroad to expiate a crime, stopping only for one night in any one place; others who fled from an avenger; or who wanted to follow the teaching of the evangelists in spreading the word abroad; they willingly gave up their homes for Jesus, and chose of their own free will a life – in a foreign land – of suffering, uncertainty and hardship. For travellers such as these life on earth could truly be seen as a pilgrimage towards the eternal home.

Whether setting out of his own free will to seek for sustenance or driven to do so, a traveller dared not lose his way in an unfriendly world. If he wanted to survive he had to study the territory he went through with the utmost care: where were the drinking places? where was food for man and beast to be found?

If he did not want to be forced to take a longer, and possibly equally difficult route, he had to have the right information as to how to find his way through woods and over mountains, and about fords, ferries and bridges; he must not lose his bearings even when sun or pole star were hidden by cloud or mist – a danger which was likely to prove even more fatal at sea than on land. Anything which was relevant, or might prove to be relevant to his journey, had to be noted as carefully as possible, for instance wind and cloud formations which would enable him to judge correctly what the weather would be like. As there is often no sun in the northern latitudes for days at a time, bearings had to be taken by other means: from prevailing winds, the moss and lichen on trees, and when at sea from birds and fish, whose appearance would give an indication that land was near. . . .

And yet, even if the traveller took every possible precaution, his journey still lasted an interminable time; at every step he made, thirty or forty thousand times a day, he was burdened by the weight of his own body, for weeks or months on end; shoes and clothing were often inadequate, and offered little protection or comfort in his daily struggle, if he was already weakened by poverty and hunger, disease and vermin – as were the majority of the population. Frustration at taking so long to reach one's journey's end is reflected in fairy-tales and romances. The concept of 'seven league boots' first appears in European literature at the end of the seventeenth century (in Perrault's fairy-tale), but the desire to cover the ground more quickly is very much older, as can be seen from *The Thousand and One Nights*, which was collected from the eighth to sixteenth centuries, or from the Faust saga. In the *History of Doctor Johann Faustus* printed in 1587, three goodly knights want to get from Wittenberg to Munich in half an hour, to be present at 'the wedding of the Prince of Bavaria's son'; normally it would have taken ten to twenty days to cover this distance. Another example of this desire to overcome the limitations of travel is reflected in a medieval romance: Alexander rises up into the air, and plunges down into the depths of the sea. At the end of the Middle Ages Leonardo da Vinci gave concrete shape to such visions, his powerful imagination pointing the way to the construction of the hot-air balloon in the eighteenth century and the development of submarines in the nineteenth.

The longing for quicker and safer means of transport must have been all the more keenly felt in the Middle Ages, because the speed of travel had become slower than in earlier centuries. In the first century BC Cicero, in Rome, received four letters from Britain; three took 27 days, one 34 days – although at that date there were neither extensive Roman roads nor a perfected courier system in Gaul. It would take 29 days 1,200 years later to get an urgent despatch from Rome to Canterbury, although in the normal way it would take seven weeks. Suetonius tells us that Caesar often travelled faster than the news of his coming. Such achievements, like the quality of the Roman roads themselves, remained unrivalled in Europe until a much later date.

So was Europe in the Middle Ages in decline? Certainly as far as communi-

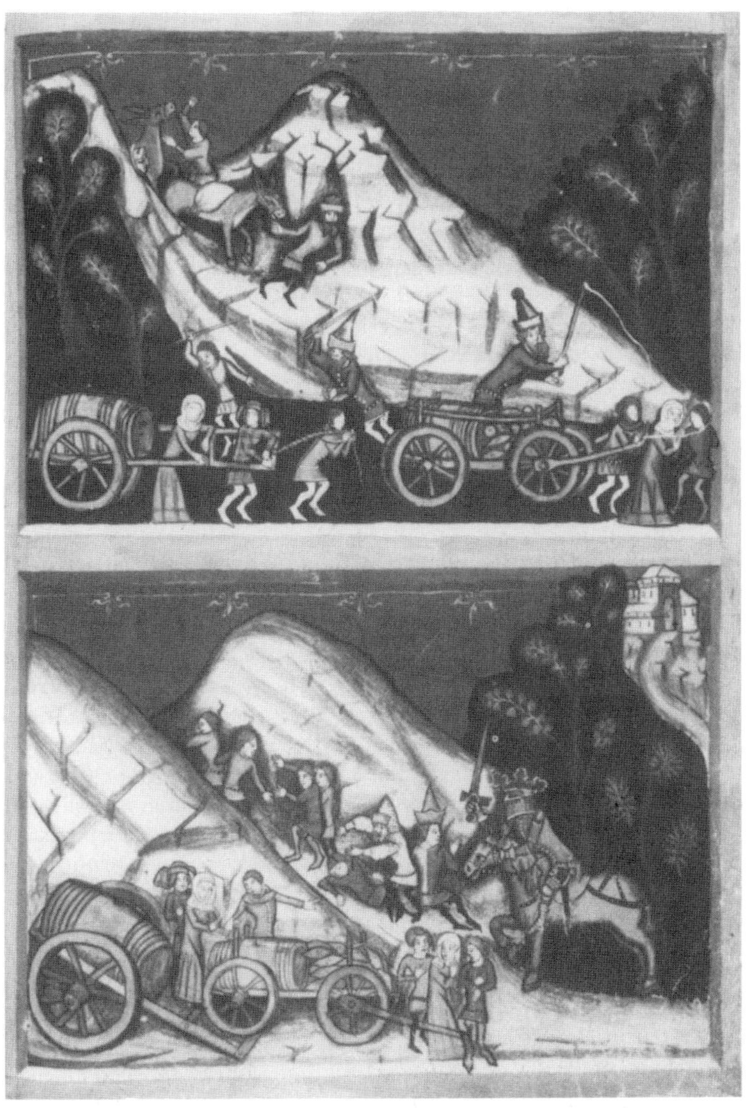

The dangers of travel. The knight William of Orange frees Christian merchants who have fallen into the hands of heathen robbers.

cations were concerned. The new regional and local rulers had none of the financial resources of the ancient empires; they were not interested in maintaining structures in good repair, let alone building new roads, bridges and tunnels. It is indicative that the great Roman constructions such as aqueducts were called 'Devil's bridges': since it was thought impossible for men to have built them, the Devil must have put them up overnight.

But the picture was not entirely black. During the Middle Ages settlers landed in Iceland, Greenland and at times even parts of North America, and explorers reached China and India. The second key date marks an even greater change. The overseas expansion by European powers which changed the face of the world became possible because ocean-going ships were built, nautical instruments invented (or adopted from other countries), crews were better instructed and capital was raised, which enabled adventurous individuals backed by enterprising rulers or trading companies to venture where none had dared to go before. But it would give a false impression of history to say that the discovery of America in 1492 was due only to spectacular advances in maritime skills. Such an outcome was only possible because developments in the fields of technology, law, commerce and society had combined to achieve an impetus which pushed back the frontiers of civilisation. Advances – and improvements in travelling conditions – were furthered by fresh discoveries, and setbacks overcome in their turn.

How do we know about the journeys people made? The Middle Ages have bequeathed us an immense number of sources in which one or more aspects of travel are mentioned – mostly in passing. Life histories, chronicles, financial accounts, liturgical matter, documents, acts, customs records, notes on the building of bridges and hospitals, complaints about innkeepers, descriptions of royal progresses . . . Such accounts are of immeasurable value, but have their drawbacks, because of the style they are written in and also because of the prejudices and interests of authors schooled in a literary tradition, so that they are not always representative. For centuries such matter was written in the manner of educated people, who used Latin words for things which closely resembled similar objects of Greek and Roman times. To quote one example: *reda* in classical Latin denotes a luxurious, four-wheeled vehicle; in the Middle Ages *reda* was a word often used north of the Alps to describe a single-axled cart, or a litter. Since one thing – the four-wheeled vehicle – was missing, another was substituted in its place; and one travelled relatively comfortably in both the luxurious *reda* and in a litter. Were statements made in Toulouse in the twelfth century also correct for Speyer in the thirteenth? Narrative sources give a far more subjective picture than documents: it is not always clear whether something is an actual description or a biased or idealised view. And many authors show little interest in just those things which we would particularly like to know. The Life of Bishop Benno of Osnabrück for instance, when describing the adventures and deprivations he suffered on a journey to Rome at the time of the disputes over investiture, says: 'If we were to describe this and other things which he did at that time in detail, our account would certainly be more lengthy than it was profitable.'

Many authors were even less interested in 'detail'. What may seem revolutionary to the historian looking back – for example the invention of stirrups, which made riding a horse more comfortable, or the development of carts with a movable fore-axle – obviously went unnoticed by the chroniclers, or they thought the matter unworthy of mention.

Written sources are complemented by miniatures on illuminated medieval manuscripts, and by seals, coins and sculpture. But pictorial images have their own drawbacks: is the artist trying to portray a ship, or a team of horses harnessed in the manner of the time? Or is he perhaps only interested in portraying the conventionally accepted symbol? A ship must be shown in such and such a manner . . . There were in the visual arts, as in written works, certain generally accepted ways of depicting certain things (for example a saint, an evil man or a pleasant place), often differing from age to age or from region to region, and according to who had commissioned the work. Medieval manuscripts, paintings and seals are finite in number (although now and then a codex is discovered in a library or archive, or a painting which has been painted over is revealed); and damage, fire and careless handling have all caused irreparable losses.

In contrast to the relatively small and dwindling stock of written sources, the number and quality of archaeological finds has grown immeasurably over the past few decades. Thanks to new methods of recovering and interpreting material, we have gained an insight into areas on which the written sources barely touch, and have a better idea of what everyday travel was like in the past. Marine archaeology has given us useful information about the appearance, size, cargoes, and technical construction of antique and medieval ships. Yet here, too, there are difficulties in interpreting the finds: was the Osberg ship, recovered in 1903, a ceremonial ship not in everyday use, or was it typical of hundreds of others? It is often even more difficult to interpret the finds where grave goods are concerned: is a chariot or ship a votive offering, a child's toy or a realistic model of something in everyday use? And if a toy has certain characteristics, one then has to ask whether it was used to teach something new? Were games and toys used in the Middle Ages and ancient world too as aids to learning and innovation?

The perishable nature of much of the material also makes archaeological interpretation more difficult. Many things which were of importance to travellers were made of materials which could be easily destroyed or burnt: bridges, houses, carts and ships were made of wood, and sometimes the fortifications along a route; clothing, maps, shoes, trappings and harness for mounts or dray animals were made of fabric and leather, and wore out in use or rotted, were burnt or lost in floods or at sea. Many fragments which are found during excavations must be interpreted, and that often means enlarged upon. Whether the experts agree in their interpretations, is another matter.

PART I
BACKGROUND AND CONDITIONS

LOCALITY AND CLIMATE

The geographical setting

Europe is richly endowed with islands and peninsulas, mountains, plains, rivers and lakes. But the map does not show that vast forests covered the lower mountain slopes until well into the Middle Ages, making them impassible, that marshy land made travelling on level ground difficult, or that until the nineteenth century river valleys were often waterlogged and therefore unsuitable for traffic. And yet compared with other continents, Europe is fortunate. More than a third of the landmass consists of peninsulas and islands; in Asia and North America the proportion is only a quarter. So the average distance from the sea is not far, less than in any other continent except the Antarctic. In Europe the average distance from the coast is only 212 miles, in Asia 469 miles, in Africa 419 miles. That is a great advantage, because until comparatively recent times it was possible to travel faster, and more comfortably, by sea than on land; the position did not radically alter until the coming of the railways, and the introduction of motor-cars and planes in the last hundred and fifty years.

Europe's many peninsulas and islands provided a challenge to the early traveller. People learnt to be at home on the water, and built boats in order to colonise islands and cultivate the land, or tap their mineral wealth. As these islands were often visible from the coast, there was less risk involved; many of them – such as Mont St Michel, the famous monastery and place of pilgrimage off Normandy – could even be reached on foot at low tide. England can be seen from Calais, Sicily from southern Italy, Cyprus from Syria – a tempting sight for daring or desperate men. There are countless islands in the Aegean between Greece and Asia Minor, and in the Baltic between Jutland and southern Sweden, ideally situated for 'island hopping'. Experience gained from sailing in relative safety on inland or coastal waters could then be called upon when venturing on longer voyages – not usually from choice however, but – as the Icelandic Sagas show – when driven by storms far out to sea towards a distant, often uninhabited country. This is possibly what happened to men from Ireland, who probably landed in Iceland in the early Middle Ages; Iceland could also have been reached from Norway: the distance from the west of that country to the Shetland Islands, from there to the Faroes and from the Faroes to Iceland is 250 miles in each case. Active volcanoes were also immensely useful to seafarers because they provided natural beacons. Stromboli – 3,038 feet high today – was the great lighthouse of the Mediterranean and could be seen at night from more than 62 miles away, providing an excellent landmark in the south-east of the Tyrrhenian Sea, in the triangle between Sicily and Calabria. But islands – so helpful to the traveller – were also useful to pirates, providing endless hiding places. The countless islands in the Ionian Sea were infested by pirates until the nineteenth century, and in the Middle Ages they swarmed over the islands of the Baltic and North Seas.

Tides and currents

Tides and currents were among the natural features which could help the traveller. The difference between high and low tide varies from about two to three metres in the Bight of Heligoland (more near river mouths and narrows), to about six metres in the English Channel. Systematically used, the tide can help the seafarer in two ways: at high tide the tide-water reaches a considerable, and very useful, speed, for example 6 miles an hour near St Malo in Brittany. And smaller differences in the tide can also be useful, as they were in the provisioning of Ravenna – which at that time lay on the Adriatic – during the Gothic war. Ships with deep draughts could sail farther inland at high tide. In medieval times, sailors dropped anchor in any suitable place, and could simply unload their cargo at low tide, without having to pay heavy port dues. The advantage of being able to reach ports lying well inland at high tide naturally did not apply where there is little difference in the tides. In some areas, such as the Baltic, ports were accessible at every time of day.

Ocean currents, thirty to eighty miles wide, flow with more or less constant speeds in any one place; out in the open the currents run at anything from 8 inches to 10 feet a second, in narrows considerably faster. A rate of 6½ feet a second means a good hundred miles a day – without any additional help from oars or sails. The vast reaches of the Pacific were crossed in primitive times with the help of currents and prevailing winds.

However attractive land on the other side of the water might seem, currents could be treacherous to those who did not know their strength, or who ignored it. It was not only the Scylla and Charybdis of the Odyssey which were feared, which were probably in the two-mile-wide Straits of Messina, and filled sailors with dread until well into the eighteenth century, because the surface current there reaches a rate of 1 knot (1 sea mile or 1.152 miles an hour) and is increased by the tide. The dangerous tides in the Strait of Dover were notorious (21 miles wide); and in the Mediterranean area currents could prove fatal to many ships sailing through the Straits of Gibraltar (9 miles wide) or through the Bosporus and Dardanelles (0.44 and 0.8 miles wide respectively). As more water evaporates in the Mediterranean than flows into it, it 'sucks in' water from the Black Sea and Atlantic (despite the deeper counter-current in the Straits of Gibraltar).

Currents all too easily drive ships out of their planned course; in the past this led to the discovery of new lands. Cabral sailed to Pernambuco in South

America in 1500, on his voyage to India, because his ship was driven off course to the west by the Equatorial current.

Climate

Europe is in the temperate climatic zone, which stretches from the Tropic of Cancer to the Arctic Circle, or roughly from the Canary Islands in the south to Iceland in the north. The sea provides warmth, ensuring hot summers, mild winters and moderate changes in temperature throughout the year. Regular rainfall allows a variety of plants and animals to flourish, and guarantees relatively stable harvests, providing good sustenance for its inhabitants compared with other continents. Rain benefited the early traveller because he could sail down rivers nearly all year round, and more importantly had no need to take a heavy load of drinking water for himself and his mount with him. Changing winds favoured travel by river and sea. Yet throughout history the movement of men, goods and ideas has been hindered but not prevented by less favourable climates, as can be seen by looking beyond the temperate climatic zone. Travel was possible in east and north-east Europe, where winters were colder, and in North Africa, where temperatures were higher and rainfall lower, and even in the dry and barren wastes of the Sahara, where the moisture from rain evaporates. Over the centuries men and animals adapted to their surroundings: Arabs were as much at home in the desert as many western Europeans on the ocean. There are many indications too, that in around the year 1000 the long voyages of the Vikings and their settlement of Iceland and Greenland were favoured by a warmer climate than that of today.

The traveller in Europe also had the advantage of having fewer natural hazards to contend with than in many other areas of the world. Pack-ice is melted by the Gulf Stream, so that ships can sail freely from Norway to Iceland. There are few major earthquakes, and consequently few devastating tidal waves caused by tremors beneath the sea; there are no tropical tornadoes, such as those which rampage across south and south-east Asia, or across the North American continent, wreaking havoc by land and sea. As a rule floods in Europe cause less damage to men, beasts and vehicles than in India or China; because of the rainfall pattern there are none of the droughts that afflict vast tracts of land elsewhere; and plagues of locusts were not in general as devastating to crops as in the Mediterranean region. Europe is free from the sleeping sickness carried by tsetse flies and so debilitating to man; and people seemed fairly well immunised to malaria – carried by the Anopheles mosquito and also present north of the Alps – in the areas where it was most prevalent. However travellers going south – such as the Emperor Henry VII – were afflicted by it in their thousands. The favourable climate much impressed travellers from abroad. In the year 1480 Laonikos Chalkokondyles wrote in his history, concerning Germany: 'Neither are there diseases which are known to arise from foul air, and which are prevalent in the East, where many succumb to them, nor do they fall prey to the other sicknesses which visit us in summer and autumn. Therefore many people are spared. Nor are there earthquakes worthy of mention.'

The seasons

SPRING

Whan that Aprille with his shoures sote
The droghte of Marche hath perced to the rote,
And bathed every veyne in swich licour,
Of which vertu engendred is the flour;
Whan Zephirus eek with his swete breeth
Inspired hath in every holt and heeth
The tendre croppes, and the yonge sonne
Hath in the Ram his halfe cours y-ronne,
And smale fowles maken melodye,
That slepen al the night with open yë,
(So priketh hem nature in hir corages):
Than longen folk to goon on pilgrimages
(And palmers for to seken straunge strondes)
To ferne halwes, couthe in sondry londes;

Chaucer, writing at the end of the fourteenth century, describes in the Prologue to his *Canterbury Tales*, feelings which were common to merchants, soldiers, messengers and other travellers all over Europe. In spring it was time to set out on the road again, after the winter's rest. The days were longer and warmer, the snow had melted in the fields and there was plenty of fodder for their horses.

Spring comes even earlier in the south than in the north; apple blossom flowers from about the tenth to nineteenth April in the Upper Rhine district, but not until a month later in Denmark. The Frankish army was summoned to a 'March Field', while it consisted mostly of footsoldiers; but from 755 the order went out to muster at a 'May Field': many sections of the army were mounted by then and could only make the long journey to the place of summons when there was adequate food for their horses. The twice-yearly synods of the Church were held in the fourth week after Easter and in the middle of October, when the churchmen could be more certain of finding enough fodder for their mounts on the way to the meeting-place.

In early spring roads which were still sodden for much of the time made the going difficult: men, beasts and carts sank deep in the mire. Only the brave ventured forth; enterprising merchants stood to gain much if they could set out on the road while lazier or more cautious rivals remained at home, fearing

A pilgrimage shrine: illumination for the month of April from a fifteenth-century book of hours commissioned by Anne duchess of Brittany.

frost, floods and that there would be insufficient food for themselves and their mounts. They could be first in the field, eagerly awaited by their clients. People who had been cut off from the world for months on end by snow and ice, were keen to see their wares and ready to pay higher prices than later in the year, when there would be more on offer.

But now travelling conditions improved almost daily. The sun, mounting higher in the sky and shining for longer, dried out the roads and made the lower mountain passes accessible again; melting river-ice and snow from the higher ground filled the rivers, which once more became navigable. Dependable spring winds were used by the Vikings, who from about 800 sailed from Norway to England each year, on the prevailing east to north-east wind; in the autumn, with the prevailing westerlies, they sailed home again.

Late spring or early summer were the favourite times for festivals. Every year from at least 1311 the solemn procession of the 'Bucintoro' and the symbolic marriage of the Doge with the sea were held on Ascension Day in Venice. In Germany major festivals were usually held at Pentecost. Great feasts were held in Cologne or Mainz by Otto the Great in 965, by Henry II in 1007, and by Frederick Barbarossa in 1184. At this time of year it was also possible to camp out overnight comfortably in temporary canvas 'cities'. The weather could be counted on, although a storm occasionally brought the festivities to an untimely end, as happened in Mainz in 1184.

SUMMER

Summer was the best time to travel. The days are longer; in central Europe the traveller has six more hours at his disposal than in winter. A variety of foodstuffs could be bought relatively cheaply in markets. Nights could be spent in the open in summer or autumn, if nothing better was available. Many passes in the Alps or Pyrenees, which in spring were even more treacherous than in winter because of avalanches, could now be crossed.

In summer the Althing, or parliament, met in Iceland, sitting for two weeks every year in the south-west of the island; many settlers took a fortnight or more to get there on horseback. In southern regions travel could now become a torture. The Islamic traveller Ibn Battuta, of whom we will hear more later, notes that in southern Russia in the mid-fourteenth century people avoided the mid-day heat and travelled for preference in the morning or evening. And in summer there were more malaria-bearing mosquitoes. There were more deaths among Germans travelling to Italy than were caused by feuding, assaults or warfare.

The summer winds over the Mediterranean, and Atlantic and Indian Oceans, also favoured the traveller. Hot air rises over the Aegean and Crete, and cold air flows down from the north; the resulting etesian winds from the north-west and north reach Force 6–7 (46–56 feet per second), usually dropping in the evening.

It was such a wind which drove Odysseus, in the Odyssey, for nine days and nights from the Island of Kythera south of the Peloponnes to Jerba in Tunisia. The same wind later enabled ships to sail from Rome to Alexandria, to fetch grain for the capital, and later still allowed pilgrims to sail to Jerusalem, and the crusaders to set out from Marseilles, Genoa, Pisa or Venice; in September or October the return journey could be made with the help of the sirocco, the hot wind from the Sahara which often blows for a month. In July ships took only a few weeks to sail from the north coast of Africa to India, using the south-east trade-wind which had been known and used since at least the first century AD; in January they returned by the same route with the north-east monsoon. At the end of the Middle Ages, Atlantic seafarers also made use of the north-east trade-wind in July to speed their return to Europe from America.

Seafarers not only made use of the strong winds such as the etesian, monsoon and trade-winds, but also used the wind-currents caused by air rising when it has been heated by day over the land, so that in the early evening the sea breezes blow towards the shore. Ships on the Tiber set sail then for Rome, to save the oxen (pulling the boats by long tow-ropes) or crew.

However, the traveller counting on favourable winds had to be prepared for the unexpected. Even today, despite all our knowledge and a careful study of wide-ranging weather forecasts, mountaineers and yachtsmen are often overtaken by a sudden change in the weather. The early traveller had of necessity to beware of such dangers.

AUTUMN

Autumn brought other advantages for the traveller on land. The days were still long, and the weather often warm enough to sleep in the open; roads were dry; the summer sun had melted the snow in the high mountain passes. As many people were out in the fields cutting the corn or gathering in the grape-harvest, and shepherds were still herding their flocks, there was much greater safety on the roads. It was natural for example, for the general chapter of the Cistercians to meet every year in September.

Thanks to the harvest, produce dropped in price. If necessary, travellers could subsist for a while on wild berries and greenstuff, and could collect nuts and beech kernels for their journey; these were highly prized as travel-rations, being nourishing (weight by weight hazelnuts contain almost as many calories as butter!), and as we know today, rich in vitamins and trace elements.

The advantages of travelling in autumn were often outweighed by disadvantages however: enemy armies might choose just that time to sally forth in search of provender or to lay waste the harvest, in order to outwit their opponents.

Pilgrims returning from Compostela in September; they carry a staff and scrip; one has a typical pilgrim hat with upturned brim, while several are barefoot, and another has an ear-trumpet. Five of them wear strings of cockleshell. From the Hours of Anne of Brittany.

By November, at the very latest, there would be rain and possibly frost. Roads became miry, without being frozen hard. Well-to-do travellers who were still far from their destination, looked around for winter quarters. But on occasion journeys had to be made in spite of bad weather or even sickness. According to Gregory of Tours, in the sixth century Childebert King of the Franks ordered the bishops in his kingdom to go to Verdun in the middle of November, to sit in judgement on one of their number who was accused of high treason; 'It was raining very hard at the time, and it was so wet that it was bitterly cold and the roads were deep in mud and the rivers broke their banks; but they had to obey the royal command.' When in 1025 a bishop pleaded illness as a reason for not obeying a summons to attend a meeting, he was told that he should have himself carried in his bed to the meeting-place.

In the Mediterranean the equinoctial and winter storms were greatly feared. From the middle of September to 10 November it was considered dangerous to be at sea, and from then until 10 March impossible; those who wanted to avoid undue risks set sail between 26 May and 14 September. Under the circumstances it is clear why in 800 Charlemagne only dismissed a legation from Jerusalem in the spring. At this time of year even urgent news could be held up for months by the weather. Even in the sixteenth century Philip II of Spain took his time over diplomatic correspondence. What was the point in hurrying when his couriers would not find a ship at Valencia or Barcelona which would dare set sail during the winter storms, and would be unable to get across the Pyrenees and Alps for months?

In winter it was more dangerous to be at sea on the Mediterranean than on the North Sea or Atlantic. Where the water-depth is only twenty-five fathoms, as between the Netherlands and England, a very large sea is unable to build up; the Mediterranean, on the other hand, is over 1500 fathoms deep between the Balearic Isles and Sardinia, and, given the same wind-speed, the sea will be proportionally higher when compared with shallow water areas. Voyages were undertaken on the North Sea until Martinmas (11 November) and then once more from the 2nd (on the Baltic Sea 22nd) February. It must be stressed that even so voyages were occasionally undertaken on the Mediterranean in winter, especially towards the end of the Middle Ages.

There were therefore several reasons why people rarely travelled by sea at this time of year. The winter storms placed men and ships' cargoes at risk; and people who had to travel could usually do so more quickly on land than by sea, because they could not count on favourable winds, as the missionary, Willibald, later Bishop of Eichstätt, found in 726 when he took more than three months to get from Tyre to Constantinople, and Henry VII, in 1312, when he took 19 days (from 16 February to 6 March) to get the short distance from Genoa to Pisa.

Ships had to be overhauled and made wind and weatherproof, which could best be done in winter in the home port, with cheaper labour and lower costs. There was also the drawback in winter that in rough seas it was difficult to get from ship to shore, quite apart from the fact that with the lower temperatures and squalls at this time of year it was out of the question to spend nights in the open, even on the Mediterranean.

In the North Sea and particularly the Baltic, winter often comes – literally – overnight; the Grettisaga shows all too clearly what that meant to the traveller. Seafaring came to a halt when the bays and estuaries in which ports generally lie, were frozen over. Low temperatures, sluggish tides and lower salt content contribute to the formation of ice. On average all seas contain 35 p.p.m. salt, the North Sea and Baltic 30 and 8 respectively, the Gulf of Bothnia (between Sweden and Finland) only 1 p.p.m. As a result some seas freeze over in winter, the Gulf of Finland and Gulf of Bothnia for five months on average; even today narrow shipping-lanes can only be kept open by ice-breakers.

In western Europe travel also came to an end in late autumn because men and horses could be fatally chilled by wading through rivers. Sources show that the exception proved the rule. The account of the life of the tenth-century Bishop Ulrich of Augsburg tells of a miracle, and miracles cannot be counted on. One day Bishop Ulrich and his mount had to cross a tributary of the Lech. Because the river was so full none of his companions except a certain Herewig dared to go by the ford, which was directly in their path, and all looked for a better place by which to cross. Ulrich however rode fearlessly through the water. 'As it was winter, he wore thick felt shoes against the cold. When they had crossed the river, Herewig, although he was on a larger horse than the bishop, was drenched to the waist. But when he looked at the bishop's clothes to see if they were also wet, he couldn't see a single damp hair even on his shoes.' Asked about the miracle, Ulrich told his companions that during his – Ulrich's – lifetime they must not 'tell anyone what you have seen'.

Many settlements were cut off from the outside world in winter, because wheeled vehicles became bogged down in the mud and slushy snow. In western Europe clothing and equipment were usually quite unsuitable for travel at this time of year. In addition most people were undernourished; if they were not padded out with fat they quickly began to suffer from the cold and from chilblains, which itched so much that they were unable to sleep at night.

If need be, merchants and soldiers proved inventive and adaptable. The Annals of Fulda note a terrible winter for fruit and crops in the year 860. Even the Ionian Sea was covered with a thick layer of ice; merchants loaded their wares on to horses and carts and managed to get to Venice. About fifty years later, during an uprising, soldiers camped in tents and hurriedly built huts in spite of the winter cold, in order to secure a strategically important mountain.

But if some things made certain forms of travel impossible in winter, those who were able to take advantage of them by equipping themselves with suitable clothes and gear could benefit. The farther rivers and seas in Europe are from the Gulf Stream, the longer they are frozen: the Rhine for days or weeks, the Vistula at Warsaw for about two months, the Neva at Leningrad and the Volga at Kazan for almost five months, as long as the Gulfs of Finland and Bothnia. There were advantages and disadvantages for travellers: they could not sail upriver or across the sea, but inland waters, rivers and marshes were no longer insuperable barriers. The Romanised Celts and Germanic tribes found this in the winter of 406 during the barbarian invasions, when they fled before the Vandals who had stormed across the frozen Rhine. The same thing happened about 500 years later to the Slavs, who were secure in their fortress of Brennabor until Henry I took advantage of the situation: the low-lying ground had been waterlogged and offered ideal protection in summer but in the winter of 928–9 it was covered with a thick sheet of ice. The Saxon army advanced unhindered and took the fortress. The Kattegat, and in 1323 the Baltic, were repeatedly frozen, so that it was possible to get to Sweden from Denmark or Germany.

Frost dried out the roads which in autumn had been muddy, and ice would bear even heavy vehicles. Large parts of Europe lie under snow in winter; the going is more even and conditions ideal for some means of transport; even heavy loads such as wood and timber could be transported. The inhabitants of north and eastern Europe, like those of the dry desert regions, were acclimatised to the weather, and took advantage of frost and snow, developing many useful implements: skis and snowshoes (at least from the tenth century in Scandinavia), skates (with blades made from animal bones) and sledges. A sledge, a forerunner of the ornate sledges used in Germany from the Renaissance onwards, was found in the Oseberg ship excavation. Sledges are not only useful in winter but can be drawn over wet fields, muddy roads and even hard ground, if one helps them along by greasing the blades with oil or alternatively wetting them with water; in cold weather the water will freeze to ice and they glide along more smoothly and are less effort to pull. The sledge was also highly prized, because – unlike wheeled vehicles – it was exempt from tolls.

In Novgorod one differentiated between summer travellers (coming and going in summer and autumn) and winter travellers. The latter set out in autumn while the sea was still navigable, or journeyed overland with the first snows to Novgorod; in the spring they returned home with the last of the snow or when the sea was navigable again. When they travelled in winter, they used light sledges drawn by dogs. If they were going to buy goods they took only essential clothing and money; there was no room for other luggage.

Snow obliterates the boundaries between one piece of land and another, and between roads and cultivated land, so that one can travel 'across country'; with snowshoes one can even travel across soft snow without harming the crops growing below. Footprints in the snow can easily be seen, which made it easy to hunt wild animals in winter, and also people; if these had been driven from their homes – their houses and possessions burnt – they could easily be hounded down by their enemies. Henry of Latvia describes sorties which European 'pilgrims' (crusaders) undertook yearly at the beginning of the thirteenth century against the still heathen inhabitants of the Baltic. After being mercilessly hunted, there would often be death by the sword (for the men), or from starvation or cold, while the women and children would be sold as slaves.

MOUNTS, DRAUGHT- AND PACK-ANIMALS

The medieval traveller used various animals as mounts or draught-animals, according to the task in hand and the climate. The most important were:

The ass, which is native to the warm regions of Arabia and North Africa; we know that it was certainly domesticated in the fourth century BC and there are references to it being used in caravan trains in the third century BC. Donkeys were also much favoured beyond the Mediterranean area, in the cooler regions north of the Alps and in Asia. They had many advantages: they are mountain animals and are therefore sure-footed and economical (feeding on thistles and straw), and so were preferred to horses in many regions; as they are smaller than horses, they can be more easily mounted. The ass was mainly used as a pack-animal and to ride, rather than as a draught-animal. It can carry about 150 kilograms, or half as much as a camel, and can be ridden by an adult carrying with him a certain amount of baggage. The horse is often associated with luxury, arrogance and war in the Bible and the writings of the early Christian authors; the donkey with humility and lowliness. As Jesus had ridden into Jerusalem on a she-ass, in the Middle Ages the ass became the chosen beast for people to ride who wanted to be the true servants of Christ; Norbert of Xanten and other followers of the medieval cult of poverty rode on donkeys, when they did not go on foot. According to Battuta however, it was considered shameful in India to ride on a donkey.

The horse, which is stronger and faster than the ass, was domesticated later than the other draught- and pack-animals, but at the latest by the end of the third century BC, possibly simultaneously in western Europe, south-west Asia and in Mongolia. It is particularly suitable as a mount and draught-animal; properly harnessed it can pull a weight of more than 1000 kilograms, although as a pack-animal it cannot carry much more than a donkey (about 170 kg). The European horse in early times – like that in Mongolia – was certainly much smaller than horses are today – possibly 52 inches (13 hands) instead of 63 inches (15¾ hands). In the thirteenth-century collection of laws, the *Sachsenspiegel*, the full testamentary capacity of a man is held to depend on whether he can mount a charger unaided from a mounting-block, a 'daumenelle' (about 15¾ inches) high. The horse was fairly rare in western Europe from the fifth to eleventh century; it is interesting that the German word 'Pferd', the designation for a horse first used in the sixth century, is derived from the Latin 'Paraveredus', or post-horse (whereas the Old High German *hros*, or modern *Ross* or charger, and the Old English *hors* are earlier). At the height of the Middle Ages, thanks to systematic

The Emperor Henry VII on his way to Rome, with baggage train. The draught-horse is in the shafts; a lead-horse is harnessed in front in the traces, as was usual when going over mountains.

breeding, battle chargers were the usual mounts, particularly in the Islamic sphere of the Orient, but also in the West. They were fast and quick to react, and so powerful that they could carry a horseman in heavy armour. As stallions were valuable 'military equipment', it was forbidden in many cases to take them into the territory of potential enemies (for example in the Carolingian period in 781 and 864; such orders were about as successful, however, as they would be today). The decades-long rebellion by the Saxons was dealt a permanent blow when the Frankish rulers ordered them to deliver horses every year (from 758 they had to give 300 horses each year to the Franks instead of the previous tribute of 500 cows). The breeding of war horses also benefited the civil population in due course, and – as the horse became more widespread – it gradually lost the character of a purely aristocratic mount. Horses were important for many reasons. Technical advances – better harness and the use of horse-shoes – gave them extra power to pull carts and farming implements. The population growth in the high Middle Ages was directly influenced by the introduction of horses into the agricultural scene. Even the difficult ground in certain areas which promised to give a good yield could now be worked; the three-field system and the cultivation of oats in turn benefited the horse. As horses can go faster than donkeys, not to mention oxen, they could be used as mounts or to draw vehicles to transport travellers more quickly; more important in the long run was the fact that perishable foodstuffs (such as fish and vegetables) could be transported from the surrounding areas to the towns, which, thanks to better provisioning, grew rapidly in size in the latter half of the Middle Ages.

But the horse had its drawbacks. In spite of its increasing importance for agriculture and transport, it remained until comparatively modern times the favoured mount of the rich, and as such was the status symbol of noblemen, knights and bishops. It is noteworthy that in 1228 the Cistercians ordered in their Constitution that 'our brothers' must not have their own carriage or horses, or stable the horses of others in their monasteries. The horse was expensive to feed: less economical than the ass, it ate oats, an important foodstuff for the peasantry; in the Middle Ages the majority of the population were not able to eat bread, but only porridge. European horses were particularly demanding in this respect. On his journey to Mongolia in the mid-thirteenth century, Carpini was advised in Kiev to leave his horses there and take Mongolian horses as mounts – only those would be able to scrape fodder from under the snow.

Successful breeding may always have its disadvantages: highly bred animals are usually more prone to disease; in 791 a campaign by the Franks against the Avars failed because most of their horses had fallen prey to an epidemic. And finally riding could be dangerous. Abelard broke his atlas vertebra falling from his horse; Norbert of Xanten fell from his horse and immediately took to 'another kind of life'. Running-costs had also to be taken into account: a traveller riding in high style on a horse had to reckon that the layout for his horse (oats, hay, stabling, bridge tolls, etc), would at least equal his own expenses for board and lodging and other necessities. He could go faster than those on foot, but appeared to be better off and could not take advantage of concessions which were provided for the needy (free lodging in hospices and elsewhere, for example).

The mule (offspring of he-ass and mare) and hinny (offspring of stallion and she-ass) are sturdy pack-animals. The mule is larger and stronger than the hinny; it is as strong as a horse, and as placid, patient and resistant to disease as the donkey; it has a longer working life than the horse, has greater powers of endurance when doing heavy work, and as a sumpter-mule can carry loads safely over difficult terrain, even in trackless mountain country. The mule was the usual mount and pack- and draught-animal for those lower in rank than a knight. In 1623, the Palatina, the famous library of the University of Heidelberg, was transferred to Rome by mule train. Even today the mule is greatly valued for its sure-footedness by the mountain troops of the Federal German Armed Forces.

The camel (it is important to differentiate between the one-humped dromedary of west and southern Asia and North Africa and the two-humped, mainly central Asian camel) has many unique characteristics. It is ideally adapted to extreme conditions, being more suitable than any other animal as a mount or pack-animal in devastatingly dry and hot areas. It can feed itself even better than the donkey on hard, thorny desert plants, and can go for a day without food and if necessary

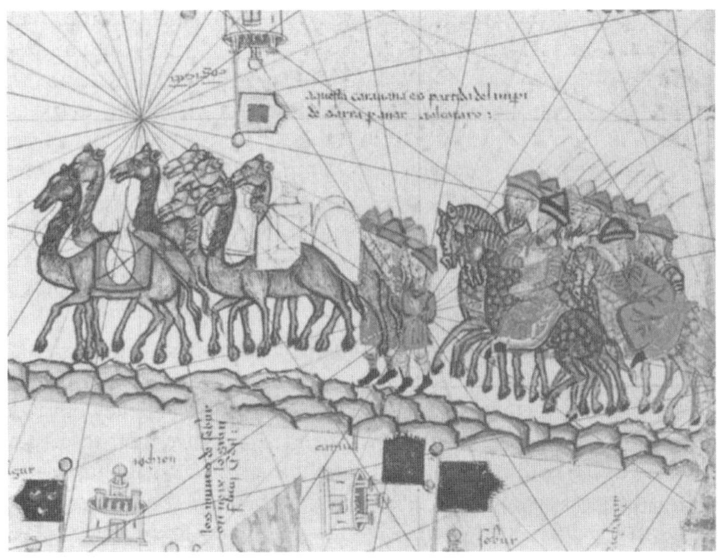

A camel caravan on the silk road in Sinkiang. Part of a map in the Catalan World Atlas of 1375.

for a week without water, drawing on the water and fat stored in its hump as it goes along. The camel provides men with milk, camelhair and meat, and in addition good fuel made from dried dung. As its body temperature can climb in the course of a day by up to 7 degrees, the camel loses little moisture in the form of sweat. It is protected from heat and cold by the fine underlayers of hair in its coat. Thick horny pads on the soles of its feet protect it from the heat of the desert sand, and allow it to keep going for a long time over the hard tracks of mountainous regions. These qualities, together with its swinging gait, have earned the camel the name of 'ship of the desert'.

Camels have probably been domesticated since the second millennium BC; there are references to camel caravans in sources from about 1100 BC. They were equally suitable as mounts or transport animals for civil and military purposes. Without the camel it would not have been possible to cross the trade-routes of the Sahara or the vast expanses of central Asia between China and Byzantium; it is clearly superior to horse, ass and mule in its carrying capacity, endurance and adaptability. It can do almost a hundred miles a day and carry a load of 270 kilograms: which bears out a saying of Battuta that with a fast camel you can get from Cairo to Mecca in ten days (808 miles as the crow flies).

The Arabs brought the camel with them to Spain and Sicily, and it was used in Merovingian Gaul, but – unlike the ass and horse – it never became really at home in Europe. The Emperor Frederick II loved to make a great show with an exotic retinue while journeying through his realm. In 1235 he took many animals unknown in Italy with him: an elephant, several dromedaries and camels, leopards, gerfalcons and hawks; the annals of Colmar note his progress through the Rhine valley 'with a host of camels'; six years later he was a guest at the monastery of San Zeno in Verona, and brought with him – to the dismay of his hosts – an elephant, 24 camels and five leopards!

The elephant, even rarer in medieval Europe than the camel, is slower than the horse, ass or mule. As an elephant can carry several people, it was used in India, according to Battuta, for warfare. The Caliph Haroun-al-Raschid sent the Emperor Charlemagne, as the status symbol of eastern rulers, an elephant called Abul Abbas; it arrived safely in the summer of 802 at the court in Aachen, where it caused great amazement.

Oxen were the most usual draught-animals in the Middle Ages, for carts and agricultural implements. It is difficult to judge their usefulness in this respect because they were certainly smaller and less powerful than they are today; it was some while before stock-breeders paid as much attention to cattle as to horses. Oxen, harnessed in pairs alongside each other or one behind the other, are easy to drive and control, but they go more slowly and have less endurance than horses; it is said that you could not expect them to do much more than 9 miles a day. In his Life of Charlemagne, Einhard mocks the last Merovingian king, who was too poor to be able to have noble chargers: 'Wherever he went, he had to go in a cart, drawn by a yoke of oxen and driven by a cowherd, as if he were a farmer. He drove thus to the palace, and to the open council of the people, which sat annually for the good of the realm, and then returned home again in the same manner.' Guibert of Nogent, a chronicler of the First Crusade, tells with a mixture of ridicule and pity, how inadequately many of the participants were equipped and how they had many illusions as to the length of their journey: 'In truth you would have seen many strange and laughable things at this time. Poor people shod the hooves of their oxen with irons like horses, harnessed them to two-wheeled carts, loaded their few provisions and small children on top and so led them forth; and as soon as the little children saw a castle or a town, they asked eagerly whether that was the Jerusalem, to which they were going.' Despite such accounts, one must not forget that oxen were indispensable as draught-animals for the 'small farmer' until the twentieth century in the West; the agricultural economy of Europe would not have been possible without them.

So long as there were no tolerably good streets and roads – and in mountainous country that meant until the nineteenth century in Europe – people had to depend on pack- or sumpter-animals to transport themselves and their goods. The beasts had to be nimble and agile enough to go along often very narrow tracks, and also to be strong, docile, able to carry heavy loads, and sound of foot. Mules and hinnies were the best beasts of burden. The weight which they could carry was often used as a unit of measure (about 150 kilograms varying considerably from country to country). Even over level ground sumpter-animals were often more practical than ox-carts, despite the fact that an ox could pull as much in a cart as could be carried by two horses. Because the oxen were so slow, the wages and food for their drivers and fodder for the beasts mounted up over long distances. But pack-animals had their drawbacks too: they could only cross rivers with very light loads, or they and their packs would be damaged. A loaded cart can be left overnight, and the driver can set off with it again the next morning; but it takes time to look after a pack-animal. After a day's journey, when its owner is also tired, it has to be unloaded, fed and watered; next morning it has to be loaded up again; care has to be taken to distribute the load evenly, so that it does not unbalance the animal. The Franciscan monk William of Rubruck experienced such difficulties on his journey to see the Mongolian Khan. Having reached the Crimea, in 1253, he had to decide how his baggage should be carried. Merchants from Constantinople persuaded him of the advantages of a kind of covered wagon, of the sort Russians used to transport furs in, and which could be left loaded. With hindsight, Rubruck regretted having followed their advice. He took two months with the teams of oxen to cover the first long stretch of the journey; with pack-horses, he reckoned that he could have covered the distance in half the time.

Bearers – possibly prisoners of war or slaves, who were also (reluctant) travellers in medieval times – were used when even sure-footed pack-animals found the going too hard in the high mountain areas. The word 'slave' is derived from 'Slav': captured in the Slav territories, in the early Middle Ages slaves were sent via Verdun to Islamic Spain; to make them more 'profitable' they were loaded with goods such as furs from the eastern European countries; valuable slaves, such as those Liutprand of Cremona was commanded by Otto I to present to the Byzantine Emperor, would have been handled as carefully as other 'goods' on the journey. At the beginning of the tenth century the toll tariff of Raffelstetten (on the Danube in Upper Austria) speaks of 'slaves, horses, oxen and other carriers'. To judge from the listed regulations, a man sometimes carried a quarter of the weight which was put on a horse.

Besides the above-mentioned animals, goats and sheep were also used as pack-animals if necessary, for example on a crusade; they were particularly useful because they would have been taken anyway to provide fresh meat and were killed as needed, although as the journey went on they yielded less and less meat, having used up their reserves of flesh and fat on the way. Finally, in north and eastern Europe hounds drew light sledges, and the semi-domesticated reindeer heavier ones.

How did women ride, when they had to travel in this way? The capital of a pillar in Autun shows the Holy Family on the flight into Egypt: Joseph leads a donkey, on which Mary, with the baby Jesus in her arms, is riding side-saddle. So this was clearly considered seemly, as a remark of Rubruck concerning the Mongols also confirms: 'The women ride like men, astride their horses.' Women were not supposed to sit astride in public; in Europe this was considered shocking until the twentieth century. But did women really only ride side-saddle? Horses and donkeys could not be guided so well when the rider had to depend on a switch rather than pressure from the thighs. And not all horses were prepared to amble gently along carrying a lady's saddle stiffened with wood. And not all women who had long journeys to make, could stand such a saddle. If it was a question of safety, considerations of modesty were set aside, even in the West. According to the pictorial evidence of the Emperor Henry VII's journey to Rome, the Queen rode 'like a man', at any rate over the Alps.

The flight into Egypt. Capital of a column in the cathedral at Autun (1120–30). Out of respect for the Holy Family, they are shown richly dressed; the leather harness of the donkey is finely worked.

JOURNEYS BY LAND, RIVER AND SEA

Travel on land

In the heyday of the Roman Empire, about three thousand miles of road radiated outwards from the golden milestone in the Roman Forum; many European states did not have an equivalent road network until the eighteenth century. Plutarch describes the appearance of the ideal Roman road, and how Caius Gracchus in planning roads was concerned with usefulness, beauty and comfort. 'The roads ran through the land in a straight line, and were paved with hewn stone or laid with sand deposits, well stamped down. Hollows were filled in; where mountain torrents or ravines cut through the countryside, viaducts were built, and as both banks were made parallel, the whole construction had a symmetrical and harmonious appearance.' Milestones marked the distances; mounting-blocks placed at frequent intervals on either side of the road, enabled riders to mount their horses unaided.

These roads compensated for the small number of troops, allowing those in the interior to be used to maximum advantage: a legion could quickly be deployed from the Rhine to the Danube or Euphrates. The roads were not designed for civilian traffic, being less suitable for wagons and draught-animals because their surfaces became slippery when wet; the animals stumbled and their unshod hooves quickly wore down. Another disadvantage of the roads became apparent during the barbarian invasions: once the border defences had been stormed, the roads made it all too easy for the invaders to advance into the heart of the realm. So to counter possible raids, the Roman roads in the border regions were allowed to fall into disrepair in Late Antiquity (but not in central Gaul, Italy or Spain), or were used as quarries. Farms were sited at a distance from them and connected by a new road network. As land was measured by means of roads, Roman roads often served as boundaries ('*limes*' means both 'boundary-line' and 'road'). The kingdom of Alfred the Great and the English territories of the Danish king Guthrum were divided by Watling Street, the old Roman road.

In spite of their lack of interest in road-building, the secular and spiritual powers of the early medieval states, as well as merchants, were interested in good communications; only these would allow them to keep order and retain their positions, and would enable ideas and merchandise to be sent out into the world. But soldiers, missionaries and merchants carrying luxury goods over long distances, made do with narrow roads along which they and their mounts

St Martin rides out of a town and gives half his cloak to a beggar at the wayside, from a fifteenth-century German painting.

could go. In the eighth century, Sturmi, abbot of Fulda, travelled with his ass through the trackless wilderness around Fulda. Every evening he had to fell trees to make a fence, to protect his mount from wild animals. Most travellers had to adopt similar tactics, if they wanted to walk or ride safely from one place to another – irrespective of whether there was a beaten track, let alone a made-up road.

We can get a fairly accurate idea of the stages of princely journeys from the places and dates listed in documents, annals and chronicles; but we do not know very much about the exact location and condition of the roads. There are many gaps in our knowledge and we have to fill in the picture by studying traces in the landscape, field names, indicators of resting places or inns, archaeological remains, old maps, aerial photographs and other details. And even when we have

isericordia autem domini ab eter
no: ⁊ usque in eternum super timen
tes eum
Et iusticia illius in filios filiorū:
his qui seruant testamentum eius.
t memores sunt mandatorum
ipsius: ipsius: ad faciendum ea:

A royal carriage, from the Luttrell Psalter. The figure holding a squirrel may represent Philippa of Hainault, wife of Edward III, and the carriage has the

discovered an 'ancient way', it is often difficult to know whether Charlemagne or Gustavus Adolphus would have travelled along it. For roads have changed course even more frequently than rivers; if a new toll was raised or bridge built, roads which had until then been well used would be ploughed up again. The removal by force of the bridge over the Isar at Oberföhring eight miles upstream to Munich in 1158 by Duke Henry the Lion of Saxony was a major contributor to the blossoming of that town on the Isar in the twelfth century.

To cross streams, there would be at best a plank for those going on foot, or they would wade across, as they did across river fords. In the latter case travellers were lucky if they found a rope stretched from bank to bank to hold on to, because the water might sometimes be so deep that it came over their heads. Even small rivers were insuperable barriers when they were flooded. To

imperial double-headed eagle on its sides. Two horsemen drive the team of five horses harnessed in single file.

build bridges and keep them in good repair was expensive. It was only possible to have a ferry, if the ferryman and his family could subsist on the fares. There were of course cases where ferrymen lived very frugally or had other means of support; in this respect the legends about ferrymen have a kernel of historical truth: Christopher bore travellers across a river; Julian atoned for the murder of his parents by working as a ferryman in a foreign land.

Even the roads called 'street' were generally only about four or five metres wide, so two vehicles might meet in the middle. Proper maintenance of roads was not carried out in Europe – with a few exceptions – until the end of the eighteenth or beginning of the nineteeth century; until then pot-holes were filled in with earth and brushwood when necessary. Such roads had some advantages over the paved Roman roads: they were less susceptible to frost, easy to repair and provided a better surface for horses and pack-animals which were shod.

In general roads did not run through the waterlogged river valleys, because there floods posed a constant threat to any kind of construction works. And people feared the bad air. It was not known that mosquitoes carried malaria, but people stayed as far as possible from stagnant water. For this reason too, roads were laid above the river valleys and along the lower mountain slopes, as for example along the edge of the Black Forest, or at the foot of the Vosges

Tree-felling and bridge-building. Land clearance benefited travellers, who were threatened by robbers, murderers and wild beasts in the forests. In the illustration a road links two towns.

Two St James's pilgrims on the road. From a pilgrim's guide, Leipzig 1521.

or Apennine mountains (Via Emilia Piacenza–Rimini), or the ancient salt way (*Hellweg*) already used in Charlemagne's day (later the *Reichs – und Bundesstrasse 1*), high above the marshy Lippe valley in the Haarstrang region. Staging posts from the time of the Frankish conquest are threaded along the road like pearls on a string, each not more than a day's journey from the last: in the ninth century the king and his envoys on their travels, and later other travellers, could be sure of finding food and shelter, repair workshops, and above all water for themselves and their mounts in Steele, Bochum, Dortmund, Wickede, Werl, Soest, Erwitte, and so on all along the route.

As trade and traffic increased around the turn of the millennium, there are single instances, and then more frequent mention in the sources, of road-building by church and secular powers. Road and bridge builders were even gradually spoken of as saints – Dominic, who built part of the pilgrim's way to Santiago de Compostela, or Benedict, who had a bridge built over the Rhône at Avignon. Bishop Benno of Osnabrück had 'dry and well levelled roads' laid

A simple thirteenth-century French travelling-cart. The driver looks round for instructions.

'through several swamps, of which there are many in these parts'. From the turn of the millennium, roads had to be 'level', so that heavy, breakable goods such as stone for the many churches being built or enlarged, and later for palaces and bridges, could be carried along them. The stone was mostly hewn in quarries, so that it would be less heavy to transport and less hard on wagon-wheels and roads; the rubble could then be used to fill in pot-holes. That was the method Michaelangelo was still using in 1518–19, when he had a road built to transport blocks of marble.

Towards the turn of the millennium, many things led to a revolutionary improvement in means of transport, although it was nevertheless a gradual revolution. The traveller now had at his disposal mounts and draught-animals which had been bred on the farms, better harness, horse-shoes, better vehicles, relatively level roads, an increasing number of bridges. The improved means of transport and improvements elsewhere were mutually beneficial: more people could be fed economically because food could be produced more cheaply and transported with less expense of energy and without loss of quality to the burgeoning towns.

Until the nineteenth century the majority of people travelled on foot, because they had no other way to go. Many even went barefoot, from poverty, or because of the heat or uncomfortable shoes, or as a penance. Well-to-do people only travelled on foot when they wanted to identify with the weak as a sign of humility, or in order to get into conversation with their fellow-men. Bede tells how Bishop Aidan (d. 651) 'was wont to traverse both town and country on foot, never on horseback, unless compelled by some urgent necessity; and wherever in his way he saw any, either rich or poor, he invited them, if infidels, to embrace the mystery of the faith; or if they were believers, to strengthen them in the faith, and to stir them up by words and actions to alms and good works.'

To ride in a wagon was considered unmanly, especially perhaps as despite many improvements it was still an uncomfortable means of transport; only women and those men who could not go any other way – the old, the sick and prisoners – travelled in this way. The fine lord or prelate rode on horseback. If he was old, sick or wanted to make a show, he was carried in a litter. The impression this made, as late as the mid-twelfth century, can be seen from the life of an archbishop of Trier. In 1148 Albero appeared at a synod in Rheims 'in such splendour that all gaped at him in astonishment. He sat in a leather litter hung with fine linen within and drawn by two horses.'

PREPARATIONS

The higher the traveller was in the social scale, the longer and more elaborate would be the preparations for his journey. A king or pope usually planned his route well in advance; people and institutions from whom he expected help would then be prepared, and those at home or abroad who wanted to contact him would know where they could find him.

What luggage did the medieval traveller take with him? As little as possible, especially for those going on foot. Marco Polo tells how the Tartar horsemen carried two leather flasks for milk, a pot to cook meat in and a small tent in case it rained. Tents were too heavy for most travellers: if there was no barn in which to spend the night, they would look for somewhere sheltered from wind and rain, wrap themselves up in their cloaks and try to get some sleep. Pilgrims – the prototype of the medieval traveller – were often shown dressed in a long cloak, which would serve as a blanket at night, with a broad-brimmed hat to protect the face from the sun and stop the rain running down their necks, in stockings and strong or not-so-strong shoes, with a scrip in which passes and other papers could be carried, together with one or two coins (sometimes quite a lot of money), and a few provisions and other bits and pieces; and with a staff in their hand, which could be used when climbing mountains or for wading through deep rivers, vaulting across smaller streams or to ward off attacking animals. The pilgrim would also have a (table) knife, possibly a leather beaker, stones with which to strike a spark, so that fish caught in a net on the way could be roasted over a fire. A letter of introduction to relations or acquaintances was better than any amount of luggage; it might lead to an offer of free food, drink, shelter, ferry crossings and so on, and be as good as a magic wand for many a pilgrim. Nor were robbers interested in pieces of paper, so it was safer than ready money or valuables.

Plenty of rain and the widespread forests meant that the traveller in Europe could usually quench his thirst without too much difficulty. Adults normally need two and a half litres of water a day, part of which is obtained from food. Hard work or great heat increase the amount needed to five to thirteen litres. And during sieges and on the crusades, travellers from Europe learnt the true meaning of thirst. Lone travellers usually carried a small reserve of water, in hollow gourds or animal bladders, in stone vessels or glass flasks; groups, especially in southern regions, used light and unbreakable leather containers in which to carry their water. Even in central Europe travellers had to plan where they could get water from: Ekkehard remarks in passing in his accounts concerning the monastery of St Gall, how the monks there went about building a fortress to defend themselves from the Hungarians: 'Where rushes used to grow, they dug a very deep well, certain that they would find water, and they did indeed find there the purest water.' Bede tells in his *Ecclesiastical History* of the unusual step King Edwin took in caring for his people in the 620s: the Anglo-Saxon king had brass drinking-bowls – of the kind still seen today – hung by clear springs near the highways for the use of travellers. Ships had to go into harbour frequently, to take water on board. If a journey was to be through dry or desert regions, the provision of water had to be carefully planned a long way ahead.

Bread and cheese were useful foods, which could supply the required amounts

A merchant gathers his goods in preparation for a journey: note the carefully-roped bundles, the solid barrel and sacks.

of carbohydrate, protein and animal fats. Nuts have already been mentioned in the section on the seasons.

Inland waterways

Trade and traffic in Europe are greatly facilitated by navigable rivers. Until the nineteenth or twentieth century the rivers wound along – as the Loire does today – between islands and sandbanks. In spite of being so shallow even rivers which we consider insignificant today were useful to travellers, for example the Ill between Colmar and Strasbourg. Dugouts made from oak or pine trunks, such as are still constructed, boats, barges and rafts had shallow draughts; their loading capacity was often little more than three quarters of a ton – or as much as could be loaded on an ox-cart.

A good illustration of what the medieval river network was like can be seen by looking at Switzerland. The stretch from the North Sea along the Rhine, Aare and Rhône to the Mediterranean was navigable – except for a distance of

Travel by land and river: at Paris, a consignment of wine is delivered from barges, while a carriage full of people enters the city gates. From a fourteenth-century French manuscript.

A ship being towed. From an anonymous painting, Cologne 1450–60. St Ursula and her companions are travelling by river to Cologne. The travellers could recognise the town from a distance by its characteristic silhouette and from the three crowns on the banner flying from the bailey tower and the arms above the town gate.

about 18½ miles – for approximately 1,243 miles: you travelled up the Rhine to Waldshut, turned into the Aare at Koblenz and along Lake Biel to the Lake of Neuchâtel, whose south-western tip is only about a day's journey from the Lake of Geneva; from there you could go down the Rhône to the Mediterranean. If you wanted to go to the north of Italy, you travelled 12½ miles up the Aare to the Limmat and through Lake Zurich and Lake Walen See to Walenstadt; or up the Aare and Reuss, past Lucerne and through the Vierwaldstätter See to the Flüela Pass; or up the Aare past Bern through Lake Thun to Lake Brienz. On the other side of the Alps the Italian lakes offered a reprieve after crossing the mountains. A large part of western and central Switzerland was connected to the great waterways of the Rhine and Rhône, and many other rivers were navigable. Apart from one day's journey overland, you could travel by boat from the delta of the Rhine to that of the Rhône.

This did not necessarily mean that travellers remained on board all the time. There was hardly room to move in the small, unsteady boats. It was a relief to stretch one's legs from time to time, at any rate in the evening, when going on land to sleep. At low water (particularly in summer, the most usual time to travel), at river divides, rapids and waterfalls, the boat would be unloaded and dragged or carried overland, as the Vikings did between the Dnieper and Düna, and merchants between the North Sea and Baltic, or the Turks at the siege of Constantinople in 1453, and the pioneers in the American West in the eighteenth and nineteenth centuries. At Hedeby in Schleswig, at the narrowest point between the North Sea and Baltic, a kind of container was probably already in use, so that freight could be loaded and unloaded quickly and safely. But although convenient in some ways, there were disadvantages in carrying or dragging boats overland: time was lost; in unfriendly territory travellers were exposed – as were the Norsemen at the rapids on the Dnieper – to attacks from the local inhabitants. On the other hand places of work gradually grew up around the rapids and other stopping places. Schaffhausen owed its growth into an important town to the fact that at the Rhine Falls ships had to be unloaded and their cargoes transported by land; in Russia a separate proud community was formed by those who carried the boats of Novgorod travellers over the rapids of the Volkhov.

Boats were allowed to drift downstream. They were steered by a helmsman in the bow with a steering oar. It is clear that they could make good way with the river currents. The Rhine at Strasbourg flows today at a speed of 7 feet a second at half tide. Earlier it flowed more slowly and ran in countless arms into the valleys, as it does today into the water-meadows of the Rhine valley; but between Karlsruhe and Mannheim the course of the river was shortened by 31 miles by Tulla's regulation of the Rhine. If one reckons on a rate of 6½ feet a second, that is something over four miles an hour; theoretically at that rate one could have covered a good hundred miles in twenty-four hours. It is rather doubtful if this was actually achieved; but rudders, poles and sails helped to speed up the journey, and in fine summer weather one could travel by day and night. Travellers covered great distances in a very short time along rivers which they knew well. Liutprand of Cremona travelled from Pavia to Venice in three days in 943 – at least 200 miles along the waterways of the Po and Adriatic. A boat once covered the distance from Metz to Trier in one night; on land it would have taken at least two days. Charlemagne usually travelled from Ingelheim to Koblenz in one day, and Frederick Barbarossa travelled in a day or a day and a half from Frankfurt along the Rhine and Main to Sinzig (84 miles) after being elected in 1152. The serfs of the Ingelheim palace admittedly took a week to tow Charles's boat back to its 'home port'. A flat barge took two to five days to go down the Rhône from Lyon to Avignon (125 miles as the crow flies); to tow it back took about a month!

To go upriver sails were used (sailing barges can of course still be seen in Holland and on the east coast of Britain), or oars (as when Boniface's corpse was transported up the Rhine), or barge-poles or tow-ropes. Horses, oxen or men towed the boats, which were held on course by a steersman; horses could do a distance of 9–12 miles a day, oxen and men a little less. Serfs – which included most of the population – were bound to render dues and services to their lord. A serf living by a river had therefore to provide horses – or himself – to tow his lord's boats.

The advantages of inland navigation for communications and trade were so obvious, that even in antiquity natural watercourses had been linked by canals to form a waterway network. According to Tacitus the Romans wanted to join the Saône and Moselle by a canal. Centuries later, Charlemagne enlisted all the resources of his realm to build a Main-Danube canal. After immense labours, of which the traces can still be seen in the landscape, the project was given up – attacks from Saxons and Avars no longer threatened on two fronts. In the late Middle Ages, traffic increased so much that it paid to build canals. A forerunner of the North Sea–Baltic Canal, opened in 1895, the Stecknitzkanal between Lübeck and the Elbe, was completed in 1398. How helpful it was to navigators can be judged from the fact that a part of the north-west coast of Jutland is called 'Jammer' or 'Misery' Bay.

It was generally possible to travel not only more quickly along the inland waterways but also more cheaply and comfortably than on land. When Boniface went to Friesland along the Rhine, Yssel and Zuider Zee, it was clearly because travelling on a river boat was more comfortable for an old man. Bulk goods such as corn, wine and salt, which often cost more to transport on land for a few days than the value of the load, could be economically carried by boat over long distances.

Conveyance by water was also comparatively cheap because for a long time no expensive construction works were needed. Traffic on land meant that roads and bridges had to be maintained, although this was often neglected. Rubble embankments where smaller rivers ran into the larger waterways or the sea usually served as landing-places for river craft. The boats were landed by running them aground; a trap was let down from the bow, to make unloading simpler; similarly constructed craft were used by the Allies in 1944 in the Normandy landings.

Transporting goods and people was achieved particularly economically when the prime purpose of the journey was to take wood downriver to areas where the forests had already been felled or in which there was no wood of the right quality. At the end of the journey – the Rhine delta perhaps – the rafts used could be broken up and the wood sold; the rafters then travelled back to their homes on foot. It is interesting that the wood for the Hanseatic cog built in 1380 and discovered in 1962 during dredging works in the lower reaches of the Weser, came from the mountain country of Hesse, and was therefore probably floated down the Fulda and Weser. Rafts were used as welcome alternative means for transporting people until the nineteenth century. Simple cabins offered a minimum of protection for the passengers from wind and weather.

River travel was not without its risks, however. The still untrammelled reaches of the rivers were longer and shallower than they are today; the larger rivers often changed their course from one year to the next, so the boatmen had to be able to re-find their bearings. A boat could easily run aground and sink. Which is why sources – such as the Lives of Charlemagne or Albero of Trier or the Grettisaga – lay such great stress on the ability of their heroes to swim. In 1062 a river boat was used in a coup d'état. The German court was on the Rhine island of Kaiserwerth. According to Lampert of Hersfeld's account, Archbishop Anno of Cologne invited the twelve-year-old King Henry IV on to one of his magnificently appointed boats; Henry went unsuspectingly on board. 'Hardly had he boarded the ship, however, when the Archbishop's accomplices surrounded his position, the oarsmen quickly took up their posts and threw themselves with all their strength upon the oars, driving the boat with the speed of lightning into the middle of the stream. The King, disconcerted and bewildered by the unexpected turn of events and thinking that he would be taken by force and murdered, threw himself head-first into the river, and would have drowned in the rushing torrent, had not Count Ekbert, unmindful of the danger into which he was rushing, leapt after the drowning man, and used all his strength and skill to save him from going under, dragging him on board. Then the King was reassured by all manner of friendly words and brought to Cologne. The rest of the people followed on land.' The legend of the Loreley and their rock on the Rhine tells of other dangers which sailors had to fear; it was not until 1832–34 that a deeper channel for boats was dug in the river-bed at Bingen; at low water the reefs can still be seen.

Considerations which affected travel in general, also applied to inland and ocean navigation. Man-made obstacles could be more of a nuisance to travellers than naturally occurring hazards. Opposing interests had to be accommodated: bridges were invaluable for travel on land, but their pillars were a danger to boats, causing backwaters and whirlpools as the river ebbed and flowed. Bridges were also built so that if necessary rivers could easily be barred, as the Seine was in the ninth century against attacks by the Vikings. As well as providing a means of transport, rivers were useful in supplying food, energy and toll-money. Fishermen spread their nets from the banks; weirs supplied mills with a regular, fast-flowing stream; ecclesiastical and secular authorities showed no lack of inspiration when it came to thinking up taxes for various uses of a river, and they even barred the way with ropes or chains. In 1157 the Emperor Frederick Barbarossa complained that citizens and merchants had made representations to him that 'from Bamberg to Mainz on the Main, new, untraditional and totally irregular tolls were being demanded in very many places from merchants and that they were being robbed by this means.' After due consideration it was agreed by the princes that a ban should be made on all levies for a period of time, until their validity should have been proved; as on the appointed day none of the new toll-lords appeared at court, 'all tolls from Bamberg to Mainz, according to a decree by the princes, were banned for ever and ever', except for those at Neustadt, Aschaffenburg and Frankfurt. Barbarossa added his imperial weight to the ban, saying that 'no one should hinder the merchants who travel up the Rhine or who pull a towrope along the bank, which is acknowledged to be the king's highway, on the pretext of demanding a toll or in any other way.' The Emperor naturally took it as of right that towpaths were king's highways (*via regia*), and that anyone who committed an offence on them, came under the royal jurisdiction.

Things which made things easier for travellers, could also help their enemies. In the ninth century there are repeated references to Viking raids deep into the Carolingian Empire. Arles and Valence on the Rhône, Angers and Tours on the Loire, Rouen and Paris on the Seine, Lüttich on the Maas, Cologne, Bonn and Mainz on the Rhine, Trier on the Moselle were plundered or sacked; Prüm, Stablo and Aachen, which were farther from rivers, fared no better. These raids made it painfully clear to both rulers and their people that coolly audacious, bold and merciless men in seaworthy boats could often sail inland faster than messengers could bring the fearful tidings of their coming, so that their unfortunate victims had no time to defend themselves.

Ocean navigation

In many respects travel by sea offered even greater advantages than on inland waterways. With a favourable wind distances could be covered at a speed which the overland traveller could not hope to rival.

Individuals, groups and peoples learnt to make full use of the opportunities which seafaring offered. At the time of the barbarian invasions the inhabitants of inland countries often showed an astonishing capacity to learn and adapt. The Vandals advanced through a large part of Europe, and then, in 429, crossed the Straits of Gibraltar with 20,000 warriors and possibly 80,000 followers, to North Africa, where they founded a kingdom that would rule vast tracts of the Mediterranean. In the seventh and eighth centuries Arabs were equally at home on the sea, as the inhabitants of Constantinople, the Lombards, Romans and Franks soon learnt to their cost. Saracens (often equated with pirates in the sources) from North Africa and the islands of the Mediterranean, terrorised the seas, and the coasts of Italy and southern France. People also went by sea when driven by necessity to do so, as a remark of Adam of Bremen shows: he had been assured on good authority that there were people who had travelled from Sweden overland to the Byzantine Empire – 'but the barbarians on the way render such journeys impossible, for which reason men venture to take to their boats.'

As in other fields, there is little to show what seafaring was like for the ordinary traveller. Millions of people travelled by sea in medieval times, but we know nothing about them; the few who have left us accounts of their journeys, often gave no details of their lives at sea. So we must study the 'background information'.

The greatest advantage of travel by sea, until the invention of the steamship, was that a cheap form of energy could be used to maximum effect. Sailing is defined in a modern nautical dictionary as 'The art of propelling a boat at the greatest possible speed by using windpower alone and by progressing in all directions possible.' A sail had to be strong enough not to be torn by a sudden gust of wind, and was also used on board and on land as a tent. The size and shape of sails, and number and position of masts, had to be determined by long experience. Additional power could be gained from paddles or oars, currents and tides. But more important still to the sailor was the whole build of the ship, the way in which wooden hull, sails and rigging worked together at sea. Thousands of pieces of wood, held together only by wooden pins and bolts, had to be able to withstand the ever-changing force of wind and waves.

Suitable wood for shipbuilding was often difficult to find, especially as tall trunks were needed for mast and keel. Seams and joints between the planks were caulked with tow (a byproduct from the combing of flax), and the hull protected from weather and woodworm so that it would not rot, with tar (from natural pitch-products or birch trees).

Accounts of shipwrecks show that ships' crews were usually very highly skilled, and were able to construct one or more boats from the timbers of a stranded vessel, whether they were Norsemen at the height of the Middle Ages or Portuguese seafarers voyaging to India at the dawn of the modern era.

In the Mediterranean there were oared or sailing galleys as well as large hulks for carrying merchandise. Irish and Scottish fishermen, from the fourth to ninth century, used coracles – made from animal skins stretched over wickerwork – which were extremely seaworthy. Irish monks sailed to Iceland in them, and possibly even – according to the account of St Brendan's legendary voyage – to America.

The so-called Viking longship in Scandinavia was perfected from the eighth century onwards. Developed from the open rowing boat, it was seaworthy but could also be used for travelling upriver (with a draught of only 1 metre when fully laden); because it was so light it could easily be carried on land. With a length of 45–66 feet, occasionally up to 82 feet, and a beam of at most 16½ feet, and with its great square sail it must have been able to reach a top speed of about 11 knots, more than 12 miles an hour. Bows and stern were practically the same, so that it was easy to land and push off again without turning the boat. The oars could be used when there was no wind, or the sail set to take advantage of the wind direction. In 1893 an Atlantic crossing made by a ship built as a replica of the Norse ships proved how seaworthy and adaptable under sail they were, and that the ship could easily be steered with the steering-oar on the starboard (steerboard) side.

There were two main types of such ships. Those of the Norse warriors had to be fast and were long and narrow, with space for many oarsmen. Ceremonial craft for 78 or even 120 rowers have been found in graves, but these were hardly likely to have been representative of the ordinary Viking ships. Although the speed increased with the number of rowers, supplies of water and food had to be replenished more often. Trading vessels were broader and shorter, and deeper, with plenty of room to stow the cargo; in order to have as much room as possible for freight and passengers, the number of crew was purposely kept as low as possible, with consequent loss of manpower. The wind was all important: if the boat was becalmed for too long those on board might die of thirst. Grettir may have sailed from Iceland to Norway in such a ship. In the mid-eleventh century Duke William of Normandy sailed across the Channel to conquer England in ships similar to those the Vikings had used for centuries. The Bayeux Tapestry shows many details of his vessels. As the freeboard was often less than 3½ feet above the water, shields were often fixed over the sides to stop the waves washing over the boats. And swift troopships were also used to transport horses and supplies.

French ships with half-decks built up with breastworks, and passengers in a rowing boat.

Detail from the Bayeux Tapestry. The illustration shows open troopships, bringing Duke William's soldiers and their horses to England. The ships have only one mast, with a square sail laced to the yard. There are holes in the sides of the ships for oars.

At the height of the Middle Ages this type of ship was gradually replaced in the North Sea and Baltic by other types of craft, which may have been developed from coastal vessels and to which the Hanseatic cog also belonged. This was no faster, but certainly larger and more serviceable than the Viking ships; with its stern rudder it was easy to steer and could carry about ten times as much merchandise (it is estimated that the Gokstad boat found in 1880 had a displacement of about thirty tons, the cog about 270 tons). Half-decks in stern and bow (where the pilot took up his position), and the main deck, helped to protect passengers and cargo from the waves. The half-decks were later built up with breastworks into castles and were well integrated into the main part of the ship. Such ships were called hulks, and had replaced the northern cog by the beginning of the fifteenth century. They were first seen in the Mediterranean at the end of the twelfth century, when an English and French fleet took crusaders to the Holy Land in 1188. The northern ship aroused interest because of its large carrying-capacity, simple rigging, the small number of crew required and consequent low running-costs; it was adopted in the Mediterranean as a trading vessel (or *nao*). It was in ships such as these, which were still quite small, that Columbus sailed to America and Vasco da Gama to India at the end of the Middle Ages. The cog was about 98 feet in length and with a beam of 26 feet, Columbus's flagship the *Santa Maria* 75 by 23 feet, and the smaller of his two accompanying ships, the faster-sailing *Niña*, about 56 by 20 feet. There were various types of sailing-ship, all belonging to the general category known as 'caravel'. Influenced by Arab and northern-European models, they evolved from the small trading and fishing vessels of the south-western (and windiest) corner of Europe.

With the construction of ships which could weather the tides and rough seas of the Atlantic, medieval seafarers were not only carrying on the shipbuilding traditions of antiquity, but surpassing them in many respects; comparable advances in land transport were not forthcoming until centuries later. There was even a certain degree of comfort in that the ships were no longer open. Most passengers (and crew) admittedly still had to find somewhere on deck, fore or aft to sleep in fine weather – as Grettir did – or even had to fight for a place; but on well-known routes – such as that from Venice to the Holy Land – arrangements were made to accommodate well-to-do pilgrims. They would rent one or more cabins and stowage room for their baggage and provisions in advance; if that was not possible, William Wey had advice to give them: 'Furste, yf ye goo in a galey make youre covenaunte wyth the patrone by tyme, and chese yow a place in the seyd galey in the overest stage; for in the lawyst under hyt ys ryght smolderyng hote and stynkyng.'

The fast speeds of which the ships were in theory capable, were very rarely achieved however, because until comparatively modern times, for reasons of safety and comfort, they did not sail a direct course but went along the coast or from island to island, in a series of loops, with stops of varying lengths in port. If a storm threatened sailors wanted to be in the shelter of a harbour, or at least protected from the wind by an island or cape. On land there was fresh water, food and wood for a fire to cook by, so that a hot meal could be prepared without endangering the boat; perhaps additions to the menu could even be made, and meat and game provided as well as fish; on board cooking arrangements – if there were any – were primitive. It was also more comfortable to sleep on land (without smells or the early morning mists and cold). Major repairs could be made to the boat; there was wood for the hull or rudder, and lianas, rushes and other materials with which to caulk the planks or mend the sail. And finally it was more easy to calculate one's position accurately on dry land than on a rocking boat, where calculations of the geographical latitude could be wrong by up to five degrees.

Compared to the efforts which went into shipbuilding, very little was done for a long time to improve the infrastructure. Many of the lighthouses built by the Romans still stood in medieval times – near La Coruña in north-west Spain for example, and at Dover and Boulogne on either side of the Channel; but it is uncertain whether they were used. The imperial records show that in the year 811 Charlemagne had the 'age old' pharos which stood at Boulogne, and 'which showed seafarers the way, put into use again, and ordered a beacon to be lit on top of it at night': but we do not know how successfully his orders were carried out. In the Mediterranean area beacons and other aids to navigation were better maintained than in the north, because most of the population lived very near the coast, and the sea was therefore more important as a means of livelihood and transport than in the countries north of the Alps. The situation improved as travel and trade increased in the North Sea and Baltic. Exceptionally high church towers which were visible from a long way off served as expressions of civic pride and as navigational aids for seafarers.

We do not yet know exactly how the Vikings navigated on the high seas. The knowledge gained by the helmsman on his many voyages must have been all important, and would have been enhanced by the experiences of other travellers. It was even more important for the seafarer to be at one with nature in all its aspects than for the traveller on land. He had to make a careful study of wind and clouds, sun and stars, the state of the water (colour, salt content and flotsam), flora and fauna. Columbus wrote in his journal that the Portuguese discovered most islands by a study of the flight of birds. Birds of passage may have shown the Irish monks the way to Iceland. It was possible to learn from experience the 'sphere of activity' of birds and fish, and to know which birds slept at sea or on land. A way of discovering where the nearest land lay by means of birds which the traveller took with him, goes back to at least the second millennium BC; Noah is often shown in pictorial images setting free the dove from the ark. The compass, which had been used for navigation in China since the tenth century, is first mentioned in the West in 1190; but as technological discoveries were often ignored by the literary-minded chroniclers, one may assume that the compass was also probably used earlier in Europe, possibly even by the Vikings. One wonders if they even perhaps had a better means of calculating their position, which they kept secret or which has been forgotten over the centuries; it is interesting that on their voyages from Norway to England they were clearly able to hold to their course without too much difficulty, in order to land at a particular place determined in advance. From Norway to Greenland the Vikings possibly travelled along a parallel of latitude; the geographical latitude can be calculated in an open boat simply by observing the altitude of the sun. On voyages in the North Sea and Baltic other methods had to be developed as navigators could not count on seeing the sun by day and the pole star at night, as it was so often misty. An important navigational device was the sounding line with a lump of tallow at its base, for measuring the depth of the water and assessing what the seabed was like; the nature of the bottom deposits – sand, rock, shingle of various colours – helped the navigator to determine his position, especially if he also studied the other indicators.

Written sailing directions, such as those which had been known in antiquity, were not available until the late Middle Ages, and most helmsmen could neither read nor write; even in the sixteenth century there were many illiterate seamen among the trusty Portuguese navigators who sailed to the East Indies. But medieval navigators had an incredibly rich store of experience to call on. Important information was handed on by word of mouth, from one person to another and from father to son, and in due course was written down. Parts of the Icelandic Sagas are like sailing directions, woven like set-pieces into the narrative by their authors. 'From Hernar in Norway' – the island of Hennö near Bergen – runs a sailing direction of this kind from late medieval times, 'you sail to the right, to Hwarf in Greenland (Cape Farewell on the southern tip of Greenland). In doing so you sail as far north as possible above Hjalvland (the Shetland Islands), so that it can only be seen on a clear day at sea; then to the south of the Faroes so that the water between is half the height of the mountains, and south of Iceland where you can still see its birds and whales.' Until the mid-fifteenth century details of routes were passed on by word of mouth, then they were written down by hand, and the first sailing directions only printed in 1541. In sailing manuals important information such as descriptions of the coastline, land and sea marks, depths of water, navigational instructions, was included and could be supplemented and added to after each voyage.

A navigator who had to make his way between many islands and shallows, needed more than a lead-line; Battuta writes that it was the custom to have a pilot when sailing among the Maldive Islands in the Indian Ocean. Centuries later, Vasco da Gama was lucky enough to obtain the services of a famous Arab scholar in East Africa, for his voyage to India. In the Pacific, charts must have been in use from early times; Marco Polo remarks that 'clever seamen, who voyage on those seas' had described the islands and drawn them in on maps. During his voyage through the West Indian islands, Columbus completed as accurately as he could charts of the places he visited.

Unlike the Vikings, Columbus had a rich store of navigational instruments and theoretical knowledge to call on during his voyages: cross-staff, astrolabe, quadrant, compass (whose variation he noted on the way), chronometer, charts and globe. Leading on from the works of Arab scholars, astrologers in the West had developed instruments to measure the position of the constellations. During the course of the Middle Ages, these instruments were further refined and were used for navigation. But one must remember two things: firstly, most ships still sailed with no instruments on board, trusting only to the navigator's experience and in God's help. And secondly, that it was difficult to take a position on a heaving boat. On the other hand Portuguese accounts show that in the sixteenth century many passengers had the ability and the instruments with which to check the navigator's pronouncements.

There were more difficulties to overcome in calculating geographical longitude than geographical latitude; there were no instruments to measure time and speed accurately. A sandglass had to be turned every half hour or eight times during a watch, which the seaman might often forget to do. Speed could only be judged by the time it took the ship to pass something floating in the water; it is questionable whether the log-line was known at the end of the fifteenth century. Tidal streams made it considerably more difficult to calculate a position. What it was actually like to chart a course is described by the Venetian envoy Quirini in 1506 in an account of the first Portuguese voyage to India: 'The astrolabe tells them when they have reached the equator. When they have passed it, they sail southwards for about two thousand one hundred miles, until the astrolabe shows that they are 35 degrees from the equator and therefore in the latitude of the Cape of Good Hope. During this long voyage they steer by the chart using compass and magnets. And although they lose our Pole Star from sight, they can still use the compass, because wherever the lodestone is, it always points to the north. In this way they can judge the winds more exactly than if they

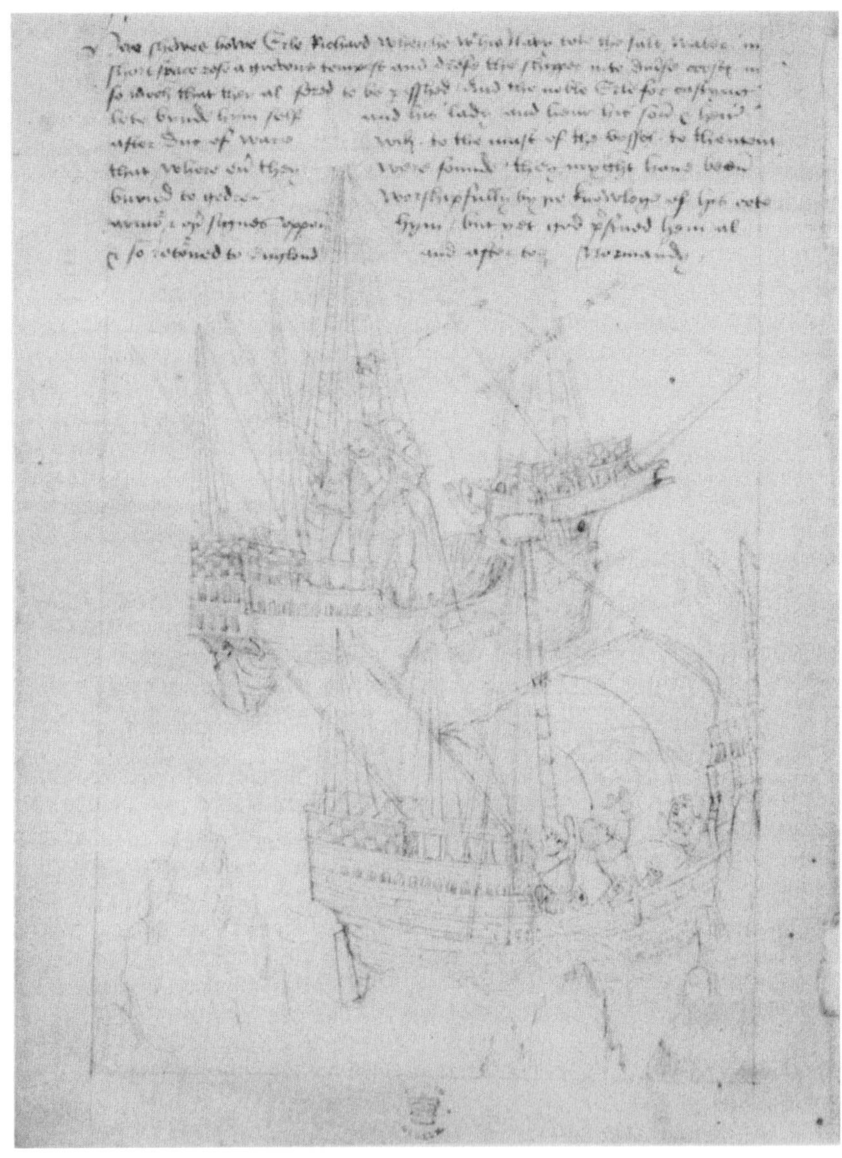

The dangers of travel by sea: Richard Beauchamp, earl of Warwick, encounters a dreadful tempest at sea, and ties himself, his wife and his son to the mast 'with the intent that when they were found, they might have been buried together'.

had not lost the Pole Star from sight. With the astrolabe they can also judge the altitude of the sun. At midday they can thus see how many degrees they are from the equator, and therefore know how far they are from those places which they wish to avoid, or to the desired ports.'

The island journeys of the Irish monks in their nutshell-like coracles, the voyages to Greenland and America of the Vikings in their open longships, the early voyages of discovery of the Portuguese and Spaniards are all the more amazing in that they were carried out without the help of such aids, or only with the help of very rudimentary calculations and instruments.

Realistically, the traveller had to expect discomfort during his sea voyage, if not danger to life and limb. He had to put up with the perpetual creaking and groaning of the wooden ship, and the slamming and crashing of the waves against the hull; with the disagreeable scrabbling of rats, and still more disagreeable bouts of seasickness; with the nauseating smell that rose from the bilges when it was hot or windless, the maggots with which all foodstuffs became infested on long voyages, the penetrating stink of rat urine which hit you when you ate the ship's biscuit, and the foul water. True, drinking-water and wine were kept in wooden casks lined with clay, but after a month's voyage it was no pleasure to quench one's thirst from these.

Besides hunger and thirst there was the danger of storms blowing up and of dead calms, and the risk of pirate attacks and mutiny. The typically sceptical 'landlubber' was given a graphic warning of this in the chronicle of Joinville, who had set out to sea on a crusade in 1248: 'In a very short time the wind had filled the sail and blown us out of sight of the land of our birth. And I tell you now, that anyone who sets out on such a dangerous course, is foolhardy. For at night you fall asleep without knowing whether you will find yourself the next morning at the bottom of the sea.'

It is no mere coincidence that poets so often used images of 'stormy seas' and 'safe havens', and that artists so frequently depicted storms at sea; St Nicholas came into his own as the patron saint of seafarers, whether they were merchants or pirates – many were in fact both – and was greatly revered. Travellers counted themselves lucky if they had even made the 'short' voyage across the Channel from England to the Continent safely. Storms often blew up so quickly that the crew hardly had time to react. If the sail was torn and the rudder broken, only a miracle could save the ship from going down. Bede tells how in the mid-seventh century during a storm, travellers cast some holy oil which Bishop Aidan had given them, foreseeing a storm, onto the sea; immediately the waters became calm. On his return from his first voyage to America Columbus was caught in a hurricane; finally in desperation, since no other help was forthcoming, he vowed to go on a pilgrimage if saved.

Coastal inhabitants who knew the sea well, had special prayers which – to the seafarer – might sound more than a little ambiguous. On the south-east coast of England in an area where many ships ran aground, a prayer was said in stormy weather: 'Oh God, protect ships at sea from the storm – but if they must run aground, let it be on our shore.' Such people were usually poor, scratching a meagre living by tilling the land, and fishing. A wrecked vessel was a bonus, and the right of wreck might give the right to seize the ship and its merchandise, if not the shipwrecked mariners themselves. The appropriate lights were often placed in the wrong position, to cause ships to run aground. If the local inhabitants had the right of wreck to the ship and its cargo providing the crew were all dead, the seamen who had just escaped death by drowning, were in mortal danger. Seafarers were understandably anxious to restrict the right of wreck – making it a privilege for a narrow or wider circle of beneficiaries (as by the Lübeck Charter of 1224, and the Hanseatic Treaty of Stralsund in 1370; or under the Charter of the Cinque Ports in England).

Problems also arose when passengers were suspected of harbouring a disease. Sebald Rieter travelled to the Holy Land by sea in 1479. As the plague was rife in Venice, the port of departure, when the pilgrims left, they were not allowed to land during the voyage. They could often only get permission to visit the holy places at their ports of call by offering bribes.

Vasco da Gama and his men more than once had difficulty in getting drinking-water on the coast of Africa, during their voyage to India; once they even had to obtain it by force. Another time the local people came from a distance to help them. Whereas many explorers named places after feast-days or saint's days – for example Santa Cruz or Natal (the land of the Nativity) – Vasco da Gama and his men gave a strip of land in East Africa the name *Terra da Boa Gente*, or Land of the Good Men. Many a ship's crew died of thirst after terrible sufferings when their ship was becalmed. The story of Tristan and Isolde tells of the misfortune of being becalmed and suffering from thirst.

There are many descriptions of pirates. At sea the borderlines between legitimate force and unlawful attack were as loosely drawn as on land. People were often slow in attempting to control the pirates effectively – especially as almost everyone had some connection with them or found to their delight that they had wiped out a rival. Neither Charlemagne in his attacks against Saracens and Vikings, nor the Hanseatic League against the league of pirates known as the Vitalien brüder and other raiders, were as quick, aggressive and effective as Caesar had been, according to Suetonius, against the pirates of the Mediterranean.

If Christians and Moslems met at sea, the vanquished could hope for little mercy. In 1394 Hans Schiltberger fought against the Turks in Hungary. His army was routed; Schiltberger and many of his men took to flight, hoping to save themselves by getting across the Danube by boat. The events he describes must have been typical of many shipwrecks. There was no question of solidarity among Christians: 'Then the ship was so full, that they wouldn't let anyone else on board, and they beat off the hands of many who tried to get onto the ship, and they were drowned in the water.' Schiltberger was taken prisoner by the Turks; as he and his fellow sufferers in prison were likely to have their noses and ears cut off and be chained as galley slaves to their banks, they fled. From a mountain

A storm at sea. A Bible illustration (Mark 4, 38), which any medieval traveller who had been to sea would recognise at once. In a storm, passengers in an open boat were at the mercy of the ocean. The picture reminded people that in such situations they must put their trust in God.

by the Black Sea they saw a Christian ship; when it grew dark they signalled to the crew from the mountain by making a fire. The 'master' of the ship sent a boat to find out what the signal meant. Schiltberger and his companions stated that they were fellow Christians, who 'had been taken by the heathen and had by God's help escaped this far, so that they might be returned to Christendom'. The boat's crew tested their credentials in an interesting way: they 'asked us, if we knew the Lord's Prayer and the Creed. So we had to say the Lord's Prayer to them, and the Creed.' The sailors wouldn't immediately take the five refugees with them, but went back to get further orders from their captain. Finally the five were taken on board, and shared the fate of the ship: it escaped from three Turkish vessels with difficulty, nearly sank in a storm, and was driven far out to sea so that they all nearly perished from hunger and thirst. 'Then we came to a rock in the sea, and found snails and spider-crabs there, which we collected and fed on for four days.' At last Schiltberger reached Constantinople (still Christian in those days) and could travel further in 'foreign lands'.

A Lübeck chronicle tells how in 1453 a ship with about 300 pilgrims on board

Columbus lands in the New World. His flagship the Santa Maria *and two accompanying ships the* Niña *and* Pinta *are seen in the background. Indians offer goods, and others flee from the disembarking Spaniards.*

which was travelling back from the Holy Land fell into the hands of Saracens: the 'wicked men' fell like wolves upon the Christian pilgrims, killing all the men who refused to believe in 'our god Mohammed'. They spared the women, 'so that they might force them to be used for their pleasure'.

During the long voyages undertaken by explorers, there were two further dangers to contend with: mutiny and scurvy. When Columbus's westerly voyage dragged on too long, the crew grew restless; in retrospect, Columbus realised he had had a mutiny on his hands. Columbus had been able to enlist volunteers for his three ships; Vasco da Gama had a crew of 148 on his voyage to India and another twelve men who had been sentenced to death or banishment, who were spared on condition they were willing to undertake dangerous duties during the long voyage. A mutiny was more or less inevitable, but Vasco da Gama was able to put it down.

He was unable to get the better of another problem, because he had had no previous experience of it. Vasco took three years' provisions with him. The daily ration for the crew was: 750 grammes of ship's biscuit, 500 grammes of salt beef or 250 grammes of salt bacon, $1\frac{1}{2}$ litres of water, $\frac{3}{4}$ litre wine, $\frac{1}{10}$ litre olive oil, $\frac{1}{20}$ litre vinegar, with beans, flour, lentils, sardines, prunes, onions, garlic, sugar, almonds and honey, in order to be able to prepare a wider variety of dishes. On long voyages the ship's provisions became increasingly inedible; and worse still was the fact that there were no fresh fruit or vegetables to provide the crew with Vitamin C. Scurvy became a fatal sickness; of the 160 who had set out, only 55 returned home alive (on Magellan's first world circumnavigation only 18 of 237 survived, but in that instance some of them, including Magellan himself, fell in battle).

Vasco da Gama's crew first suffered from scurvy at the mouth of the Zambesi in East Africa; they had been sailing for five and a half months since leaving San Tiago, one of the Cape Verde islands. Later, the Portuguese were given oranges and lemons in Mombasa by the king there. 'It pleased God in his mercy, to heal all of us who were sick at that time, while we lay near the town, because the air in that place was very good.' The Portuguese naturally saw no connection between their eating of citrus fruits and the alleviation of the sickness. As they were able to get fresh fruit and vegetables farther along their route, those who remained ill quickly recovered. During the short crossing (in 23 days with the south-west monsoon) there were no further cases of scurvy, and none during their stay in India. The return voyage took a very long time, because the Portuguese did not yet know that they would have to wait until November/December for the north-east monsoon. They left six weeks too early. Constantly becalmed or driven back by the wind, the voyage back to Africa, which took 'three months less 3 days' became a torture. The whole crew became ill: 'Their gums grew so swollen over their teeth, that they could no longer eat; their legs swelled up as well, and they had great sores all over the body, which made them so weak that they died, without having any other sickness.' On the voyage out Vasco had lost 30 men; now 30 more died. 'And those, who were still on duty on each ship, were but seven or eight men, and they were far from being as well as they should have been . . . We had come to a point, where all discipline failed. While we travelled on thus in deadly danger, we made many vows on board ship to the saints and mediators.' The ship's captains were wondering whether to sail back to India on the next favourable wind, when at last the east wind (the north-east monsoon which had now set in) took them back to Mogadishu in Africa, where in a few days, on 2 January 1499, they had dry land under their feet again, 'at which we were as happy, as if it had been Portuguese soil'.

The anonymous author to whom we owe this account, describes with clinical accuracy the Vitamin C deficiency which was feared for so long: bleeding gums, skin and musculature, sores on the lower leg, lack of energy, disinclination for work. In a modern medical handbook it states laconically: 'If untreated scurvy inevitably leads to death.' The body can store a certain amount of Vitamin C; on a diet totally deficient in Vitamin C it takes about three months for the first clinical symptoms of scurvy to appear. Vasco da Gama's return voyage across the Indian Ocean took just under three months, but perhaps the crew were still so weak from the voyage out, that the sickness took less time to manifest itself fully.

In the mid-fourteenth century, Battuta had noticed during his journeys through eastern Asia, that the sailors on Chinese ships stowed 'greenstuff, vegetables and ginger' in wooden barrels. This was probably a preventative measure to ward off the disease, to which more seamen fell prey between 1500 and 1800 – that is after the introduction of longer, uninterrupted voyages – than all those killed in battle and other disasters at sea put together. The preventative and healing properties of citrus fruits were only recognised in Europe from the middle of the eighteenth century; in 1795 the British Admiralty ordered supplies of lime juice to be carried on all warships.

The natural landscape and cultivation of the land

Towards the end of the first century AD, Tacitus pointed out in his *Germania*, how inaccessible much of Germany was: 'In some parts it is quite different, it is true, but in general the country is made terrible by its primeval forests or hateful by its bogs.'

The vast and impenetrable forests were inimical to the Romans. During the Middle Ages large stretches of woodland were cleared, but on a lesser scale in Germany than in the Mediterranean countries. 'Hateful bogs' were probably not waterlogged swamps but flooded watermeadows and the ancient ox-bow river channels in the valleys of the Rhine, Danube and Elbe. Roads had already been made through woods and even across swamps in Tacitus's day; without them it would have been impossible to bring the much coveted amber from the North Sea and Baltic down to Italy, or for Germanic warriors to have sallied forth against the Romans. Although the picture Tacitus draws needs modifying in other respects also, it does give an accurate idea of what many regions were like, up until nearly a thousand years later in fact, as the few written and more numerous archaeological sources show.

In 1080 Lampert, a monk from the Hersfeld monastery in Hesse, describes in his annals the danger in which Henry IV found himself in 1073. The Emperor was besieged by the Saxons high up in mountainous Harzburg, which could only be reached by a very treacherous path. 'The other sides of the mountain were shrouded in darkness by a terrible expanse of forest, which stretches from there as continuous primeval woodland for many miles right to the borders of Thuringia.' To trick the enemy, the Emperor began to parley with them. While they were still unsuspecting, he fled by night with a small troop of men. 'For three days, it is said, they travelled without food through the primeval forest along a narrow, little known path, which a hunter who led the way had discovered when he was making his way through distant parts of the wood in the heat of the chase.' Exhausted by hunger, lack of sleep and the exertions of the long journey, they came on the fourth day to Eschwege, where they recovered a little; the next day, when many followers were already coming to join the Emperor, they went on to Hersfeld. 'Here Henry stayed for four days, waiting for the troops which he had summoned from the whole realm for a campaign against Poland.'

The account is noteworthy for several reasons. Long after the first woodland clearances of the early Middle Ages, there were still extensive primeval forests in central Germany at the end of the eleventh century. There was probably more than one path known to the hunters who followed their quarry all day through the forest; some of our modern roads probably go back to the early game paths. The forest was considered terrible by Lampert, used to the comforts of the great monastery of Hersfeld; for he was armed not with bow and arrows or axe, but with a pen. A monk a hundred or two hundred years before Lampert had described country similar to Tacitus's *Germania* in Fulda, the neighbouring district to Hersfeld.

In earlier centuries the forest was not as totally uninhabited as it is today, for even Henry and his followers expected to meet with sudden attacks at any moment on their way. Henry's flight was in the middle of August; at that time of year there were charcoal-burners and resiners in the woods, turfcutters and coppicers, potash-burners, shingle-makers and swineherds. Protection was sought there by men who preferred a rough life and liberty to a more comfortable existence in the service of a hated lord, and by outlaws and the hunted. Peasants hid stores in the woods, which would enable them to survive if robber bands or soldiers threatened their homes; Charlemagne was possibly thinking of such hoards when he warned the administrators of his imperial domain to take care that no one hid seedcorn in out-of-the-way places. Possibly Henry and his companions found some such hoards on their way.

In Germany at the time of Henry IV's flight there were about five to seven inhabitants per square kilometre, fewer in Thuringia with its extensive forests.

In spite of that it is unlikely that the small troop met no one during the three days, especially as they went through the anciently inhabited oak woods; quite the opposite must have been the case, otherwise loyal followers of the Emperor would not have gathered to meet him in Hersfeld.

In many regions – for example in the Paris basin or in the Rhine-Main triangle – there was already a thick network of settlements in the early Middle Ages, which often lay within sight or even within calling distance of one another. It is difficult to stress too strongly the importance for the medieval traveller of these clusters of dwelling-places, only one or two miles away from each other. The next stopping-place was always within sight; the traveller could count on finding water to drink in hot weather and a roof over his head when it was wet; if he was overtaken by fog, snow, or darkness, a distant light or the barking of a dog or crowing of a cock would show him the way to the nearest shelter. As time went on, many of these places grew large enough to have a church, whose bells would be rung during stormy weather or the hours of darkness, so that travellers would not lose their way; the E-chime of the five-hundred-year-old 'Gloriosa' of Erfurt cathedral could be heard, when the wind was in the right direction, from over twelve miles away! But even when there was no sound of a dog barking or of bells ringing to guide the traveller, he could tell from the boundary stones, and from the meadows, fields and gardens, which lay round the settlements, that he was nearing the homes of men.

One of the greatest achievements of the Middle Ages was that isolated clusters of dwellings gradually became linked by a better and ever-growing network of roads. The roads were not, of course, definitively fixed for a long time. If a road was not used – because it was dangerous or because there was a better way, or because prohibitively high tolls were demanded on the way or it was blocked by trees blown down in a storm – it soon became overgrown again. And that applied to long-distance routes also.

Over the centuries single farmsteads were enlarged into royal manors, palaces or monasteries. It is true we are frequently told that this or that monastery was surrounded by a desert wilderness. That would be an accurate description of a monastery such as the one in the south of France with the apposite name of Saint-Guilhem-le-Désert, St William in the Desert, an important stopping-place on one of the routes to Santiago. It was less applicable to Prémontré in northern France: the founder monastery of the Premonstratensians was said to have been built in a barren, totally uninhabited region, in country that was full of scrub and swamps, and which was altogether uninviting – except for a small chapel, a little orchard full of fruit, and a small pond! In the neighbourhood of the later Cistercian monastery of Maulbronn, robbers were said to have been rife and to have fallen upon travellers; where robbers can make a 'living' there must be people, which is not surprising in an area ideally placed for traffic, through which a motorway, railway and main roads run today. With the founding of monasteries and royal courts the character of the landscape changed (with the building of official buildings and churches, planting of vineyards and orchards, and making of fishponds and other necessary features), and traffic increased; messengers, churchmen and lay people came and went.

Fortifications built as a refuge – sited for example to offer protection from Hungarians, Norsemen or Saracens – were often permanently settled later; they served to alter further the patterns of the countryside and to make the network of settlements even more dense; some of the farming communities below the walls of such forts developed over the centuries into urban settlements, such as Freiburg in Breisgau.

The Upper Rhine area is a textbook example of how urban communities developed: gaps of more than a day's journey between places were gradually filled in. The deciding factor in whether a place became a town or remained a country settlement was neither size nor number of inhabitants: there were large villages and small towns. Of primary importance were the rights which the citizens of the community held, above all the right of self-government and self-jurisdiction, followed by the right to hold markets, to be a staple town, raise tolls, have a mint and erect defences.

As a traveller approached a town, if the citizens had the right to fortify their community and separate it from the surrounding countryside by a defensive wall, and the right to lay down laws and carry out sentences forthwith, the facts would be clearly in evidence. The traveller would see the town walls from afar, often set off by richly decorated towers and gateways, which were a mark of self-esteem, and prudence, since the watchman at the gates would ask the identity and purpose of those who wished to enter. A gallows in close proximity to the common thoroughfares warned the newcomer to obey the laws laid down by the community; the seats of justice also told him, however, that he would have a fair hearing if he were falsely accused. The authorities kept the peace: it was a punishable offence even to draw a sword. Special laws protected those visiting the town markets, and on their way there and back; the safety of travellers was of concern to the community, even when they were outside the town walls. Urban communities shaped the character of their citizens; they favoured the rise of a self-confident, daring breed of men, who would stride down the years as merchant adventurers and explorers, to give us Marco Polo and Columbus.

In the regions where there were plenty of towns – northern Italy, southern France, Westphalia, Flanders – the traveller could count on finding an inn for himself and a stall for his mount each night, and a shoemaker, a wheelwright (for repairing wheels or carts), a money-changer, a barber, baths, and a girl of easy virtue. He could get information at the market about bridges and ferries, about the safety of his ongoing route and the food supplies in various regions; the authorities kept an eye on prices, but in town records there are numerous complaints by strangers about having been cheated in such and such a place. The traveller might also find sympathetic people or institutions in a town, who would help him if he had been robbed on the way or been destitute when he set out. Guilds offered support to colleagues in the same trade (travelling craftsmen for example), religious brotherhoods devoted themselves to other, more saintly,

Easy going: a fertile, well-farmed countryside with good paths and bridges and settlements not too far apart.

travellers (members of the Brotherhood of St James in Paris supported pilgrims from other lands as well), and Hospitallers had expressly undertaken to help all those who were weary and overburdened.

As against the advantages to be found in a town, one must not forget the darker side. Despite the threat of draconian reprisals, there was much crime, due to poverty; and a greater risk of infection because of inadequate hygiene, overcrowded buildings and indescribable dirt. There were neither sewers nor means of garbage disposal, and usually no paving stones. At best one might hope to be able to jump from stone to stone when it was wet, to avoid getting shoes and clothing sodden in the mire.

In the first half of the fourteenth century Europe had a considerably denser network of settlements than it has today. Failing communities were abandoned, as soon as the pressure of population decreased, particularly after the Great Plague in the mid-fourteenth century. One example will show how this process of 'depopulation' affected a small area: in the southern Fulda–Werra mountain country, between 1300 and 1500, in an area of about 290 square miles, 169 single and group settlements disappeared. If there had been 180 settlements in the area in about 1300, in about 1500 there would have been only about 80 villages left. As a result of this decline, the traveller had farther to go to the next settlement where he could find food, shelter or help. Compared with other areas however, the European traveller was still in a fairly favourable position. Rubruck notes, that on his return journey from the court of the Mongol Khan, he saw neither a settlement nor any trace of a building in two months and ten days.

The deserted villages and towns were a great loss to the traveller. On the other hand one must not forget the greater security and comfort which was brought about by cultivation of the land during the course of the Middle Ages – the clearing and draining of forest and marsh to cite but one example. The fairy tale of Hänsel and Gretel lost in the wood and in mortal danger from wild beasts echoes the fears felt by people for many generations. And in the course of centuries thousands of soldiers, pilgrims, merchants and ordinary men and women fell prey – and not only in Italy – to the 'bad air'. It was not known how malaria was carried, but people realised there was a connection between the incidence of the disease and swampy areas in the heat of summer. By draining swamps, the breeding places of the malaria-carrying mosquitoes were also destroyed. The relief at finding – contrary to expectations – 'good air' in low lying country is expressed in the name of the Argentinian capital: Buenos Aires, the exact opposite of 'Mal /aria'.

THE IMPORTANCE OF RELIGION, TRADE AND COMMUNICATIONS FOR TRAVEL

Singly or in groups, many thousands of people were on the road in medieval times, travelling in the service of one of the three great monotheistic religions, or taking merchandise or news abroad.

Religion and travel

In the area covered by this book, both Christendom and Islam held sway. Both had an exceptional dynamism in their early days, Islam even more so than Christianity; a hundred years after its foundation the Mohammedan faith had spread from the south over the Pyrenees and east as far as Persia. Jewish scholars and merchants worked in both the Christian and Islamic worlds.

The Church had always had rather an ambiguous attitude to travel. On the one hand it warned people (especially women) of the dangers of being on the road, and on the other it sent millions of people out into the world. On the whole the positive side was uppermost, particularly because of the many precedents which Christians could find in the Old and New Testaments, from Abraham to the Holy Family, and the disciples sent by Jesus into 'all the world'. In his account of his mission to the Mongols, Rubruck quotes from the Apocrypha: 'he will travel through strange countries; for he hath tried the good and the evil among men' (Ecclesiasticus 39.4). Benedict demanded that his followers should settle in one place and remain there; but even he allowed for travelling monks who were to be sent out in pairs; and the abbot should ask for a letter of recommendation from visiting monks who called in on their way. Monks from priories associated with the abbey at Cluny had to take their vows in the presence of the abbot of Cluny. Synods mobilised thousands of people; the late medieval reforming councils of Constance and Basle were the most important of the medieval congresses. Many Cistercian abbots travelled with a great retinue, accompanied by armed servants, to the annual general council at Cîteaux. Pious Christians wanted not only to visit shrines, but if possible to bring back relics as well. This was often a highly political matter. Widukind of Corvey, one of the most important chroniclers of the tenth century, writes that abbot Fulrad of St Denis, on a visit to Rome, had discovered the grave of Saint Vitus, taken the relics and brought them back to West Francia; from there they were taken in a ceremonial procession to Saxony. As the Saxons now 'possessed' the mighty intercessor, the standing of the (Western) Francs went downhill, and that of the Saxons was enhanced (*ex hoc res Francorum coeperunt minui, Saxonum autem crescere*).

The officiating Church body disregarded the difficulties of the journey, at least if it was a case of spreading the word, but also if there were bishops or churches to consecrate, Christians to confirm, synods to attend, or books or other objects to fetch. That the Church expected Christians to travel, is clear from the fact that priests had their own portable altars and bishops were duty bound to set aside a third or quarter of the income of their churches for the sustenance of travellers and the support of the poor (which was often the same thing).

Christendom was the strongest influence in medieval Europe; in spite of countless schisms it has left its mark on the countries of Europe until the present day. Since the Great Schism of 1054 it has been divided into the Roman and Greek Churches; the Church of Rome was repeatedly challenged by new heresies. Doctrines from the Orient which proclaimed a community of the 'pure' (Cathars), caused division among countries, communities and families. The Benedictine Order, important for the cohesion of western Christianity, was weakened in the twelfth century, when Cistercians and Premonstratensians aspired to a new 'ideal of life'.

The Christian Church set the pattern of the year and week with festivals and holy days; it covered Europe with a network of churches which – with all their local differences – were uniform in design. It influenced the behaviour of people to the needy; and created unifying ideals which broke through linguistic, cultural and social barriers. In praying to God, in honouring God's Mother, the apostles and saints, men felt themselves to be of one community. Travellers felt 'at home' when they heard the Latin words of the Mass or Absolution. The right of asylum in churches and churchyards could be a life-saving factor for travellers threatened by 'summary justice'.

The influence pilgrimages had on travel in the Middle Ages cannot be over-stressed. Christians, Moslems and Jews all travelled to holy places to pray. In the Islamic faith pilgrimages have an even greater significance than for Christians: every Moslem is duty bound to visit the holy shrines of Mecca at least once in his lifetime, in a spirit of reverence; year in, year out, millions of people flocked along the roads to Mecca, becoming aware of their common purpose only as they went along or when they reached the holy building of the Kaaba at Mecca itself. The eastern and western Christian Churches were united, despite their other differences, by their worship of communal saints, such as the apostles or St Nicholas: pilgrimages by Christians to the Holy Land, to Rome, Santiago, Canterbury, Einsiedeln . . . meant that there were constantly moving crowds of people and created an international brotherhood of men, triumphing over differences of colour, language, legal or social status, age, sex and any other differences.

The Jews formed an important link between East and West. As the only

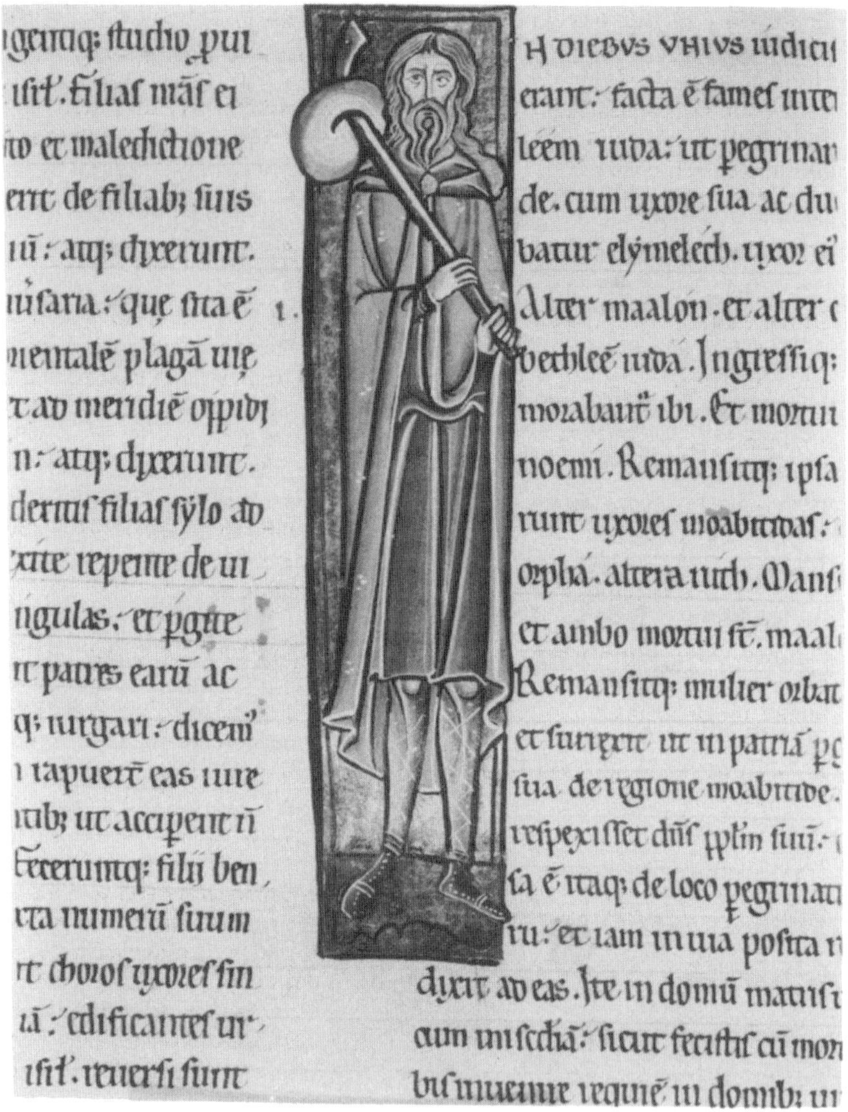

A twelfth-century traveller with his bundle hooked on his staff and a good travelling cloak.

non-Christians in a community which regarded those who did not follow the true faith as guilty of a crime punishable by death, they were in a precarious position throughout most of the Middle Ages. They had to trust in the dearly bought protection of the particular ruler of the day; they were often hard pressed and repeatedly – as at the time of the crusades and the Great Plague – intolerably humiliated and persecuted.

Trade

In the early Middle Ages, long-distance trade in the Mediterranean and Kingdom of the Franks was in the hands of Syrians and Jews. The words 'mercatores' and 'Judaei' were often used synonymously. Jews were held in high regard as merchants, moneylenders and doctors, so long as there were no Christians with comparable qualifications. The Syrians and Jews had inherited the skills of the Phoenician and Greek traders; they often spoke several languages; and they were adept at making their way in both the Christian and Islamic worlds. In 797 Charlemagne sent Isaac the Jew with his emissaries to the Caliph of Baghdad; Isaac was probably a merchant, who served as interpreter and guide. After the death of the two other leaders of the legation, he brought Haroun-al-Raschid's presents back to the Emperor.

Since the eighth century European traders – especially the Frisians – had been making trading contacts, although they were descended from families whose members had only recently laid waste great tracts of Europe through murder, plunder and rapine. They had learnt from experience that the exchange of goods in a peaceful manner was more paying in the long run.

The reputation of traders was constantly under attack, even from the Church. A sermon made by Peter Damiani, one of the leaders of the religious reform movement, at the Feast of St Nicholas in 1057, is noteworthy; St Nicholas being one of the patron saints of merchants. Peter Damiani fulminated: 'You flee from your homeland, do not know your children, and forsake your wife; you have forgotten everything which is essential. You are covetous, wanting to acquire more, and gain only to lose, and in losing, bemoan your lot.'

Despite such abuse, merchants were not only welcomed by civil and church leaders as the bringers of luxury goods, but also because they knew foreign languages and countries, and could often give useful information about possible enemies and allies. So they were granted privileges by rulers, such as exemption from heavy ship's duties, tolls on vehicles and pack-animals, fees for passes, and other dues, and through special protection. At the end of the twelfth century the Prince of Novgorod guaranteed Germans and merchants from Gotland safety and legal protection in the Novgorod territories; they would be safe from robbery and attack, 'unharmed and untouched by anyone'. In 1269 the Hanseatic merchants were allowed to fell trees whenever they chose, for the repair of ships or for building: 'So when the guest comes to the Neva and needs wood or a mast, he may cut them on either bank of the river, wherever he will.' Such privileges were the cause of envy among the 'underprivileged'. A levelling process gradually took place. Special privileges had barely been granted to certain traders, before others aspired to them or to even greater concessions; what had originally been the privilege of one class of people became in the course of time the right of every citizen.

As a royal safe-conduct was only valid where the ruler held sway, traders had to be able to protect themselves; they formed guilds or leagues; the members took a solemn oath to be true to one another until they returned home safely – or until death. United, and if necessary armed, they were no longer at the mercy of bandits and pirates. They formed caravans on land or convoys at sea. Passes offered or extracted from rulers during the late Middle Ages, were only valid for as long as the money paid for them would guarantee safety; often enough the payment was treated as a tax, and the letter of safe-conduct used as a means of extending the state's power. In the first half of the thirteenth century, the *Sachsenspiegel* states that the ruler will give compensation for losses due to robbery; but this compensation was only paid if the injured party was in a position to wield power and influence. He could get his own ruler to put pressure on the indemnifying party on his behalf; or he could join with others needing protection in order to trade safely. The threat to boycott the streets, roads, and bridges, markets and fairs, goods and services of the defaulting party to a contract, was no meaningless gesture, as the Hanse showed in its quarrels with Bruges in 1388–92.

After making such perilous journeys, traders wanted to rest in peaceful surroundings, and they built houses of their own in the important foreign trading centres. Venetian traders had such houses in many places in the eastern Mediterranean and by the Black Sea, north German traders in Venice at the Fondaco dei Tedeschi, the Hanse in Bergen, London and Novgorod; and in Bruges there were many Germans scattered throughout the town. The German establishment or 'kontor' in Novgorod measured about 180 × 100 feet, and was therefore about the same size as the houses with courtyards of the rich boyars. The buildings were surrounded by a high stockade of wooden stakes. It had only one gate, which was shut at night by the watchman. Bloodhounds were used to keep 'friends' at a safe distance from the valuable merchandise (in Venice there was a house belonging to Germans, whose watchdog began to growl angrily as soon as it heard anyone speaking any language other than German!). At the centre of the property was St Peter's Church, and the whole establishment was called the Peterhouse. The church, being the only stone building in the 'kontor', offered a safe haven and a quiet place in which to pray, and was often a last place of refuge, when aggressive Novgorodans tried to assert their rights by force. All the other parts of the property were built of wood: the simple dwelling quarters, each with sleeping space and dining-room, provided shelter for eighty to one hundred and twenty merchants with their servants. There were individual common-rooms for merchants and their female helpmates ('nurseries'), store-rooms, shops and cellars (also used as a prison, although the Novgorod authorities were officially responsible for arrests); a common dining-room, a brewery, a sick-room and bathroom, forming a relatively autonomous community. An alderman held office each trading season; he was chosen from among the ranks of independent traders on arrival at the Neva, and from the mid-fifteenth century appointed by Lübeck. The clerical work was done by the priests of St Peter's Church.

The establishment was typical of others which merchants kept in common in foreign towns. Guests found a home from home, and their bodily and spiritual needs were well cared for: the cooks would serve them with their native dishes, the hymns they knew would be sung in church or chapel, and the sermon preached in their mother tongue, in which they could also confess their sins and gain absolution. The personnel in such houses were from the merchants' homeland, or could at least speak their native language; they could help a visitor in his dealings with the merchants, tradesmen and officials of the town in which he was staying.

The name 'feast' or 'fair' illustrates the importance of the church calendar for trade in the Middle Ages. When people flocked together for one reason or another, on a saint's day or to celebrate the anniversary of the dedication of a church, merchants and pedlars from far and near would be among the crowd, and would find a public eagerly awaiting their wares in the market place. Trade fairs which drew people from outside the region were held in large towns (such as Frankfurt and Leipzig) and smaller places (such as St Denis to the north of Paris and Zurzach on the High Rhine).

Expensive goods made up the major part of long-distance trade until the height of the Middle Ages: noble metals, finery (precious stones, amber, coral, pearls, silks, furs), slaves (sold as objects), incense and spices. Spices were needed to conserve foodstuffs, introduce variety into a limited diet and to mask the odour of meat which was no longer fresh; many spices were much sought after as aphrodisiacs, narcotics and for medicinal remedies. Pepper played such an important part in trade for a time, that customs-duties and taxes on it rose, and merchants were rudely referred to as 'peppersacks'. The voyages of discovery in the late Middle Ages were carried out as part of the search for a direct route to India and its spices.

Wares that were needed for religious ceremonies played a special role in foreign trade: thousands of Christian communities needed wine for mass, oil for consecration and incense for religious celebration. The need for incense meant that unbroken trading contacts were maintained for centuries between the Christian and Islamic worlds, over a distance of often more than 4000 miles – although this did not entail Icelandic traders having to go to Arabia. Just as amber had been taken from the earliest times from the Baltic to the Mediterranean, without traders from Samland going to Phoenicia, so incense could be handed on from trader to trader. As merchants wanted to make full use of their loading capacity both on the outward and return journeys, two-way

A merchant plying his wares. Long-distance traders dealt in valuable goods which had to be carried by one or more pack-animals. The merchant, seen here talking to a noble lady, also conveyed news and information: another reason why medieval rulers granted privileges to such travellers.

trade was undertaken. Iceland for example exported fleeces, wool, hides, pelts, meat, tallow, butter, cheese, fish, whale-oil, falcons and brimstone. The Church's need for wine, oil and incense led to the development of a world-wide economy – of a very basic sort – which could thrive despite barriers of language or culture or (in the case of incense) religion.

Since the crusades, markets had been opened up in other areas for expensive merchandise. And goods in daily use, such as corn, wine, fish and salt, were carried in ever increasing quantities. While it was principally a matter of transporting small quantities of expensive goods, the state of the roads was not particularly important. The amber trade between the Baltic and Mediterranean, the silk trade between China and Byzantium or India, the trade in incense between the Yemen and Alexandria could be carried on without roads being built: simple paths were adequate for bearers and camel caravans. But as more goods were traded, and the loads became larger and heavier – casks of wine or barrels of herrings for instance – roads and transport became all the more vital. In the latter part of the Middle Ages a much higher priority was given to roadbuilding and the provision of stable vehicles, both of which benefited the ordinary traveller as well as merchants. Place names such as Salz(salt)burg and Halle (a Hallore was a German salt-maker), and the salt-streets to be found in many places are a reminder that travelling merchants passed that way with the most important preserving material and seasoning of all. Joint fleets sailed from the Hanseatic towns to fetch the salt which was needed for fish-curing from the Atlantic coasts of France. Such journeys created bonds between the North Sea and Baltic areas and with the European countries bordering on the Atlantic.

As a lack of wood had been experienced in the Mediterranean regions for some time, leather containers had to be used for many goods – such as wine – which were carried in wooden casks in the north and which had been put in amphora in ancient Greece and Rome. The leather containers mentioned in the Bible and in the 'Thousand and One Nights' had several advantages over earthenware jars: they were light and unbreakable; if necessary they could be blown up and used as an emergency lifebelt or float when crossing rivers. Battuta tells how inflated leather bladders were tied together to make life-rafts in the Indian Ocean.

Throughout history, there have been conflicts of interest between politics and trade. Monopolies, embargoes, extraterritorial rights and the imposition of duties could all lead to clashes. China imposed the death penalty on anyone who tried to break the country's monopoly of the silk trade. Monks reputedly succeeded in smuggling silk-moth eggs hidden in their staves into Byzantium, where a thriving silk industry soon arose. Willibald, later Bishop of Eichstätt, was endowed with a high degree of native cunning; in 720 he got round an export ban, by putting balsam into a vessel and masking its characteristic smell with the stronger smell of petroleum. Byzantium, as the only 'true seat of empire', claimed a monopoly on the royal colour purple; a distinguished envoy, Bishop Liutprand of Cremona, had purple material which he had legally purchased taken from him when he left and was reimbursed with the cost price, and told that foreigners had no right to go about decked in purple. Merchants were tempted to avoid paying duties. As the houses of merchants in foreign towns had many privileges which the local population did not enjoy, clashes were almost inevitable, as for example over the punishment of offenders. (Who would sit in judgement and whose laws would pertain in cases of murder, robbery, theft, criminal assault?) On more than one occasion merchants pretended to be pilgrims, in order to avoid paying tariffs and duties. In such cases the authorities usually demanded the payment of an – even higher – tariff. Records exist however from tenth-century Germany and fourteenth-century China, of orders confiscating the goods and vessels of the offending party.

Foreign trade narrowed the gap – in distance and time – between producer and consumer, supply and demand; it bound together through the exchange of goods peoples of different races, religions and cultures. Along many of the routes discovered by traders, soldiers, artists and missionaries later travelled, as did St Ansgar in the ninth century on his missions to Scandinavia. The maxim, to travel with as little ready money as possible, applied to merchants as much as to others; it was in fact trade which led the way towards the cashless methods of payment which other travellers, such as pilgrims to Jerusalem, later enjoyed. Until the seventeenth and eighteenth centuries, the boundaries between robbery and trade were often somewhat ill-defined. The re-emergence of piracy or hijacking today shows that the powers of peace-keeping authorities must be continually reinforced against individual or collective attack; what has been gradually achieved in some areas is in others still – or once more – unattainable.

Sending messages and imparting news

Among our travellers were both messengers and envoys. The former were mostly of modest origin, and were not empowered to make business transactions; the latter – often nobles, churchmen, rich merchants – were in many cases authorised to make contracts on behalf of those who had sent them.

Rulers both great and small were interested in having information which was as full, accurate, up-to-date and speedily conveyed as possible; they wanted to be able to assess enemy positions and those of their allies correctly and to avoid unnecessary expense. It was unfortunate, to say the least, when an expensive legation heard after a long journey that the ruler to whom they had been sent

A messenger, from the Ursula Cycle. According to the legend, Aetherius, a heathen prince, sought the hand of Ursula, daughter of the English King. In the illustration a courtly messenger is handing over a sealed letter. The spurs on his heels show that his message has been brought with all speed.

had died long ago, or that the power who had sent them had been overthrown in the meantime. City states were also keen to get news quickly: one has only to think of the celebrated messenger who brought the news of the victorious outcome of the Battle of Marathon to Athens in 490 BC.

In the Persian empire the state roads and messengers were under the authority of the ruler, not the private citizen. Greek, Roman, Byzantine, Islamic and Ottoman rulers adapted the Persian system of carrying news and letters to their own particular circumstances; in the Mongolian empire and in the empire of the Great Mogul of India a messenger system was set up in the tradition of that of the Persian empire but which worked much more efficiently; it was possibly surpassed in that respect only by the relay-runner system of the Inca state.

In the West the tradition of state messengers ceased with the dissolution of the Roman empire, at the latest by the Carolingian era. From the tenth to eleventh century onwards there was a new system of sending messages in which the messenger of the temporal power was only one among many. According to the charter of Limburg of 1035, every member of that monastery was bound to ride out each day wherever the abbot sent him. Cluny, in the eleventh century, founded its own system of emissaries to maintain the links with its daughter-houses. Every large trading or banking company had a messenger system in operation, to keep communications open between the central office and its subsidiaries. The same applied to large towns. At the universities it was of vital importance that students should be able to contact their families so that funds could be sent from home; professors and students organised their own university courier systems, which received protection and privileges by royal decree.

The position of the Church became all the more important in the dissemination of information, the more it became centralised in the supreme power of the Papacy, and the more the latter asserted its authority over the new orders of Franciscans and Dominicans, who were themselves bound by a central unifying structure. By setting up a courier system, the Papacy, which had inherited the traditional standing of the late Roman state, was able to keep in touch with its own concerns and those relating to bishops and monasteries. Thus Rome was the best-informed city in Christendom in the late Middle Ages; news was gathered from countless sources, studied and disseminated further through the appropriate channels. As the curia continually drew further powers to itself, more and more churchmen and lawyers were forced to travel to Rome for official or personal reasons. The great monastic orders had their own houses in Rome, from which – often in direct conjunction with the Papacy – missionaries were sent out, whose reports would then be sent back to the central hub in Rome. Since the days of antiquity, pilgrims had visited Rome, among them counts, dukes and kings, abbots and bishops, and the information they handed on was carefully assessed.

The curia not only demanded that bishops should visit Rome on a regular basis, but also sent out official nuncios to the churches, who would impart papal decisions and make themselves acquainted with the affairs of clerics and laymen, bishops and kings. These legates appeared in all the finery of pontifical robes and insignia, 'just as if the Pope himself were arriving', it says in the *Vita* of Bernward of Hildesheim; their horses' saddles were 'covered with a purple cloth in the Roman manner, like that of the Pope'. In any case the pope himself often appeared in person; since the reformation of the church in the eleventh century the papacy had added progresses to its pastoral duties, in the manner of royalty. Pope Urban II instigated the crusading movement at a council at Clermont.

A regular ambassadorial system was first introduced by Venice. A decree of 1288 ordered Venetian envoys to submit within fifteen days of their return a complete account of their activities, experiences and conclusions concerning the foreign country, including everything which they had been able to find out by official or unofficial means about the place they were visiting and which they had learnt on the way. It was no coincidence that an innovative future trend in diplomacy was first introduced in Venice: the appointed representatives of the powers taking part in the Fourth Crusade found themselves in Venice in 1201 with sealed blank documents from their rulers, on which the agreements made with the Signoria were then written.

An individual courier system was expensive to maintain. Money had to be laid out for horses, overnight accommodation, road and ferry tolls, not to mention subsistence and other necessary expenses. It might be necessary for instance, in order to speed up a journey, to persuade the master of a ship to set out earlier than intended or to sail at an unfavourable time of year. If Venice wanted to send a special envoy to Rome at the beginning of the sixteenth century, a sum had to be provided equivalent to a month's salary of a high state official or a year's keep for a family of three adults. An individual could hardly afford such sums, and they were sometimes even beyond the means of towns, universities and kings; there was on occasion insufficient money for the maintenance of the 'head office' messengers.

So interested parties got together, or people made use of chance messengers. Merchants could win or lose a fortune by learning of the sinking or safe arrival of a ship sooner or later than their rivals. So in Florence in 1357 seventeen trading companies founded a joint messenger service, the 'Scarsella dei Mercanti Fiorentini' (the Messenger Packets of the Florentine Merchants), which was soon followed by similar organisations in other places. Any traveller might be made use of, when the opportunity arose, to carry a verbal or written message, whether he were a king or bishop, merchant or captain, monk or pilgrim, travelling bard or shepherd (the Life of the traveller monk Norbert tells how shepherds left their flocks to bring the news of his coming). When Bernward of Hildesheim travelled to Rome in 1000–01, he took with him letters from 'all the bishops on this side of the Alps'; when he returned home, the Emperor Otto III could safely entrust his discreet ex-teacher with information he wished to impart.

Certain qualifications were required. Only men were suitable as messengers. They had to be fit, tough and resourceful, adaptable and able to work under stress, in order to be able to cope with the hardships involved; dependable, so that they could be entrusted with secret information; if possible with a knowledge of several languages. Clerics were suitable for dealings with the Pope, bishops or abbots, since they could read and write, and knew Latin and modes of address. Messages from the Franks to the Saxons and Slavs were entrusted to men who had been brought as hostages to the Frankish empire and who adhered to the Frankish cause. Charlemagne occasionally employed non-Christians as envoys, for example Isaac the Jew, as previously mentioned. In many instances messengers took an oath to serve only the master who had sent them, and to let themselves be tortured and cut to pieces rather than betray their message. Loyalty and self-sacrifice were not to be expected from badly treated bondsmen.

Envoys had to protect the sender's interests without harming those of the parties who received them. They had to promote the cause of the mission by 'suitable' conduct. Thangmar, a priest who was sent to Rome, knew how to serve the cause of his bishop, Bernward: he prostrated himself on the ground before the pope and emperor. On the other hand, the Franciscan Rubruck had initial scruples about honouring the Mongolian Khan with a genuflexion.

Messengers were expected to collect as much information as possible while travelling in a foreign country – at the same time avoiding all accusations of being engaged in espionage. The Byzantine emperor Nikephoros openly accused Liutprand, Otto the Great's emissary, of stirring up conflict and of having been sent 'as a spy (explorator) under the guise of peace' – in which he was not far wrong. In the pamphlet which Liutprand wrote concerning his abortive mission, he was openly, and by implication, advocating war.

A regular communications system was thus only possible if both envoys and host country observed certain rules. Procopius sets out two duties and a right of envoys: they must not commit any offence against the king or have relationships with married women; on the other hand they might speak out freely in the name of their patron, even if they had something unpleasant to say.

The following were the 'ground rules'. The sanctity of the king: as 'murderous' envoys were frequently sent, messengers could tell by the roughness with which they were searched before an audience, how they were regarded.

Relationships with women: the ban only concerned married women in the host country. Women were often offered to foreign officials as a gesture of hospitality, if not actually forced upon them.

Freedom of speech: that this was by no means a universal right, is shown by later sources. In the *Nibelungenlied* emissaries expressly beg permission to deliver an unwelcome message.

Safety of the messenger: life, health and freedom were only assured to the envoy on the journey to and fro and during his stay at the foreign court, if he observed other rules beyond those set out by Procopius. Messengers must create no disturbances, must not get involved in 'internal affairs', smuggle out news, or befriend enemies. And even if they behaved impeccably, they could not be certain that their lives would be safe, as two examples show. Bede tells in his *Ecclesiastical History* how at the end of the seventh century two English priests were sent to Friesland to a local ruler, to ask permission to preach the gospel there. On the way they stayed for a few days with a steward, who promised to take them as requested to the local lord. But when the people saw that the priests observed another religion, they feared that their lord would force them to adopt the new faith, and that they would have to give up their old gods. They slew the missionaries and threw their bodies into the Rhine. The respect in which messengers were held is illustrated by the way in which the villagers were punished. Angry that the 'strangers who desired to come to him' had been killed, the chief put all the offending peasants to death and burnt their village. In a tense situation one party could announce its intention of breaking off 'diplomatic relations', or give advance notice of breaking faith by killing the representative of the other side, if possible in a particularly brutal or shameful way. In 798 the 'Norsemen beyond the Elbe', who had until then been very loosely allied to the Franks, gave unmistakably to understand that they wanted to shake off the Frankish yoke. They revolted and took King Charles's envoys, who were in the country at the time, prisoner, 'in order to gain satisfaction'. This mode of expressing themselves possibly implied criticism of the behaviour of the envoys; perhaps they had been too abrupt and had thought that boasting about the might of their ruler would serve instead of tact. Some of the envoys were slain at once, others were spared to be exchanged for ransom money later; some of the latter managed to escape, and the ransom demanded was paid for the rest. Those who sent envoys were therefore well advised to demand guarantees for the safe journey there *and* back of their messengers, if possible by taking hostages (and even that was no absolute guarantee of the safety of their own people). Jan Hus was one who learnt how little a solemn assurance was worth in certain circumstances. He travelled from Bohemia to Constance in 1414, with a promise of safe-conduct from King Sigismund – and was burnt to death there in 1415.

The protection of envoys was occasionally taken to extreme lengths, as is shown by a purposeful statement of civil liberties which Lampert of Hersfeld attributed to rebellious Saxons. In 1074 Henry IV sent the abbot of Hersfeld to the Saxons who were rebelling; he was to find out if the King's representatives could travel there in safety and be assured of returning home. The proud boast of the Saxons was that, 'they were not so stupid, not so without respect towards the common rights (*jus gentium*) acknowledged even by barbarian peoples, that they did not know, that even during the most bitter feuds no harm must be allowed to be done to foreign envoys.' In this statement Lampert was going beyond the rules laid down by Procopius. Liutprand had taken advantage of such freedoms to abuse the Byzantines.

An envoy could reckon on payment for good news, and must allow – despite all assurances to the contrary – for being blamed or worse when bringing bad news. Bishop Otto of Freising tells of a sympathetic trait of Berthold of Zähringen: if a messenger hesitated over giving bad news, 'as often happened, he would say "Speak up! Speak! I know that bad news always follows good, and good bad, so it is all one to me, whether I hear the bad news first, because I know I will hear the good news afterwards, or whether I hear the good first and then the bad." '

Messengers had to prove their identity by means of gestures, objects or written testimonials. Ekkehard of St Gall gives interesting details of a convoy of gold brought from Verona to St Gall; the officials were to reply to demands for alms with 'palmed thumbs'. The six most trustworthy messengers among the St Gallers should travel two by two along three different routes to Verona and give themselves out by their clothes and speech to be pilgrims; if they had been recognised, the gold would have been tied to their legs 'with their own thigh sinews'. Since ancient times, messengers had identified themselves with half a coin, which had to match the other half. When the Landgrave Louis IV set out for the crusades, he arranged with his wife Elisabeth that she should trust the messenger who presented himself before her with a certain ring.

A good example of a frank letter of credence is that which Pope Innocent IV sent with Carpini, his ambassador to the Mongols, in 1245. The Pope exhorts the Great Khan to keep the peace, criticises him openly for his previous conduct, and recommends his envoy to him. Quoting natural laws, the Pope first calls for peace (while at the same time he was actually gathering his forces to do battle against the Emperor Frederick II!): Men, dumb animals and even the elements of the universe are 'bound together as if by a natural bond and . . . distinguished by an eternal and unbreakable bond of peace which surrounds all their different spheres'. There followed an accusation that the addressee 'had plundered and laid waste many lands of both Christian and other peoples' and still stretched out his 'bloodthirsty hands' towards other countries, 'without regard to the natural bonds of brotherhood which unite all nations, and without respect for sex or age'. The Pope demands that the Khan should give up 'such attacks and especially the hounding of Christians for once and all'; he should fear God's anger and make atonement for his previous misdeeds. Only then does the Pope present his 'dear son, Brother John, and his companions'. 'Receive them kindly in God's name, as if you were receiving us personally in their persons, treat them honourably and put your faith and trust in that which they have to tell you on our behalf. Attend with all success to the above named matters with them, and particularly to all which concerns peace'. The Khan should let the Pope know, 'quite straightforwardly and openly' through the envoys, why he had driven out other peoples and what he intended to do in future. Finally Innocent asks for support for his envoys: 'Grant them safe conduct on their outward and return journeys, and all that they need during their stay, so that they can return to us safe and sound.'

Messengers could in general move around freely at a foreign court – as freely as hostages that is, and within the limits of certain previously laid down or expressly stipulated conditions. In one respect they were not at all free: their return depended on the express pleasure of the ruler, who often kept them waiting without giving any reason. Charlemagne received an Arab legation in Aachen in 797, but only let them depart from Saxony, and in mid-winter; in doing so he was letting the envoys see at first hand that the Frankish empire was by now solidly based between the Rhine and Elbe and that the Saracens should have no false hopes of enlisting the Saxons as possible allies against the Franks. There were many opportunities to play tricks on envoys, without overstepping the rules, as Liutprand, who was very sensitive in this respect, shows in his account: envoys could be kept waiting in order to soften them up; this could be very annoying. if the funds for their stay were running out. Every means could be employed to humiliate them – by watching them, limiting their movements and giving preferential treatment to ambassadors from other countries, by prohibitions (from riding on horseback, or wearing their favoured headdress), by giving them a less good place at the ruler's table (lower down, without a tablecloth), by putting obstacles in the way of their return journey (horses to be supplied only for the men, and not their luggage, and so on). According to Liutprand, he himself took his revenge and deeply offended the Byzantines by speaking dismissively of their ruler as the 'Greek Emperor', by insulting them verbally and satirising them.

Envoys could be engaged in the delicate mission of wooing a bride for their lord in a foreign country, and accompanying her on the long journey home. Even Norbert of Xanten, a monk, was once engaged to woo a bride for his friend, Count Theobald. The complications which could arise in such situations are illustrated by the story of Tristan and Isolde. In the latter Middle Ages and later, it was not unusual for an envoy to stand 'proxy', and represent his lord in a betrothal with the bride.

Professional and chance messengers were also of course useful in bringing news. Instead of having to send one's own messengers abroad at great expense, strangers could be questioned when they entered the country; skilled spies could quickly ferret out useful information at inns, crowded markets and places of pilgrimage. The less well paid the messengers were, the easier it was to 'tap' them.

Professional messengers were easily recognised. In the Mongolian empire the relay-runners wore a belt with bells on it, so that the next in line could get himself ready in time. Non-professional messengers were often easily distinguished also. Their personal appearance and accoutrements (dress, finery, horse, saddle, harness, etc.) were designed to impress their hosts, possibly to honour them. In the *Nibelungenlied* especially rich clothing is prepared for the messengers. Travelling in a foreign country, messengers were bound to be noticed because of their different dress and speech, the mounts they rode and their different habits. If they wanted to remain incognito, they had to disguise themselves and risk life and limb. But those who announced their identity also had to be prepared for things to go wrong. Messengers to the Mongols, repeatedly found that things did not go as expected. While travelling the thousands of miles on their journey there and back through the Tartar kingdoms, Rubruck and his companions were dependent on the goodwill of local chiefs who showed an absolutely insatiable hunger for the 'presents' which were intended for the true recipients of the mission. Those who wanted to proceed in safety had to be both steadfast and glib, and above all experienced in the ways of men.

Important news was often entrusted to two messengers travelling separately (since one of them might get ill, die or fall into enemy hands), or was sent in code, hidden or passed on through an unlikely person or someone having special protection. Messages could be hidden on one's person, in clothes or in some object which was carried. A letter could be hidden for example under the wax coating of a wooden tablet. Pilgrims repeatedly misused the special protection which they enjoyed even in the non-Christian world. Silk-moth eggs were smuggled out of China in a staff, or secret information carried. Archbishop Albero of Trier hid a highly political Papal document in a supposed reliquary; officials were reluctant to examine it more closely. As even the highest church dignitaries did not hesitate – in the interests of a 'good cause' – to take advantage of the respect in which their fellow men held sacred objects, in effect they might all, even the most apparently harmless of pilgrims, fall under suspicion of being engaged in smuggling, espionage and subversion. Authorities reacted with stringent controls, and made no bones about imposing terrible punishments, of which being kept confined in cold, damp and dark oubliettes with little food or air was one of the most harmless. St Colman fared worse, according to the legend, which was probably true in this respect: travelling as a pilgrim from England to the Holy Land, he was held near Vienna under suspicion of being a spy and hanged forthwith.

Envoys did not arrive empty-handed. Presents and gifts in return had to be suited to the person concerned and to his social rank. In 757 the Emperor Constantine sent King Pippin an organ, probably the first such instrument to be heard in the West in medieval times. In 798 King Alfonso of Galicia and Asturia, with whom Charlemagne was friendly and who enjoyed a lively exchange of ideas and presents with him, sent him a tent 'of wondrous beauty'. In the same year he sent him 'in the winter', after he had sacked Lisbon, as a token of his victory, armour, mules and Moorish prisoners. A present must not be purely worldly in spirit. The envoys who came to Charlemagne from Jerusalem in the year 800, brought with them relics, representing an assurance of the protective presence of a saint, if not of Christ himself: the envoys would have been welcome if all they had brought was the blessing of the Patriarch. A large present, such as the elephant which the Caliph sent Charlemagne from Baghdad, would be regarded as a status symbol. In 944, Liutprand, later Bishop of Cremona, travelled in the service of his then lord, the Margrave Berengar of Ivrea, to Byzantium. There he found himself in an awkward position: the presents he had brought with him would not bear comparison with the gifts other envoys had brought; he quickly made up his mind, and presented his own more valuable gifts as those of his patron, with a flattering speech – the presents were nine suits of armour, seven shields with gilded buckles, two gilded silver beakers, swords, lances, spears and four slaves from the Khorasan area south of the Sea of Aral. The Emperor prized these above all else. Liutprand explained that 'What the Greeks call Khorasaners are unmanned young eunuchs robbed of their sex, of the kind merchants used to get from Verdun at great expense to send to Spain.' Five hundred years later in India Vasco da Gama was to give presents from his king to the Samorin: when the king's steward saw what the Portuguese had brought with them – twelve pieces of striped cotton material, four hoods of scarlet-coloured cloth, six hats and four branches of coral, together with six metal bowls, a chest of sugar, and two flasks each of olive oil and honey – he laughed at them and said these were not suitable to be given to the King; the poorest merchant from Mecca gave more than that. Vasco saved the situation by explaining that the presents were from among his own possessions; when the King of Portugal sent him back again, he would give him more valuable presents to bring with him.

Spiritual and temporal rulers were often on the road; but they relied on messengers to carry out the business of their realms. A personal visit was often ruled out simply by the vast distances involved. That was the case in Charlemagne's dealings with the Caliph of Baghdad, or those of Saint Louis with the Great Khan of the Mongols. It was also often the job of envoys to prepare the way for a visit by their lord. Such 'summit meetings' deserve a brief consideration.

When the meetings were to be between rulers of equal rank, they were often held on the border between the two countries. As rivers often divided two realms – forming 'natural' boundaries between lands and peoples – summit meetings very often took place in the middle of a river. Gregory of Tours tells of a meeting between Alaric King of the Visigoths and Clovis King of the Franks, on an island in the Loire, near Amboise. Centuries later the 'King of the West Franks' Charles III, and the 'East Frankish King' Henry I met near Bonn. 'After discussions between both their envoys', it was agreed that the meeting should be held on the Rhine. On Sunday 4 November 921 the leaders came face to face, regarding each other from opposite banks, 'to honour the oath made by their retainers, that they would hold the promised meeting'. On the following Wednesday, the kings allowed themselves to be rowed from the western and eastern banks to the middle of the river; both rulers then stepped into a third boat anchored there, and supported by their nobles, pledged an oath to uphold a treaty which had been agreed in advance. There were many similar meetings, sometimes held in the middle of a bridge. It was a visible means by which rulers could give reciprocal acknowledgement of each other's territories.

Communication through envoys helped to make countries and cultures better known to one another. It awakened curiosity and an awareness, at least in some quarters, of new ideas. Through the exchange of ambassadors and the accounts which envoys brought back with them, Europe became more receptive towards the outside world than were other regions, such as China, which were more thoroughly convinced of their own superiority.

COMMUNICATION ON THE WAY

In the Middle Ages the educated traveller in the West could make himself understood in Latin amongst his equals, whether he was in Iceland or Sicily, Portugal or Poland. A knowledge of Greek was also useful in the Byzantine sphere of influence: southern Italy (where there are still Greek-speaking communities today), Sicily, the eastern Mediterranean, parts of south-east Europe, the coastal regions of the Black Sea. Those who could speak Arabic could make their way in the Islamic world, which in the late Middle Ages reached from Spain to Indo-China. Archbishop William of Tyre (1130–84) spoke French, Latin, Greek, Arabic and could read Hebrew; as far as languages were concerned, he was supremely well equipped for his office.

A knowledge of Arabic was not particularly usual in the West, although far-sighted scholars such as Peter the Venerable, abbot of Cluny, recommended the study of the Koran in the original as a preliminary qualification for the military and spiritual fight against Islam, and at least a rudimentary knowledge of Arabic was needed for the crusades, and also for trading and scientific dealings with the Islamic world. Those who travelled in Arabic-speaking countries or who were taken captive by Saracens and wished to survive, had to make out as best they could.

Jews often spoke at least two languages, that of the country in which they lived, and that of their own race. As a result they could make themselves understood to their brothers in faith in other countries. As Hebrew was little known among Christians, the Jews thus had a secret language, which could be very useful in business correspondence or at times of crisis; although their strange speech and writing, not to mention different lifestyle, certainly gave rise to aversion and mistrust. With Yiddish, the Jews developed – probably after the turn of the millennium in communities on the Upper and Middle Rhine, whose members had come in part from Romance-speaking countries – a dialect, which in the late Middle Ages and modern era would have great significance in the eastern-European regions as a means of communication. The vocabulary of this language contains Hebraic-Aramaic elements and words from various German, French and Italian dialects of the time. Hebrew words were introduced into German by means of Yiddish. That happened in part via the secret language of rogues and wandering scholars, who came into contact on the road with travelling Jewish merchants and moneylenders. Many words were later introduced from thieves' slang into colloquial, and then into literary, German.

Preachers such as Bernard of Clairvaux, Norbert of Xanten, Jacob of Vitry, inspired their listeners, without being able to express themselves in the native tongue of their audience. It would do the preacher monks an injustice to see, in the accounts of their contemporaries of the exceptional response that their words aroused, only a symbolic or literary echo of the miracle of the tongues at Pentecost described in the New Testament. Charismatic preachers reached out to the hearts, rather than the minds, of men; their success was also made possible because they used the language of gesture. This belonged to the ancient rhetoric, which with grammar and logic were the three arts which formed the 'trivium', which was so basic a part of medieval education, and from which the expression 'trivial' is derived.

Gestures help those who speak different languages to understand one another. The more elementary a man's need is, the more universal and easily understood are the gestures with which he expresses that need, for instance to eat or to sleep. Other signs were only understood at particular times. Guibert of Nogent, one of the chroniclers of the First Crusade, calls God to witness that he had heard it said that in 1096 'men from I know not what barbaric people had arrived in one of our ports, who spoke such an unknown language that they could not make themselves understood, and held their fingers up in the sign of a cross, to indicate without words that they wished to go forth in the cause of the faith.' In monasteries, whose importance to travellers can hardly be overstated, sign language was systematically used; it could also be used when there was a rule of silence. In his statutes (Laws Pertaining to the Rule of Benedict; c. 1080), Abbot William of Hirsau writes: 'The sign for bread: make a circle with both thumbs and both index fingers, to indicate a round loaf of bread.' Young novitiates always had special signs, such as 'Look out, the abbot is coming!' or 'There is no one in the larder.' In such instances the colloquial speech of a monastery was closely allied to thieves' cant.

Where there is no defined, traditionally accepted system of sign language, there is a limit to understanding by this means. On his voyage of exploration through the West Indies, Columbus took natives on board, so that they could learn Castilian, and the Castilians the language of the islanders. However, Columbus soon adopted a sign language. He repeatedly notes in his journal: 'I asked by signs', 'I could find out by means of signs'. But more than once he discovered only what he expected to discover, and saw that he could not understand the natives, or misunderstood them – and they him.

Merchants, craftsmen, pilgrims had to have a working knowledge of certain languages. In the Hanseatic area Low German was used. In the ports of the near-East and in Byzantium the international language was French (Frankish); the treaty of 1229 between the Emperor Frederick II and the Sultan, guaranteeing Christian pilgrims the right to enter the holy shrines freely, was written in French. In Cyprus the so-called *lingua franca* was developed from French, Italian and Greek elements. In the Indian territory explored by Marco Polo (whose *Il Milione* was published in French) and Battuta, Urdu had been added to by the soldiers' slang of the Moslem conquerors and by smatterings of Turkish, Persian and Indian words to form a distinct and widely understood means of communication.

Those who travelled on foot in a foreign-speaking country, had at least one advantage. By getting into conversation with travelling companions they could listen and feel their way into the foreign idiom, and learn to speak it. The first Franciscans travelled on foot, inspired by the new ideal of evangelical poverty. When they came to Germany they learnt that however sacred the cause, it does not necessarily prevent serious misunderstandings. To the question as to whether they were heretics, they answered with Franciscan simplicity using the only German word that they had learnt and which might have got them burnt at the stake – 'Yes!'

The traveller in a foreign country did well to learn more than the word for 'yes' before setting out. Merchants and missionaries, messengers and pilgrims were well advised to get to know the rudiments of a foreign language, which they could then add to later. An added difficulty was that in most countries several languages were spoken – in England for instance, in the eighth century, according to Bede, there were four. The nation-wide official languages have only been adopted in comparatively modern times. Nevertheless a 'basic vocabulary' in one of the languages was an added advantage for the traveller, and also gave him additional safety. In the course of the centuries countless phrase-books have been written, which, if they were any good, have shared the fate of good maps: they have been much used and lent, worn by wind and weather, and eventually lost or left behind. There were probably many better maps and phrase-books than those which have survived the years in libraries and archives.

Among the aids which have come down to us, which were made in the Romance-speaking countries for travellers to 'Germany', are the so-called 'Conversations in Old German' of the ninth and tenth centuries, which can be cited here as an example. They give a word or phrase in Old High German and Latin; the Latin, mixed with the colloquial idiom, would still have been understood by many people in central France and Italy.

In the first part single words are given, in Old High German – Latin (the Old High German word or the Old High German phrase is only added below in brackets, when it is easy to recognise or particularly striking): head, hair, ear, eyes, mouth, tongue, teeth, beard, hand, glove, breast, belly, full belly (*follo guanbe*, or *Wanst*), help! my lord (*fro min*), good (or bad, fine, quick), vassal.

Then followed phrases which would have been used when travelling and in lodgings. With the obligatory 'Who?' and 'Where from?' a friendly interchange could be entered into.

Who are you (Wer pist du)? Where are you from (Wanna quimis)? From which direction have you come (Fona weliheru lantskeffi sindos)?

Where are you from, brother (Guane cumet ger, brothro)? – From my lord's house.

From what country do you come (Gueliche lande cumen ger)? – I was in France (or I was in another village).

What were you doing there? – I was sent there.

I didn't see you there. – And I didn't see you there either.

Where did you find lodgings last night? – In the Count's house.

Did you see my master at early mass? – No.

Where is your master? – I don't know.

My master wishes to speak to you. – I want to speak to him too.

I want to ride on now (E guille har uthz rite); give me my horse (Gimer min ros); saddle my horse (Guesattilae min ros); give me my shield (my spear, my gloves, my staff, my knife, a candle).

The horseman is usually not travelling alone, but with his wife:

Where is your wife (Guar es taz wip)? Why weren't you at early mass? – I didn't want to go.

You went to bed with your wife. If your master knew that, he would be angry with you, I warrant! – What did you say?

Listen, you fool!

When entering a tavern or inn the following phrases were needed:

I would like something to drink (Erro, e guille trenchen). – Would you like some good wine?

Yes, I would. Have you fodder for the horses? – Yes, I have (or no I haven't, or not enough, or a little).

Mend my shoe (emenda meam cabattam).

The rendering of the word for companion (*guenoz*) with 'conpagn', indicates that in the author of the phrase-book's homeland (today's central France?) bread was already the staple food (rather than oatmeal): a companion is one with whom one shares one's bread (*pain*). 'Conpagn' has come down to us today in words such as 'company' and 'companionable', and (in French colloquial speech) as *copain* or *copine*. Another word also throws light on eating habits: the question 'Have you eaten today?' (*Adst cher heute?*) does not seem to refer to many meals in a day, and its rendering by *disnasti te hodie* has additional cultural significance. The modern French word *dîner* (to dine in the evening) goes back to *disjunare*, or literally to 'unfast' or 'breakfast'; *disnare* originally referred to the first meal in the day; as the main meal was eaten later and later, it then became the word for the midday and then for the evening meal. Another word was then needed for the first meal of the day – *déjeuner*, from the same root, originally the first light meal after rising in the morning. This gradually became more substantial and was eaten later in the day, and so the first meal (which has remained breakfast in English) became in French the present-day *petit déjeuner* or 'light breakfast'.

Generalisations are made in the phrase-books, which show that the Romance-speaking author knew how to gain the sympathy of the 'natives'. You had to praise them and pour scorn on their enemies. He begins fairly harmlessly, but then really gets going; in the final words of this section the author's irony can clearly be seen.

> A wise, *or* foolish man : spaher *or* toler man
> The Latins are fools, the Bavarians wise : Tole sind Walha, spake sind Peigira
> You find little wisdom amongst the Latins; they have more folly than wisdom.
> Think of yourself! – I always do think of myself.

The phrase-books end with greetings, and wishes with which to say farewell.

> God greet you. – God bless you.

As the books show, medieval travel not only broadened the horizon, but also provoked animosity, suspicion and hatred. Travellers who felt themselves to belong to a better, more educated, more cultured group and whose 'us against the rest' attitude depended mainly on a shared language, despised all those who could not speak that language. (*The Pilgrim's Guide to Santiago*, which illustrates such prejudice, is described later.)

Many travellers must have experienced a feeling of total impotence when travelling as strangers in a foreign country: as foreigners they were immediately open to suspicion; and they had no means, other than that of making gestures which might be misunderstood, of convincing the inhabitants of their friendly intentions.

HOSPITALITY AND INNS

Where will I sleep tonight? What sort of welcome will I get? Travellers down the ages have asked themselves these questions. The second was more urgent in the past because people's attitudes to strangers tended to swing between two extremes. A stranger who was seen as a doomed individual bringing with him evil or sickness might well be killed without warning like an enemy. But a stranger could also be seen as a god – a precept that was also a part of the Christian ethic: 'He that receiveth you receiveth me.' (Matthew 10.40).

Besides the spontaneous welcome which might freely be given to travellers, there had always been forms of hospitality which were 'organised' to a greater or lesser extent: shelter given to those of the same faith, hospitality for visiting officials and commercial lodgings.

Hospitality

Dressed in rags like a beggar, Odysseus returned home after his long wanderings. In his house he found his wife being wooed by over a hundred insolent young men, who mocked the stranger; many meaningful conversations took place between the protagonists, which touched on the rights and duties of the guest. When Antinous, the leader of the suitors, struck Odysseus with a stool on the shoulder, his companions rounded on him: 'Wretched one! supposing he is some god from heaven! Gods do disguise themselves as strangers from afar, and wander through the towns in many shapes.' Penelope welcomed the stranger courteously: she had a settle fetched, and a rug laid on it, and invited the guest to sit beside her; she asked his name, his family and where he was from; she ordered her maids to attend him: 'Wash him and prepare a bed: a mattress and covers and gleaming sheets . . . and give him a bath early in the morning.'

Homer's classic story, the Bible, the laws of Celts, Teutons and Slavs, shed light on the theme of 'hospitality as it was known among ancient communities'. Basically the guest had to obey certain rules. The young men in Odysseus's house could expect to receive hospitality. But over the years they had transgressed against the rules of the house: they had broken certain taboos, when they made an attempt on the life of the son of the house, slept with maidservants, tried to force the lady of the house to marry again although her husband might still be alive; they had turned their welcome into one won by force, and had continued their stay for longer than was seemly; they had behaved as if they were the masters of the house, ordering maids and servants to wait on them, and squandering goods and chattels.

As a stranger, Odysseus had to 'prove' himself, and declare his name, origins and circumstances to his hostess. For a host must know to whom he was offering shelter, since it was his duty on occasion to protect his guest in turn from attack, as Penelope angrily reminded her suitors. The lengths to which this duty could be taken are shown in the Book of Genesis (19.8), from a different cultural sphere: Lot is prepared to deliver his own daughters to the Sodomites, rather than the guests whom he is sheltering.

From this law of hospitality, stemmed rights for the host: if a visitor died in his house, his goods became the property of the host – a right that innkeepers claimed well into the Middle Ages: however, the Emperor Frederick II ordered that a foreigner retained the right over the goods he had with him, and that his heirs could not be cut out from their inheritance by a landlord.

Odysseus asked for that which until recent centuries no one could decently refuse a traveller: shelter and water. Depending on the region the guest could also ask for fire (to prepare a hot meal for himself, and for protection at night against the cold and wild beasts) and for directions as to the right way. Penelope went far beyond what was necessary in her treatment of her guest: she invited the stranger to sit by her as an equal and tell her his story, since she was still hoping for news of her lost husband. Every stranger was also a messenger: directly or indirectly he brought news from the outside world into his host's house.

Penelope ordered a bath to be prepared for the visitor. This was more than just 'freshening up': the bath as a ritual cleansing ceremony is part of many religions. The pilgrim to Santiago, directly before arrival at the burial place of St James, washed the dirt from himself in a river, and today hundreds of thousands of Hindus still take a cleansing bath yearly in the holy waters of the Ganges. Odysseus let his feet be washed by a faithful old servant, his one-time nurse. In the Carolingian era, an abbot was once able to recognise some young men, although they were dressed as beggars, during the ritual washing of feet ordered by the Benedictine rule, seeing by their 'tender white legs' that they were nobly born. A courteous host invited his guests to wash at least their hands before sitting down at table. Before, during and after meals in well-to-do houses a servant poured water (often perfumed) from a special vessel, the aquamanile, over a visitor's hands, which was then caught in a basin by another servant: this ritual has been preserved as part of the celebration of the mass, down the centuries. In monasteries there was often running water, as in the beautiful well-room at Maulbronn, directly opposite the refectory.

Hospitality among friends and relations has existed from time immemorial. This kind of shelter was of prime importance for travellers, for instance at the time of the crusades, when nobles travelling to the Holy Land found friendly accommodation with relations in Germany, Hungary and Byzantium. But even real strangers could count on finding food and shelter; in past centuries, it was all the easier the more primitive the society of the foreign land. In the mid-twelfth century, Helmold tells from his own experience how hospitable the Slavs were: 'They eagerly receive all visitors with one accord, so that no one need ask for hospitality. Whatever they have got from farming, fishing or hunting, they give with open hands.' If anyone could be proved to have turned away a stranger, 'his house and possessions may be burnt'.

Hospitality was shown in widely differing ways. There were the many instances, only rarely mentioned in the sources, when complete strangers were offered shelter, water and fire, or were allowed to pitch their tent on another's land. There were cases of cannibalism, as Raoul Glaber tells with horror, recounting the famine year of 1033: 'Many travelled from one place to another, to escape starvation. If they had found lodgings on the way, they would have been killed at night by those who had taken them in, and eaten.' There was extended hospitality when the lady of the house invited a guest to share board *and* bed with her – as described in the Odyssey in the story of Circe and Odysseus, in the Life of St Bernard and also by Boccaccio in his realistic tales.

Lodging with those of the same faith

External pressures strengthened the links between Jewish communities of different linguistic and territorial regions. These communities maintained rest-houses alongside their synagogues for travelling members of the faith. The Jew Abraham whom Boccaccio describes in one of his most striking tales (I, 2), may have stayed in such lodgings in Rome. A Christian merchant in Paris was trying to convert the Jewish trader Abraham, an honest and upright man, to his own faith. Before he allowed himself to be baptised, Abraham wanted to see what it was like at the 'head office' of the Church into which he was to be brought. In order to observe the lives of Pope and cardinals, he travelled on horseback to Rome, where he 'was welcomed by his brothers in faith in the most honourable manner'. The example set by Jewish communities may have decided Christians to develop similar forms of hospitality.

Countless passages in the New Testament urge people to shelter strangers and care for the needy. The commandments did not go unheeded, and men have been constantly reminded of them down the centuries in literature and art.

In the first centuries after Christ, Christian communities were enjoined above all to shelter those of their own faith. The faithful should offer hospitality to messengers who carried letters and holy books from community to community, pilgrims who were visiting holy shrines, and delegates who were attending synods – without charging them, naturally. As this rule was soon abused, conditions were laid down: the visitor must bring with him a letter of recommendation and – if he wanted to stay for longer than three nights – do some work there. The fact that bishops and priests, monks and laypeople were given strict injunctions over the years to obey the rule of hospitality, clearly indicates that such a reminder was often necessary; and the repeated reminders ensured that the rule was obeyed, as other sources show.

Religious hospitality: monasteries

Religious hospitality has been practised in the ancient, medieval and modern worlds, and runs like a thread through the history of civilisation. We are better informed about the nature of such hospitality than about that offered by the nobility and burghers: in monasteries there were many monks who were scribes; the manuscripts they wrote were kept in the special care of the Church and its associates; documents were better preserved and did not run the risk of being divided up among several heirs.

The Church's hospitality was particularly important for travellers when hermitages, or monasteries (founded on the same site), were built in areas where there were no other habitations. 'All guests, who come, must be received as if they were Christ; for He will say: "I was a stranger, and you took me in." And show to all the respect due to them, especially to your brothers in the faith, and pilgrims.' If a visitor is announced, the abbot and brothers must go to meet him, 'in complete fulfilment of their loving Christian duty'; they must give each other the kiss of peace only after praying together. 'In the greeting itself, great humility should be shown towards all guests: when they come and when they leave, bend your head or prostrate yourself on the ground before them, and so honour Christ in them, since in them you receive Him . . . Show especial and particular care in the welcome given to the poor and to pilgrims, for in them you receive Christ in the truest sense: for the imperious bearing of the rich compels respect of its own accord.'

Benedict of Nursia founded a monastery at Monte Cassino in 530, whose Rule 816 was applied to all monasteries in the Frankish kingdom, even if they already had other rules. Norms were thus set for hospitality in the centuries which followed, as Section 53 cited above shows, continuing as follows: Abbot and monks must wash the visitors' feet, the abbot must pour water over the hands of guests, and even break his fast for the sake of a guest. And a special kitchen must be built for him and his guests: 'so that visitors who arrive at any time, and of whom there are always some in a monastery, don't disturb the life of the brothers'.

As Benedict's rule only offered a more or less general framework, monasteries had to set their own rules according to the climate, custom and special conditions of their foundation. In the ninth century it was no longer considered seemly in Benedictine monasteries to wash the feet of important guests; the washing of feet was reserved for a few (often twelve) or for all poor people; a bath was prepared for more important guests who wanted to refresh themselves.

Accommodation, service and care should be suited to the visitor's rank: 'for it is not right that bishops and counts should be placed with poor people, abbots and strangers', as a commentary on Benedict's rule states. If means allowed, a separate bedroom should be offered. The plan of the monastery of St Gall was used as a model: if a new monastery was to be built, it could be used as a pattern so that nothing important would be forgotten at the planning stage. The plan provides for cells for visiting monks, lodgings for the poor and a house

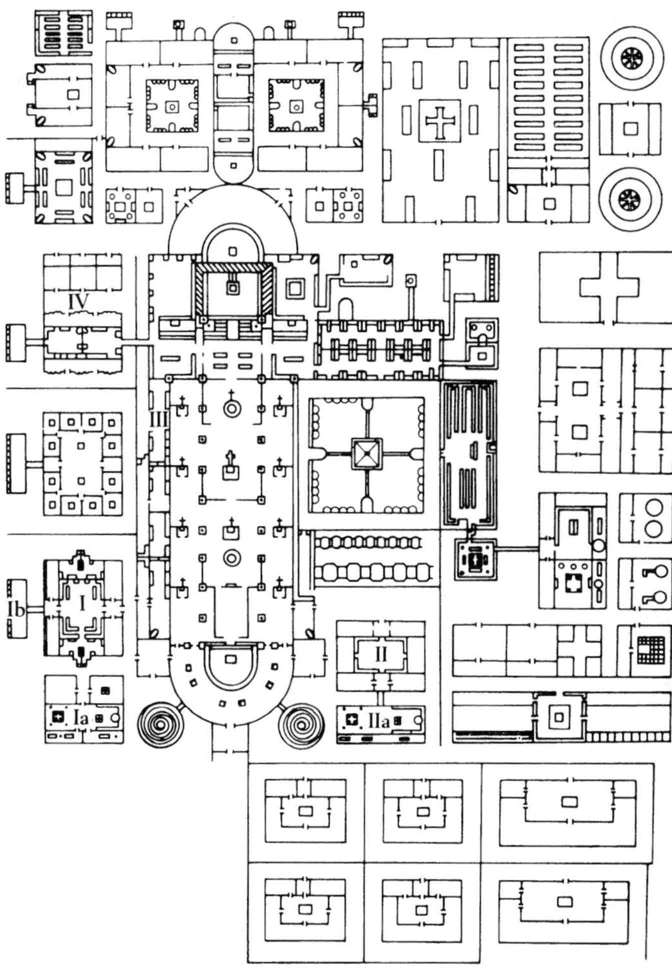

Plan of the monastery of St Gall (c. *820*) *showing, amongst other things, the following quarters: the house for important guests* (*I*), *its latrines* (*Ib*); *accommodation for pilgrims and the poor* (*II*), *with their kitchens and brewhouses* (*Ia and IIa*); *the lodgings for brother monks from other orders* (*III*); *and the abbot's house* (*IV*).

for important guests. This has a dining-room in the centre, with fireplaces, and bedrooms at the sides, which could be heated, together with quarters for servants and horses; a neighbouring building houses a kitchen, cellar, bakery and brewhouse, set aside for these distinguished guests; the plan is practical and provides for a latrine for eighteen people.

As guests were not subjected to monastic discipline, in particular the rule of silence, it was often very lively in their quarters until late at night. For this reason the guesthouse had to be built as far as possible from the monks' sleeping quarters and the bare cells of visiting monks (by the north wall of the church). Lodgings for the poor were designed in a similar way to the guesthouse, but on a smaller and simpler scale: there are no stables in the plan (the poor were not expected to arrive on horseback), and no heating arrangements in their bedrooms, and no latrines. Poor travellers could relieve themselves out in the stables (as was customary in country districts of central Europe until the middle of this century), or pass water against a tree.

If there was a large retinue to accommodate, tents they had brought with them or which were provided by the monastery would be erected for servants and baggage. Or servants would find somewhere warm and dry to sleep in the grounds. Monasteries which lay on the much frequented pilgrims' ways, also provided rest-houses. And rings, which can still be seen in the cloisters of monasteries in south-western France, probably indicate that horses as well as pilgrims found shelter there. If there were great crowds of people at a shrine even the church would be thrown open to provide overnight accommodation; synods repeatedly warned people to behave in a seemly and orderly manner at holy shrines, by night as well as day.

The food offered, as well as the accommodation, differed according to rank and position. One privileged to eat regularly (if modestly) might turn away in disgust on seeing what the poor could stuff down in a short while when they got the chance to eat their fill; he might then write as a commentator did on the Benedictine rule: The poor cannot show moderation; to let them eat as much as they like is to incite them to gluttony; that would be no merit on the part of the monastery, but a sin. So one should cook 'beans or some other peasant dish' for the poor, and certainly less than for the rich. According to the financial state of the monastery, the dues that were paid to it and the attitude of the monks who were responsible for provisioning guests, and also the number to be fed, the nature and amount of food offered varied even for the poor: as a bare minimum they ought to be able to count on some soup; if they were lucky they would be given bread and cheese, bacon, meat or fish, wine or beer, and sometimes there might even be money, wood or cast-off clothing . . .

A sound economic basis was essential if monasteries were to fulfil the mission given them by Benedict, of receiving Christ himself by receiving the poor and pilgrims. The basic precept of taking in strangers and giving them free lodging, laid a considerable burden on the foundations. But Benedictine monasteries tried to fulfil this duty laid down by the Gospels and by their rule even when they were in economic difficulties; the sources give examples of monks grumbling when there was only thin soup instead of solid food left over for them. The cause of their complaints was probably the fact that the monastery had overreached itself, particularly if it had been feeding the poor and pilgrims as well. In times of need monasteries were especially besieged. Norbert of Xanten sent money from a preaching tour to Prémontré, his first monastic foundation, so that during a famine 120 extra needy people could be fed in addition to the 400 already being given food there.

Many monasteries had reluctantly to offer hospitality in the grand manner, for instance when they had to lodge the king and his followers or a diplomatic legation for some time, which meant providing suitable food and accommodation and possibly even appropriate gifts. Well-to-do visitors showed their gratitude in many ways: rulers guaranteed protection, granted privileges, assigned property or rights to the holy brothers; rich guests gave votive offerings, which could later be melted down and minted. Lesser visitors brought candles, a hen or a few silver pennies.

On the whole important visitors were probably less burdensome than the daily mass feeding of the poor. At Cluny and the monasteries associated with Cluny it was usual on the anniversary of a monk's death to give a poor man the same food as that given to the monks. As the number of dead to be commemorated took on alarming proportions during the course of the centuries, the living were almost beggared by the dead and special rules had to be made: lodgings were no longer to be offered to 'all visitors' as Benedict had ordered, but to 'all, whom one can house'; limits were set for the daily food rations to be given to the poor, and for the length of time any one guest might stay; parts of the monastery's income were set aside which might not be used for entertaining visitors, so that enough would be left for the proper maintenance of the house itself.

The monastic community could be put in a difficult position by the welcome given to visitors: for the brothers were ordered to devote themselves to prayer, study and work, *and* to honour Christ in every stranger. Charity was in at least one instance woven into the name of a foundation: a great French monastery was called not after a place (like Maulbronn) or a river (Fulda) or a saint (St Gall), but after its function: *Caritas super Ligerim*, *La Charité sur Loire*, or *Charity by the Loire*.

Religious hospitality: xenodochia and hospices

In the ancient world there were no special homes for the sick (their families were supposed to care for them), but there were lodgings for travellers and strangers: xenodochia. This changed in late Roman times when Christians undertook to house all those who were weary and heavy laden. So to the existing buildings – such as the *xenodochium* often built beside a church – others were added, where care could be given not only to strangers, travellers and pilgrims, but also to local beggars, widows, orphans, the old, sick and frail. Until modern times there have always been these competing claims for help from such institutions: it was only in the eighteenth and nineteenth centuries that the accepted role of such houses with their range of different functions altered so that different institutions took on different duties – the care of orphans or the blind for instance.

Hospices probably originated with Scottish pilgrims, who felt the need for suitable accommodation on their journeys to Rome, and who founded 'hospitalia', for their own countrymen in the first instance. In about 800, *xenodochium* and hospital were alternative words for the same thing, but later the names hospice and infirmary were introduced. How vague the terminology was for a long time is illustrated by the meaning of the word *hospitium*: a house, billet, shelter, hospice, rented room. From the twelfth century onwards references to *hospitium* usually mean 'guesthouse with board and lodging for travellers'.

There are references to hospitals in Italy from the eighth century onwards: in the eleventh century they increased greatly in number; in the Lucca area, in central Italy, there was sometimes a hospice every two or three miles along the main road leading to Rome. From the twelfth century the hospital became a charitable institution in the widest sense.

Hospices needed land tenure and a regular income; for both of these they had to thank donors and testamentary dispositions. From the height of the Middle Ages there were increasing numbers of hospices which were founded in their own right; they had the right to their own funds, to have a seal and accept legacies. Hospices, like churches and monasteries, feared the annexation of their property. Private citizens, and Church or temporal rulers, freely appropriated buildings, vineyards, land or moneys. There was also a problem when bequests were made especially for the support of needy travellers, but the funds used for charitable purposes in a wider sense. As travellers were most often on the road in spring, summer and autumn, but poor people locally needed help all year round, and the hospices had to work within existing capacity, there was bound to be a conflict between supply and demand.

We know little about the appearance of *xenodochia* and early hospices for two reasons: archaeologists have only recently become interested in making a systematic examination of guesthouses; and they are often not easy to find, because there has often been further building on the same site. Many a traveller owed his life to the fact that he found a continuously occupied habitation in the mountains a little below a pass (or from the eleventh century onwards at the top of a pass). Here he could warm himself and find some nourishing soup, dry out his clothing and shoes, and shelter overnight from the cold, snow and wind. Whether such a house had one or more rooms, was occupied by one person or a family with servants, was unimportant.

From the turn of the millennium towns and knightly orders, and later brotherhoods, founded large hospitals in many places – such as Milan – for several hundred people, like a town within a town. In such large establishments

Charity given by St Joachim and St Anne. Part of a polyptych, c. *1490. St Joachim (on the left) and St Anne (in the background on the right) are giving alms, to a beggar cripple and pilgrims.*

there were usually separate sleeping-quarters for men and women; even married couples would therefore sleep in separate rooms. In many places there were separate open fireplaces at which men and women could warm themselves.

A traveller staying in a house where the sick were also cared for could expect advantages and disadvantages. He could reckon on getting his board. But there

A guest warms his feet. Unsuitable clothing and insufficient food often caused travellers to suffer from chilblains and frostbite. An open fire was a blessing, however simple the house might be.

was a risk of infection, particularly since standards of hygiene were primitive; when he continued his journey he might be carrying a disease to an area where it was not yet rife. In the short term, the spread of infection might cause thousands to die; in the longer term the comings and goings of travellers led to the (partial) immunisation of the European population against many diseases. The value of this was clearly shown when at the beginning of the sixteenth century, the Indian population in the New World was dreadfully decimated by the introduction of smallpox, scarlet fever and diphtheria.

The provisions for travellers varied from region to region and according to the material well-being of the establishment. In England the visitor might be offered beer, in France wine and in many places in Spain new cider. If few travellers passed by and the hospice had abundant supplies (for the time being), the visitor would be offered varied and nourishing food; if there were many waiting to be fed, the duration of their stay had to be limited (often to three days only), and they would be offered only soup, a dish of peas or beans or a pap of millet and oil. Many hospices in outlying districts gave other invaluable help to travellers besides food and shelter. They maintained bridges, marked paths, and escorted travellers through treacherous country.

In the course of centuries millions of strangers enjoyed the hospitality of monasteries, hospices and hospitals. Whether rich or poor, they were personally welcomed, often greeted in the most friendly manner, and given nourishment and often shelter as well. When commentaries on Benedict's rule speak of 'the poor', they mean poor travellers as well. Bishops and priests, cathedrals and abbeys, increasingly offered hospitality in hospitals and hospices from the height of the Middle Ages onwards. Travel in medieval times was not the prerogative of the rich. The poor also undertook long journeys; for when they set out they knew that at least once in a while they would be offered free bed and board – if only some soup – on the way.

The establishment of hospices for pilgrims points to an increased amount of travel from the eighth and ninth centuries onwards, for which monasteries alone could not cater. From the twelfth century onwards towns overtook monasteries as the focal point of social activities. It was there that brotherhoods were formed, hospices sited and charitable orders founded. But even in the late Middle Ages and in the modern era, Benedictine monasteries have remained true to the ideal of their founder: they honour Christ in strangers, mindful of the warning to be prepared for the Day of Judgement: 'I was a stranger, and ye took me in.'

Although Europe was strewn with monasteries, although since the height of the Middle Ages many hospices had been founded especially for pilgrims, private hospitality must have increased also. One reads about it in passing in the sources. The *Pilgrim's Guide to Santiago* makes it the duty of all the faithful. The spectrum of medieval hospitality ranges from free overnight accommodation and board in a monastery or hospice, to lodgings with a priest or widow, at a farm in the straw, in a still-warm bread oven, to the offer of bed and board in exchange for a few days' work in the harvest field (another good reason for travelling at that time, as many hands were needed on the land), with some travelling money on departure or an invaluable recommendation to friends and acquaintances farther along the way.

Inns

Just as there was no 'typical' innkeeper, so there was no 'typical' inn. If a hostelry wished to be regarded as such, it had at least to be able to provide a bed for visitors. An occasional host, as described by Boccaccio, had a bed in his room for himself and his wife, another for his fifteen-year-old daughter, and a third for passing strangers; his one-year-old son slept in a cradle. If the guest wished to have an evening meal, he had to bring his own provisions with him and cook them himself. And there were guesthouses elsewhere, where the guests had to prepare their own food, as an episode in accounts of the crusades indicates. Returning from the Third Crusade, a shipwreck forced King Richard the Lionheart in 1192, to travel back to England via Austria. As he had grievously offended Duke Leopold V of Austria at Acre, he travelled in disguise. In order not to attract attention he even took on the 'servile opus', the menial task of cooking at the inn. But he betrayed himself by forgetting to take off a valuable ring. The mistake cost him two years in prison and his vassals the incredible sum of 150,000 marks (about 35,000 kilograms of silver) in ransom money.

In the later Middle Ages there were also hostelries which offered every necessary comfort to travellers, their servants and mounts. They consisted of

Arrival and sleeping-quarters at a hostelry. The inn can be recognised from a distance, by the sign hung outside it. Even well-to-do travellers, arriving on horseback, had to make do with communal sleeping-quarters, as can be seen from the bedrooms shown here.

a large complex with guesthouse, bakery, slaughter- or brewhouse, with stables and barns and of course a yard in which carts could be left. At the end of the fifteenth century an edict was passed in Spain, setting out a minimum standard (not reached everywhere) of comfort to be provided at inns. The kitchen for instance had to have a chimney and fire, saucepans, frying-pans and spits, light, a table with cloths, wooden or stone seats, soup-bowls, plates, salt-pots, cups, jugs, tubs, kettle and wooden buckets. If a traveller wanted to be sure of being comfortable and getting good food, he could send retainers on ahead, who would take beds, covers and carpets with them if necessary, and see that everything was ready for their master's arrival.

It was less practical to send on an advance party if one was sleeping in different places every night, and the situation was more difficult if one was travelling at a time when thousands of people were on the road – all vying with each other for suitable accommodation. It was not only paupers who had to put up with what they could find. Erec, a knight of the Round Table, crept into an 'old ruin' that appeared to be inhabited; instead of a greeting he introduced himself to his future father-in-law by saying: 'Good sir, I need somewhere to sleep!' The rich could offer to pay more, but money could not buy everything. Arnold of Harff who was on a pilgrimage only learnt on the way that oats were unobtainable between Burgos and Santiago. So the horses had to be left in Burgos, the company mounted donkeys and mules and rode as quickly as possible to Santiago and back, so that they could get on their horses again at Burgos for the homeward journey. It was hardly surprising that pilgrims called northern Spain the 'land of penance'.

The names of inns in Europe had an international flavour. A traveller could stay at the 'Krone' in Germany, at the 'Couronne' in France, at the 'Crown' in England. Names such as the 'Star' or 'Black Horse' could be found north or south of the Alps. The 'Lion' or 'Eagle' might refer to the local manorial coat-of-arms. At the 'Wheel', carters might be especially welcome. Other names referred to specific events: the 'Three Kings', 'Three Crowns', 'Stars', or 'Moors' could be seen in the Rhine valley in particular; they were reminders of the bringing of the holy relics of the Three Kings, patron saints of travellers, which Rainald of Dassel brought in 1164 from Milan via Chur to Cologne.

Commercial guesthouses were usually sited in cities, market centres or larger towns, as they depended on regular trade; in major ports and other places where there were constant streams of traffic, inns could make a good living from the passing trade. Commercial hostelries also served as places in which to do business, as places of entertainment and as meeting-places for the local population. Sometimes inns were officially built by the authorities to protect the safety of the public. In 1286 the Danish King Eric V Clipping was murdered in a barn because he had not been able to find lodgings on the way. Remembering this act, in 1396 Queen Margaretha I ordered an ale-house to be built at intervals of every four miles. The hotel at Översee in Schleswig is the successor to one of the 113 royally approved inns, whose foundation in her day proved such a blessing to travellers.

The larger towns in the south of France, where there was a lot of traffic, had each at least twenty or thirty hostelries in the late Middle Ages. In 1370 Avignon had even more – about sixty inns; the large number was due to the fact that at the time the Papal court resided there.

The more travel increased in the late Middle Ages, the more clearly defined were the different kinds of hostelry. In England in about 1400 one could differentiate between three types: one could stay at an inn, and possibly also eat there; it was at the Tabard Inn in Southwark, south of the Thames in London, that Chaucer's pilgrims met before setting out for Canterbury. You could get wine at a tavern, and beer at an alehouse. An inn was often divided into several rooms with different functions: a common room, perhaps directly connected to the kitchen, the landlord's bedroom and one or more rooms for guests. The

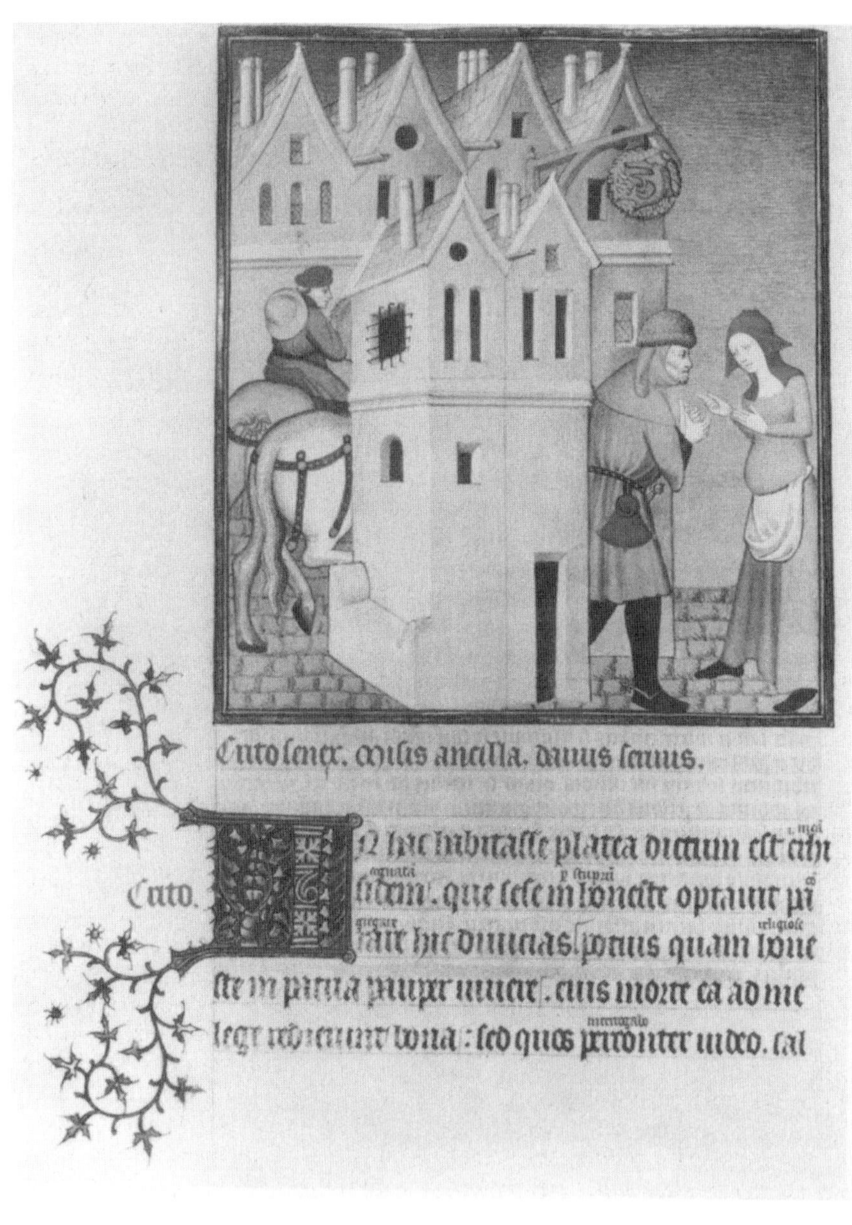

A traveller arrives at an inn, perhaps The Dolphin *from the sign, and bargains with the innkeeper's wife for accommodation while his servant attends to the horses.*

number of beds differed from inn to inn. In Aix-en-Provence in the first half of the fifteenth century there were eleven inns, of which two had 18–20 beds, six 7–12, three 3–4. A minimum number of three beds was required in many places for a house to be recognised as an inn.

The furnishings of the bedroom depended on the standards of the house and the climate, varying according to time and place. In southern countries light bedcovers were adequate; in northern latitudes feather pillows or several fur rugs were needed. Notes on the domestic arrangements of the Hospice of the Order of the Knights of St John in Jerusalem include references to freshly laundered bedlinen; possibly greater care was taken over hygiene there, as was usual in comparable Moslem establishments. We do not know how often bedlinen was changed. It is unlikely that it was very often, particularly when one considers the circumstances surrounding the fight against puerperal fever: even in the second half of the nineteenth century Philipp Semmelweis was still attempting to get sheets changed for every woman in childbirth.

We know about different types of bedclothes from many different sources. The *Sachsenspiegel* lists among army equipment, a bed, pillows, linen (including tablecloth, with two washbasins and a handtowel). Abelard advised Heloïse to equip the beds in her convent with mattresses, under-bedding, pillows, covers (if necessary a cloak could serve as a cover) and sheets. Meanwhile the *Vita* of Norbert of Xanten was talking about the brothers of the first Norbertine monastery sleeping on beds of bracken. Beds of freshly dried bracken could be more comfortable and hygienic than mattresses whose covers and straw-stuffing had not been changed for a year.

Even in the twentieth century in central Europe not every child had his own bed. There was not enough room, and there were not enough beds and bedding – or heating. The phrases in the Bible: '. . . if two lie together, then they have heat: but how can one be warm *alone*?' (Ecc. 4.11) are based on age-old experience. The heat of another's body was also welcome in bed because people usually slept naked without the additional warmth of a night-shirt or nightgown. A saying that arose from this generally accepted custom of sleeping in a communal bed was a 'cold shoulder'; if one was tired of talking or had had a quarrel, one could move apart, turn over and offer this to one's neighbour. In hostelries beds were usually for at least two people, and often for three, four or five, if not ten people; in 1520 Dürer was shown a bed in Brussels for 50 people, which was possibly intended for drunken guests. In 1385 a house in Arezzo (central Italy) listed 180 overnight visitors in 19 days, or four to fifteen a day; there were four beds and one mattress for the guests! Sleeping several to a bed was not considered demeaning; otherwise the sculptor of the capital of a pillar in Autun would not have considered it right to show the Three Kings lying in one bed under a single bedcover.

When several beds were placed close together in a small space, and were slept in by a number of people, there were bound to be awkward or happy encounters. Stories and comedies mirror the social realities of the scene.

The Three Kings of the Nativity. Capital of a pillar in Autun Cathedral. Even rulers could not be certain of getting a bed to themselves when they travelled abroad. The Three Kings are shown sleeping peacefully together under a richly worked cloak.

Lighting was expensive and dangerous; candles might be lit at night in the guestroom of a monastery, but not in inn bedrooms. Not every hostelry could offer a convenient 'chamberpot'; those who wanted to 'go outside' at night had to feel their way around in the yard or stables and could easily lose their way coming back in the dark to a strange house among the many beds cramped together in a small space, or might purposely get into the bed of a loved one, as Boccaccio describes in the story mentioned above.

The sanitary arrangements in hostelries in the Middle Ages must have been similar – just as they are today – to those of the general public. Bodies were neglected rather than cared for – rich food and lavish clothing notwithstanding. With the dissolution of the Roman empire, the Roman habit of bathing disappeared, at least to the north of the Alps. Washing and bathing the whole body was still done, but was the exception rather than the rule. Monasteries which carried on many elements of classical civilisation into later eras, usually had latrines and bath-tubs. The latter were rarely used as they counted as luxuries and were held to be contrary to the monastic spirit of asceticism. In the constitution of Hirsau it states: 'Otherwise it is usual for men to take a bath when they have shaved themselves. We need not say much concerning our brothers. Anyone may freely take a bath twice a year only, without asking permission, before Christmas and before Easter. Otherwise anyone may bath with permission, if it is necessary for his health.' William of Hirsau also laid down rules for washing in the morning: the monks were to 'wash their hands, and if they wished, also their faces.' Different towels were provided for priests, for deacons, for subdeacons and simple laymen, and a fourth for those 'whose hands are not sound'. It was not considered seemly to turn up one's nose at the towel designated for one's 'class'; one had to understand that the towels provided were for drying the hands only, and that this was an important hygienic measure in preventing the spread of skin diseases.

Latrines have been mentioned in connection with the plan of the monastery at St Gall. Individual roofed privy areas were introduced as a luxury in Europe, and were gradually adopted by the nobility and burghers; it was easy to do without a 'private place' as there were chamberpots – and servants to empty them, into the streets in towns, sometimes over passers-by, as complaints by town authorities (even at a later date) show. According to a story by Boccaccio – who can be considered a reliable witness in such matters – in Naples in the mid-fourteenth century a house had as its privy two boards strung across a street high in the air; a starry-eyed suitor, sitting on this perch at night to relieve himself, considered himself lucky not to break his neck when he fell in the mire. The continuation of the story is also on the theme of hygiene: to get rid of the intolerable stink, the poor lover washes himself and his clothes in a well, from which in the morning townspeople will draw drinking water. The use of lavatory paper, like pyjamas, was something Europeans first learnt from China; until then hay or soft straw must have been used, as Ekkehard notes in his annals of St Gall.

Lavatory and bath, which we take for granted in hotels today, would only rarely have been found by the medieval traveller in a hostelry. In towns there were public baths, which at least in the later Middle Ages had a rather doubtful reputation: the distinction between brothel and bath-house was somewhat blurred. As there was little bodily hygiene – even in the baroque era perfume was often used instead of washing – people had a strong body odour; this was perhaps less noticeable, as everyone was used to it from the earliest age, and it mingled with all the other unpleasant smells that were around. In town streets people had to pick their way round animal dung, dog and cat corpses, blood from bloodletting, the detritus from kitchens and slaughterhouses. But that medieval people were not totally insensitive to smell is shown in John of Hildesheim's 'Story of the Three Holy Kings' (second half of the fourteenth century), in which the incense which the magi bring to the newborn Jesus is seen as a means of dispelling the 'bad air' of the stable.

Many inns were run by immigrant landlords. A traveller from Cologne would be delighted if he found a German host in Lyons. He would be able to speak his own language and eat native dishes, and could count on advice and help if he needed to book a place on a boat going to Marseilles or deal with authorities, merchants and tradesmen. The interests of local authorities in keeping a very simplified control over foreigners and the interests of travelling merchants coincided, since the latter had their own trading establishments, especially in ports. In many places 'German', 'French' or 'Spanish' merchants were expected to stay in their own 'national' inn. They had no objections to their freedom being limited in this way providing that the landlord had a good reputation or the hostelry was maintained by fellow merchants. One of the most famous trading bases was the Fondaco dei Tedeschi, the obligatory inn for German merchants in Venice, where they could find all they needed for themselves and their businesses. Here they could eat, drink, sleep, keep their stock, pay duties and sell their wares. The Fondaco (the word probably comes from the Arabic 'funduq' – inn, warehouse and custom's hall all in one), in one of the most expensive areas of Venice, consisted of kitchen, dining-room, wine-shop and rooms which merchants could also rent for longer periods.

There was an even greater difference than that between a simple hostelry in the mountains and a grand inn in a town in the range of foods offered. A lowly traveller had to be content with bread and a bit of cheese and perhaps some soup here and there as he went along, but at the beginning of the sixteenth century among the purchases for the Archbishop of Salzburg's stay in the Tyrol were: beef, lamb, pork and veal; tongue; capons, geese, hens, eggs; various sorts of fish; bread, flour, oatmeal, barley; milk, cream, cheese, lard; pears and apples; greens, turnips, cabbage; vinegar and mustard, yeast, cinnamon and many other spices. Banquets with twenty or thirty courses were not exceptional.

If someone had stayed in a place for some time or was a frequent guest, he would give or be treated to a farewell meal, often accompanied by music from singers or wind instruments, reminiscent of a feast of ancient times: the *Odyssey* tells us that the gods created the lyre to 'accompany a banquet'.

Landlords come off badly as a rule in literature. Students used to chant a comparatively harmless Latin-German jingle: 'Hospes illum amat, qui vil trinkt und modice clamat' (a landlord loves those who drink a lot and only grumble in moderation). More serious was a bitterly angry complaint by Bishop Liutprand of Cremona: the wine in Byzantium was undrinkable, because it was adulterated with pitch, resin and gypsum. Liutprand knew that in the west, honey and herbs and other substances were also added to wine, but was not prepared to allow others the right to their different tastes. There were also dire accusations of deceitfulness and murder. (How accurate the complaints of guests may be is a question which it is still difficult to judge in our own day.)

There may be several reasons why there are so many references to the unpleasant side of staying in hostelries abroad. A prime reason was possibly the arrogance of the educated people who wrote such material when they found themselves confronted by the simple folk on whom they were dependent in a foreign country. And people are particularly sensitive and hard to please when it is a question of food or drink or sleeping away from home. While people gladly put up with inconveniences at home, bad experiences with regard to staying away seem to imprint themselves more forcibly on the memory than happy events, particularly since a bed has had to be paid for which at home would be free. This has to be remembered if one wants to assess travellers *and* hosts of bygone days fairly.

SPEED OF TRAVEL

How fast did people travel in the Middle Ages? Averages are difficult to estimate, as an extreme example will show. In twenty-four hours the well-organised relay courier service in the Mongolian empire was supposed to cover 235 miles (the Roman state post, the 'cursus publicus', did 'only' 190–210 miles). But there were also cripples who crept forward inch by inch with the help of small stools, which prevented their hands from getting cut to ribbons on the road. The St Elisabeth of Hungary miracles, which are relevant to the history of travel, tell of a twenty-one-year-old cripple who in 1232 dragged his lame body from Grünberg in Hessen to Marburg in five weeks, over a distance of 17½ miles as the crow flies, about 22 miles along the road. The speed of travellers in the Middle Ages therefore varied from under 1 to nearly 100 miles a day!

Most people travelled on foot until well into the nineteenth century; at a speed of 2½ to 4 miles an hour they could do 20 to 25 miles a day. On horseback a traveller could cover 30 to 35 miles a day. But an example will show that one cannot draw general conclusions from these figures. The aerial distance from Hildesheim to Rome of 750 miles must have meant a road distance of at least 930 miles in the Middle Ages. If one divides this distance by 20 or 30 (daily distances covered, at the lowest estimate, for those on foot and on horseback), one gets about 45 or 30 days. Only very few travellers on foot would have covered 930 miles in seven weeks. And Bernward of Hildesheim, who would certainly have had the use of very good horses, took rather more than two months for the journey there (2.11.1000 to 4.1.1001, via Trent) and a little under two months for the return journey (16.2.1001 to 10.4.1001 via St Maurice d'Agaune in the upper Rhône valley). Rubruck's return journey on his mission to the Great Khan of the Mongols was considerably faster: from the camp in Karakoram to the Middle Volga took him ten weeks (9.7 to 16.9, about 2,500 miles as the crow flies), which would be an average of about 35 miles a day. Rubruck's statement that the ground he covered each day was equivalent to the distance from Paris to Orléans (seventy miles as the crow flies), is probably correct.

Reckoning by averages does not give a true picture, because it does not take into account rest days (desired or unavoidable), or longer breaks, which are often mentioned in accounts of journeys. Men and mounts needed to refresh themselves; a traveller might want to enjoy the hospitality of a relation, another to pay his respects at a shrine or visit holy relics in situ, a third visit a (trade) fair and make contact with his business associates; others would be held up by sickness, floods, snow, customs problems; their horse might be stolen, there might be trouble with the landlord, or a ferry might run aground . . .

Planning a journey realistically, allowance had to be made for delays in the mountains and certainly on reaching the sea. In mountain passes 2½ to 3 miles a day, depending on the weather and time of year, and the traveller's constitution, would be quite an achievement. One reckoned on at least four to six days for the journey from Chur to Bellinzona (about fifty miles in a direct line) over the San Bernardino Pass; in the first half of the nineteenth century it still took a week to travel in an elegant carriage from Innsbruck to Bregenz over the Arlberg Pass (eighty miles in a straight line).

Nineteen miles a day was a good average for travellers on land. Even on horseback it was only possible to do more than two hundred miles in ten days if a traveller changed his horses and had no rest days, even after four or six days. It was only in the eighteenth century, thanks to better roads, and the introduction of staging-posts where horses could be changed, and of comparatively comfortable carriages, that the upper classes and the ever-growing middle classes could travel more quickly; in the nineteenth and twentieth centuries travel was revolutionised by the introduction of steam-power and motor-engines.

Delays at sea were unpredictable. One could wait anxiously for a favourable wind for days, if not weeks. In 1249 Saint Louis took 23 days instead of the three expected to get from Cyprus to Damietta (250 miles). Marco Polo was forced to stay in Sumatra for five months because of bad weather.

Although it is difficult to estimate average daily distances (particularly because of the different length of daylight in winter and summer), mean times would be known; temporal and spiritual authorities, individuals and corporations, who had urgent news to hand on would bear these in mind when working out their journeys. A table of such times is listed; daily distances judged by speed per hour have consciously not been overestimated.

The relatively low 'average' for sea journeys is accounted for principally by the fact that ships seldom steered an ideal course; and travellers frequently called in to land on shore on the way. One reckoned on nine days' sailing time from Lübeck to Bergen during a journey of three to four weeks. With a favourable wind day and night one could do up to 875 miles in a week (Lisbon to the Canary Islands). The copy of the Gokstad ship, in which the Atlantic was crossed in 1893, had a sail and twenty-eight oars with a crew of sixty men. It set sail from Bergen on 30 April and arrived in Newfoundland on 27 May. The Norwegians knew the winds and currents and had modern instruments and maps. In spite of that they only did an average of about 94 miles a day on the approximately 2,625 mile long crossing.

Ibn Jubair, an Arab traveller, took thirty days to get from Ceuta to Alexandria in the twelfth century; on the way he had called in at the Balearic Islands, Sardinia, Sicily and Crete (about 2,375 miles). The return journey was less successful. The ship took 50 days to get from Acre to Messina (1,250 miles) because of bad weather. Jubair tells how the passengers suffered greatly from hunger; prudent travellers had taken provisions for thirty days with them,

A cripple on the road. (Pen and ink drawing by Hieronymus Bosch, 1516). Cripples used many different artificial aids. 'Stools' made from a branch with four smaller branches, were easy to make and therefore within the means of the poor.

but others only enough for twenty or even fifteen days. Those who had brought provisions for twenty days must have counted on doing sixty miles a day, and those who had brought food for fifteen days counted on doing at least eighty miles a day. So the journey described by Jubair lasted at one point at least three times as long as the optimists had hoped. This corresponds to mean times listed by Italian ports: from Venice to Candia in Crete (c. 1,000 miles) took eighteen days with an exceptionally good wind, but normally 23–30 days in summer and 45–60 days in winter. One reckoned on taking a month for the journey from Genoa to Acre (1,750 miles). In the Indian Ocean with a fairly favourable wind the journey from Muscat to Quilon (in south west India) took a month (1,562 miles or about fifty miles a day).

The increasing speed of travel in the late Middle Ages and early modern era had many causes: the breeding of faster horses, establishment of staging-posts, the building of roads and bridges, regularly operating ferries, better provisions for men and horses on the way, the building of faster (and more comfortable) ships. An express messenger from Rome to Florence (144 miles in a direct line) still took 5–6 days in the mid-fifteenth century, but only one day in the second half of the sixteenth century. Exceptional messengers are said to have done 160–190 miles daily at that time; the west had caught up with the centuries-old lead of the Asian kingdoms.

One must also consider whether there were not other, less expensive, perhaps even quicker methods of carrying news.

In his *History of the Saxons*, Widukind of Corvey tells how the Hungarians sent messages during their military campaigns in Germany *suo more*, in their customary manner, by sending smoke signals; in the empire in the tenth century this method of sending information was less well known. According to Marco Polo pirates in the Indian Ocean used smoke signals to send messages from ship to ship to notify each other where booty was to be found. Columbus noticed on his first voyage to America that the Indians communicated by smoke signals, 'like soldiers in wartime'. This way of transmitting news was known in many regions; it is still used today in the West to announce the election of the Pope. But the waiting crowd has in this instance more than once misinterpreted the signal – of white or black smoke. In earlier times these 'smoke telegraphs' were used to advantage: the message had to be as clear and unequivocal as possible, for example 'Prepare to attack' or 'We are in danger'. The German king's troops outnumbered under attack in Italian cities repeatedly found the only way to attract help was to light a fire; the light warned the troops camping in the surrounding countryside of the danger (for example in Pavia in 1004 and Ravenna in 1026). In the Mediterranean area smoke and fire signals were also used successfully. The Byzantine empire had set up a chain of beacons on mountain-tops so that the capital could quickly be warned of a Moslem attack. In the tenth century Arabs were said to have sent news by means of fire signals from Alexandria to Ceuta in one day (about 2,200 miles in a direct line; the 'telegraph' distance must have been longer because of the lie of the coast). The 'crusading states' in the Holy Land always built their castles within sighting distance of one another. But smoke and fire signals also had obvious disadvantages: they could be seen by the enemy; they could not be distinguished in mist or fog and were less easy to send when the land was flat.

At sea flags were used for signalling. Columbus mentions that he took pains on the return from his first voyage to America to keep in contact with the *Nina*, his second ship, at night for as long as possible with flare signals. He does not go into details – as to whether for instance whole sentences could be communicated by this means. A real light telegraph was not invented until 1782, by Christoph Hoffmann (1721–1807), ten years before the Frenchman, Chappe.

In the sixth century Procopius stated sadly that the 'art' of sending messages with trumpets was 'now' lost. Simple commands were still of course given to troops in battle by means of trumpets, and the Hungarians did this, as the Life of Ulrich of Augsburg notes. In Africa, up until the present century, drums were used to transmit news over very long distances.

Carrier pigeons were possibly used in the East as early as 1000 BC; they were used for military purposes in the first century BC and for civilian communications by the fourth century AD. Although pigeons were ideal in the pre-industrial era for carrying messages – being very fast, cheap and economical to keep – they were not bred specifically for this purpose. The Islamic states realised the advantages of using them in the ninth and tenth centuries. Sultan Baybars (1260–77) used carrier pigeons in hitherto unknown quantities in his war against the other crusading states.

Things which we take almost for granted today – travelling faster than sound, telephoning with the speed of light – were the stuff of dreams for men in earlier ages; all they could do was wish for a magic ring, which would carry the wearer wherever he wanted to go.

Traveller	Speed m.p.h.	Daily distance in miles
Traveller on foot	2–4	15–25
Runner	6–7	30–40
Horse galloping	12–15	
'Average traveller' going slowly with followers and baggage (e.g. merchants)		20–30
Able-bodied rider, in a hurry		30–40
Mounted couriers with change of horses		30–50
Mounted relay messengers in the Mongolian empire, 13th c. (according to Marco Polo)		235
Relay runners in India 14th c. (according to Ibn Battuta)		190
Papal express messengers 14th c., on level ground		60
The same, in the mountains		30
Express messengers in France and Spain 14th c.		95–125
Inca relay runners	6	150
Mounted Spanish courier in 16th c. in South America		30
River boats, downstream, on Rhine or Po		65–95
Galleys, with rowers only		
1 hour at 4.5 knots	5	
then 1.5–2.3 knots	1.7–2.6	
with sails 6 knots and over	7	
Sailing ships	3	75–125
Sailing ships, with wind, currents and oarsmen at a rate of 6–7 knots	7–8	
Viking longboat, 1893 copy, at 9–11 knots	11–13	95
Hanseatic Cog 4.5–6.8 knots	5–8	

SOVEREIGNTY AND LAW

The Roman empire had united the Mediterranean world and reached out as far as Mesopotamia in the east and to the borders of present-day Scotland in the north-west. Within this empire travel was as safe and commonplace as it was to be once again in the nineteenth century – notwithstanding St Paul's unfortunate experiences. A merchant had inscribed on his gravestone in Hierapolis/Phrygia (in present-day western Turkey) that he had travelled seventy-two times from Asia Minor to Rome in his lifetime.

The unity of the Mediterranean area was broken by the barbarian invasions, the founding of the Germanic kingdoms in the place of the *Imperium Romanum* and the expansion of Islam from the seventh century. The Roman state lived on in almost unbroken continuity in the Byzantine empire for almost a millennium more, until the fall of Constantinople in 1453.

The Germanic, Slav and Arab rulers took from the culture of lands they had conquered those things which they found useful. The Church adopted the speech, law and administrative practices of Rome. The Germanic kingdoms which arose in the place of the *Imperium Romanum* took on the Roman concept of the state. Rivalling Byzantium, the Franks even revived the western empire in the year 800, giving a clear sign that there was a new centre of power in the north-west of the one-time Roman empire.

Under attack from external enemies and from tensions within, the Carolingian empire broke up after the death of Charlemagne. In the tenth century a new empire arose in central Europe based on the old East Frankish kingdom, and binding together parts of the old Roman empire and the ancient free *Germania*, Roman, Germanic and Slav speaking regions in a united whole, which, after successfully beating off external enemies, took on imperial status once more in 962. In the west the 'French' monarchy of the Capetians arose from the West Frankish kingdom. Common to both new realms was the fact that the rulers shared their power with temporal and church leaders who had power in their own right.

Although the medieval kings had before them the example of the Church, with its universal centre in Rome and regional centres in the episcopal seats, it was centuries before fixed royal residences were established; the king practised his office for the most part on the road. The perpetual travelling made heavy demands on the stamina of the ruler (and his wife!). If so many rulers died as young men, it was partly because they were not up to the strains imposed by travel.

The medieval kingdom had in general neither the personnel, nor the financial means or will to try to lessen natural obstacles to travel by building roads, bridges and tunnels as the Romans had done. A ruler could count himself lucky if he had made travellers in his kingdom safe from attack from their fellow men. Forests, mountains, floods, mist and storms at sea cost travellers fewer lives than warfare and feuding, robbers and bands of vagrants. Nobles who felt their rights had been infringed sought to get compensation by force from people from whom they could extort ransom money or whose goods they could appropriate. The number of beggars, vagabonds, homeless and those who had been driven to crime by poverty was simply too great for the safety of the general public to be permanently upheld on streets, and in inns.

Far-sighted rulers tried to mitigate the dangers by seeing that at least a minimum of order was upheld on the high road. A typical problem was that faced in 1236 by the Emperor Frederick II and his princes: 'Is it ever permissible for people travelling to a market along public roads to be summoned and forced by others to leave this public road to go to their markets along their private roads?' The question was clearly answered in the negative. Most rulers would go as far as giving travellers free passes which would exempt them from their own tolls and ensure goodwill from their officials, and would recommend them favourably to the rulers of the lands they travelled through, so that burdensome rights such as groundage and right of wreck, if not wholly waived, might at least be modified. The latter right granted wrecked ships and merchandise to the finder; according to the former a ruler could claim merchandise if the axle of a cart had touched the ground; those who enjoyed such rights obviously had no interest in seeing that people travelled along well-kept roads.

In the second half of the eleventh century there are signs that there was a great increase in traffic *and* an increased awareness on the part of powerful local rulers that the practice hitherto adopted of shamelessly robbing the weak and strangers or killing them without mercy was not in keeping with a Christian way of life. The Truce of God movement arose, which was started by the Church in south and central France and in the course of a few decades was adopted as 'pacts of peace' throughout Europe by secular authorities who wanted to uphold law and order in the land. Certain groups of people were placed under special protection (clerics, monks, women, merchants, pilgrims, farmers, Jews), and also certain times (Thursday to Sunday every week, Advent and times of fast, festivals) and special places (churches, churchyards, mills), and pack-animals, farm implements and other articles. The extent of the measures taken can be seen in the Truce of God announced by the Archbishopric of Cologne in 1083. If nobles broke the peace they were to be punished where it hurt them most: they had to leave the land and forfeit their feudal tenure. 'Have-nots' forfeited life or limb: 'Mutilation of the hands must not be carried out on boys who are not yet twelve years old, but can be executed on those who at this age, that is twelve years, have reached maturity.' Robbers and highwaymen were to be excluded from all protection, but they too could enjoy the right of asylum; a

The dangers of the road: noble ladies attacked and bound by brigands; a fourteenth-century French miniature.

robber or thief could not be killed or taken prisoner in churches or churchyards, 'rather he should be kept there until he is forced by hunger to give himself up.' Difficulties began when high ideals had to be incorporated into everyday reality. Who would decide what was theft or highway robbery? Who was prepared to bow before authority, or take a stand against the powerful?

Local rulers were usually keen to consolidate their own position, without regard to neighbours or even the central authority (such as it was). As if travellers had not enough to contend with, they were confronted by artificial barriers which hindered travel far more effectively than the climate, forests, rivers or mountains: to fill coffers there were tolls, staples (foreign merchants must show their wares there), escorts (who had to be accepted, even when they were not wanted), vexations over not heeding some order or other, or the – unwitting –

breaking of the law. Such 'law' was often difficult to differentiate from arbitrary actions, theft and highway robbery.

People reacted in different ways. If possible they voted with their feet and avoided the areas in question; if that was not possible, individuals often banded together in groups – often on a temporary basis – and towns or cities formed federations. These groupings would help ward off danger from natural causes, heighten the risks for potential attackers, and help to make sure that the travellers were not defenceless if they were caught up in the endless confrontations between feuding nobles and soldiers.

Difficult questions confronted the traveller. Could he be sure that the ruler through whose land he rode would really protect life and limb, goods and chattels? Or more specifically, should he, ought he to travel with or without weapons? Both had advantages and disadvantages. Those who travelled without weapons, gave the authorities and inhabitants of the territory they were going through clear evidence that they deserved to be trusted and invited them to reciprocate; in cases of feuding or warfare it was easier to prove one's neutrality and therefore perhaps to escape with one's life. On the other hand such a stranger might be regarded with mistrust: was he a spy? thief? murderer? Was he perhaps carrying an infectious disease? And those without weapons could not ward off an attack. Authorities and travellers both tried to find a compromise. Where it was at all possible, people did not set out alone on the road, and also if possible did not carry any valuable objects with them. Church and secular authorities regarded attacks against the defenceless – such as women and pilgrims – as particularly reprehensible.

Authorities locally often demanded that travellers should follow specific routes. Anyone caught off such roads was held to be avoiding tariffs (if a merchant) or lost his right to the king's protection (pilgrims to Santiago in northern Spain). These routes were naturally also known to thieves. As if it was not enough that traffic was limited to certain roads, if one wanted to travel without suspicion, one often had to give certain signals such as calling out as one went through a forest – and thus perhaps attracting the notice of any miscreants who were around!

The great outward expansion of Europe from the fifteenth century onwards was preceded by other population movements and trading and military expansion. Parallel with internal developments were the conquests in the east, the voyages of the Vikings to Iceland, Greenland and North America, the development of the trading interests of the Hanse and the re-conquest on the Spanish peninsula and the crusades. With these the Church of Rome was stretching out to ancient, densely populated cultural spheres beyond Europe. With the greatest self-confidence explorers took possession of the new – but already inhabited – lands on behalf of their kings. They staked their claim by giving new names to countries, islands and rivers, decorated pillars with the arms of their king (the Portuguese) or hoisted the flags of Roman Catholic kings (Columbus).

The expansionary movements sketched above were not particular to Europe or Europeans. The Mongols founded an empire in a few decades in the thirteenth century that stretched from the lower Danube to Peking. While the Islamic rulers were driven out of Spain, the Turkish empire spread to eastern central Europe.

In the thousand years between 500 and 1500 the European states were (relatively) undisturbed from threats from outside and could develop unifying elements which benefited travellers. Some of these developments were not initially due to European initiatives but owed much to a favourable position and borders; to erstwhile poverty, which made the region less attractive for conquest; and to world history which favoured Europe. Huns and Avars, Hungarians, Mongols and Turks – migrating to Europe from Asia – it is true caused much harm; but the essential development of Europe was not damaged in the longer term, because peoples and kingdoms in the east and south-east bore the brunt of the attacks with heavy and far-reaching material and personal losses: Europe is deeply indebted to Russians, Poles and Hungarians, who in the thirteenth century so weakened the Mongols that central and western Europe escaped their ravages; the Byzantine empire held the Turks at bay for centuries, and was regarded by Europeans with a mixture of wonder, envy, religious hatred and feelings of inferiority. When Byzantium fell in 1453, Europe was by then so much stronger that it could fight off attacks by the Turks in the centuries which followed; unlike Africa, America and Asia, Europe was not subjected to invasion from without in the following five hundred years.

IMPROVING CONDITIONS FOR TRAVELLERS

Ferries

A woman from Sittard in the Rhineland, according to the *Miracles of Anno*, collected in about 1185, was returning from Santiago de Compostela and came to a ferry across the Rhône. Because of the 'negligence or greed' of the boatmen, four hundred men and women, and horses, mules and donkeys got into the boat. When the 'fairly large ship' set sail and 'was making its way with difficulty in the torrential waters, it sank in the stream, as it wasn't built to carry such a load, and took all who were on board down with it.' Only the woman from Sittard was saved; she said it was thanks to the mediation of St Anno, Archbishop of Cologne (1056–75).

Such accidents were for centuries accepted fatalistically along with other misfortunes. Ferries have to cross the flow of the stream; the stronger this is, the greater is the danger of capsizing. Even today one may read in the papers of hundreds of lives being lost in a ferry disaster on an African or Asian river. For his part the author of the Miracles logically accuses the ferry crew of 'greed or negligence'. An overladen ship in a fast-running river is difficult to steer and therefore doubly at risk. In spite of such dangers there were no fixed bridges between Basle and Rotterdam on the Rhine until the mid-nineteenth century.

In the Middle Ages individual men took on the post of ferryman, to carry people across a river or lead them across fords or – as in the *Miracles of Anno* – to take them across in a boat. The sources usually say little about the men who carried out their duty day by day, and far more about those who fell short of expectations. The ferrymen mentioned in the *Pilgrim's Guide to Santiago* were said to have handled pilgrims roughly; others were said to have unscrupulously taken the pretty wife of a poor pilgrim as payment.

The problems which crossing a river posed to an army, are described in one of the great medieval epics. In the Nibelungenlied (written down in about 1200) the twenty-fifth 'adventure' has a central position; for Hagen is convinced at this point that only one of them will see his homeland again.

Twelve days after leaving Worms, the Burgundians come to the Danube. The King asks Hagen to find a ford through the fast-flowing water. For a ford not only decided where settlements would spring up, as place names such as Frankfurt (-ford) and Schweinfurt, Ochsenfurt and Oxford show; sources frequently tell how people were only able to continue their journey when they miraculously discovered a ford at the appropriate moment. Legends of a stag or doe showing the way across a river may have had a kernel of truth.

A miracle comes to Hagen's rescue: two 'mermaids' warn him that no one will escape with his life except the chaplain; they tell him that he will find an inn and a ferryman farther upstream, an 'evil-tempered' man, whom one must treat with politeness and to whom an appropriate payment must be made. Shouts such as 'Who will take us across to the other bank?' are of no avail, as the ferryman is not willing to be of service. By cunning and murder Hagen takes possession of the ferry. But all is not yet well, as Gernôt's cry shows: as there is no boatman, he fears the death of many dear friends. Hagen comes to the rescue once more; he lets the horses swim across the river and takes 10,000 men across – a round figure which stands for 'very many' men.

The Danube ferry was said to take four hundred people, about as many as the Rhône ferry in the story in the *Miracles of Anno*. If one considers that the fast Viking longships had forty to a hundred warriors on board, and that a ferry had no need for speed, ferries must have been able to take more than a hundred passengers. A large raft could also be made use of as a ferry. Since there were such difficulties in crossing rivers, as we can see from the *Miracles of Anno* and the *Nibelungenlied*, it is understandable that in the ancient world those using ferries threw coins into the water, to propitiate the river god: the site of ferry crossings could be ascertained from finds of such coins.

Finally Hagen decides to test the most important part of the mermaids' prophecy. Despite the cries of protest of his companions, who cannot follow his reasoning, he throws the one man who is supposed to escape with his life ruthlessly overboard, and even pushes him under; although the king's chaplain cannot swim, he is rescued: 'he was saved by God's hand.'

When they have disembarked from the ferry, Hagen smashes it to pieces. When he is asked reproachfully, how they will get home, he replies evasively: 'If there is a coward among them who wishes to flee, 'der muoz an disem waege liden schemlichen tôt' (he will suffer a shameful death in this way).

Bridges

In his *Histories*, the Benedictine monk Richer remembers a journey which he made in the spring of 991 from Rheims to Chartres, accompanied by a servant and a messenger who knew the area. After many adventures – they got soaking wet, lost their way and a horse died – Richer came in the evening to Meaux, about a day's ride to the east of Paris. When he saw the bridge over the Marne there, he was in further difficulty. 'There were so many and such large holes in it, that even those who knew it well hardly dared to cross.' His careful guide looked in vain for a skiff; finally he 'risked going over the bridge and with God's help brought the horses safely across. Where there were holes he put his shield or bits of plank under the horses' hooves, and half bending, half upright, running forwards and then back again, he managed to get the horses and myself across.' Richer's story illustrates the fact that bridges had to be kept in good repair if traffic was to be kept moving and men and animals brought safely across them.

From the eleventh to thirteenth century a considerable number of bridges were built – for economic, military and altruistic reasons. Trade and traffic was increased in order to make profits; bridges and barbicans were taken into consideration when planning the defences of a town; and finally bridge-building at the height of the Middle Ages was considered a work of neighbourly love, like that of taking in strangers or paying ransom for prisoners. Delays and danger on the road should be avoided as much as possible, and those going on foot and pilgrims protected. A ferry accident could sometimes lead to the building of bridges by those with the means to do so. In 1080, at about the time that the woman on a pilgrimage to Santiago mentioned above nearly drowned, stone bridges were built over the Gers not far from the Rhône; the reason for doing so was expressly given as the wish to save lives when the river was flooded. In 1130 the Count of Blois built a bridge over the Loire for the health of his soul. As a consequence of all this, people were inspired to make testamentary bequests of part of their estate for the building of bridges. In the late Middle Ages countless bridges were paid for by legacies, and examples show that there was an increased awareness during the latter part of the Middle Ages of the need to build and maintain them, and that spending on major construction works was considered of as much importance as more conventional means of saving the soul (paying for masses, despatching emissaries or pilgrims).

Against this background it is hardly surprising that a legend arose around the building of one of the most renowned of medieval bridges, the Pont Saint Bénézet at Avignon, the famous bridge of the song, whose stones more than almost any others have given wing to the imagination. Bénézet (= Benedictulus or Little Benedict) was herding sheep, when he suddenly had a vision, and the following conversation took place:

> Lord, what do you want me to do?
>
> I want you to leave your mother's sheep, which you are herding; for you are to build me a bridge over the River Rhône.
>
> Lord, I don't know the Rhône, and I daren't leave my mother's sheep.
>
> Haven't I told you that you must believe? Be brave, for I will see that your sheep are safe, and I will send you a companion, who will lead you to the Rhône.
>
> Lord, I have only three pennies, and so how will I build a bridge over the Rhône?
>
> I will show you how.

It was not the only time that a great undertaking was inspired by a vision, in which a child of the people was asked to carry out an unusual task. The children's crusade of 1212 was set in train by a vision in the same way, as was the final expulsion of the English from France, led by Joan of Arc. And the

The famous bridge across the Rhône at Avignon; built of stone, it originally had twenty-two arches, of which four still stand.

story of Bénézet is not the only legend which tells how something was built by a humble youth which would lead to the greater safety of travellers (we shall come to the story of the hospice in the Arlberg Pass later).

Like the heroes of other legends, Bénézet at first refuses to obey the command: he cannot leave his job, does not know the Rhône, has no money. His arguments are of no avail, and finally Bénézet sets off, obediently following the voice. The way is shown by an angel dressed as a pilgrim, with staff and scrip; the angel leads Bénézet to the place in which he is to build the bridge for Jesus Christ, and will show him how to go about it. When Bénézet sees how wide the river is, he loses heart and says that it is not possible to build a bridge. The angel encourages him, and promises him the help of the Holy Spirit, and shows him a boat, in which he can cross. In the town of Avignon he is to present himself to the Bishop and people. So Bénézet goes to the boat and asks the boatman 'for the love of God and the blessed Virgin Mary' to row him across to the town, as he has something to arrange there. The boatman, a Jew, replies: 'If you want to go across, give me two large pieces of gold (*nummos*), as all the others do.' Bénézet repeats his plea, 'for the love of God and the blessed Mary' to be taken across. The Jew retorts: 'Don't give me your blessed Mary, for she has no power, in heaven or on earth. Three pieces of gold mean more to me than the blessed Mary, and besides, there are a lot of Marys.' When Bénézet hears that, he gives him his three coins. The Jew sees he will not extort any more from him, takes the money and rows the boy across to the east bank.

Such conversations must have taken place a million times in the course of the centuries. A ferryman cannot live on 'God bless you's', let alone feed his family. Two religions meet here. The unbelief of the Jew, and his inability to distinguish between the various Marys are not criticised; only the word 'extort' apportions blame. Bénézet has to give all his worldly goods to get across, while the ferryman is in fact only getting a few coins of little value.

Bénézet presents himself to the Bishop as having been sent by Jesus Christ and is met with scorn. One of the Bishop's officials mocks him: 'You poor fool, you poor wretch, you say you want to build a bridge, which neither God nor Peter, nor Paul, nor Charles, nor anyone else has built!' Bénézet holds his ground, and agrees to be put to the test: if he can carry a heavy stone from the Bishop's palace, they will believe that he is also capable of building the bridge. In front of the Bishop and a great crowd, Bénézet goes to the stone 'which thirty men could not shift from its place', lifts it up, carries it as easily as if it were a stone in the hand, and places it at the site of one of the future piers of the bridge. 'All, who saw it, were amazed, wondering at God's greatness and the power of his works.' The Bishop's official who had mocked Bénézet a short while before, is won over and places a considerable sum of money at his disposal.

God testifies to his messenger's authority, by letting the blind see, the deaf hear and the lame run. The building of a bridge over the Rhône at Avignon was indeed a considerable feat; the argument – how can you hope to build what neither God nor his saints, nor Charlemagne have built? – could not easily be refuted; it took so long because God had not intervened. Being put to the test in the sight of God was not only known to contemporaries as a means of apportioning justice: they knew that God would give his chosen ambassadors superhuman powers to prove their authority through miracles, as Jesus had done. Many sources tell how immovable obstacles were overcome in this way.

A circle of friends, supporters and patrons formed a brotherhood, which like the medieval guilds included men and women, lay people and clerics (the latter mostly not in leading positions). Bridge building – like the building of churches and hospices – also meant that a legal adviser was needed, to take charge of contributions, devises and testamentary bequests. The building of the bridge caused a coming and going of people, who travelled by road and river to Avignon or left there in throngs: craftsmen, needed at the building site, and representatives who could collect contributions in the appropriate dioceses from rich and poor alike to further God's blessed work. On their return, they had to lay their purse first of all on the altar; then the contents would be counted in the presence of witnesses, and the collector would receive his share. After a while the owners of the ferry could be paid off with a lump sum. The bridge was built in a record time of only eleven years.

The Pont d'Avignon, completed in 1185, impressed people by its size, and because – unlike many other bridges – it was built of stone: twenty-two arches spanned the Rhône, of which since a flood in 1669 only four still stand. The bridge-builder Bénézet belongs to the not very numerous ranks of lay people canonised by the Church: and he was laid to rest in the chapel on 'his' bridge, which can still be visited.

A medieval highway code

'The king's highway shall be wide enough, for one vehicle to make way for another. The empty cart must give way to the loaded one, the less heavily laden to the heavily laden. A rider must give way to a cart and a pedestrian to a rider. If they find themselves on a narrow road or on a bridge or if they are following a mounted man or someone on foot, then a cart must wait to let others pass. The vehicle that is first onto the bridge, may cross first, whether it is empty or laden.'

The earliest highway code in Germany – consisting of a few sentences – indicates that there was a great deal of traffic – both people and vehicles – on the roads; strict rules were needed, if confrontations, especially over 'right of way' were not to break out to disturb the peace. This ruling is to be found in the *Sachsenspiegel* which Eike von Repgow drew up in the first half of the thirteenth century. In essence he collected together unwritten Eastphalian laws, taken from judicial practice and daily usage. The collection was referred to until the twentieth century; many sentences have become bywords. The final sentence of the paragraph quoted above reads: 'He who gets to the mill first, shall grind first.' We can consider Eike's code in greater detail as a reflection of the customs in the duchy of Saxony.

He distinguishes between the 'king's highways' – forerunners of later main roads – and other roads. King's highways – which were also called public ways or military roads – were usually broader than other roads. There was a standard width: a vehicle should be able to make way for another vehicle; the minimum width should therefore be about thirteen feet. As 'road' and 'way' were often used to describe the same thing, there cannot have been a great deal of difference between the two.

For the traveller, the legal status of the road was more important than its width. On the king's highways and national roads 'road users' were under special protection. The *Sachsenspiegel* states very clearly that from time immemorial there was protection 'at all times and on all days' for the property and life of priests and church people, of women and girls and Jews, and also for churches and churchyards, villages bounded by a ditch and fence, ploughs and mills and 'all the king's highways on land or water: these all stand under special protection, which extends to all those who go there (i.e. into churches, churchyards, mills, villages).' The special protection of persons and places was maintained in letter and spirit. Lawbreakers were beheaded or broken on the wheel, according to the gravity of their crime (murder, assault, attack, robbery).

The *Sachsenspiegel* tries to strike a balance between the interests of farmers and travellers. The interests of the landowner, who has cultivated his fields and pastures, are given priority. The traveller's wishes are recognised in general, but considerably limited: 'Anyone going over unploughed land, if it is not an enclosed pasture, may do so freely . . . Any traveller, who lets his animals graze corn in a field . . . must pay for the damage according to its worth.' Anyone taking the wrong path over a cultivated field, must pay a penny a wheel, the mounted man must pay a halfpenny. If the crop is already standing, the fine would be higher; 'there may also be distraints'. If the levy is unlawfully withheld, the transgressor may be seized and will have to pay at least three shillings (the equivalent of a sheep or 100 kilograms of rye).

One can easily imagine how unpleasant such measures could be. The trespasser might have committed the damage unwittingly, because he did not know his whereabouts in a foreign land, or because the way was not marked or was badly marked. Possibly the owner of the piece of land was only looking for an excuse to seize a 'trespasser' and extort a high ransom from him. On occasion he might not even give his captive an opportunity to contact his own people.

Anyone caught stealing hay or corn at night – especially if he tried to take away the stolen goods – had, according to the *Sachsenspiegel*, forfeited his life. An exception would only be made when a horse was exhausted; in that case a traveller might 'cut corn which was within reach when he was standing with one foot on the path, and give it to the horse to eat'; but he must not take any corn away. But who would decide, whether the horse's collapse was not perhaps due to negligence, possibly because the traveller was too mean to feed it properly that morning? Casuistry was a highly developed art in law and in the confessional, but it was not Eike's purpose to set out a binding rule for each and every eventuality; he only wanted to set a framework, within which people could live together more harmoniously.

There also had to be rules for liability for injury when someone was attacked by a domestic animal; Eike's recommendations on this subject are still accepted today; if anyone harms or kills a dog, boar or other animal because it has attacked him, bitten him or bitten his livestock on the street or in a field, he is conditionally indemnified from paying damages or from other punishment. He must take an oath on sacred relics that he acted in an emergency and could not defend himself in any other way. The danger was greater for early travellers than it is today, because iron dog-chains were expensive, and there was no barbed wire or electric fencing to make it easier to keep boars and bulls under control. The owner is responsible for his animals. 'Anyone owning a bad-tempered dog, a tame wolf, stag, bear or ape, must pay for any damage that it does.'

The worst injuries were still perpetrated by men, however. Medieval authorities had no proper official network, and the complex multiplicity of rulers made it difficult until the nineteenth century to pursue lawbreakers and prevent crime. Travellers often asked individual authorities for protection in their territory. The *Sachsenspiegel* is on the traveller's side in this respect: 'By right anyone is exempt from paying for safe-conduct, who is risking his life or goods.' That Eike is talking about a fee – a sum, as opposed to a tax, with which a particular service is paid for – is shown by the following clause: anyone taking money for safe-conduct must protect the traveller from harm in his territory, or he must pay him damages in return.

In this connection Eike mentions other dues which repeatedly led to aggravation and abuse: bridge and ferry tolls. In the paragraph quoted at the beginning of the chapter, he states that there are many bridges; otherwise a 'right of way' would not be necessary. As authorities usually lacked the necessary ongoing funds for building and maintaining bridges, the right to run a ferry or build a bridge was usually leased, sold or given. The owner of this right then levied a toll from those using the bridge or ferry. Eike was as against ferry or bridge fees being forcibly levied as a toll or tax as he was against safe-conduct taxes: travellers in vehicles, riders or pedestrians who used neither a boat nor a bridge, should not pay.

Eike introduced scales into ferry and bridge tolls: a full vehicle paid twice as much as an empty one; ferry tolls could be twice as high as bridge tolls; these should be ¼d for a pedestrian, ½d for a rider and 'four pennies, to go over and back again' for a loaded vehicle. As a comparison, a pound of butter at that time might cost twopence, a hen twopence or threepence.

Priests and knights were, the *Sachsenspiegel* said, to be exempt from ferry and bridge tolls. The 'underprivileged' soon wanted these privileges too. What was originally the right of a certain class, was given to more and more people – exemption from bridge and ferry tolls for example, to pilgrims, monks and nuns and eventually to merchants also. Anyone trying to avoid such tolls, had to pay fourfold (the recommended fine for avoidance of a market toll, however, was a fixed sum – 30 shillings, or the equivalent of six pigs or 1,000 kilograms of rye). Possibly 'avoidance of tolls' was also directed at those who disguised themselves as priests, monks or nuns.

Hospices

At the beginning of the fourteenth century, the opening of salt workings at Halle greatly increased the traffic over the Arlberg Pass, which is about 5,250 feet high. The nearest stopping places, St Jakob in the east and Stuben in the west, were so far apart that people were continually having accidents in snow and avalanches, storms and mist. Help was brought about not by the Church, or secular powers, or by an order of monks or brotherhood from the valley, but by 'Henry the Foundling', whose story reads like a legend. But in the later Middle Ages legend and reality went hand in hand; young people of lowly birth being inspired by visions to achieve the hitherto impossible.

Henry worked as a swineherd on a mountain not far from the Arlberg Pass; the foundling boy saw how travellers lived, and died. A publication of 1647 says: 'They brought down many people, who had died on the Arlberg; the birds had pecked out their eyes and torn out their throats. This grieved Henry the Foundling sorely.'

Henry saved up his wages for years; he put down fifteen florins towards the building of an inn at the top of the pass, but was given the cold shoulder by everyone. So he turned to Duke Leopold of Austria – and was greeted with success. The Swiss lands of the Hapsburg duke could be quickly reached from Innsbruck via the Arlberg Pass, and Leopold knew the pass from having travelled over it himself. In 1385 the Duke made an announcement in which he notified all those concerned both then and in the future that: 'The poor labourer Henry of Kempten, who was a foundling when a child', had come to him and had told him that he wanted to build a house on the Arlberg, and live there himself, for the sake of the 'poor wretched people, who might shelter there.' Storm and sickness would no longer 'strike down, as they had hitherto', these poor travellers. The Duke had considered the plan, and came to the conclusion that 'many good things had been brought to pass' by simple folk. He allowed Henry to build the house and asked all those living near and far, but particularly all those who rode or walked over the mountain, to back the undertaking. He recommended Henry to the special protection of his Austrian officials; no one should hinder or harm him.

The foundation stone was laid on the Feast of St John the Baptist, on 24 June 1386. In the course of time further buildings, a chapel and graveyard were added to the simple hospice. The chapel was placed under the protection of St Christopher, the patron saint of travellers, ferrymen, sailors and pilgrims.

Later the new complex on the Arlberg – like hospices and hospitals elsewhere – was put on a firm institutional footing. Provision was sensibly made for the time when Henry, and a certain Ulrich of St Gallen, who had joined him, would no longer be able to undertake their responsibilities. A community – the Brotherhood of St Christopher – was to run the hospice. The brothers were to support with their charity the 'inn in which both poor and rich may stay'. Priests were to say masses in the chapel for the dead brothers and sisters of the community, and were to be given the equivalent of 18 kreuzer.

In the same way that people were sent out to collect money for the Rhône bridge, Henry and his colleagues travelled through Germany, Italy, Hungary and Poland, to enlist support and collect money and materials. Relics were bequeathed to the chapel, and special indulgences authorised for those who visited it, as for those who visited the chapels on bridges. The Swabian city of Esslingen considered that its contribution to the hospice on the Arlberg was 'a good investment'. The members of the brotherhood had their names entered in a book: name, rank, coat-of-arms, escutcheon, crest, background, contribution while living and after death, any additional contributions, date of joining. In this way an invaluable document was created: the approximately four thousand coats-of-arms make up the largest and most valuable German heraldic collection of the late Middle Ages still in existence.

In the winter Henry and Ulrich left the house evening after evening, carrying lanterns and long staves, and with round or oval thonged wooden snowshoes on their feet, tied to their shoes with strips of leather or with a girdle. These 'snowshoes' prevented their feet sinking in the soft snow; and they also left tracks in the snow which could be seen when they went farther from the house. 'And whoever we find in the snow, we take to the "traveller's rest" and give him charitable help until he can go on again.' In their first winter there, Henry and Ulrich saved seven men from death, and in the first seven years they saved 50 lives – both being 'holy' or 'round' numbers. The sources do not tell us how many people died or froze to death, in spite of the help now available.

Later the innkeeper had special responsibilities: it was his duty to give travellers information about conditions on the road and to give them cheap food and drink (which was to be free for the poor). In bad weather he must always, and in winter every morning and evening when the bell rang for the Ave Maria, go out with a helper; they were to take bread and wine with them, to appointed places and from there call out four times 'with a clear, loud voice, to see if anyone needed help'. And if they heard or saw anyone, they must accompany or carry the person in need as quickly as possible to the inn, 'and restore them with the necessary food and cheer (which they must pay for, but which is to be free for the poor)'. If the innkeeper neglected his duty, he would be judged by the brotherhood and 'punished', and if necessary even 'dismissed'. Finally the innkeeper must give a verbal and written account of everything important that had happened 'in that wild place' to the priest at Zambs as head of the brotherhood.

European history is reflected in the story of the St Christopher Hospice. Like the road over the Arlberg it lay neglected from time to time; it was burnt down several times by accident or in war, and was rebuilt. Today there is still a Brotherhood of St Christopher on the Arlberg; in medieval times the dukes of Austria were foremost amongst its members, today they include illustrious names from politics, industry, society, the Church and the arts.

TRAVEL IN THE MOUNTAINS

The Alps, the mightiest and most varied of Europe's mountains, form a natural boundary between different climates and types of vegetation, cultures and peoples. As most of the passes lie at a height of between 6,230 and 8,200 feet, they were difficult to cross in winter. The rivers carved out new routes with each spring's floods in the waterlogged river valleys, which were blocked by boulders and undergrowth; as in other valley areas, people travelled mostly above the valley bottoms along very rough, steep paths clinging to the mountainsides, which were unsuitable for vehicles. Every year avalanches rolled down the slopes, so that it was pointless to build roads; if a path had crumbled away or was blocked, another way would be chosen the following spring. Under a heavy fall of rocks, which had probably trapped a trader in its path, the Erstfeld hoard was found, with four richly decorated necklaces and three bracelets.

It is difficult to draw general conclusions from source references and details on maps. The Alps and Pyrenees rose up like insuperable barriers before travellers going from France to Spain or from Germany to Italy. Despite that, crossing the Alps was often described in matter-of-fact terms, as if deserving no further mention. On the other hand Einhard gives terse details of the difficulties and hardships which Charlemagne and the Franks experienced in the war against the Lombards, 'when they went over the pathless mountain peaks, with their boulders reaching to the sky and the rough rocks underfoot'.

There were no signposts, such as were found, in a very rudimentary form, on level ground, particularly as the locals did not need them and the regional rulers had no interest in them and no money to put them up and keep them in good repair. Sometimes, from the goodness of his heart, a traveller who knew the way would make four stones into a small pyramid – like those you can still see in the mountains – to prevent others losing their way and freezing to death.

Nature, as elsewhere, is not entirely inimical in the Alps however. There is usually enough water to drink, and even at high altitudes one can generally find shelter from the burning rays of the sun, as the tree-line (today) runs up to between 4,600 to 6,500 feet, and trees in the central Alps are found at 6,800 to 7,300 feet. According to the region, the Alps can be both friendly and unfriendly to travellers, attractive or unattractive to settlers. The growing amount of traffic over the Alpine passes in the Middle Ages led to increased cultivation of the land. With the introduction of agriculture it became possible for people to settle in the central Alps at heights of occasionally up to 4,900 feet, but usually not more than 3,900 feet. Living conditions and traffic were further assisted by the Alpine lakes which are rich in fish, and run deep into the heart of the mountains, and whose shores offered ideally fertile ground for settlers. Lake Maggiore and Lake Garda are today about thirty miles from north to south (in earlier times they reached farther into the mountains); and it was possible to cover distances easily in one day in a boat which on land would have taken several days. It was as if nature was inviting travellers to enjoy the pleasures of the lowlands for the last time before beginning the arduous ascent to the high passes, or offering them rest in beautiful surroundings when they had wearily made the descent from the major obstacle to be met with on their journey.

People who were prepared to work the land in the Alps had to be more frugal than those elsewhere; they could not be expected to pay out large sums of money. Because settlements were inevitably scattered and because of the nature of the land, mountain farmers were difficult to control; if you wanted something from them you had to give more in return than to people in the fertile pastures on the plain. If you made enemies of them, it was a serious matter. You were up against a tough race of men who knew the land and were excellent climbers, who knew every hiding-place and could quickly lure the unwary into a trap, as the rearguard of Charlemagne's army found to its cost. The *Song of Roland* tells the sad tale: their dismay at finding themselves in the impenetrably dark ravine in the Pyrenees must have been typical of other travellers in other regions: 'The mountains are high and the valleys deep, the rocks sombre and the ravines sinister to behold. That day the men from France rode through them with great pain.' When they saw Gascony, they thought of 'their daughters and their noble wives. There was no one among them who did not cry with emotion.'

Impenetrable territory favoured bandits. In the ninth and tenth centuries Saracens had a bridgehead in Fraxinetum, in the French Alpes Maritimes, from where they made sorties to plunder, burn and slaughter in the Rhône valley and Burgundy. They achieved a spectacular 'coup' in 982, when they seized Abbot Majolus of Cluny in the Great St Bernard Pass. It was no coincidence that in 1240 the Emperor Frederick II put all the inhabitants of Schwyz, later one of the original cantons of the confederation, under the special protection of himself and his empire; this region was very important to the German kings on their travels.

As many people were now going over the Alps, various trades grew up around their needs, although it is difficult to know at what dates these became organised. There were carriers who knew the countryside and the Alpine routes, to carry goods – especially those of value – over the mountains, and possibly people in litters as well. The more traffic there was, the more practical it became to invest in helping travellers. In the mountains, unlike other areas, finding reliable shelter is quite simply a matter of life and death. In Roman times state rest-houses were established, of which some possibly still existed in the Carolingian era. To guarantee a minimum of safety and help for 'private' travellers – pilgrims, merchants, adventurers – monasteries were founded during

Robbers lie in ambush for a party of travellers in hilly and wooded country. Large parties might offer better protection, but could also be a more interesting target.

the Middle Ages at the foot of several passes, below the hospices on the passes themselves (which from the eleventh century might be at the very top of a pass). Monasteries and hospices were if possible sited so that travellers only had a day's journey between the last lodging before going over the pass to the first stop on the other side. By the Gotthard Pass in the Urserental there is a place with the suitable name of Hospental (guesthouse valley; 4,868 feet); from there one could go in a day without too much difficulty over the top of the Gotthard Pass (7,961 feet) to Airolo (3,772 feet); the climb and descent together consisted of a vertical climb of 4,920 feet, of which the wearisome, steep descent consisted of about 3,800 feet. The monastery at Disentis was founded in the eighth century at the juncture of the Vorderrhein and Medelser Rhine, at the foot of several passes, including the Lukmanier Pass leading to Bellinzona and Italy. Disentis shows too that in siting such houses people's powers of endurance were taken into consideration. The height of a pass was of less importance to a traveller than the relative steepness of the final stage of the climb. If he had rested at the Disentis monastery (at 3,749 feet), he 'only' had another 2,525 feet height to climb to the top of the Lukmanier Pass (6,284 feet).

One of the most important Alpine crossings is the Brenner Pass, which at 4,500 feet high can be crossed with tolerable ease even in winter. In Roman times there was first a mule-track over the pass, and between 195 and 215 a military road built from the Etsch valley to Augsburg. It is typical of the two-sided character of good roads and easily crossed passes that the Brenner was one of the main gateways for Germanic invaders during the barbarian invasions. The south Tyrol was continuously occupied by Teutons; as a result the border between germanic and romance speaking peoples today lies well below the Brenner Pass, south of Bolzano.

The Franks were interested in safe Alpine crossings and therefore brought under their control very early on (575) the Mont Cenis Pass and the Great St Bernard Pass (Mons Iovis) together with the southern Alpine approach at Aosta. The German kings and emperors preferred when going to Italy to use the Brenner Pass and the Bündner Passes (Julier, 7,491 feet and Septimer, 7,576 feet, between the Rhine Valley at Chur and Chiavenna and Como); large military forces had to be taken along different routes and over different Alpine passes, in order to make rapid progress and avoid difficulties in obtaining supplies on the way.

It was only in the late Middle Ages that individual rulers bothered once more about building Alpine roads, as the Romans had done over a thousand years before. The money to be obtained from traders proved tempting. Among the roads constructed was a path in the Schöllenen Defile, which opened up the Gotthard in about 1200, a way cut through the Eisacks Defile to the Brenner in 1314, and a cart-track to the Septimer made in 1387. With very few exceptions, until the end of the Middle Ages, the Alpine passes could only be crossed by bearers and pack-animals

Valleys channelled traffic; where they narrowed travellers could easily be seen and the way barred to enemy armies. In the eighth century the Lombards tried to block the comings and goings between the Pope and the Franks where the Alpine valleys run into the plains of the Po; envoys had to go round via the Tyrrhenian Sea. If one way was blocked, a detour could always be made by one of the other passes; but these were mostly less convenient and higher, to say nothing of the time lost by going out of one's way. The emperors Henry IV and Henry VII were forced in the winter of 1077 and autumn of 1310 respectively, to go over the Mount Cenis Pass to Italy; but this, at 6,882 feet, is at least 2,296 feet higher than the Brenner.

Many travellers were faced with the problem of whether they would get across the mountains before winter set in. On his first journey to Rome, Boniface was able to leave 'the snowcapped peaks of the Alps' behind him just in time. Decades later the Jewish merchant Isaac did not dare risk crossing the Alps in October with a valuable elephant. But Hannibal had shown a good thousand years before (in 218 BC) that one could cross the Alps with elephants even in winter.

The 'great ones' of history travelled with their retinues, and had the means to take on extra help and knowledgeable guides when necessary – and their exploits were bound to be noted by the chroniclers. There is little mention of the 'ordinary man' in the sources; if ordinary travellers fell to their death, or perished from cold or starvation, a chronicler would in general see little need to note the fact. At best, the traveller's mortal remains might be found when the snow melted, and laid to rest in a churchyard.

Lampert of Hersfeld tells of a dramatic crossing of the Alps. In the autumn of 1076 the Emperor Henry IV had the choice of either being pardoned from excommunication by the Pope by 15 February 1077, the anniversary of his excommunication, or losing his throne. Rival princes had invited his opponent, Pope Gregory VII, to Augsburg on 2 February 1077. Henry wanted to make an unusual gesture of reconciliation towards the Pope and cross the Alps in winter to meet him. He had heard that the powers opposing him had 'put guards along all the routes to Italy and the passes that are called defiles, in order to deny him any possibility of getting across.' So he decided on the western route, which had the added advantage that he would have the support of relations in Burgundy. He celebrated Christmas in Besançon and then started off:

> The winter was particularly severe, and the fearsomely high mountains with their tips practically in the clouds, over which the path went, were so covered with terrible drifts of snow and sheets of ice that on the way down over the icy, precipitous mountainside neither horse nor rider could proceed in safety.

There was nothing for it, but for Henry to achieve the impossible. Lampert renders full justice to the King, towards whom he usually shows no great friendship; he describes in detail the difficult and costly journey, particularly the dangers of the steep descent. Henry took on locals as guides, who knew the mountain well, and could lead his retinue over the snow and rocks, and give every possible assistance to Henry's followers.

> When they had been led by them with great difficulty to the top of the mountain, it was impossible to go any farther, because the precipitous side of the mountain was, as already mentioned, so covered with frozen sheets of ice that a descent appeared quite impossible. Then the men attempted to overcome all the obstacles by sheer bodily force: they crept forwards on hands and knees, then they supported themselves by clinging to the shoulders of their guides, and often when their feet slipped on the icy ground, they fell and rolled down for a way, but finally, after being in imminent danger of losing their lives, they reached the plain.

The chronicler tells how the ruler's consort had to share the discomforts with her husband. Coming down Mont Cenis 'the Queen and the other ladies accompanying them' were placed on cow-hides and the guides leading the party pulled them down the mountainside in that way. They lost many horses. These were either let down 'with the help of certain devices', or dragged down with their legs tied together; many collapsed, and others were badly hurt, 'only very few survived the dangers safely and unharmed.' It is interesting that Lampert allots considerably more space to the horses than to the women in his account; but it was not customary to waste many words bemoaning women's lot.

In Canossa – probably on 28 January 1077 – Henry was reprieved from excommunication; he ruled for another twenty-nine years. His penitential journey to Canossa is among the best known journeys of the Middle Ages, but that he stood about in the snow for days in sackcloth and ashes certainly belongs to legend. Lampert gives us the true account in describing the wintry Alpine crossing. Anyone who had to go over the mountain ranges in the winter must have been faced with similar difficulties to those of Henry IV and his followers, and to even greater dangers, because very few people could count on getting as much help as the Emperor.

INNOVATIONS

Many civilising technical achievements were lost in late antiquity and the early Middle Ages, because the new rulers were accustomed to the 'simple life', and showed no interest in running water and good drainage, luxurious baths and underground central heating.

Against these losses one can set definite gains in three main areas of development in medieval times: ironworking, the breeding of horses, and shipbuilding. The first two were important for greater efficiency in battle, the last for acquiring wealth. On the whole the Middle Ages were not favourable towards innovation. It is true the command in Genesis to 'replenish the earth, and subdue it' was followed literally in the felling of forests; but innovation was often regarded as synonymous with temptation; it meant changing one's ways and threatened work practices in a world in which hundreds of beggars had no hope of lifting themselves out of poverty in the most literal sense of the word. A large landowner who could requisition limitless cheap labour was indifferent to technical developments. When labour shortages arose, in the twelfth to thirteenth centuries, people were more inclined to look favourably on the new.

Different attitudes are illustrated in the lives of two bishops. In the life of Bruno, Archbishop of Cologne (953–65), the brother of the Emperor Otto the Great, it says condescendingly that in their day the Greeks were always trying to hear or discover something new. Quite the opposite is said in the life of Bernward, Bishop of Hildesheim (993–1022): 'He always had, when he was at court or going on a long journey, talented and unusually gifted men in his entourage, who had to study whatever seemed to them of value in any particular field.' It is not surprising therefore, that Bernward possibly even practised the despised 'mechanical arts' himself and that his artists and craftsmen succeeded in making pioneering advances and rediscoveries in metalworking. In Hildesheim the bronze doors of the cathedral and the Bernward Pillar show that craftsmen in the workshops set up by Bernward had mastered the techniques of monumental bronze casting which had not been practised since antiquity. If men of the ruling classes had all shown equal enthusiasm for innovation, the economic, technological and social developments in Europe would have come about much more quickly – but whether this would have been to the advantage of Europeans and mankind in general is another matter.

How can one measure the speed or slowness with which technical achievements are introduced? If one looks at the question from a purely European point of view, one is bound to take account of things which had already been discovered, but which were not put into use – either because groups of people would not accept the new or because the old ways were too powerful to be overthrown. It would give a far too sketchy picture of the historical perspective if one were to consider a few innovations at the time of the Renaissance alone, without considering the developments which made these changes possible.

Many advances of medieval times have already been mentioned; we can enumerate them briefly and look at others in more detail. For overland travel these were: the selective breeding of horses; the use of anatomically and technically appropriate harness (collar-harness, possibly already developed in China in the fourth century BC), so that the horse could use its full strength for pulling and also use the harness as a break when going downhill; parallel to that the development of actual breaks. The development or adoption of aids to make travel safer and more comfortable: stirrups (previously young, active men alone were catered for); horseshoes (horses could cover longer distances, and were more sure-footed on icy patches and mountain paths); upholstered saddles (making riding safer and more comfortable for horse and rider); the (re)discovery of the movable fore-axle (less wear and tear; lessening of the enervating creaking of unlubricated axles) and of the coach-body slung on leather straps (to alleviate bumpiness; additional comfort for women and the old and sick).

For sea voyages, there was the development of seaworthy ships, which could transport many passengers or a large amount of cargo over long distances with a small crew. For this two things were necessary: an intuitive understanding of certain natural laws, in order to be able to sail close to the wind; and the construction of ships with several masts and sails, which could offer a maximum of speed and safety with the minimum of operational demands. Compass and stern-rudder were probably invented in China and introduced into Europe from the twelfth to thirteenth century. Dependable timepieces were developed (there were wheel-clocks from the end of the thirteenth century), and also appropriate instruments for ascertaining the position of a ship. The development of efficient equipment to pump water out of the bilges was possibly derived from Roman techniques, and from machinery which was used in mine-working.

The first mention of a technical development in a written or illustrated source gives us no indication of how widespread it was. The stern-rudder, which could be turned on one or more axis and which made possible accurate steering with less use of force, was known in Europe from the eleventh century; in many regions, however, it was still regarded as an 'invention' at the beginning of the fifteenth century.

Regarding the world itself, people had to choose between the theories of the geographers of antiquity and those of Christian authors. Should the world be seen as flat or as a globe? Only if the globe theory was correct, would it be possible to sail in a westerly direction to India. The divergences of opinion over this question led to conflict with the guardians of the official faith. In the

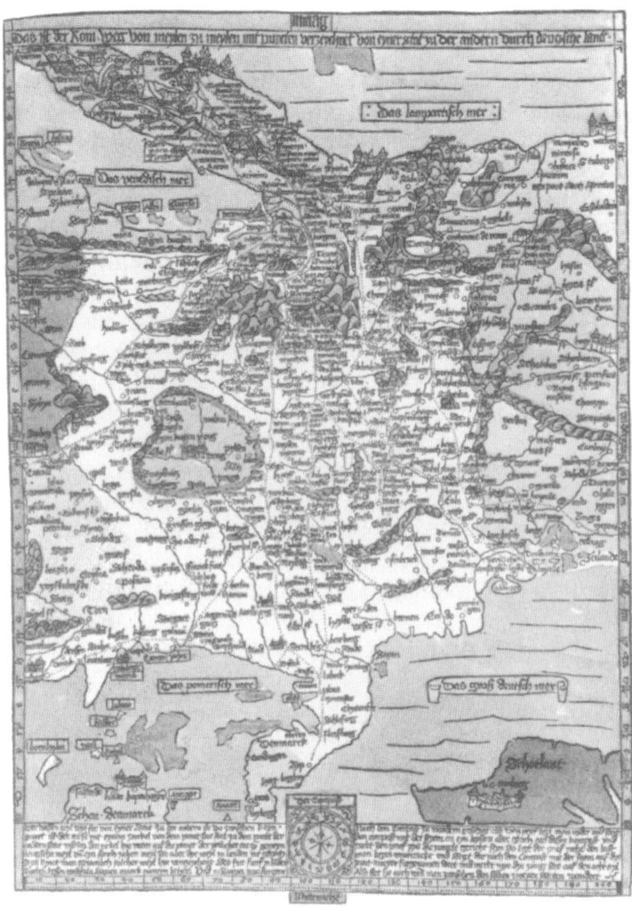

Map of the route to Rome by Harald Etzlaub, Nuremburg 1502. Etzlaub was a pioneer in the art of making route maps, the forerunners of our road-maps. The map is reversed south to north. At the top is Rome and the 'lampartisch Mer' (Lombard, Tyrrhenian Sea); below is Denmark.

Middle Ages there was a different attitude from that of today to the binding nature of religious doctrine. Anyone questioning the basic tenets might come up against the Inquisition; burning at the stake would all too often be the outcome of a trial. It is true that since the introduction of scholasticism, subtle arguments among authorities were the order of the day, but it was not accepted that contradictory ideas as to the theory of the world should be weighed up as thesis and antithesis and finally resolved by synthesis. Experimental thought only very slowly gained ground over the accepted doctrines. And the spread of knowledge was as important as innovation. Compared with the great number of journeys made in the Middle Ages there are only very few accounts of such journeys. If travellers were to inform their fellow men of their experiences, these had to be written down or – at the end of the Middle Ages – printed. Maps were known in antiquity and in the Middle Ages, and were helpful to those who knew how to read them. When a cathedral was built a plan was given to the bricklayers and stonemasons to help them in their work, and a pilgrim to Jerusalem would draw an exact plan of the Church of the Holy Sepulchre, so it is probable that travellers too sketched maps in order to help them remember the way, just as we might do today: first you go in this direction . . . then turn to the . . . here you come to . . . then you will see . . . Good maps were much used, locked away, lost. In all probability there were maps in everyday use; in those that have come down to us, in maps from the height of the Middle Ages kept in libraries, Jerusalem has a central position as the most important place in the religious world. Around the Holy Land the then-known continents of Europe, Asia and Africa are grouped in a T shape. The possession of such maps was an advantage, as new places and further discoveries concerning distances, positions and coastlines could be added. But only tentative use was made of the ability to add such corrections. However by the end of the Middle Ages there were maps for various purposes: land maps for pilgrims to Rome, sea charts for medieval sailors. The former showed the towns, rivers and mountains which were important for pilgrims; the latter were designed for the needs of seamen, who had to be able to recognise characteristic landmarks and coastlines from the decks of their ships.

EXPLORING THE WORLD

The discoveries of travellers and scholars of earlier times were transcribed in the Middle Ages, and translated and commented upon. Classical authorities often proved an obstacle for medieval scholars however; new discoveries were classed as 'impossible' after Herodotus, Pliny and others had been consulted, or were 'matched' so closely to the sources that theory no longer bore any relation to what people had themselves observed. The limits of their own knowledge were in general not admitted, but concealed behind a barrage of arrogantly inflated fantasy (it is not at all unusual even today for the theorising of experts concerning uncertain data to lack a qualifying question mark).

In the fourth century BC Alexander was accompanied on his Indian campaign by many scholars; their accounts were mostly lost over the centuries. The vision of a rich, mysterious land was embroidered like a fairy-tale and incorporated into the Alexander myth. Alexander was even supposed to have flown through the air and travelled to the bottom of the sea. These tales naturally helped feed curiosity, scientific enquiry and the desire for conquest. According to visual medieval representations, Alexander had no truck with the magic paraphernalia that are part and parcel of the 'Thousand and One Nights' and of the Faust legend: he had no magic ring, or magic password, but only plausible or realisable means: large birds bore him into the air in a basket; he was lowered into the depths of the sea in a container. The legend made use of ideas which from the time of the Renaissance onwards would be thought through and eventually developed.

In their desire to explore the earth, men have from time immemorial risked life, health and freedom. Who were the men who travelled the world in medieval times, and what drove them to make their journeys of exploration? The striving after pure knowledge and discovery played a lesser role than in ancient Greece. For both Christian and Islamic travellers – such as Rubruck, Marco Polo and Battuta – the greatest spur to travel was their overwhelming desire to get to know foreign lands and peoples; their willingness to experience the new can however be seen as a legacy from the classical past, which educated Christians and Moslems possessed as their birthright.

Most travels were rooted in definite missions. Foremost was that of proclaiming the Word: Christian missionaries carried the Gospel, as Jesus had bidden them, possibly as early as the first century, to India, in the seventh to China, and in the eleventh to Greenland. Among the missionaries who took the time and trouble to describe their experiences and discoveries on their long journeys for those who came after them, are Boniface and Rubruck.

Lack of land in which to settle may have driven the Vikings in the ninth and tenth centuries to discover and settle in Iceland, Greenland and parts of the coast of North America, extending the horizons of the then known world.

Desire for profit encouraged merchants to find new markets and discover new wares. Their knowledge of Greek and Roman authors helped the Arabs, who in extending the boundaries of Islam discovered India; by 'India' medieval writers in the west, following the ancient geographers, usually meant the Indian subcontinent *and* south-east and east Asia together with China. Popular interest in the real and supposed riches of India was heightened at the end of the thirteenth century in Europe by Marco Polo.

Many journeys which must be numbered among the voyages of exploration were undertaken for political reasons. Carpini and Rubruck, for instance, were exploring the possibility of winning over the Mongols to Christianity and as allies against the Turks.

Religious, trade and military interests combined in the crusades, which did much to open up the near east. The crusaders got to know the Levant, an area still fought over today, a hub of international traffic of great significance: here the trade routes from the Black Sea, from China, India, Ethiopia and the western Mediterranean countries met.

Sometimes a journey turned into a voyage of exploration by chance. It was known towards the end of the fifteenth century that the best way to sail round Africa was to sail in a wide arc to the west before rounding the southernmost cape. While sailing on such a course in 1500, Cabral went too far to the west; he landed unintentionally between Bahia and Pernambuco on the coast of South America. This example shows that it was not geographical factors alone which determined the exploits of explorers. In 1427 the Portuguese discovered the Azores, to the west of Lisbon, about 1,250 miles from Portugal in the Atlantic. If it had only depended on wind and currents, they would have gone on to discover America too. A number of favourable factors combined at the end of the fifteenth century in Spain to enable the Spanish to be the first to land in the New World: the end of the burdensome war against the Moors after the fall of Grenada in 1492, the interest of the crown in innovation, together with a readiness to give material and spiritual support to an undertaking which according to scholars at the universities was doomed from the start; and finally the courage, self-confidence, experience, missionary zeal and enterprise of one man, who was convinced of the truth of the theory which he wanted to prove – that there was a shorter route to India than the one barred by the Arabs to the east, which could be found by sailing in a westerly direction.

About many of the medieval voyages of discovery, probably most of them, we know nothing. Many travellers were never heard of again: they were lost in the primeval forests, smothered by sandstorms, drowned in the sea or rivers, fell prey to disease, died of thirst in the desert or on the ocean. Many journeys must have been cut short by death, which today – if they had succeeded – we would

The medieval world-view: an early thirteenth-century map with Jerusalem at the centre: Europe lies at the bottom of the page, while the five great rivers, including the Ganges, the Euphrates and the Tigris, flow down from the top of the map.

have hailed as voyages of discovery. In the Icelandic Sagas we are repeatedly told that this or that person set out on a voyage but was never heard of again. In 1521 Magellan was killed in a fight with natives after being the first to sail round the world.

As most medieval people were unable to read or write, many accounts of journeys were retailed by word of mouth, perhaps purposely not written down so that rivals would not get to hear about new sources of wealth. Many discoveries may have gradually become known over the years, and – as the knowledge was handed on from person to person – have become more and more distorted with fantastical details. The belief, held for centuries, in a land ruled by women led to one of the mightiest rivers in the world being called the Amazon.

To an educated Roman at the height of the *Imperium Romanum* in the second century AD, the following areas of the world would have been known: the whole Mediterranean region, mainland Europe as far as the Vistula, and the British Isles in the north west (the land lying beyond an imaginary line from Königsberg to the northern bank of the Caspian Sea, was more or less shrouded in outer darkness). To the east, large parts of the Arabian peninsula were known to some extent, and also the coastal fringe of India, the Malay peninsula and parts of Sumatra and the Indian Ocean north of the Equator; to the south-east, south and south-west, the Somalian peninsula, the Upper Nile Valley and Abyssinia, a wide coastal strip in north Africa and the west coast of Africa.

During the following millennium little happened to widen the horizons from the European point of view. From the seventh century the voyage to Africa and Asia became difficult. In Europe people were preoccupied with settling and fortifying their own lands and took little interest in what happened beyond the bounds of Christendom. Until the year 1000 Europeans in the north and north-west knew of Scandinavia, Iceland, Greenland and the north-east coast of North America, and to the east, Russia as far as the Urals.

In the high Middle Ages the horizon broadened out, thanks also to the accounts of Carpini, Rubruck and Marco Polo. Many details about central Africa, Arabia and Indo-China, handed on by Islamic scholars, merchants and travellers, trickled through to the Christian world, often becoming more and more fantastic in character the farther they got from the original source. The Black Death in the mid-fourteenth century caused only a slight slackening in the pace of expansion. In the second half of the fourteenth century and particularly in the fifteenth century, there was a great explosion of world exploration, led by Portugal at first, followed by Spain, England, France, the Netherlands and Germany. Portuguese navigators sailed in a few decades from cape to cape along the coast of Africa, and then in 1497–99, discovered the sea route to India. Columbus searched for a westerly sea route to India and in 1492 reached the 'West Indian' islands, the New World. By about 1500 parts of central America and the north-eastern coasts of South America, as well as the sea routes to India and Africa, were known.

DEPARTURES AND ARRIVALS, AND THE JOURNEY HOME

Hunger and thirst, heat and cold, exhaustion, sickness and death – all were ever-present dangers for medieval people, and more especially for travellers. A traveller setting out on a long journey had to consider the possibility of death. When making a will before leaving, he would make provision for his own spiritual salvation. Masses would be said, and psalms sung, food given to the poor and care to the sick, the homeless sheltered and pilgrims sent to distant shrines. The traveller put his house in order, made peace with enemies and warned feuding factions to settle their differences; he appointed someone to take charge while he was away, and got together money, clothes and letters of introduction to take with him. When he had done all that was in his power, he asked God and the saints to protect him: he visited churches, asked friends and relations to pray for him, and if he was powerful, asked for the prayers of the monastery in his domain.

If the sources so often stress the importance of prayers for help, it was not only because most of the accounts were written by clerics; it was rather because such prayers could alleviate the traveller's daily experience of being alone and in danger: he could feel that he was part of a great company of hoping, praying people and interceding saints. Benedict ordered that before setting out monks should ask for the prayers of their brother monks and the abbot, and that the monastery should specially remember each day all those who were absent. Boccaccio tells of a cheery merchant, who sought the protection of St Julian every morning before setting out. Columbus made an express habit of 'christening' every new pen with a prayer: 'Jesus cum Maria sit nobis in via' (Jesus and Mary be with us on our journey). On his first voyage to America he went even further: he placed his flagship under the special protection of the Virgin Mary, and called it the 'Santa Maria'; Vasco da Gama, on his first voyage to India, sailed with the 'São Gabriel' as his flagship, and with a 'São Raphael'; the archangel Raphael was honoured as a patron saint of travellers.

In the course of centuries spontaneous requests became formulated into specific prayers, which were included in votive masses; these masses were celebrated in certain places to honour the patron saints of travellers – the Three Kings, Raphael, Tobias, Christopher and others. The prayers illustrate the practical difficulties of travel, and God is asked to safeguard the traveller from danger to body and spirit, particularly from robbers and storms, assault and wild animals, and at sea from pirates and storms, and from being driven off course by men or devils. The following prayer is a typical example: 'Holy Lord, almighty Father, eternal God, leader of all saints, who directs the godly into the paths of righteousness: send the angel of peace with your servant (your servants) N., to accompany him (her/them) to their appointed goal. Let him be a happy companion (comitatus jocundus), so that no enemy may drive them from their way; let the wicked not come among them and may the Holy Spirit accompany them.' God, his saints and his holy angels are to accompany the (named) travellers over mountains and through valleys, and to keep them from all dangers of rivers, fords and ferries. After the happy outcome of their undertaking God will lead the travellers, blessed with earthly and heavenly goods, safely home again.

Parting was a sore trial for those who loved one another. The *Nibelungenlied* tells how Queen Brunhild tried to dissuade her husband from travelling to the court of Etzel and Kriemhild:

> His fair wife begged the King to stay.
> At night holding close her loved one in her arms.
> Early in the morning came the sound of flute and fiddle.
> Now they must follow: now they must leave.
> Who has his love in his arms, holds his love close.
> Once King Etzel's wife mourned too, in parting.

In 1248, Joinville, a French nobleman, followed King Louis of France on a crusade, which the King had vowed to make when he recovered, contrary to expectations, from a mortal sickness. Before leaving, Joinville invited friends and retainers to a rousing, four-day feast; on the fifth day, a Friday, he begged any of those present whom he had wronged to forgive him, and offered to recompense them. Then he set out, barefoot, in a penitential shirt, with a pilgrim's staff in his hand; at the graveside of saints he begged for protection on his journey. Later he wrote: 'When I left I did not let myself turn back, to see Joinville once more – for fear my heart would break at the sight of my castle, which I was leaving with my two dear children.' He travelled down the Saône and Rhône on a boat, and embarked at Marseilles. When the horses had been taken on board, heaven's blessing was called down upon the ship – Creator Spiritus meaning here as well as God's holy spirit, a favourable wind: 'The ship's captain called to his crew in the bows of the ship: Have you finished making ready? Aye aye, sir. Let the priests and clerics come forward. When they had assembled, the ship's captain called to them: Sing, in God's name. And as with one voice they all sang "Veni Creator Spiritus". Then he ordered his men: Set sail, in God's name. Which they did.'

Friends who met on the way – even if they were on horseback – greeted one another with a passionate embrace and kisses. In a monastery it was more orderly. Benedict makes practical distinctions between the arrival of important visitors who demand entry by knocking on the door, and the requests of the more humble poor. The latter should be greeted by the porter at the gate with

The entry of King Sigismund into Bern on 3 July 1414. The King and his followers approach the town on horseback; they can be recognised from afar by the banners they carry; lance bearers demonstrate the ruler's might, and trumpeters announce his coming.

a 'Thanks be to God', the former he must go to meet, in order to ask their blessing. A newcomer is bound with a prayer and the kiss of peace to keep the peace of the monastery.

Commentaries on Benedict's rule from the Carolingian era clearly set out the protocol: a brother shall go to meet a brother, a high official a high official, the abbot the King, a bishop 'or any other from among the powerful', and all the monks must prostrate themselves on the ground before him. 'When the Queen comes, a monk must not greet her thus, but must kneel on one knee and bow his head humbly before her.'

Those who wished to be greeted with due respect, had themselves announced well in advance; that applied particularly to a ruler and his followers. The arrival (*adventus*) of Emperor and Queen, Pope and bishops, sometimes of counts and other nobles and charismatic figures such as Bernard of Clairvaux was a festive occasion. In a ceremonial developed at the court of imperial Rome, abbot and monks (or bishop, clerics, monks, nuns, men and women of a town) came forth in a procession to greet the newcomer a long way off, gave him presents, greeted him with praises (*laudes*, while calling on the saints, as in a litany) and led him in in state. Important parts of this ceremonial were later incorporated in the Corpus Christi procession: with the processional cross in front, with candles, incense, relics, then clerics, nuns, lay people – according to rank and name, two by two; in the place of honour in the middle of the procession the royal or imperial pair riding or walking beneath a baldaquin; the guests of honour led between the ranks of cheering, singing and chanting bystanders, with solemn ringing of church bells, into the church to give thanksgiving.

The rank and position of the visitor would be clear from how far one went to meet him, and from the rooms, servants, utensils and so on which were allotted to him for the duration of his stay. The Emperor Otto III rode out to meet his one-time teacher Bernward two miles from Rome; when he went home, the Emperor accompanied him on his journey for two days; then Otto took his leave from the Bishop of Hildesheim, but gave him men to accompany him from among his retainers, who would be able to tell him later how Bernward was and how his journey had gone.

A high ranking guest could expect to receive the best treatment on offer. This caused problems for bishops (and also for monks and priests), since the ideal they sought to emulate bound them to practise humility and modesty, whereas their high office justified a show quite equal to that offered to secular potentates. Ekkehard IV tells of a Bishop Peter of Verona who one day visited the monastery at St Gallen. Possibly this bishop never existed, but the story has a kernel of historical truth since it describes the expectations of a bishop. On his arrival, the brothers offered him an evangeliar, which they considered one of their 'better copies'. Their guest thought they were insulting him; he had heard a great deal about the monastery, and privately took offence at the cheap copy. For the mass, a 'better' silver cup was produced. After the mass Peter brooded angrily about the cup too. Finally the monks gave him what they considered to be an extravagant meal. After they had eaten Peter lectured the brothers (the abbot was away): they had treated him in a friendly manner, 'but the evangeliar and cup, which were offered, were so inferior, that I was dumbfounded. However lowly and unworthy I myself may be, I am still the bishop of a not unimportant place.' The brothers could only with great difficulty make him understand that their house, of St Gall, had nothing better to offer.

Finally they managed to soothe the bishop's ruffled feathers; Peter promised to try to help the monastery with a consignment of gold to be sent over the Alps, which they had already discussed.

The return of a traveller was as ceremonial as his departure. Word would get about that he had returned safely from his arduous journey. A labourer would perhaps be met at the town gate by his work companions, the king a mile from the town by all of rank and standing. The ceremony was repeated with greetings, private prayers of thanks and public thanksgiving in the church. Benedict states that monks should ask for forgiveness on their return for all their sins, for any stray words, thoughts or deeds. Boniface's letters to his friends in which he tells of his safe return – and announces further travels – show clearly the anxieties about such undertakings which travellers felt. Crusaders who got home safely, sometimes expressed their thanks by generous gifts to the Church, for example by founding a monastery. Just as Joinville held a feast before he set out, Charlemagne held festivities in 787 when he had returned safely from his second journey to Rome. The otherwise rather prosaic author of the Frankish imperial annals tells of the joy of the happy homecoming: 'And this most gracious King came home to Queen Fastrada at Worms, where they rejoiced together, and feasted, and praised God's mercy.'

Many travellers died on the way – from weakness or an illness, drowned or murdered, struck by lightning or wrongly executed, like a German pilgrim to Santiago in Toulouse . . . Pilgrims often did not even regard it as a misfortune to suffer hardships during their journey; the saint in whose honour they were travelling would see them safely to a heavenly home. In many places there were special graveyards for those who had died on their travels; the Campo Santo Teutonico in Rome, in the shadow of St Peter's and dating from the eighth century, must be the oldest and best known of such graveyards still in existence today.

A dead traveller would usually be buried at the spot where he died; anyone dying on board ship would be wrapped in cloth and committed to the sea. The mortal remains of great lords were usually taken to a place named by the dying man or his heirs; Otto III for example was taken in a ceremonial cortège from central Italy over the Alps to Aachen in 1002 and laid to rest in the cathedral there. The heat in the Mediterranean countries and the long distances involved, meant that it was not usually advisable to take the whole corpse home. The body of the Emperor Frederick Barbarossa, who died on 10 June 1190 on the third crusade, was embalmed and taken to Seleucia where it lay in state for four days; the entrails were left in Tarsus, the flesh in the cathedral at Antioch; the bones continued on their journey to Jerusalem where they were to be laid to rest; they got as far as Tyre, where they vanished. A few decades later Louis IV of Thuringia died on his way to the Holy Land. As his life and that of his wife are well documented, his final farewell, death and the conveyance of his body are described – and his widow's grief. It is rare in the sources to find an account of the effect of a traveller's death on those he left behind him.

Goods being unloaded from a ship by porters and by men using a wheeled trolley, while the sailors furl the sails.

The body of King Louis IX, who died on a crusade in 1270, being put on board ship in Tunis. Illumination from the 'Great Chronicle of France'.

Louis set out on the crusade on the Feast of St John the Baptist, the 24 June 1227, from Schmalkalden. Elisabeth accompanied him for a few days for part of the way; she could not tear herself away from her dear husband. Their parting deeply moved their contemporaries; in 1233 a woman told how she had heard a 'song in the German language of the tearful farewell of the Landgravine' sung at the beginning of the year on her way to Marburg to the grave of Elisabeth. The crusading troop did an average of about twenty-five miles a day, a good distance, especially as they had to cross the Alps and do over half the journey through the July heat of Italy. On the third of August Louis met up with the Emperor Frederick II in Troia (Apulia). They went on together. In Brindisi, where the crusaders were to embark for Palestine, there was a terrible fever

Parting. Marburg, the Elisabeth window in the Elisabeth Church. Elisabeth and Louis, in a fond embrace, cannot bear to part from one another. The Landgrave is clung to on either side by his grieving wife and his companions in arms.

raging, to which both the Emperor and the Landgrave succumbed, the latter so badly that he had himself prepared for death with the last rites, the holy oil being dispensed by the Patriarch of Jerusalem. Louis died on 11 September. After solemn prayers for the dead, his body was wrapped securely in rich coverings and left for the time being in Otranto; his followers then continued their crusade to the Holy Land.

Messengers must have brought the news of Louis's death to Thuringia by about the middle to end of October 1227. The Reinhardsbrunn chronicle – based on a contemporary account – tells how Elisabeth received the news. So that she would not hear the sad tidings from an unexpected source, her mother-in-law sought her out. Elisabeth must be courageous, in order to bear stoically what 'has happened to your husband, my son, by God's heavenly dispensation.' 'If my brother (she called Louis this since they had spent their childhood together) has been taken prisoner, he can with the help of God and our faithful followers be freed.' 'He is dead.' Elisabeth's hands clenched. 'Dead? The world and all its glory is dead for me.' She got up suddenly; ran violently across the room, as if out of her senses, and threw herself against the wall, sobbing bitterly.

On their return from the Holy Land Louis's followers fetched their lord's body from the tomb. The mortal remains were prepared in the manner that was usual when a lord died far from home. The body was dissected, and boiled until the flesh fell from the bones. Then the entrails were buried on the spot, the heart usually in a particularly holy place such as a church. Louis's snow-white bones were laid in a costly shrine, carried by a pack-animal and guarded at night in a church, with many prayers; in the morning a mass was celebrated and sacrificial gifts made, and the troop continued their journey homewards. The Bishop of Bamberg, an uncle of Elisabeth, was informed that the funeral cortège would come through his town. The Bishop, with priests, monks and nuns went out to meet it in a solemn procession. Amid prayers and sorrowful chants, and accompanied by the doleful ringing of bells, the shrine was taken into the cathedral, and opened by Elisabeth. In the presence of the bleached bones she acknowledged her love, and expressed the crusading piety of her era. She does not begrudge God the life of one who set out of his own free will and with her blessing for the Holy Land. 'God knows that I would have preferred his life to all the wonders and joys of the world, if God in his goodness had spared him to me.' If she could have had him back, she would gladly have given up the whole world for him and lived as a beggar with him in direst poverty.

Meanwhile, at Reinhardsbrunn, the local monastery of the Landgrave to the south-west of Gotha, a great crowd of people had gathered. Here too monks and clerics came out to meet the cortège in a solemn procession with prayers and chanting. The ceremonies for the dead were in the age-old Christian tradition, uniting care for the soul of the departed with provision for the bodily needs of the poor: the celebration of masses, prayers, nightly singing of psalms, gifts to the monastery, alms for the poor. In the presence of his widow, his mother and brothers, Louis IV was finally laid to rest in the family burial place.

PART II
DESCRIPTIONS OF TRAVEL IN THE MIDDLE AGES

In the chapters which follow the picture of medieval travel will be rounded out with relevant source material. The accounts are based on well-documented facts about individual people or groups of people. This part of the book begins with a description of a flight in the sixth century, and ends with the journeys of later travellers, but there is no strict chronological order. It seemed best to let passages dealing with similar subjects follow on from one another.

A FLIGHT

Attalus, from a well-to-do Gallo-Roman family, was sent as a hostage to endorse an agreement, to the court of a Germanic lord in the Trier area. When the partners to the contract – the kings Theodoric and Childebert, sons of King Clovis who had died in 511 – fell out, the hostages became the property of the state; those who were keeping them could now use them as servants. Attalus consequently had to work in the stables of a 'barbarian'. His uncle, Gregorius Bishop of Langres, tried in vain to free his nephew; his new master demanded an impossibly high ransom. Then Leo, the Bishop's cook, thought of a plan: he had himself sold to the 'barbarian', and by means of his skill in cooking, soon won his master's confidence. One night after a feast which he had prepared, he and Attalus escaped. They took their master's horses and a bundle of clothes. Coming to the Moselle, they left their horses and clothes on the bank and swam across the river supported by their shields. Having reached the other side, they ran on towards Reims, by day and night, without a bite to eat. After three days they managed to get some fruit from a plum tree to build up their strength. One night they heard horsemen coming towards them, but managed to hide themselves behind a bramble-bush in time to overhear what the men were saying. One of them was their master, who cursed the fleeing men and swore that he would hang the one and cut the other to pieces with his sword. The same night Attalus and Leo reached Reims, where they sought the help of a priest. The latter, an old friend of Gregorius, had been warned about them in a dream; he looked after them and hid the two young men for a few more days, as their master had got wind of their whereabouts again. After another short journey, Bishop Gregorius was able to embrace his nephew with tears of joy; in gratitude to Leo for freeing him he gave him and his descendants their freedom and some land of their own.

Gregory, Bishop of Tours from 573, from the same distinguished Gallo-Roman family, tells this story of an episode in the life of his great grandfather and the latter's nephew (Gregorius, before he became a bishop, was a count in Autun). In the Middle Ages hostages were exchanged in their thousands, or simply taken and deported abroad. Many managed to escape, but few reached their goal. Paulus Diaconus, a contemporary of Charlemagne, remembers that his great-grandfather when taken hostage had been able to escape from the overlordship of the Avars. Half starving during his flight, he was taken in by an old Slav woman, who hid him and carefully fed him back to health; when he had regained his strength, the old woman gave him a parcel of food and directed him on the way to his homeland. Later, the Waltharius epic tells of the successful flight of Hagen, Walter and Hiltgund – characters in the *Nibelungenlied* – who as hostages escaped from Attila. All the hostages who escaped had the same burning desire to be free among their own countrymen once more.

The account of Gregory of Tours is embellished with legendary details, such as the dream motif, and many things which do not quite match. The fleeing pair are supposed to have left on a Sunday and to have reached the priest on a Sunday also, but at another point it says that they reached Reims after only four days. Much more important than such inconsistencies however is the fact that in many families the details of the successful flight of a member of the family were still remembered generations later (just as today in some families the story of the escape of a father or grandfather from a wartime prison-camp may be retold).

To get an idea of travel in the Middle Ages, pieces of information from all the various sources have to be pieced together as in a mosaic to build up the overall picture. Unlike many of the chroniclers, Gregory tells us many things which are of interest precisely because of their 'everyday' nature; we can look at some of these 'stones' in the mosaic which he gives us, in more detail, and in the context of the contemporary scene.

Attalus and Leo belonged to the millions who were on the road in medieval times: soldiers and merchants, slaves and hostages, exiles and messengers, scouts and spies, thieves and murderers, bridegrooms and pilgrims, religious and political refugees, men and women, young and old, the healthy and the sick . . .

Attalus and Leo differed from most of the above however: they hid in the woods by day and travelled if possible by night; they took pains not to be recognised by anyone. It was usual to ask travellers their name, where they were from and where they were going. War and disease had decimated the population in late Roman times, so that the small number of people left were mostly well-known to one another, like Bishop Gregorius and the priest in Reims. The pursuing 'barbarian' therefore had a better chance of retaking the two fleeing men.

The two men only took the horses as far as the Moselle. Perhaps they did not want to be accused of stealing horses and also wanted to confuse the men following them, because anyone who worked in a stable would certainly have known to get a horse to swim across the Moselle. It is true there was a bridge at Trier which had been built by the Romans, and whose pillars still carry traffic today; but the few bridges available channelled traffic and made it easier to keep track of travellers. Such a bridge, on which perhaps a toll would also have to be paid, was out of the question for people on the run. To swim across the Moselle – it was high summer, because the plums were ripe – was no problem for young men, especially as they had their shields to buoy them up, which were probably made of leather stretched over lime-wood. The river, which was not dammed or forced into a narrow channel, wound between many islands and sandbanks, which made the crossing easier.

People travelling on foot even now consider carefully what they will take with them. Besides the horses, the two men left their bundles of clothes behind. In August and September they could count on warm nights; and if it grew cold they could keep moving and rest in the daytime in the shade of a wood; for they had to cross the southern outlying spurs of the Ardennes. Food was more of a problem than clothing. They would not have had any money (not even the 'token money' which more modern prisoners might have been given and which is useless outside prison). Leo and Attalus, like other travellers, would also have been wary of robbers; they took their swords and shields with them, which they grasp when they hear the group of horsemen approaching them at night. Even if they had had any money, they would not have been able to buy food, because it would have given their whereabouts away to their pursuers. So they had to make do with what they could find on the way – such as ripe plums. It is not very likely that these were their only food. Various foodstuffs can be found in the woods in summer, which a cook would know how to recognise – fruit, nuts, roots, wild herbs. The most surprising thing is that the two escapees had not taken a light net with which to catch fish, or even birds. When Saint Gallus at about the same time was looking for a suitable place in which to build his cell in the forests to the south of Lake Constance, his companion cooked him a simple meal: he caught fish, which he then roasted over a fire; he clearly had a net and material with which to light a fire with him in his baggage. Gallus and his companion made a meal with the fish and some bread they had brought with them, which would correspond to the minimum modern nutritional requirements: carbohydrate, protein, fat, trace elements – with water to drink. There is no mention of fish however, in the account of Attalus's flight. And Attalus told the priest sheltering them in Reims that that was the fourth day they had had no bread or meat. The 'barbarian's' larder was so richly stocked that even a stable-lad could reckon on getting some meat every day. But for many people until comparatively modern times meat was an occasional extravagance, if not an impossible dream. Even bread, especially white bread, was for a long time reserved for the rich only; the poor usually had to make do with oatmeal.

Attalus and Leo had a good knowledge of their whereabouts. They would have taken their bearings by the stars at night, and the sun by day. The time of year favoured them too, because in mid-summer the sky is so bright that one can find one's way along a road even without moonlight. And there was a road. A Roman road ran from Trier via Arlon to Reims, a distance of about 125 miles in a straight line, which would mean about 137 miles along the road; the fleeing men would also have had to make detours round the usual stopping-places. Possibly Attalus and Leo followed this road, which would explain the meeting with their master. Young men could easily have done 137 miles in a week.

Attalus and his travelling companion were lucky: their flight succeeded. But to win their freedom the two had to overcome many dangers. They were lucky enough to be able to escape starvation and death, partly because – like Paulus

Diaconus's ancestor – individual people were ready to offer them protection. In the sixth century only ruins remained of the organised staging-posts of the Roman empire north of the Alps; beyond its borders there had probably never been any inns, so individual people were all the more hospitable. Monks and hermits would also offer overnight shelter as did the Reims priest and the old Slav woman in the eastern Alps.

BONIFACE'S TRAVELS

Boniface, born in about 675, could have had a career as an abbot or bishop. But he decided to follow the example of Irish and Anglo-Saxon monks, and to exchange his ordered life in his English homeland for the difficult existence of a missionary and church official on the Continent. His life is better documented than that of most of his contemporaries; in his letters, in church acts inspired by him, and in the account of his life, there are countless illustrations of the theme 'Travel in the Eighth Century'.

From 716 until his death in 754 Boniface was for almost forty years continually on the road. He went to the holy city three times, undertaking his third journey to Rome in 737/38, at the age of over sixty. He worked as a missionary in Friesland, as organiser of a disorganised church in Bavaria, the Frankish kingdom, and Thuringia. As a reformer of the Frankish church he had to deal with majordomos and the King, bishops and archbishops, abbots and priests, not to mention his dealings with the curia in Rome. His many activities necessitated personal attention, that is journeys by himself, or the sending of trustworthy colleagues.

Countless religious emissaries were killed on the Continent by heathen Teutons – by reason of their faith, like the Anglo-Saxon missionaries about whom Bede writes, 'Black' and 'White' Hewald – or were slain by robbers, as was Boniface. The latter did not seek out martyrdom, but aimed throughout to carry out his carefully planned and wide-ranging missionary and reform work, as the correspondence shows which he entered into with church and secular authorities; letters are quoted here as examples of letters of recommendation, which travellers would seek to obtain before setting out on a long journey. Bishop Daniel of Winchester appealed in 718 to 'the most pious and gracious Kings, to all dukes, and most dear and honoured bishops as also to all godfearing abbots, priests, and spiritual sons, in Christ's name.' Citing all God's commandments and the story of Abraham in particular, Daniel made a specific request for hospitality: to fulfil one's charitable duty towards travellers is a work pleasing to God. All thus addressed were requested to show charity to the bearer of the letter, to the servant of Almighty God Wynfrid – the latter would only take the name Boniface in Rome in 719 – as God Himself loved and commanded them (*caritatem ei, quam Deus et diligit et praecipit, exhibetis*). Those who offered hospitality to Boniface were following the words of the Gospel: 'He that receiveth you receiveth me'. Bishop Daniel stated that those who fulfil this commandment will receive eternal praise. He ended with the blessing: 'May the Grace of God be with your highness for ever more.'

Boniface could present the letter to the highest temporal powers and officers of the Church from simple priests to bishops. Providing that is, that the recipient could read and had a knowledge of Latin – which was not always the case even with clerics. Thirty years later some Bavarian bishops informed the Pope about a priest, who received people into the Church with the following words: 'I baptise you in the name of the Fatherland and daughter and the Holy Spirit.' (*Baptizo te in nomine patria et filia et spiritus sancti.*) Temporal rulers could seldom read or write, even more rarely knew Latin; for that reason they often had clerics at their courts.

Bishop Daniel was content to ask for hospitality (hospitalitas) for Boniface. Four years later Pope Gregory II added to the request, clarifying it further: those addressed should supply Boniface with 'everything necessary', give him 'men to accompany him on his journey, and provide him with food and drink and anything else he might need'. Anyone making difficulties for Boniface or putting obstacles in his way was threatened with eternal damnation. Charles Martel too, the effective ruler (though officially only majordomo) of the Frankish kingdom, foresees in his letter of recommendation Boniface being faced with obstacles: no one shall harm him or do him any wrong, and he shall be kept safe and free from attack under the protection of the majordomo at all times.

It is clear from the letters of recommendation which Boniface gave his own emissaries when they set out, that a traveller was better served with a wide-ranging general request than with special pleas. The king of Mercia, an important Anglo-Saxon kingdom, was asked to give a messenger help and support in any eventuality which might occur. Boniface asked a count to let a messenger going to Rome travel unharmed through his territory and to help him in any possible need, 'as you have done for our earlier emissaries and as they have reported to me on their return.'

If one looks at the letters written on behalf of and by Boniface, it is clear that a request for hospitality included everything that travellers might need abroad: to be supplied with food, and fodder for their horses, with clothes, lodgings and if necessary heating, medicines, an escort through a particular territory from stage to stage, an escort in special circumstances (robbers, bogs, forests, mountains, snowstorms, mist); safe-conduct for the journey out *and* back; exemption from tolls and dues; recommendations to ferrymen to take the traveller willingly and without charge across his river and so on. Hospitality also entailed expert advice to the traveller about his route and the dangers and risks he might expect; finally it might include comfort in adversity (the word *solatium* is repeatedly used in the sense 'help in the widest sense' which would include comfort), help for the dying and a suitable burial.

Hospitality of the kind Boniface might claim relieved the traveller of the necessity of carrying money; he was also far less likely to be attacked if he could tell highway-robbers with a clear conscience that he had no money or valuables on him; the letters, incomprehensible to ordinary robbers, were on behalf of one person only. Boniface's letters of recommendation were therefore at least as valuable as many universally accepted credit-cards today.

How was it that Boniface – a man with an edgy, abrasive temperament – was given disinterested support for so many decades? How did he enjoy such universal hospitality? Boniface was working in an area that was still imbued with Germanic, and already with Christian, ideals; in both ideologies hospitality played a leading role as the descriptions of Tacitus – which were certainly not purely idealised – and the exhortations of the Gospels illustrate. Moreover Boniface's work was welcomed by the Frankish rulers; he was helping to develop the countryside when he founded bishoprics and monasteries, led synods, admonished corrupt churchmen, sent for educated men from his homeland to come to the area where he was working, who were prepared to undertake altruistic enterprises. He also had much to offer: his advice was sought, and his prayers, and sometimes even his gifts. Boniface knew how to win favour with rulers by giving suitable presents: he sent King Aethelbald of Mercia a hawk and two falcons – for the royal hunt – together with two shields and two lances, which would certainly have been richly embellished. King Aethelbert II of Kent begged Boniface to send him two falcons and sent him a silver, gold-lined drinking beaker three and a half pounds in weight and two 'shaggy doublets'. Boniface sent Archbishop Egbert of York via the messenger who delivered his letter 'instead of a kiss two flasks of wine': bishop and brothers were to have a happy day, mindful of the love which bound them to Boniface. In other letters, Boniface related that he had arrived safely in Rome; he sought comfort and advice from his countrymen in England; he asked the monks of Monte Cassino, to remember him in their communal prayers; he asked the Pope for his decision on complex questions of faith or church discipline; he asked for prayers for his missionary work, for helpers from his homeland, for relics of saints, for certain books (lives of the apostles, martyrs, church fathers, Bede), he asked for clothes, incense, spices . . .

The many existing letters, written by and to Boniface, throw light on the comings and goings of the emissaries of secular and spiritual powers. It would do the letters an injustice, to dismiss them as merely 'communications media'. When messengers brought one of Boniface's letters, they were helping to alleviate the loneliness and often superhuman workload of a 'lone warrior' and to welcome him into a community of praying, interceding, hoping and waiting people. The letters reveal a many-layered tapestry of relationships which in the course of centuries bound the West ever more strongly together, uniting it despite all its differences, and which maintained the links between the European and the outside worlds. A correspondent from the Roman curia sends Boniface cinnamon, pepper and incense; the gifts show that overseas trade with India had not been broken off in the eighth century, in spite of the inroads of Arabs into the Mediterranean area.

Since late Roman times, women could be numbered among the pilgrims going to Rome to seek forgiveness for their sins. They faced even greater dangers on the road than men. It is noteworthy that even an abbess asked Boniface for advice about pilgrimages to Rome. The Abbess Eangyth writes in about 720 that she had for a long time felt a longing, like so many of her colleagues and relations, 'to visit the one-time mistress of the world, Rome, and to ask for forgiveness for our sins there, as many others have done and do, and myself most of all, who am already older and have sinned and failed far more in my life.' Eangyth openly admits that she would be blamed by many for undertaking such a journey; she also knows that Church edicts state that each person shall serve God in the place where he or she took their vows. Despite this she wants Boniface's opinion as to whether it would be best and most useful for her 'to stay in her own homeland or to go abroad' (*sive in patrio solo vivere vel in peregrinatione exulare*). Nearly two decades later the daughter and successor of this abbess, clearly driven by the same feelings of unrest, also asked Boniface for his advice. He did not dare, 'to forbid you myself to go on a pilgrimage, nor to advise you unhesitatingly to undertake it.' He advised patience and waiting until there was no longer any danger from Saracens, and caution; if Bugga has weighed up her enterprise in prayer, she must do whatever her love of God bids her. Boniface expressed himself more openly than in his letters to women in a long epistle to Archbishop Cuthbert of Canterbury in 747: he could not conceal from him his anxieties concerning female pilgrims and begged him urgently to forbid by means of synods and royal command married women and nuns to go to Rome. It is clear that Boniface had been observant during his travels and that he had spoken of his worries with other people: the women pilgrims to Rome fail for the most part, and only a few remain pure. 'For there are only very few towns in Lombardy, in Francia or Gaul, in which there is not a woman who has broken her vows or a whore from among the race of Angles. And this is a nuisance and a shame for your whole Church.'

Boniface frequently used the means recommended here – synods or a ruler's command – to fight abuses in the Church and elsewhere. Such synods met twice, or a minimum of once a year; that meant that year by year churchmen (and lay people) flocked along the roads, to discuss questions of faith and custom in an appointed place, perhaps to bring accused brothers to justice, and finally to write down their deliberations into tenets which are called the 'canons' of church law. The repeated re-statement of certain commandments shows that the social reality did not correspond to the ideal. At the so-called *Concilium Germanicum* in 742 the 'servants of God' were forbidden to carry weapons, to fight, to go on a campaign or fight an enemy; exempt are only those who are forced to do so in order to celebrate the mass or transport holy relics. A prince shall therefore have one or two bishops and the priests of the royal chapel with him, and every commander should have a priest 'who can pronounce sentence on those who confess their sins, and make them atone for them'; five hundred years later a house chaplain still belonged among the followers of powerful crusaders. In 742 the *Concilium Germanicum* also forbade 'all God's servants to hunt or go about in the woods with dogs, or to keep hawks or falcons.'

There were corresponding commandments which reflect the great mobility of certain groups of people, according to the framework laid down by authority. Every priest was to render an account to his bishop at times of fast as to the way he carried out his office, his life, his faith and his teaching. If a bishop was travelling through his diocese, to confirm people in their faith, abbots and priests were to receive him and support him in every way. Bishops were asked to know their way about their dioceses, and archbishops to be concerned with their whole church province. A Bavarian synod of the mid-eighth century called for peace (with a ban on cursing, drunkenness, use of immoderation or force) and finishes with a commandment and promise to all Christians: 'to take all strangers and visitors into their house. If they do all this, they will receive an eternal reward and the misery which we experience in this world will with God's help be more bearable.'

After many successes – to which the reform of the Church in the Frankish kingdom through the synods and the founding of the Abbey at Fulda belong – and many failures – Boniface was not invited to be present at the spectacular visit of Pope Stephen II to the Frankish kingdom, although he more than anyone had promoted the links between the Franks and the Pope – Boniface wanted, now that he was eighty, to resume the missionary work which he had started in vain in Friesland forty years before. The account of his life gives details of travelling along inland waterways and of the provisioning of a group of missionaries: Boniface went down the Rhine with several companions; travel by boat made it possible to take more baggage and comforts than was possible on land. A good number of books were among their luggage; Boniface also took relics on all his journeys. At night the group always sought a harbour. They went down the Rhine and the Zuider Zee – which was smaller in his day – to Friesland, where Boniface now had more success with his preaching.

The missionaries slept in tents, as secular lords and churchmen would do for centuries on their travels; the necessary provisions, including a flask of wine, were carried on the boats. Why wine? one might ask. Water was known to be often polluted and unhealthy, whereas wine, drunk in moderation is healthy and good for the circulation; it was no coincidence that Little Red Riding Hood took her grandmother a bottle of wine. Also, Benedict had expressly allowed his monks to enjoy wine, which was drunk as a matter of course in the Mediterranean regions. Above all, however, Boniface had planned the journey carefully; in the last chapter of his *Vita* it says that lack of fresh water 'in almost all Friesland' was causing men and beasts great hardship, for ground- and river-water were brackish. On the day on which the newly baptised were to be confirmed, Boniface and his companions were slain by robbers. The *Vita* ends with a miracle: at the spot at which Boniface died, a wonderfully fresh-tasting spring suddenly burst forth, 'quite contrary to the nature of this land'.

The body of Boniface was taken by boat to Utrecht and laid there provisionally; a little later it was rowed solemnly 'with psalms and songs of praise and without great pains on the part of the oarsmen' up the Rhine; thirty days after his death the mortal remains of Boniface reached Mainz, or perhaps – the authorities contradict each other on this point – even Fulda. Boniface had named this foundation as his resting-place a long while before.

People streamed from far and near to honour the dead man. His saintliness immediately proclaimed itself when the sick, cripples, the weary and heavy laden were healed at his graveside. As a place of pilgrimage Fulda was at no time comparable to Canterbury; but in the course of centuries St Boniface's grave was also visited by millions of men, seeking help in their need or to thank for mercies received. Today the German bishops still travel year by year to Fulda, to deliberate at Boniface's graveside on questions which concern Church and society in Germany.

ROYAL PROGRESSES

Charlemagne on the road

And the said gracious King celebrated Christmas at the court at Herstal, and Easter also . . . in 779 King Charles travelled through Neustria and came to the court at Compiègne. . . . The diet was held at the court at Düren and then they went to Saxony. The Rhine was crossed at Lippeham, and the Saxons tried to offer resistance at Bocholt; by the grace of God they did not get the upper hand . . . The Saxons from the right bank of the Weser . . . offered hostages and pledged their oath. And then the aforenamed illustrious King returned to Francia. And he celebrated Christmas at Worms, and also Easter. In 780, when he set out to bring order among the Saxons, King Charles came to Eresburg and then farther to the source of the Lippe, where he held an assembly. From there he went on to the Elbe and on the way . . . many were christened. And he reached the Elbe at the mouth of the Ohre, and there made dispositions for the Saxons and also for the Slavs, and the aforesaid most excellent King returned to Francia. Then he decided to go to pray at Rome, together with his wife, Queen Hildegard. And he celebrated Christmas in the town of Pavia and . . . in 781, at the end of the said journey he celebrated Easter in Rome . . . And when King Charles returned from there, he came to the town of Milan, and here his daughter Gisela was baptised by Archbishop Thomas . . . And from here he returned to Francia.

Similar entries can be seen year after year in the official account of the history of the Frankish kingdom, the 'Imperial Annals'. Charlemagne was – like his father and grandfather, his sons and grandsons, many abbots and bishops, and sometimes the Pope – annually on the road, for weeks, often months at a time. The route, or itinerary, of many secular and church officials can often be reconstructed from such records and particularly from documents which give meeting-places and dates. It has been estimated that in the four and a half decades of his rule, Charlemagne covered distances which together would equal the distance round the world several times over. Similar details are known about an Islamic ruler of the time of the crusades. In the seventeen years of his reign (1260–77), Sultan Baybars was said to have led thirty-eight campaigns, fought in fifteen battles himself and travelled in all about 25,000 miles.

Charlemagne would have done most of the journeys which the Imperial

Annals mention for the years 779–81 on horseback; there were many navigable rivers in the Frankish kingdom but their courses only corresponded for short distances to the routes that the king and his followers had to cover in the year 780. It was only centuries later that fit and healthy rulers had themselves carried in litters once more in Europe; the example of Byzantium may have had a strong influence in this respect, since many practices of the Roman Empire had never fallen out of favour there.

It was only in the last two decades of Charlemagne's reign that the palace at Aachen became more of a permanent residence. But even then the King still carried out his duties mainly by travelling round the kingdom – as French and German kings did later. In Germany, unlike France, no capital city grew up. There were only quasi-capitals, such as Magdeburg under Otto the Great or Prague under Charles IV. The lack of a capital with powerful authority and working officialdom, archives and buildings both favoured and indeed made necessary the mobility of medieval rulers. An empire such as Charlemagne's would have been difficult to rule from a central capital; Paris took on the functions of a capital city at times during the Middle Ages, but the area to be governed was very much smaller than that of the 'Empire'.

A glance at a historical atlas will show how large the dimensions of the Carolingian empire were after the addition of the kingdoms of the Lombards, the Saxons, and the Spanish March: Barcelona to Hamburg is 937 miles in a direct line, Nantes to Linz 750 miles, Hamburg to Rome 812 miles. Because of bad roads, the lack of bridges, extensive forests, marshes and mountains which were difficult to cross, a messenger going from the Ebro to the Elbe would take at least a month to get there; it would take him another month to take the king's reply back over the Pyrenees. So the hub of the Carolingian empire was well placed; it shifted in the years of Charlemagne's time as emperor from the area between the Marne and Oise/Aisne to the areas between the Rhine and Maas or Rhine-Main area; the imperial annals quoted above take Compiègne, Düren and Worms to represent these areas in the year 780.

In the seventh to eighth centuries a striking change took place in the Frankish kingdom, a break with the classical town culture. The Merovingian kings who preceded the Carolingians had resided in Roman towns – Reims, Soissons, Paris, Orléans. The Carolingians preferred to live on the land. Herstal, Compiègne, Düren are representative of countless royal demesnes, whose importance for the royal progresses can hardly be overestimated and which therefore deserve to be studied more closely. For a start, it is clear that the demesnes had to be large enough for the king and a sizeable retinue to be entertained there even at the great annual festivals.

If these festivals had been unimportant, the author of the annals would have passed over them, as over many other details, in silence. As is clear from other sources, and from other countries – England after the Norman conquest for example – rulers laid great store by having their divine right honoured at the great church festivals and making their majestic presence visible for a while to all their people, rich and poor alike. A stay at Christmas or Easter at a particular place would be planned long in advance, and foreign legations would also be congregated there, whom the King wished to meet 'with official honours'. When Charlemagne spent Christmas in Pavia and Easter in Rome, he had highly political reasons for doing so: Pavia was the capital of the Lombard kingdom only annexed a few years previously, and Byzantium had not yet waived its claim to Rome.

In 779 a diet was summoned at Düren. As Charlemagne also appointed bishops and abbots and even joined in learned arguments over dogma, it was appropriate that all questions which concerned the empire should be discussed and decided at such diets; the final separation between regnum and sacerdotium, the offices of king and priest, was only completed centuries later, being partly realised after the dispute over investiture. So worldly *and* spiritual authorities were usually present at a diet. Royal demesnes such as Düren, Frankfurt, Ingelheim had therefore to be sited where great gatherings could be held. There would be a perpetual throng of officials, messengers, suppliers of provisions, traders, pedlars and entertainers.

The living quarters, stables, barns and workshops of the demesne chosen had to be suitably appointed for the king and his family to be comfortably accommodated. Specially fine buildings were usually only added to the 'palaces', which often hardly differed from the royal demesnes. In a palace an *oratorium* would also be expected, a chapel in which religious services for the ruler could be held. If the king spent Christmas and Easter at Herstal, the demesne would certainly have had its own chapel.

Stone, as a building material, was reserved, until well into the Middle Ages, for churches. Even the living quarters of palaces and demesnes were for a long time made of wood, wattle and daub, which are good insulating materials so that it was cool in such houses in summer and easier to heat those rooms which had heating facilities in the winter; the buildings also had drawbacks, like some old country houses today: they were not insulated against rising damp and there was a greater risk of fire than in stone buildings; the imperial annals record that in the year 790 the palace in Worms burnt down.

As only a proportion of those attending the diet could be put up in the living quarters, even high church and state officials had to find their own accommodation, as at the meeting in Lippspringe in 780; they put up tents, as Boniface did in Friesland and the guests of the Emperor Frederick Barbarossa at the great court feast in Mainz in 1184. Sleeping in one's own tent, under one's own covers or furs, would have been much more pleasant than spending the night in airless, badly ventilated rooms, not to mention damp bedclothes and vermin. Today many well-to-do people would rather sleep in a – preferably very comfortable – tent, than in a hotel. In Charlemagne's day they would have had no choice.

Diets were often convocated by Charlemagne in the area in which he was drawing up his forces for a campaign: in 773 before the campaign against the

Lombards in Geneva, in 779 before the Saxon campaign in Düren, and in 780 even in Saxony. The idea of these arrangements was to spare those summoned an unnecessarily long journey; even a great empire had to tread carefully in its dealings with its limited number of helpers and back-up support.

Until modern times campaigns in central Europe were carried out if possible in the spring or summer. In the spring there was still a danger of swollen rivers and floods, which caused the Frankish army much trouble in 784 and 785. In summer the roads were in a better condition than in the rainy seasons of autumn and winter, and it was easier to find shelter. The ordinary soldier could sleep happily under the open skies, wrapped in a pelt; if there were problems with supplies, the troops could feed themselves in summer for a few days on what they could find in the woods and fields. However a drought in the summer of 772 almost proved fatal to the Frankish army in Saxony; contemporaries regarded it as a miracle that enough rain fell just in time to save the army. In late summer the enemy's harvest could be gathered or destroyed, making survival more difficult for them and so making them easier to defeat. The army was usually disbanded in the autumn, because to feed and house a large number of men through the winter was difficult. There was also another consideration: medieval kings had a great passion for hunting; this royal sport combined pleasure with regular physical training in readiness for war. The imperial annals for the year 804 for example, record that Charlemagne disbanded the army and went to Aachen; then he set out to hunt in the Ardennes, and returned later, probably at the onset of winter, to Aachen again. There were exceptions to such rules: Charlemagne quite often led winter campaigns, to surprise the enemy, in 784 against the Saxons, in 787 against Italy; ten years later he went in mid-November to overwinter in Saxony – the enemy had visible proof that the Franks were there to stay in their country.

In 779 the Rhine was crossed at Lippeham, near Wesel. The event deserved no further mention from the chronicler. But in 778 it had been noted that the Frankish army had gone through a ford on the Ebro. Even in a dry summer the Lower Rhine had too much water to be crossed by means of a ford – unlike the Main for instance. As according to the imperial annals the Frankish army had built two bridges with secure bridgeheads over the Elbe in 789, and three years later a pontoon-bridge over the Danube, and as there was no fixed bridge, the army must have crossed the Rhine in 779 on boats and barges, which would have been brought there specially.

The annals give no details of the further route, or of the way by which Charlemagne later returned to 'Francia'. There had been roads since time immemorial in the lands on the right of the Rhine – which were not comparable with the Roman roads in the lands to the left of the Rhine which had been kept in more or less good repair – but along which Charlemagne and his contemporaries were able to travel. It notes in the annals in connection with a diet at Paderborn, that Charlemagne had streets and roads 'cleaned up' in Saxony and that peace reigned 'on the open road' (785). In the year 797 it says that the Frankish army had to go through bogs and 'impassable terrain' in Saxony, which is another indication that they could usually travel along roads.

In the year 780 the imperial annals record: 'And many were baptised on the way.' The baptism could be carried out by clerics, whose presence with the army had expressly been provided for by the reforming synods instigated by Boniface. Such baptisms were not a question of conversion: the 'inner Christianisation' of Europe only began with the Church reform movement in the eleventh century, was further advanced by the mendicant orders from the thirteenth century and only reached a certain depth with the Reformation and Counter-Reformation in the sixteenth century. The baptism of Saxons bound them to the Frankish empire in two ways: by the oath of allegiance to the Emperor and the baptismal vow; a relapse into heathen ways was punishable by imprisonment, fines or sentence of death. Henry of Latvia tells what sometimes happened at mass baptisms in his Livonian Chronicle for the year 1216: beleaguered Estonians were forced by hunger and thirst to surrender. They were granted peace on condition that they accepted the Christian faith. The Estonians announced that they were prepared to do so; a priest was sent in to them in their fortress, who blessed them and spoke as follows: ' "Will you," he asked, "give up your idolatry and put your faith in the one God of the Christians?" And when all answered, "We will", he sprinkled them with water and said: "Now you are all baptised in the name of the Father, the Son and the Holy Ghost." When that was done, they were granted peace, and after the sons of the eldest had been handed over as hostages, the army withdrew with all their spoils and booty and the prisoners back to Livonia, and praised God, who is glorified eternally, for the conversion of the heathen.'

That Charlemagne was not content with the overthrow of the Saxons, that he saw himself as a tool in God's hands, was part of his acceptance of his role as ruler, that made the spread of Christianity a duty.

Charlemagne, it says in the annals for the year 780, wanted to go to Rome 'to pray'. The journey was not a result of a despairing cry for help, like that which in 755 and 756, summoned his father Pippin to fight the Lombards on behalf of the Pope, or like that of 799 when Charlemagne was summoned to go to Rome for the third time by an exiled Pope under a cloud. Prayer was given as his main reason, but it was possibly a cover for political or military motives. The homage to Rome by the Franks dated from Merovingian times, and was greatly encouraged by Boniface. It was important for every ruler who valued his own salvation and that of his kingdom to have a good relationship with 'the heavenly gate-keeper'. Dealings with bishops, abbots and secular princes could also be carried out during such journeys, and the opportunity would naturally be seized to 'fly the flag' or demonstrate one's sovereignty in the metropolises of two kingdoms at Christmas and Easter. In 786 the imperial annals announced once more that Charlemagne had 'gone to Rome, to pray at the threshold of the holy apostles'; and it added 'and to put the Italian affairs in order and deal with the Emperor's emissaries concerning their arrangements, and this was done.'

At a time when church and secular spheres were so closely interwoven, there were usually several – political, religious and other – motives for any 'state action'; the historian has to take the religious element into account. The same sources tell that Charlemagne's father, Pippin, seriously ill in 768, went home from Saintes, via Tours, where he said a prayer to St Martin, and then 'he came to Saint Dionysius and there died.' This mode of expression shows the close relationship people had with the saints. Pippin did not go to Tours and Saint-Denis, but to the saints Martin and Dionysius. St Martin was the most important saint of the Carolingian empire; his relics were even carried into battle to guarantee victory. St Dionysius was held in equal veneration; according to the legend he took his head in his hands after being beheaded and went to the mountain which was called in his honour and that of other saints, *mons martyrum*, Montmartre.

The sources do not tell us Charles's route, or which Alpine passes he took on his journey out or back, or the time of year, or the size of his retinue, or whether there were or were not pack-animal handlers; they do not tell us at what point the ruler himself had to dismount and continue on foot the wearisome journey along steep, narrow paths.

Charlemagne took Queen Hildegard with him to Rome. That was unusual, and the annals record the fact. The information we have highlights the burdens which in the Middle Ages fell on both a ruler *and* his wife. Those in leading positions paid a high price for the respect in which they were held because of their office. They had to travel in wind and weather and even in summer could get drenched to the skin; a chill might rapidly turn into fatal pneumonia. Nights were spent in shabby inns or windy tents; wrapped in damp bedcovers and plagued by fleas, bugs, the scrabbling of rats and mice, perhaps painful chilblains – not to mention restless bedfellows – there was little sleep to be had. Although they could not count on getting refreshing sleep, they had to appear calmly the next day: give orders to servants, send messengers, receive secular and spiritual princes with due ceremony. These would throng round the ruler's retinue on the way, begging, beseeching or threatening, trying to get a hearing for their petitions – and trying to win the Queen's sympathy to promote their cause. It states repeatedly in the records that this or that gift, sanction, or endowment was made 'at the request of our dear wife'. Then they had to pack up again, set off and travel farther. Everything that had to be transported had its proper place on a certain pack-animal, or later, in a certain vehicle. The methodical loading and unloading was a routine task, which is only indirectly mentioned in the sources.

We are quite well informed about Queen Hildegard, who accompanied her husband to Rome; so we can illustrate the theme 'women travellers', by taking details of her journey as representative of the travels of other women, about whom the sources are silent. Charlemagne had taken the thirteen-year-old Hildegard as his second wife in 771. In the twelve years of her marriage to Charles she bore him nine children (from his other marriages Charles had at least nine other children); at the birth of her first child Hildegard was fourteen or fifteen years old; Gisela, mentioned in the extract quoted above, was the penultimate child of the royal pair, born in 781. As Gisela was baptised in Milan, we can take it that she was born between Rome and Milan. This would mean that her mother was heavily pregnant when she had to travel along roads and tracks, over passes and rivers, through mountains and woods. It is understandable that with at least nine births in twelve years and that kind of journey, Hildegard only lived to twenty-five: the many demands of motherhood, travel and stressful court life must have worn out the Queen before her time, like many others who shared her fate.

A wife could not accompany her lord on all his travels, so her joy at the celebrations for his happy homecoming was all the greater. Extra-marital relationships were also fostered by the long and frequent separations of married partners. Charlemagne had four wives and at least six concubines in the course of his life.

Military undertakings were so successfully completed in Bavaria and Saxony, that the brief entry in the annals for the year 790 – no military campaign, celebration of Christmas and Easter in Worms – could be appropriately fleshed out by anyone who understood the annals. People expected the king to travel round; for the time of his stay in an area he was judge, and could bring local rulers to justice when necessary and possibly also help the 'ordinary citizen' to get his rights. And additionally, the idea which went back to pre-Christian times, that the king was a saviour, and could bring fertility to fields, cattle and men by his presence, lived on for centuries after the baptism of Clovis and his Franks in 496, overlaid to some extent by Christian ideals, like many another feast and custom. So for the year 790 the imperial annals could be rewritten as follows: 'In order to dispel the idea that he was doing nothing and wasting his time, the king went up the Main by boat to the palace which he had built in Germania at Salz on the Frankish Saale, and then returned along the same river back down to Worms.'

The king's envoys

Although the king was so constantly on the road, a realm as large as the Frankish empire in 800 needed information if it was to keep law and order under control. In 802 the office of the *missi dominici*, the 'emissaries of the lord king' was instituted. 'Clever and wise men' from among the circle of church and state high officials were to travel through appointed parts of the empire to keep an eye on them. There were similar institutions in later empires – the daily journeys of the middle-ranking administrative officers through villages in the nineteenth century, or Gogol's 'Government Inspector'.

The 'emissaries of the Lord Charles' had to make investigations on the spot in each place and then send a report back to the King; if they could not put a stop to malpractices, they must bring the affair without more ado under the jurisdiction of the Emperor; it must not happen that 'sycophancy, bribery, nepotism or fear of powerful men prevent justice from being done.' God's holy churches, the poor, and especially widows and orphans were held to be particularly at risk.

In 803 the abbot of Saint-Denis and the count of Paris were the king's envoys for the areas of Paris and Rouen. It is worth looking at the questions they had to deal with. Abbot and count were to investigate whether bishops, priests, abbots, monks and nuns were living according to the precepts of the Church and fulfilling their duties or whether they were neglectful and lazy; whether the priests knew the psalms, whether they instructed those who wished to be baptised in the Christian faith, whether they were in a position to adapt prayers for special masses – for example for the dead – according to the sex and number of those for whom the prayers were intended; the king's envoys must test how well the priest instructed his congregation in his sermons, what penances he gave to sinners and what reparations were demanded for any damage done. 'More important than anything else, however, is that they investigate the manner of life and chastity of priests, and whether these are a model and example to their Christian communities.' The king's envoys must find out whether lay people had taken church property; whether unity and friendship ruled among bishops, abbots, counts, abbesses and the king's officials or whether they were in conflict – over, one imagines, their rights and property. The envoys were also to find out whether there had been cases of perjury, murder, adultery; whether poor men had been oppressed by officials with regard to their military duty, by for instance being forced to do service year after year, so that they could not cultivate their land or pay their dues and were forced to give up their freedom; the king's envoys must also see that the required ships were being built at the coast . . .

A long list of instructions accompanied the envoys on their way. And these were only the main categories. They must make careful investigations to see that everything was in order with regard to Church and state. This method of control could only function under specific circumstances: behind the emissary there had to be a powerful authority which would guarantee that only men of honour and integrity were sent as envoys; the envoys must be known to be capable of punishing offenders without regard to their person, and equally of appointing suitable people to office; the central power must be able to protect the controllers it sent out from every kind of attack. These conditions were, when matters were at their best, present in Charlemagne's empire. The *missi dominici* must have put right many abuses and helped many innocent men to obtain justice; the sources are, however, full of complaints about oppression and injustice, probably for the most part because of a lack of suitable controllers. For there was always a danger of stopping one gap and opening another: if the abbot of Saint-Denis was travelling as a king's envoy month after month, he could not at the same time look after the affairs of his own monks.

THE VOYAGES OF THE NORSEMEN AND THE GRETTISAGA

In the year 800 the Imperial Annals record: the King 'left the palace of Aachen in the middle of March, travelled through the coastal regions of Gaul, had a fleet built in these waters, which had become unsafe because of sea-raiders, and set up a watch there, and celebrated Easter in Centula (St Riquier).' It was the year in which Charlemagne was to be crowned Emperor. In the European–near-Eastern area there were now three great powers: the caliphate of Baghdad, Byzantium and the Carolingian empire. The legations which came to the Carolingian court from far and near were proof of the recognition paid to the emperor; people wanted to be on good terms with Charlemagne; at the very least they wanted to know with whom they might have to deal. At precisely this time the official Frankish records announced the appearance of a new danger. 'Sea-raiders' would trouble, plunder and ravage the Frankish lands and the British Isles for more than two hundred years. It is true that there is talk of building a fleet, but Charlemagne reacted to the threat in a different way than towards Saxons and Lombards, Moors and Avars. Possibly the decision not to lead an offensive campaign against the 'sea-raiders' and follow them into their lairs, destroy their bases and make their sorties impossible, shows something of the 'rustic' attitude, which can be seen elsewhere among the Carolingians. Who were these sea-raiders? How was it possible that they – along with Hungarians and Saracens – became *the* scourge of the West for decades?

In the course of the barbarian invasions, in the mid-fifth century, some of the Angles, Saxons and Jutes had built ships, terrorised other lands and looked around for places in which to settle. In England they had been recruited as soldiers by the Romans and – after their departure – by the British princes, and eventually established their own settlements and territories at the expense of the Romano-British inhabitants; they founded kingdoms, adopted the Christian faith and were even soon sending missionaries themselves to convert the Germanic peoples on the Continent; Boniface was one of them. The consciousness of a common heredity has remained alive; Anglo-Saxon sources repeatedly refer to the inhabitants of the territory between the North Sea and Lippe, Elbe and Rhine as 'Old Saxons'.

Other Saxons, towards the end of the fifth century, carried out raids up river estuaries, as did 'Norsemen' four hundred years later; raiding and plundering, killing and laying waste, they spread terror and alarm. The monks of the monastery on Noirmoutier were forced to leave their island to the south of

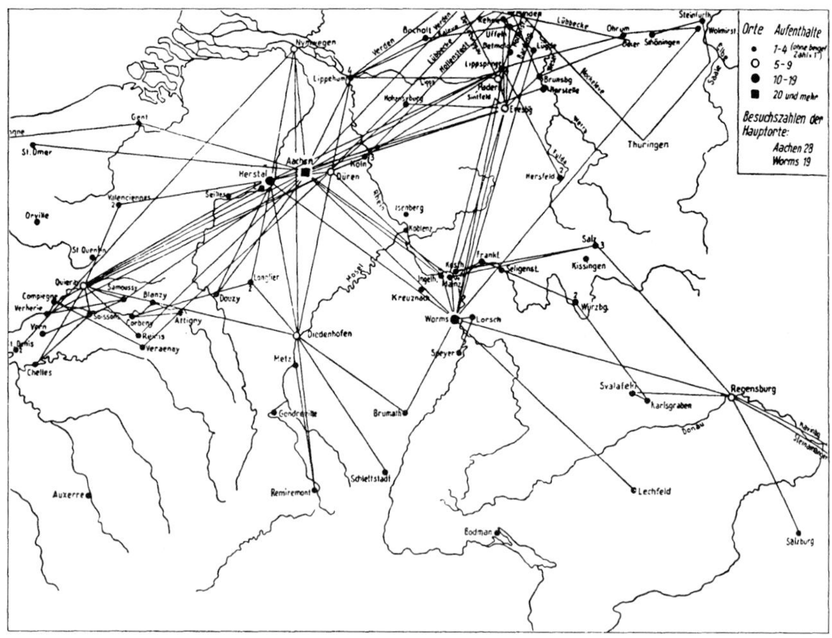

Charlemagne's Itinerary. The route-map of Charlemagne's journeys gives an idea of the burden laid on medieval rulers. The itinerary is incomplete; the journeys to Rome, amongst others, are not marked.

the mouth of the Loire; after an Odyssey lasting ten years they finally brought the relics of Saint Philibert by various stages to Tournus in Burgundy, where they hoped to find peace at last; centuries later they were attacked here too by Hungarians and Saracens.

Originally the Saxon seafarers set out in early summer and returned home in the autumn. Then they gradually began to spend the winter on the spot, perhaps on an easily defended island. The surrounding areas were not in a position to offer active resistance; they counted themselves lucky if – like the inhabitants of England in the ninth and tenth centuries – by giving hostages and paying high ransom money they could rid themselves of the pestilence at least for a while. Finally the sea-raiders settled permanently; they took root and became part of the population of the country; they were anxious themselves to preserve peace and order and to ward off enemies from outside.

This pattern of events – seafarers getting to know a country by carrying out raids, then settling there during the winter and finally settling for good – repeated itself in the ninth century. At the beginning of that century 'Norsemen' made England a half-Danish country. There were what could be called 'push and pull' effects. The Norsemen were 'pushed out' of their country by a (comparative) overpopulation; by an increasingly strong central kingship which took over from the previously independently ruling minor kings, chieftains and large landowners; and because breaches of the peace and other serious crimes were no longer left to be bloodily avenged as was the custom by a single tribe, the unholy chain of murder and revenge being instead brought to an end through temporary or permanent banishment. Young, strong, adventurous men were 'pulled' by the prospect of finding booty elsewhere, land to settle in or freedom – at the expense of those who were weaker, as the Anglo-Saxon Chronicle relates.

> 997. In this year the enemy army went round Devonshire to the mouth of the Severn, and there plundered and laid waste the land, and killed the inhabitants as also in Cornwall, and also in Wales and Devon . . . the enemy brought about great devastation . . . they burnt and slew everything that was in their path; . . . and took incalculable booty on board their ships.
>
> 998. In this year the enemy turned eastwards again, to the mouth of the Frome, pushing into Dorset, wherever they wanted to go. Often forces were drawn up to oppose them; but when the battle was about to begin, the command to withdraw was given, and in the end the enemy was always victorious. Then they had for a time their permanent camp on the Isle of Wight and got their supplies at that time from Hampshire and Sussex.
>
> 999. In this year the enemy came again into the mouth of the Thames, and . . . they took to horse and rode across the land, wherever they would, and plundered and laid waste almost all of West Kent . . .
>
> 1002. In this year the King and his council decided to pay tribute to the fleet and to make peace on condition that they ceased from their mischief . . . a tribute was paid of 24,000 pounds . . .
>
> 1003. . . . Exeter was destroyed . . .
>
> 1004. . . . fleet to Norwich, plundering and burning the whole town.
>
> 1006. . . . after Martinmas the enemy drew back to their stronghold on the Isle of Wight . . .
>
> 1006. The King . . . ordered that . . . provisions should be guaranteed them . . .
>
> 1007. In this year 30,000 pounds tribute was paid to them . . .
>
> 1013. . . . the Archbishop Elfeah (of Canterbury) was martyred . . .
>
> 1016. In this year Cnut came with 160 ships . . .

Death and destruction went on for a few months longer, but the death of King Aethelred and his successor Edmund in the same year made it possible for the real holder of power Cnut to take the English crown in 1016. The yearly tribute payments were rather higher, but a certain degree of peace and security returned to the country after decades of war and devastation. In the year 1028, the Anglo-Saxon Chronicle announced: 'Cnut left England with fifty ships for Norway, where he drove out King Olave and took possession of the country for himself.' So Cnut then ruled over Denmark, England and Norway; he had founded a thalassocracy, a great empire founded on the sovereignty of the seas. He was helped in this by the fact that for centuries the art of making seaworthy ships had been perfected in the North Sea and Baltic regions. Fast troopships and slower merchant vessels with a large loading capacity were available, and he could effectively rule over an empire whose parts were separated by hundreds of miles of sea (Denmark to England being over three hundred miles). The ships, and crews who knew how to sail them, made it possible to raise levies and transport them from one part of the empire to another.

A picture of the everyday world of the Norsemen is revealed in the Icelandic Sagas, a literary genre combining chronicle and fictional work. The story of Grettir the Strong was, it is true, only written down in about 1300, but it contains many details about sea voyages in about 1000 which are not to be found in the chronicles and annals. Grettir was a real person: he was born in 996 in north-west Iceland; from his youth onwards his path was strewn with those he had slain; in 1011 at the age of fifteen he was outlawed first for three years, and in 1016 for life. After many years of wanderings he was killed in 1031.

The combination of remarkable seafaring skills on the one hand, and great helplessness and inability to take bearings on the other is illustrated in the following brief extract from Grettir's story. A ship had sailed within sight of Iceland after an arduous voyage; as it cruised towards the coast, it was caught in a storm and blown far out to sea; it was tossed there by wind and waves all day long. Finally the wind changed, and they were able to sail towards land again. Experienced members of the crew recognised the coast and knew where they were.

Grettir had been banished (for the first time) and had to leave the country. His father had found him a place on a ship that had spent the winter in a river estuary, belonging to Haflidi, who undertook trading voyages to distant countries; regular journeys between Norway and Iceland were already necessary, as there was no iron or timber on the island. All his father gave Grettir for the journey was some rough wool cloth and provisions; for everyone had to fend for himself. The luxury of being able to cook hot food on board was only experienced centuries later. As his father had refused to give his son any weapon, his mother gave Grettir when he left a valuable sword which had belonged to her family. Amid good wishes for luck and safety, Grettir boarded the ship.

'They put out to sea as soon as they were ready and had a favourable wind; and when they were out of the shallows they hoisted the sail. Grettir made himself a bed under the boat behind the mast, and didn't want to budge from there, either to help to bail out the water that had entered the ship or to set the sail, or to do any other work on board as everyone else had to do; nor did he at all want to buy himself off the work.' So one paid for a passage with money or by working; in any case this paid only for the passage itself. During the voyage each man had to find a suitable place and somewhere to sleep at night. The dinghy, under which Grettir camped, would usually be towed from a ship on a rope. It was used for going from one ship to another, for loading and unloading, and if necessary as a lifeboat; it was useful if one wanted to land on a rocky shore or make repairs to the outside of the ship; and the boat could be rowed to tow the ship if one did not want to set sail or could not do so.

Grettir's ship got caught in a storm. 'The ship was rather leaky and they could not withstand the heavy seas; the crew were in a bad way.' Grettir could not believe that he and the rest of the men would have to 'sit in the same boat'. Instead of setting to, to help out in their danger, he taunted the sailors with mocking verses, which sprang easily to his lips. One day the weather was particularly stormy and cold; the men complained of having frozen fingers; Grettir scornfully refused their pleas for help; he remained lying in his lair, fondling the pretty young wife of the steersman and continuing to mock the others about their arduous work. The tension on board grew; the frozen men threatened bitterly to throw Grettir overboard. The ship's captain became worried; as well as the storm and a leaking boat he was now threatened with a fight on board.

After a long talking to, Grettir changed his mind and proved that he was both strong and steadfast. 'At that time' – the author is writing of many centuries earlier – 'you didn't empty water from ships by pumping it out, but with tubs or casks; this was called "bailing out". It was heavy work and the men got very wet doing it; they would have two tubs, and one would be handed down while the other was brought up. Grettir was asked to fill the bails and hand them up; they added that now they would see what he could do. "Small trials are the best," he answered.' So Grettir climbed down into the bottom of the ship and filled the tubs; after a little while the two men to whom he was handing them to be emptied were completely exhausted. So they tried with four men. 'So some say that in the end eight men at a time were emptying the tubs that Grettir handed up; and the ship was soon pumped dry.' From that time on Grettir lent a hand with the work wherever he was needed, and the crew adopted a different attitude towards him.

'They voyaged farther to the east and were always surrounded by thick mist; one night they suddenly noticed that they were running aground on a reef, and the whole bottom of the ship was torn out; the boat was lowered into the sea and the women put in it and everything that could be taken from the ship. Not far off there was a small island, and they transported as many of their goods and chattels there as they could during the night.' When it grew light, they tried to discover where they were. Seamen who had travelled before from Iceland to Norway, realised that they had reached Söndmör in Norway. 'There was an island close to them between them and the mainland, which was called Harhamö. There were many small farmsteads on the island, and the local chief lived there.'

Having escaped the storm, the seafarers had seen themselves confronted by a new danger: not every fog-bank indicated land and so they had paid little attention to it. It is clear that they were very uncertain as to speed and distances, especially when ocean currents or a storm had driven the ship off course; the steersman had only managed to go more or less in the right direction; after all, Norway from Tromsö to Bergen is over 750 miles. It was only centuries later that the better-equipped ships had the means to fix their position as they went along. A ship such as the one on which Grettir sailed was navigated in a haphazard way by studying the stars, birds, flora and fauna in the sea and objects which drifted past . . .

When the ship ran aground on the reef, the dinghy came into its own; it is mentioned incidentally, and deserves notice, that the women were taken to safety first; the maxim 'women and children first' may be very old. From the island the ship could be seen floundering. So Thorfinn, the local chief, had a large boat launched. 'Sixteen men could row on each side. This time nearly thirty men were on board; they rowed as fast as they could and saved the merchants' goods. But the ship then sank, and many things were lost. Thorfinn brought all the people from the ship to his steading; and they stayed there a week and dried out their goods. After that the merchants sailed southwards, and are not heard of again in this story.'

Charlemagne had also made helping those in trouble at sea the duty of those who lived by the coast in his empire. It is in any case a natural reaction for people who are themselves often at sea and will perhaps have to depend on help from strangers the next day. In an earlier part of this saga there is talk of the ship's crew of a ship wrecked off Iceland building a new ship from the timbers; 'but it was no easy task; the ship was narrow at bows and stern but broad in the middle' – like a real merchant ship. But it is worth noting that a ship's crew had the necessary skill in carpentry, and tools, to build a ship and felt themselves capable of building a seaworthy craft. Haflidi's ship was lost, and with it part of the cargo. However, no lives were lost. The shipwrecked men enjoyed a week's hospitality with Thorfinn, who had enough room to offer them bed and board. At a time, and in an area, where there were no organised commercial guesthouses, hospitality to strangers could be expected, as in the Benedictine monasteries in the early Middle Ages; but there it was mostly limited to a stay of three nights at the most. The merchants would have repaid their host with presents, and despite their losses possibly did good trade farther along their route; even by the tenth century the success or failure of a businessman was beginning to depend not only on the quality of his wares, but also on his experience, sales network and knowledge of human nature. There is no mention of right of wreck in this story. The ancient right by which objects – such as wood or whales – washed up on the shore belonged to the finder, would have been taken for granted by the author of the Grettisaga.

In a later part of the saga Grettir once more travelled with some merchants on their ship, this time at the beginning of winter. They often had to contend with bad weather; one day they were even caught in a snowstorm, followed by a heavy frost. After great danger and many tribulations, and quite worn out by their exertions, they reached land; their goods and possessions and also their provisions were saved. The merchants bemoaned the fact that they had no fire; they were certain that their lives and well-being depended on getting a little warmth. Risking his life, Grettir swam across the sound and fetched fire from another group of travellers; strangely nothing was to be seen of these next day but a row of charred corpses. Grettir saved his less robust companions from catching a chill, possibly even pneumonia.

Although by about the year 1000 it was possible to sail across the open sea from Norway to Iceland or from there on to Greenland and America, people stayed for the most part within reach of land, especially as there was then no need to take large quantities of drinking water on board. At night travellers would go ashore, like Boniface on his last journey down the Rhine. Grettir and his companions could not light a fire, as the man with St Gallus was able to do. This is surprising, as there would have been plenty of wood. The saga also indicates that there were good reasons for reaching one's destination in good time in the autumn; winter could literally come in overnight. Grettir and his travelling companions clearly did not take a sail with them, with which to make a tent. This is also surprising, as merchants would usually build a 'booth' when they went ashore, or at a market-place, made from a pair of posts or walls of piled up grass sods, with a cloth stretched across them.

After countless wanderings and misadventures, and many killings and slayings, Grettir was finally so weak that he could barely defend himself when Thorbjörn executed justice on the dying outlaw by killing him with his own valuable sword; Grettir's skull was so hard, that a deep notch was cut in the blade of the weapon. Thorbjörn severed the head from the body, put it in salt during the winter, and produced it triumphantly at the next court-day. He met with a cool reception however; people accused him of only having been able to kill Grettir by magical means. The price on the latter's head was not paid; and Thorbjörn left the country to avoid a continuation of the blood feud.

As he went along he boasted everywhere of having vanquished Grettir the Strong. Without realising it he was thus leaving a trail, and a relation of Grettir's followed him. This Thorstein Dromund was determined to avenge the cowardly slaughter. Like many Norsemen Thorbjörn decided to join the Varangian Guard at the Byzantine court, a kind of Foreign Legion, until the Grettir affair should have blown over. Possibly he followed the old Varangian Way through Kiev, or went through the Empire, or took the sea-route across the North Sea, Channel, Bay of Biscay, Atlantic and Mediterranean. Pursuer and pursued were welcomed in Byzantium, as soon as it was known that they were Norsemen. For a long time Thorstein sought his prey in vain; he was in despair that he would never succeed in tracking down the murderer he had never met. One day his unit was ordered to take part in a campaign. Their weapons were mustered for inspection beforehand, according to an ancient custom. Thorbjörn boasted again about the sword he took from Grettir, which was much admired; he described how the notch in it was made. Thorstein was certain he had found the wanted man. He too asked if he might examine the sword more closely. Thorbjörn had no objection, as he thought the other would admire his courage and valour, as nearly everyone else had done. 'Thorstein took the sword, swung it up and struck Thorbjörn. The blow struck his head and was so violent that the sword sank in up to his back teeth; Thorbjörn Angle fell dead on the ground.'

The saga of Grettir is the only example of a 'journey of vengeance' which will be included in this book. Byzantium is more than 2,500 miles as the crow flies from Iceland. The avenger travelled for months, perhaps even years, in order that justice should be done. In that respect, the journey was not all that unusual. In the Middle Ages pilgrims too travelled from Iceland to visit the holy shrines of Rome or Jerusalem, among them possibly travellers who were carrying out a journey as a penance. Just as Thorstein felt himself duty-bound to avenge Grettir, and restore the honourable peace shattered by a cowardly murder, so did men feel themselves duty bound to go on long, dangerous journeys to make retribution for their sins. After doing penance they could once more enjoy the peace and tranquillity of life in their community.

CLERICS ON THE ROAD

Journeys to Rome and ecclesiastical visitations: Bishop Ulrich of Augsburg

It was the duty of bishops to confirm believers in the faith, dedicate churches, and visit communities, monasteries and priests regularly. These duties necessitated long journeys. Whereas Italian dioceses often consisted of one town and the surrounding area only, those of German bishops were often much more spread out; the diocese of Constance, for example, spread from the middle of the Neckar in the north to well into present-day Switzerland (about 156 miles), from the Rhine in the west to the Iller in the east (about 125 miles). The diocese of Augsburg, over which Bishop Ulrich was in charge for fifty years (923–73), stretched for 'only' 144 miles from north to south, and 62 miles from east to west. Ulrich was constantly on the road during his lifetime. Among his duties as incumbent of an imperial bishopric was that of being present at court-days and diets; as a member of the college of bishops he must not fail to attend synods; for the good of his soul, he must visit the shrines of saints whether near or far.

Ulrich frequently went to Rome, for the first time in 909 when he was nineteen. His *Life* gives no details of the length of his stay, lodgings, Alpine crossing or particular incidents; from the baldness of the account one can draw the conclusion that the journey from Swabia to Rome was nothing out of the ordinary for a young man: 'Meanwhile the desire awoke in him to visit the graves of the holy Apostles St Peter and St Paul. He went thither and was well received by the Pope.' Ulrich made his third journey to Rome in 971 or 972 as an old man of at least eighty; 'for the good of his soul he wanted to pay a pious visit to the graves of the Apostles Peter and Paul.' The account of his life gives more details of this journey. At the beginning Ulrich could go a short distance in a wagon; then – one imagines in the Alps – the way became difficult. 'He could only continue his journey when he had been laid on a bed, which was carried by horses. Although this seemed a very dangerous way to travel to his aides, he managed by the grace of God and the holy Apostle Peter to get without accident to Rome by this means.' One could add: where there is a will, there is a way. If necessary, a way could be found and a litter improvised, although there are few references to these in western sources at this time. Princes of the realm such as bishops usually travelled mounted on horseback.

Every four years Ulrich made a journey of inspection through his diocese in a wagon: a seat was fixed for him in the body of the vehicle with ropes. Ulrich was said not to have chosen this means of transport initially because he could no longer ride, but because the crowds of his followers disturbed him while he was at prayer 'with their idle chatter'.

Ulrich was always accompanied by several priests and chaplains, so that every day a proper act of worship could be celebrated, and by some of his most capable retainers. After consulting them, Ulrich counted on being able to make the right decisions whenever there were church or secular matters to deal with. The duty to offer advice and help (*consilium et auxilium*) was not only a part of the king's role, but also that of bishops. Archbishop Bruno of Cologne always took a library of books with him on his travels; Bishop Bernward of Hildesheim was accompanied by able craftsmen and artists.

In Ulrich's retinue there were also attendants to lead the dray-animals and to walk on either side of the wagon to protect him; protection was possibly necessary as the wagon-train would carry tithes for the bishop. Finally he was accompanied by the ordinary people of his diocese, on horseback, in a vehicle or on foot. In fact on many days there was an impressive column on the move. The planned arrangements made for the king, or advance announcements made as a matter of course on behalf of a successful preacher such as Bernard of Clairvaux, would also be made for the visitations of one such as Ulrich of Augsburg: the route was settled well in advance; retainers would see to lodgings and make

Pope Urban II travelling to the Synod of Clermont in 1095. The Pope is riding on a grey horse, and has a comfortable saddle with back support. He is accompanied by cardinals, who can be recognised by their broad-brimmed hats, and by monks.

sure that food for men and beasts had been sent on ahead from the Augsburg church farms.

On his arrival the church bells would ring and Ulrich would be given a copy of the gospels and holy water and greeted with all the ceremony the inhabitants of each place could muster. The arrival of a bishop was as much an event as that of the king or of a saintly man. Ulrich knew how to care for the upkeep of his Church and churches literally and metaphorically: the right tool had to be laid out for him, so that he could carry out a part of the necessary improvements to church or monastery buildings with his own hand.

Then the mass would be sung. Ulrich would be seated. His authority would be made visible to all since he would be enthroned in majesty while all the rest stood. The people would be summoned and the 'wise and trusty' questioned under oath; they should tell him frankly 'what needed improving in that parish, and anything that had been done to offend against Christian law'. Offences were punished according to the judgement of the bishop and the other churchmen present, without regard to the offender's standing, and Ulrich, according to his biographers, would be guided by the advice of St Paul, to sentence, rebuke and admonish 'with all patience and understanding'. In difficult cases he consulted the men who had accompanied him; he also left many straightforward cases to be decided by his helpers, especially if he had to administer the sacrament to many of the faithful whom he had confirmed. It was usually evening by then, so that the last candidates for confirmation would come before him by candlelight.

After the judgements and confirmation service had been completed, he would go to his lodgings, but would only sit down to eat when the clerics who were in charge of alms had distributed these to the poor. Word would quickly get about when a great one was on the way: the poor, homeless, cripples, and handicapped would come out to meet the procession, and possibly accompany it for a few days. For it also says of Ulrich: 'He had food set before the weak, who had come to him and sat down in his presence. And he took great care to see that his servants provided shelter for them and attended to all their other needs.'

On appointed days the churchmen of the diocese met at regional synods. As at the judgement sessions, the archpriests, deacons and most trusted church officers were thoroughly interrogated. They were questioned on the subjects which Charlemagne had already put forward and which crop up again and again in the history of the Church: questions which show that in any age the Church may need strengthening: regularity of and care concerning the daily celebration of the mass, instruction of the people, baptism of infants, visiting of the sick and last sacraments, burial of the dead; 'in what way the tithes and gifts of the faithful are used to feed the poor and weak; how they provide for the widows and children in all their needs, and with what zeal they serve Christ in the persons of visitors and strangers; whether they had not lain with women, and whether they had any suspicions to confide on this matter; whether they had hunted with hounds or falcons, visited inns in order to eat or drink, practised forbidden games, indulged in immoderate bouts of eating or drinking; whether they had not carried on quarrels, trade, feuds, or been present at worldly wedding feasts, or had been led to do anything else unworthy of their office; whether they attended to their churches in good time; whether they were obedient to their superiors and had endeavoured to do all that they could to be true to their office and to be useful . . .' Those who were on the right path were praised and encouraged, those who fell short were rebuked and warned to cease from their wrongdoing.

Travellers were helped by such decrees, which show that priests too were to honour Christ in the persons of strangers – as Benedict had stated in his rule. Other decrees helped strangers indirectly, in that they aimed to preserve church property and prevent it being dispersed – by marriage and bequests, or hunting and gaming. The ban on visiting inns is in the ancient church tradition: it is not clear whether it was merely copied from the edicts of earlier synods or whether it was in answer to conditions in certain taverns in the Augsburg diocese.

Visitations and journeys to dedicate churches often went awry, as Bishop Bernward of Hildesheim (d. 1022) discovered. Sophia, a sister of the Emperor Otto III, had entered the convent at Gandersheim; she disobeyed the rule of remaining in one place, and spent much time at the imperial court, where she 'followed the path of a loose life and caused all kinds of rumours to run rife concerning herself.' Bernward pressed her in vain to return to the convent. To avoid such unwelcome rebukes, she wanted her convent put under the Archbishop of Mainz. At the dedication of the new convent church things came to a head: Sophia stood in for the abbess, who was ill, at the ceremony. When Bernward arrived for the dedication service, the nuns, 'already in revolt', gave a display of temperament. At the offering 'they succeeded in throwing down their gifts angrily and with unbelievable expressions of rage and cast wild abuse at the Bishop.' According to his biographer's account, Bernward kept his composure. 'Deeply shaken by this untoward display, the Bishop, in tears, thought not of his own ignominy, which he considered trifling, but following the example of the true Shepherd who prayed for his flock, mourned only the wickedness of the furious women.'

Travelling preachers and monks: Norbert of Xanten and Bernard of Clairvaux

'His new way of life was greeted with amazement: to live on earth but ask nothing from the earth.' St Norbert (c. 1085–1134) was a jovial churchman, then hermit, a well-known preacher and monastic founder, and finally Archbishop of Magdeburg. His biographer describes the reaction of his contemporaries to his new way of life (novum genus vitae) succinctly, using the word astonishment (stupor). Norbert belonged to the thousands of men and women who in the early years of the twelfth century became dissatisfied with their way of following

Christianity, and mindful of its beginnings, wanted to get back to a life of apostolic simplicity and poverty.

Monks and even abbots suddenly broke away from their settled monastic existence, left their monasteries and went out into the wilderness to live a life of hermit-like asceticism; there they engendered a great deal of activity, attracting disciples and followers of both sexes, with whom they travelled through the countryside preaching as they went; they called on people to do penance for their sins and repent, and confronted the clergy with a living example of the life of Jesus and the apostles. Norbert was one of those who felt that the striving after self-perfection was not enough in itself, if discord reigned around him. In the second period of his life he strove, like other men of his time, to fulfil as a travelling preacher the gospel command to follow the apostles; renouncing all possessions he travelled through the land preaching repentance and peace, and inveighing against the misdeeds of churchmen. In a third phase he gathered together in monasteries the followers who had joined him on his way, thus helping to bring under control the movement of wandering monks and preachers about which the official Church had never felt quite easy. The differences between monks, canons, preachers and hermits had gradually become blurred, since the new ideal of the *vita apostolica* urged people to go out into the world and give up the narrow life of the cloister or a solitary existence in the wilderness.

The movement led to rifts in the Church. It became clear that it was easier to live a life of extreme asceticism and superhuman abnegation in the loneliness of a cave, than to deal with the weaknesses of fellow men, not excluding bishops and abbots. Figures such as Norbert and Abelard – a leading figure, philosopher, theologian and finally abbot, in the history of the European Church – were tempted to ask too much of their fellow men.

The challenge facing the Church at the turn of the eleventh to twelfth century, was met by the religious movement with heresies *and* with new orders. Originally it was not at all clear what was accepted faith and what was heresy. Norbert was saved from being regarded as a heretic because the highest spiritual authority in the West, the Pope, had expressly permitted him to continue his activity as a travelling preacher freely and without restraint.

The movement of the travelling preachers and monks at the turn of the eleventh to twelfth century was a symptom of the unrest which had seized the whole of western civilisation. Besides preachers, there were philosophers such as Abelard wandering through the countryside, teachers and scholars going from one university to another, merchants, crusaders and emigrants, flocking abroad. The travelling preachers' spirit of unrest remained a mystery to many contemporaries. Even Norbert's biographer found no rational explanation; he speaks as though it was fated: 'He was driven to go abroad' (*iam peregre proficisci intendens*). For Norbert and his like-minded companions – despite their vow to remain in one place, there were many monks among them – it was not the goal, but the travelling among their fellow men that was all important.

As the life of medieval churchmen is usually better documented than that of laymen, two of the most famous travelling preachers of their day are considered here: Bernard of Clairvaux and Norbert of Xanten, the former the founder of the Cistercians, the latter of the Premonstratensians. Details of their lives can also be used to illustrate modes of travel and journeys made by knights, merchants and farmers. The preachers as a rule rarely wrote themselves: because of their roving lifestyle they had, like founders of monasteries and papal legates, less opportunity for literary activity than their more sedentary brother monks. An exception was Bernard of Clairvaux, who was able to combine his desire for contemplation with continual travel and also writing.

How should one envisage the life which Norbert and his companions led in their efforts to follow in the footsteps of the apostles? After a sudden revelation, Norbert left his property, office and all his worldly goods behind and with only a small amount of silver and his priest's clothes, set out with two companions on a holy pilgrimage. Somewhere by the Meuse he shared out the rest of his money among the poor; then he walked 'clad only in a woollen robe with a cloak over it, with the two men who accompanied him, barefoot in the terrible cold of winter to St Gilles' (near the mouth of the Rhône in southern France).

There are repeated references later to the spartan clothing of the wandering preachers; Norbert allowed his monks linen hose as well as their woollen robe and cloak. According to his biographers he wanted to have no more than that which Jesus had ordered (Matthew 10,10): neither scrip nor shoes, nor two coats. Penitents went barefoot and clad in wool (usually for a specified time) – but so too did most of the population, who had no money for proper shoes (which still applied to some people in country districts at the beginning of the twentieth century).

Men like Bernard of Clairvaux and Norbert were from well-to-do families; they gave up of their own free will comforts which the great majority of their contemporaries were not able to have, and thereby gave living proof of the genuineness of their message. The well-fed prelate hardly sets a convincing example of the ideal of poverty. Many of their ascetic practices did not go unchallenged by contemporaries however; Abelard for instance declined to go barefoot. Nor did Norbert always walk barefoot, as is shown on various occasions by his biographer: when he appeared barefoot at a synod before bishops and abbots, it was in order to provoke them. He wanted to demonstrate what a life of poverty should be and in doing so was in direct opposition to the marked acquisitiveness of the official imperial clergy. Raised to the office of archbishop, he once more took his shoes off on approaching Magdeburg, and walked barefoot into the town; he was so raggedly dressed that the porter at the bishop's palace waved him away.

Norbert sometimes rode. Riding an ass as Jesus had done was a sign of humility, like going barefoot. As a prince of the realm, and the Archbishop of Magdeburg was among the greatest princes of the realm, Norbert would certainly have ridden a horse.

The provocative nature of the behaviour of men such as Norbert of Xanten becomes apparent if one compares it with that of some of his contemporaries, for example with Archbishop Albero of Trier. In 1147 Albero welcomed Pope Eugene III, the first Cistercian pope, to Trier, 'with a great demonstration of respect by clergy and people', and accompanied him 'with exceptional pomp and impressive ceremonial into the cathedral'. Albero's biographer revels in the list of celebrities who followed the Pope into Trier cathedral. 'The Archbishop entertained them all so richly for twelve weeks without a break, that they freely acknowledged that their cup of plenty was flowing over.' None of the guests left without a present. 'Can you imagine' – the biographer addresses the reader directly as he describes the Christmas festivities, 'how magnificent the procession was on this holy day when the Pope, riding on a palfrey – with the cardinals and many bishops in front of him on white-caparisoned horses – proceeded to the Church of St Paulinus?' After the solemn celebration of mass there was a great banquet, at which 'the Pope with his cardinals on the one hand and the Archbishop with his attendant bishops wearing their mitres on the other, sat at adjoining tables. What skilled mathematician could work out what it all cost?' The writer was clearly unaware how provocative this question was.

The Pope then went on to Reims, to hold a council there; Albero had himself carried in a comfortable litter. All his life he showed a gift for causing a sensation, for setting himself centre stage. Now, in view of his age, he claimed precedence among the bishops at the council; he had the superior rights of his church proclaimed and infuriated the Archbishop of Reims by so doing. A fight ensued between the retainers of the two archbishops, in which some of Albero's followers were wounded. 'Enraged thereby, Archbishop Albero threatened to go to Ivois and lay waste the diocese of Reims.' The biographer does not blame him in the least; he sees Albero as acting justly throughout. Such warlike priests were no model for men such as Norbert.

A scene from Bernard's life illustrates the closeness with which contemporaries watched to see if the words of the wandering preachers were matched by their deeds. In 1125, while visiting the Bishop of Grenoble he went on an excursion to the Great Carthusian monastery, where he was greeted effusively. But amongst all the uplifting exchanges there was however 'one thing, which rather concerned the Carthusian prior, namely that the saddle-cloth of the horse which the holy father had ridden, was too richly worked and did not at all smack of poverty.' The prior's surprise came to Bernard's ears; he was equally surprised and asked what was the matter with the saddle-cloth; between Clairvaux and the Carthusian monastery – about 150 miles as the crow flies or a week's journey – he had not even noticed it, and had no idea what it looked like. 'The horse was in fact not his, but had been borrowed from his uncle, a Cluniac monk who was staying in the neighbourhood; and the beast was saddled just as it usually was for his uncle.' The Carthusian prior was even more astonished that Bernard had been so intent on his soul during the long journey, that he had been totally unaware of what he was sitting on, although he himself had noticed it at once.

Following the precept 'attack is the best defence' the biographer turns the account into a side-swipe at the Cluniacs, who had been reproved by Bernard for deserting the rule of St Benedict. There are many such tales told of Bernard, illustrating his disinterest in his surroundings. He paid no attention to what he ate or drank (drinking oil in mistake for water for instance), nor to the scenery through which he rode. In connection with the visit to the Carthusian monastery the account says: 'He rode for a whole day beside Lake Geneva without seeing it – or didn't take in what he saw. For when his travelling companions were talking about the lake that evening, he asked them where the lake was. And they were all amazed.'

With which we come to the question of how people reacted to the scenery they saw on their journeys. If landscape painting was undertaken in Europe long before the Romantic era, and lovely or majestic landscapes described in words and images, it was not a case of reverting to an antique mode. Such descriptions were rather a sign that some people had an eye for the beauties of nature. One has to use the qualifying word 'some', because those who are suffering from hunger, thirst, cold, vermin, who are pursued by attackers, have in general no time for scenic beauty; nature is not a godsend for them but a danger. So most of those living in Bernard's day would have seen nature as a threat. But the above account shows that people discussed in the evening what they had seen that day. Although one must add that it is doubtful whether Bernard's companions enthused about Lake Geneva as much as today's tourists who can count on their four meals a day, comfortable beds, shower in the morning and glass of wine at night. That some could appreciate the beauties of nature is also shown by Abelard, whom Bernard considered a heretic but who also pursued a life of apostolic simplicity; he fled the crowded cities and even saw temptations for philosophers in the attractions of certain places: 'The rain-fresh meadows, the green leaves of the trees, the song of the birds, the gleaming waters of a pool, the murmuring brook and everything that bewitches the eye and ear, have been forsaken by the philosophers, so that they will not be led astray into sensuality and luxuriousness.'

Bernard and Norbert preached for preference out in the streets and countryside; they spoke to the mass of simple people to whom the Church with all its privileges typified by men such as Albero had nothing to say. Even if they did not know the local dialect it is clear from the accounts that Bernard and Norbert reached the hearts of their listeners with the powerful words of their sermons – although it is open to question how much of their story is 'factual' and how much is rhetoric: a hagiological, Pentecostal miracle embroidering by their biographers. At Lake Constance, on the upper and middle reaches of the Rhine, Bernard succeeded in moving his audience: 'Even the crowds of Germanic people listened to him with rapt attention, and although they spoke another language and could not understand him, they were more uplifted by his sermon than by the translation of it in their tongue, which a skilled interpreter offered them. The people beat their breasts and shed tears, which was sure proof that they understood the inner meaning of his words rather than the words themselves.' The same was said of the sermons which Norbert preached in northern France.

While the Archbishop of Trier was threatening to lay waste the diocese of Reims, Norbert was travelling through 'burghs, villages and towns, preaching, reconciling those in conflict and turning deep-rooted enmity and feuding to peace. He asked nothing from anyone; but when something was brought to him he gave it to the poor and abandoned.' As a stranger, a poor pilgrim, he preached in churches and under the open skies; it says of him once expressly that he set out on a further preaching journey when winter was over, and another time that he came at Christmas with about thirty new novices to Prémontré. Regarding food and drink, dress and lodgings the travelling preachers were more than undemanding, as were the original Cistercians and Premonstratensians; Norbert only ate one meal a day, or at most a second meal on Sundays; this would consist of rough uncooked food. In his monastery at Prémontré the monks slept on beds of bracken. Without ambition but with a limitless trust in God, Norbert and his spiritual brothers were sure that God in His mercy would provide poor 'pilgrims and strangers on earth' such as themselves with everything that they might need.

> And so there arose universal admiration for him, and love. Wherever he drew near with his travelling companions and came to villages or other places, the shepherds left their flocks and ran ahead to tell the people of his coming.

The passage throws light on the way in which news and rumours were spread. For the most part only general descriptions are given, for example in connection with Bernard's miracle-working in Italy: 'What happened in Milan, was told roundabout. The news of the man of God sped all over Italy, and everywhere it was said that a great prophet had arisen, mighty in word and deed.' No word as to who had spread the news; doubtless it was passed on by pilgrims and merchants in Italy as elsewhere – and shepherds. These were considered in the Middle Ages to belong to a 'disreputable occupation' in spite of the honour they had been accorded in Bethlehem at Jesus's birth. Perhaps it was out of gratitude that people so despised spread the news of the men who at last spoke expressly to them. Herdsmen were ideal as messengers: they were tough, with great stamina, undemanding as to food, clothing and shelter, and they had outstanding knowledge of the countryside: wandering shepherds, who herded their flocks year by year over long distances from the plains into the mountains, possibly even over the mountains – as in the south of France over the Pyrenees to Catalonia – knew every inch of the way, possibly several languages, and certainly the people they met on their route.

'When the people flocked to him (Norbert) and heard his words at the celebration of mass as to the penance they must do and the hope of eternal salvation which is promised to all men who call on God's name, then all were

Shepherds were a familiar sight to travellers in the mountains, and were often the only guides in such areas.

joyous in his presence and he counted himself lucky who could offer him shelter in his house. His new way of life was greeted with amazement.' Later, at the time of the Black Death, there was again great enthusiasm for those who adopted this hard way of life – in Strasburg people were even eager to take flagellants into their homes.

Bernard of Clairvaux had an even greater success as a preacher than Norbert. Men flocked from far and wide to hear him; a hundred years later the Franciscans and Dominicans also drew vast crowds with their sermons. It is true that Bernard asked monks to live according to Benedict's rule, although he did not himself obey one important command: in spite of the monastic vow to remain in one place, he was almost constantly on the road in Europe. Like Norbert's life, many of the descriptions of Bernard's activities may be partly hagiological, but the ability of the two men and that of many of their contemporaries to influence people by the spoken word is attested to by other sources. And so there may really have been scenes such as that which William of St Thierry describes in the first book of his life of Bernard: 'While he preached openly and in private, mothers were already hiding their sons, wives holding back their husbands, and friends taking their friends away. For the Holy Ghost lent such power to Bernard's words that no loving bond could keep his listeners from following him.' The account is believable because as abbot of Clairvaux Bernard founded numerous daughter-houses, which meant that he sent at least twelve monks to live in each.

Who was this man? Bernard had only a weak constitution, but it is said of him that he had 'more endurance than men of oak'. The ascetic life – withstanding hunger, thirst, cold, exposure and lack of sleep – had hardened him, at the expense of his health. All his life he had trouble with his stomach and bowels. When Clairvaux was first founded Bernard and his companions often made their meals 'from beech leaves. Their bread, like that of the prophets, consisted of barley, millet and spelt; a visiting monk who had been given it once took his portion secretly away in tears, to show it to all as a wonder: "These men live on such bread, and what men!" ' It is clear from such accounts that people sometimes travelled with very few provisions. Bernard was among the most influential men of his day in Europe. If such a man was content with rough bread and drank no wine, he was allying himself to the poorest of the poor and the millions of people who flocked along the roads, and who – unlike bishops and kings – could not count on being suitably welcomed at court or palace.

The account of his life gives drastic descriptions of the lodgings he found, which should not be ignored because they too point to his heroic stature; and, more important, they throw a light on the social customs of the day. At the time when Bernard was still deciding whether to become a monk and was still wrestling with temptation 'at the sight of a certain woman', a naked girl once got into his bed while he slept. Single rooms like those in hotels today or separate sleeping-quarters for men and women were the exception. Young unmarried people of either sex did not necessarily sleep in separate beds; it was usual, as we have already seen, to sleep naked. There would be several beds in a room – at most there would be a curtain for privacy. The account continues: 'When Bernard became aware of the girl, he relinquished the place she had taken in the bed without any fuss, turned over on his other side, and went back to sleep.' He refused to be moved by 'touching and tickling' and lay calmly there; finally the girl, amazed and terrified, took flight.

Another incident also shows that in Bernard's day a 'no' by a young man about to enter a cloister was not always respected. Bernard was the guest, with some friends, of a noble lady, who at sight of the beautiful young man was seized with passionate desire. As he was the most honoured guest, she let his bed be prepared in a separate room; that night she got up and went to him 'without any shame'. When Bernard saw her, he began, 'without more ado, to cry loudly: "Thief! Thief!" At his cry, the woman fled, and the whole household awoke. Lights were lit and the thief hunted – but not found. Everyone went back to bed, silence reigned, it was dark again and everyone slept peacefully, except the poor woman, who had no rest.' Bernard had occasion to cry 'Thief' twice more to escape his hostess's attentions – each time causing alarm and a search for the intruder; finally the woman gave up, 'from fear or despair'. The following day his companions reproached Bernard and asked why he had made such a to-do about thieves in the night. Bernard explained: 'Truly, there was a thief. That which I hold most precious in this life, my chastity, that incomparable treasure, was being sought after by our hostess.'

At the time when Bernard was held in high regard throughout Europe as a mediator, when he was corresponding with emperors and popes, preaching the way of truth, he often travelled with a great following of spiritual and secular leaders. On his journey through Germany in 1146 a core of eight to ten men – among them a secretary, a bishop, a university professor, two abbots, and a monk – was surrounded by hundreds, often thousands of people. His permanent followers made daily notes, which at the end of each stage of the journey were compared, collected together and sent at once to certain recipients. These notes, 'sent abroad almost with the speed of modern reports' and certainly much copied, gave rise to talk of 'miracles', enhancing the stature of men such as Bernard and Norbert and enflaming mass enthusiasm.

Eye witnesses who 'followed Bernard for a single day near Tiengen in the Konstanz area have witnessed miracles: eleven healings of the blind through the laying on of hands, ten healings of cripples, eighteen healings of the halt and lame.' This is not the place to go into the possibility or otherwise of miracles. The spontaneous healings which appeared to contemporaries like 'miracles' were reported from many places of pilgrimage; as accounts of miracles show, the witnesses often observed the cases so exactly that medical historians can derive scientifically plausible explanations for them from the descriptions; and in addition modern medical science has shown that a sudden shock can both harm and cure such things as cramp, for instance. Many of the sick had travelled far and wide to consult quacks, wise women, medicine men in vain, or even the doctors of Salerno who were renowned throughout Europe for their skill. It was said of a woman from Cologne who was blind in one eye that she had 'already given much money in vain to the doctors'. The incurably ill often had only one hope left: that God would work a miracle, either at a place of pilgrimage or through a saintly man, on whom Christ had bestowed his powers of healing.

Accounts such as those of Bernard's healing miracles provide first-class source material, which is reliable in at least one respect: they tell us about the weary and heavy laden, the sick and unfortunate, who were a burden to themselves and their communities, and who sought salvation, help and healing from the man of God: the blind, deaf and dumb, the lame, cripples and the deformed, and those suffering from gout, dropsy, epilepsy, tremors, from demons, infertility and madness; in Cologne a madman in chains was even led before Bernard. In modern terms, most of those who sought Bernard's help were suffering from disturbances of the nervous system; there was seldom talk of fever or infections, and never of leprosy, but often of being possessed by demons. The unfortunate dragged themselves painfully to Bernard, forced their way furiously through the crowd, to be seen, touched and healed by him; the sick from well-to-do circles or those who were helped by sympathetic fellow men were transported in barrows or carts to the places Bernard had chosen. His route – like that of kings and bishops – was often decided long in advance, and would become known to those he wished above all to address, men from what are today called the middle and lower classes. 'Anyone who was sick in the whole countryside round Frankfurt, was brought to him; and the throng of people was so great that King Conrad III, no longer master of the surging crowd, threw down his cloak, raised the saint in his own arms and carried him out of the basilica.'

Knowing Bernard's route, that he would go on from Frankfurt to Speyer for instance, people could easily work out where they would catch the holy man, and could hurry to the road along which he and his followers would come. In this way a lame youth was carried to the highway along which Bernard was travelling; the young man was healed and followed Bernard, until the latter ordered him to go home. Two blind sisters who had been cured by him also temporarily joined Bernard's followers. Beggars usually 'take up their post' in places which are heavily frequented, so that they cannot be missed; a lame woman who usually sat by the door of a church was cured by Bernard, and a lame old man who begged by the wayside. Shut out from society and yet dependent on it were lepers: huts had been built for them, outside towns but at busy crossroads or turnings, and in the course of time these were developed into permanent houses – like the almshouses from which many street names are derived. Travellers were reminded that they were themselves blessed with good health and were moved to contribute something towards the good of those who had been struck down by the dreadful disease through no fault of their own.

Bernard inspired great crowds of people; he loved to 'immerse himself in the crowd'. The crush was often so great that he and others were almost trodden underfoot and once his aides only saved him by hurriedly putting him in a boat and rowing out across the Moselle. A blind man who wanted to be healed, cried out from the bank that he wanted to be taken to Bernard. Hearing a fisherman row past, 'he opened the clasp of the mantle which covered him and handed it to the fisherman in order to be allowed to get into his boat.' After he had reached Bernard, his sight was restored to him by Bernard's healing hand, 'because of his great faith'. Full of amazement, the man cried out that he could see 'the hills, the people, the trees and everything else.'

Because of such tumultuous scenes, it was understandable that Bernard often wanted to travel incognito: his companions were told not to tell anyone he was with them and not to talk about him. When asked who was travelling with them they were to reply that it was some monks, or to give the name of one of the other travellers. It was usual upon meeting to exchange the greetings, 'Who are you? Where do you come from, and where are you going?'

'The Abbot of Clairvaux enjoyed immeasurable respect and honour, and all valued him as the bringer of peace . . . Wherever he showed himself on the road, noble lords came to accompany him, people called out to him, matrons followed him and all obeyed him with a willing heart.' His entrance into many towns was more splendid and joyous than the welcome given to emperor or pope. When the Milanese heard in 1135 that Bernard had crossed the Appennines and was approaching them, the population went to meet him seven miles outside the town. 'Rich and poor, horsemen and those on foot, the small man and the beggar, all streamed from their homes and the town as if they were emigrants'; group after group received the man of God 'with unbelievable demonstrations of respect'. Those who had seen him considered themselves lucky, and those who had heard him, even more so. 'They all kissed his feet.' Although this was displeasing to Bernard, the ecstatic crowds could not be deterred by gentle words or forced back by sterner commands; 'they threw themselves worshipping on the ground before him. They even tore, if they could, pieces from his clothes, snatching bits of cloth with which to heal the sick. Whatever he touched, they considered holy, and they promised themselves a miraculous cure from touching or using such objects. Thus they went in front of him and followed behind him and called to him with joyful words of acclamation.' The whole town was caught up in the scene; public life came to a standstill, no business was done, and the leaders of the warring Milanese factions were ready to call a truce.

It is difficult for literate twentieth-century Europeans to comprehend the richness of the sign language which earlier generations enjoyed – men who could neither read nor write but who were often highly educated. To prostrate oneself on the ground before someone was not an unusual form of greeting (recommended by Benedict for instance). So it was not surprising that later the assembled monks of Clairvaux went to meet Bernard at near-by Langres, and threw themselves on their knees before him.

The abstract faith riddled by doubts of educated people is one thing, the striving after firm, visible and tangible 'proof' quite another. On one occasion people were said to have brought bread and wine, to have 'had it blessed and taken it home as sacred healing objects'. Later, after Bernard's death, there was an unbearable crush around the dead man's bier: crowds of people flocked round, 'weeping at the dead man's precious feet, kissing his hands, and touching him with pieces of bread, girdles, coins or anything else they could, so that they could use these things afterwards as relics, good for all future needs.' No attention was paid to bishops, still less ordinary monks. On the day before the funeral even greater crowds gathered, sleeping overnight in neighbouring villages in order to be there in good time the next morning. The brothers feared the worst – people had often been trampled to death in such crowds – and interred the dead man earlier than was expected.

Travelling preachers such as Norbert and Bernard, travelling philosophers such as Abelard, show how very mobile some individuals were, and also groups of people (such as the students who flocked round Abelard), and the crowds which streamed to follow a charismatic figure such as Bernard. Finding somewhere to sleep seems to have posed no great problems for them; if men from the nobility such as Norbert and Bernard and many of their companions were not fussy about food and drink, clothing and shelter, it certainly did not occur to others to complain about uncomfortable conditions on the road or to let themselves be put off making a journey for fear of hunger or thirst, cold or vermin. That was one reason. Another equally important reason in the long run was that Abelard, Bernard and Norbert founded their houses in out-of-the-way places. In a letter, Heloïse praises Abelard's actions – which we can see to have been civilising, pioneering, and to have enhanced communications. 'In this barren spot only wild animals lived, and robbers lurked; there was no shelter for miles around, no farmstead in which peaceable men lived. And precisely here, among the caves of wild beasts, among the robbers' lairs, on ground which can never have heard the name of God spoken, precisely here you built an altar to our God and dedicated a temple to the Holy Spirit.' The sites of many Cistercian and Premonstratensian houses could have been described in the same way.

This was a repetition of what had happened five hundred years earlier, when Irish missionary monks had gone across to the Continent and lived there in trackless country: single cells became the central core of a community of monks, which in the course of centuries quite often developed into a great monastery 'complex'. Monastic foundations of the size of Fulda or St Gall did not in general grow from Cistercian and Premonstratensian establishments, it is true. But even a small, insignificant monastery was an invaluable help to travellers in the Middle Ages: between the Garonne and Meuse for instance there was a string of such houses often less than a day's journey one from the other. In the poorly inhabited country between the Oder and Vistula, Cistercian monasteries provided shelter and aid for the traveller at a time when there were no towns at all there. Cistercian monasteries thus helped in a very real sense in developing the European communications network.

A PILGRIM'S GUIDE TO SANTIAGO DE COMPOSTELA

Of the three great places of pilgrimage of western Christianity, Jerusalem, since the fall of the crusader states in 1291, had been extremely difficult of access; pilgrimages to Rome, where since 1300 'holy years' had been celebrated, became all the more popular, and also those to Santiago. Besides these greater pilgrimages (*peregrinationes maiores*) there were countless lesser foreign and regional pilgrimages which were undertaken, to Aachen, Canterbury, Düren, Einsiedeln, Cologne, Padua, Rocamadour, St Michel, Thann, Trier, Wilsnack and other shrines.

'The faithful, who are going on a pilgrimage to the shrine of St James, should be able to plan in advance, if they read this guide before starting their journey; they will know what conditions to expect on the way.' An extract from a pilgrim's guide, of about 1140/50, which is one in a long line of guides to holy shrines; the earliest accounts we have are from the fourth century (a Bordeaux pilgrim in 333, the nun Aetheria in 400). The Santiago Pilgrim's Guide, a forerunner of Baedeker, shows how popular pilgrimages to the north-west of Spain were by the mid-twelfth century. It is clear that besides spontaneous and mass pilgrimages there were individual journeys planned a long while in advance; the guide also shows that people no longer undertook pilgrimages – like many who journeyed to Rome and Jerusalem in the early Middle Ages – in order to die at the shrine, but that they expected to return home again safely.

A pilgrim could glean much useful information from the Santiago guide. However, one cannot reasonably suppose that every pilgrim would have such a book in his travel pack. On the other hand one may take it that much of the information given would be handed on by word of mouth, so that pilgrims would know how to set about preparing for their journey.

The book (equivalent to about fifty typewritten pages in extent) deals with everything which concerned the pilgrim. The author gives advice on roads and rivers, bridges and hospices; food and drink; saints who must be honoured on the way; finally Compostela and St James's cathedral. Legends and anecdotes – which are still recounted by guides to travellers today – are woven into the text. The author tells how a pilgrim's custom is based on a gesture of Charlemagne's: at the top of the Cisa Pass pilgrims knelt, turned to the west in the direction of St James's shrine, said a prayer and stuck a cross, of which 'there must be a thousand' to be seen here, in the ground; Charlemagne had done this at the start of his Spanish campaign. At another place spears stuck in the ground are

St Sebald as a pilgrim. Detail from a panel painting, Nuremburg 1487. The characteristic pilgrim's hat gave protection from sun and rain and allowed the wearer to display his distinctive badges, which would make it clear he was a pilgrim and as such had the right to special protection.

said to have grown green shoots; the flowering stave is a popular motif in many legends concerning travellers, for instance, in the story of Tannhäuser's return from Rome.

The cost of a pilgrimage

There is unexpectedly little in the guide about the cost of a pilgrimage, so it may be useful to quote sums which were set aside in Lübeck at the beginning of the fourteenth century for testamentary pilgrimages, that is for pilgrimages to be undertaken by a representative. For a pilgrimage to Santiago between 10 and 40 marks were allowed; for 10 marks, two(!) poor pilgrims were supposed

The badge of St James: detail from the cloister at Moissac, not far from one of the great pilgrim roads.

to be able to undertake the journey. As a comparison, we can look at some prices of about 1220 (ninety years later the prices would have been higher; the Lübeck mark was valued at 16 shillings): a horse cost about 4¾ marks, an ox 2½ marks, a cow 13, a pig 5 and a sheep 4 shillings. So each of the two poor pilgrims who were expected to undertake the journey from Lübeck to Santiago with 5 marks had the equivalent of two oxen or twenty sheep.

Pious pilgrims?

The author describes in varying detail four pilgrim's roads through France to Santiago, and gives information about the initial places of pilgrimage on each route – Saint-Gilles in the Bouches du Rhône, Le Puy in the Massif Central, Vézelay in Burgundy and Tours on the Loire. Beyond the Pyrenees these four routes joined at Puente la Reina to form the single pilgrim's way to Santiago, along which millions of pilgrims in the Middle Ages went, it is estimated at times between 200,000 and 500,000 people a year: educated and uneducated (those who had to have the directions read out to them), rich and poor, old and young, men and women (the proportion of women is estimated to have been about a quarter to a third of the total number of pilgrims), individuals and groups (the well-to-do would be accompanied by their own doctor and chaplain), the healthy and above all the sick, who had consulted in vain the medical authorities of their day; men who wanted to ask for a special blessing or fulfil a vow (perhaps to give thanks for help received in a desperate situation); pardoned criminals; adventurers; worldlings . . .

The pilgrim did not necessarily have to be pious. At about the time the pilgrim's guide was written, the Abbot Peter the Venerable of Cluny was having doubts about the spiritual value of long pilgrimages; he warned against frivolity, restlessness, curiosity, pride and the hope of material gain. Specific measures were imposed to ward off many temptations; the spiritual value of the pilgrimage was made conditional on the pilgrim fasting on the way, eating no meat, staying only one night in any one place, leaving hair and nails uncut, not having a warm bath, and not sleeping in a comfortable bed; the last two injunctions possibly also making it easier for him to withstand the blandishments of the opposite sex.

Roads, bridges and hospices

The roads mentioned in the pilgrim's guide formed the main arteries of a dense network of lesser roads. People who wanted to visit out-of-the-way shrines or to avoid overcrowded inns on the larger roads during the main travelling seasons of early and late summer, would go along the minor roads. The hospices and bridges mentioned in the pilgrim's guide or known from research, show how

The road to Compostela: the way across the hills of northern Spain remains much as it was in medieval times.

The road to Compostela: one of the massive stone bridges built to ease the pilgrims' journey through northern Spain.

The road to Compostela: a section of paved roadway. Good surfaces were the exception rather than the rule, and any paving was usually a relic from the Roman past.

much pilgrim traffic there already was by the twelfth century. Hospices such as the hospice of Sainte Christine in the Pyrenees, and the hospices in Jerusalem and on the Great St Bernard Pass on the way to Rome, were situated in places 'where they fulfil a need. They are houses of God, holy places, where the pious pilgrim may refresh himself. Here those who need it will find peace and rest, the sick comfort, the dead salvation, the living help. Therefore there can be no doubt but that the builders of such holy places will enter into the kingdom of heaven.'

It was no coincidence that an important staging-post on the route beyond the Pyrenees was called Puente la Reina; it was at the 'Queen's Bridge' built at the beginning of the eleventh century to benefit pilgrims, on the initiative of the wife of King Sancho III of Navarre that the three routes over the Pyrenees joined to form a single pilgrim's way to Santiago. The author devotes an entire short chapter to the builders of such roads and bridges, and closes with the wish: 'May the souls of these men and of all their helpers rest in eternal peace.'

The guide describes other daily stages along the route, some in more detail than others; often they could not be covered in a single day – either the author had made his notes incorrectly on the way, or he wanted to make light of the length and difficulty of the road. The announcement that there were thirteen stages between the Cisa Pass in the Pyrenees and Santiago (375 miles in a direct line) was as unrealistic as the statement that one could get from Pamplona to Burgos in two days (106 miles in a direct line). However, if it had been the author's intention to make the journey appear less difficult to pilgrims than it really was, he would surely not have referred to the dangers in such detail; the relevant passages say much about travelling conditions in general – not only those of the twelfth century.

A warning about dangers

The author warns pilgrims about dangers from nature, and from his fellow men. Death and destruction threaten the traveller and his mount in Spain if they drink water from various rivers (many of which happened to be in Navarre), or if the traveller eats meat or fish. The journey through the Landes in south-western France, for which one must allow three days, was unpleasant; 'these will be days when you will be utterly exhausted! For it is a god-forsaken, flat region with very few stopping-places, as if bereft of all the good things of the earth, without bread, wine, meat, fish, with no running water or springs. There is only sand in abundance.' However, honey could be found in plenty, and various kinds of millet, and noisy beasts. 'If you chance to travel through this region in summer, protect your face carefully from the giant flies: they are called wasps or gadflies here, and there are great swarms of them.' Those who did not take care where they walked, would quickly sink up to their knees in the fine sand which blew everywhere.

'I wish with all my heart these devils would go to hell!' The author is cursing the ferrymen at the foot of the Pyrenees; two quite small rivers could only be crossed by pilgrims with their help; the men demanded from rich and poor alike one gold coin for taking a man across and four for a horse. And their dugout boat made from a tree-trunk was very small and quite unsuitable for transporting horses. 'If you get in this boat, take care: you will soon be in the water!' Pilgrims should only get in a few at a time because of the danger of capsizing and should let their horses swim across, if possible leading them by the reins. 'After they've taken the money, the ferrymen often let so many pilgrims get in that the boat sinks and they all drown in the river. The worthless boatmen then let out a howl of joy and take all the drowned men's belongings.' The pilgrim's guide names the proper tariff: for two people, who can afford it, one small gold coin, for a horse a large coin; the poor should pay nothing. And the ferrymen should use large boats in which there was plenty of room for men and beasts.

'I wish from the bottom of my heart that they would go to the devil!' The second curse concerns 'wicked highway robbers'. The pilgrim had barely escaped the dangers of the ferrymen when he was confronted by a new hazard in the 'inhospitable and densely wooded' Basque country. 'If the pilgrim sees the local inhabitants, his blood will freeze.' They are men of barbaric speech, and rough physical appearance. And the so-called toll-men! Guarded by two or three men with lances, they approach the pilgrim and forcibly demand an unwarranted toll. 'If the traveller should think of refusing them the money they demand, they kill him with their cudgels and appropriate the sum. Then with vituperations they strip their victim naked.' The author of the guide advises pilgrims that a highway toll should never be demanded from pilgrims, but only occasionally from merchants; if the 'toll-men' were allowed to demand a levy of at most four or six gold coins, they would ask double. The author tries to remedy the matter by his writing: he begs for heavy punishments for those directly and indirectly responsible, the tax collectors, the king of Aragon and other officials – all who are in charge of highways and waterways and who let unjustly high levies be raised. 'The priests are also responsible, who know about these crimes: they give absolution to the wrongdoers, welcome them into their churches, celebrate the mass with them and give them communion.' All directly and indirectly involved, whether clergy or laymen, should be excommunicated. The ban should be announced in the appropriate bishoprics and in Santiago, so that all pilgrims could hear it. 'The offenders shall remain excommunicated until they can be pardoned after a long, public penance – and show proper restraint in their demands for money.'

Prejudices

The author does not travel to Santiago as a poor penitent, but describes the pleasures of the table to be found on the way (one is sometimes reminded of one of today's Michelin guides). There are constant references to good wine, meat and white (wheatmeal) bread, which only the rich could afford. To give an example of the way the author describes a region, its food and its people, here is a quotation from his passage on Castile: the region is rich in gold, silver, costly materials and unusually strong horses; it is 'fertile and produces a great quantity of bread, wine, meat, fish, milk and honey; the only lack is of wood. Just one word about the people here: they are ill-tempered and profligate.'

The wholesale condemnation of the local population is no exception. The author is not prepared to accept that people in other countries may have a different way of life; and anything that does not correspond to the norm in his own country is condemned. He is only pleased by one region and its people, and one may therefore take it that he is describing his own homeland. 'Leaving Tours one approaches Poitou, an exceptionally pleasant and blessed region. The people of this countryside are able-bodied and warlike heroes: they are most skilled in fighting with bow and arrows and with the lance; they are courageous in battle. They are good runners, and dress most tastefully. They strike one with their beaming faces, and cunning speech. It would be hard to find men who are more generous and hospitable than they are.' The farther to the south the author travels, the more critical his remarks about the inhabitants become; in fact the only people to find grace in his eyes besides the men from Poitou are the 'countrymen' of St James the Apostle: the Galicians have most in common with 'we men from France'.

At first the author only mocks the speech of the people he meets on the way, but then he grows more and more critical of their way of life. He refers to the 'peasant' speech of the people in the countryside around Saintes, and calls that of the people round Bordeaux 'even coarser' (good wine and fish here); then the Gascons: they are good fighters and hospitable, and have excellent bread, good red wine and sound drinking-water, but 'they talk a lot, and scoff even more. They have fallen prey to drink, gluttony and other excesses. There is a stark contrast between their extravagant eating and their slovenly dress: they are dressed in rags as if all their money and goods had been stolen . . . They eat sitting round the fire without a table. A communal flat bowl serves as their drinking-vessel. But their over-rich food and drink, and their miserable dress is surpassed by their absolutely shameful manner of sleeping: a couple of covers are spread on dirty straw, and the servants sleep there with their masters and mistresses.'

Farther to the south, the Navarrese. The author's interest in social trends is even more marked. He does not only study, as with the Gascons, table- and sleeping-habits; in addition he is shocked that the Navarrese sense of shame differs from his own. Travellers have often been amazed or angry that people in other countries dry, wash or bath themselves unembarrassedly before strangers without any clothes on (as in present-day Japan). The author adds rumour to his own observations. 'In many places, when they want to get dry, the Navarrese men and women show that which should be modestly hidden. And they also carry out shameful practices with animals. It is said that certain Navarrese fix a strap to the hind-parts of their mule or mare, so that no one but themselves can carry out these shameful practices with the animal. Neither women nor beasts are safe from their perverse excesses.' He has no hesitation in repeating the most evil slanders about his hosts: 'When we', the author recounts his own experience, 'asked about the water, they lied to us and said we could safely drink the water. So we gave our horses a drink of it; they died straight away and the men immediately skinned them.' Earlier the author had mentioned a 'salt river', which one should not approach too closely; the water would certainly kill men and beasts. If there had indeed been salt rivers in the Pyrenees, pilgrims and their horses would hardly have drunk themselves to death.

There follow other remarks about unattractive clothing (amongst other things sandals which left the heels bare) and their way of eating: 'The whole extensive family eats together, which means that servant and master, maid and mistress, all dip into one and the same bowl, in which the main dish and side dishes are all mixed up together. They don't use spoons for eating, but their hands. They all drink from the same beaker. If you saw and heard them eating you would think they were hounds or pigs.' The speech of the Navarrese reminds the writer of the 'yelping of hounds'.

Finally the author accuses the people whom the pilgrim must rely on for help of a catalogue of crimes. Before they became Christians, 'the godless Navarrese and Basques' used 'not only to rob the pilgrims going to Santiago but also to ride on them like donkeys and so drive the poor souls to death in this way'. They are still 'a strange people, different to other races in their habits and nature, bad-tempered, stupid, completely corrupt: perverted, lazy and dishonest, profligate and given to drink, accustomed to use every kind of force, wild and savage, underhand and depraved, godless and sinister, unholy and quarrelsome, a people unused to all good ways and much practised in every kind of evil and crime.' The author places the Navarrese on a level with the Getae who were a byword for evil in the ancient world and with the Saracens of his own day. 'They are totally unlike,' he continues, 'we men from France. For the price of a single penny the Navarrese or Basque will kill a Frenchman, if he can.'

A postscript, possibly by a different author, fails to mitigate the bad impression: the Navarrese are brave fighters, and they give generous offerings to the Church. The final remark – that when going about their banditry they communicate with one another by hooting like an owl or howling like a wolf – possibly hides the dread and fear felt by the author of the pilgrim's guide when he had to go through distant tracts of forest and saw himself threatened with death at every strange noise; there is good reason why the French word 'sauvage' (wild, or the English 'savage') is derived from 'silvaticus' or 'of the forest'.

Shrines

On long pilgrimages it was customary to 'pack in' as many acts of worship, absolutions and good deeds as one could. If it was possible, the pilgrim to Rome would also do homage to the Three Kings at Cologne, St Theobald in Thann, and the Virgin Mary at Einsiedeln. The author discusses this practice. Nearly a third of the guide is taken up by the eighth chapter: 'Concerning the relics to be visited on the way, and the martyrdom of St Eutropius.' The author refers extensively to apocrypha, legends and stories, in his description of Eutropius. In his accounts of martyrs and confessors he brings many aspects of Church history alive for the pilgrim. The detailed description of a now lost Aegidius shrine in this chapter has aroused the interest of art historians; one can see how such a work affected people and how things were emphasised and interpreted; the same applies to the description of St James's Cathedral in the ninth chapter.

The author realises that it is to his advantage to promote the cult of other saints, at least in moderation. Many churches held that they alone possessed the relics of certain particularly powerful saints; when it recognises these claims the pilgrim's guide comes perilously close to deriding other churches or communities or accusing them of lying about possessing relics of the saints in question. The author says for example that the Hungarians, and the monks of the monastery at Chamalières, and also the Normans near Coutances, should be ashamed of themselves, are quite wrong and should be silent on the matter – it was quite out of the question that St Aegidius's resting place should be anywhere other than at St Gilles on the Rhône . . . He goes indirectly into the matter of the widespread 'theft' of relics, the word 'theft' perhaps being misleading: if someone thought a saint was not being duly honoured at his resting-place, there was a great temptation to remove part or all of the relics, often under cover of darkness. If the saint did not want to be moved, he would know very well how to stop this happening. 'Many people' could testify to the fact that no one had ever succeeded in removing the bodies of the saints Aegidius, Martin, Leonard or James 'from their burial places'.

The question of the authenticity of relics had far-reaching, and financial, implications: when doubts as to the authenticity of the relics of Mary Magdalene grew ever stronger, the number of pilgrims to Vézelay in the thirteenth century noticeably fell off, to the great detriment of the food trade and other trades in the area. There are no traces of such doubts in the guide. The author assures his readers that Mary Magdalene rests there 'to this day' and that 'for love of the saint' God performs many miracles and wondrous deeds.

Another saint was especially revered by those travellers who had been imprisoned. The church dedicated to St Leonard (east of Limoges) must have been a strange sight: 'One looks in amazement at the beams, on which great numbers of barbaric irons are hung as if on a ship's mast. There are iron manacles and foot-clamps hanging there, neck-irons, chains, stocks and leg-irons, crowbars and other things', from which Leonard had freed thousands of prisoners thanks to his powerful mediation. He had repeatedly appeared 'in visible human form even in the places where slaves were held captive across the sea', as those men had testified whom he had freed 'thanks to God's holy power'. A kernel of truth lay behind these statements: members of certain brotherhoods gave themselves into captivity to free those who were enslaved. To the latter it might appear that St Leonard had taken on human form. Like the chains in St Leonard's church, votive offerings were hung at other pilgrim shrines, made from silver, wax or wood and depicting a jawbone or leg, or ship, as a token of thanksgiving for being freed from toothache, for having a leg healed or being saved from a shipwreck.

In the account, compiled from various sources, relating to St Eutropius, reputed to be one of Jesus's disciples, the author clearly shows that he was contemporaneous with the crusades; without thinking he includes in his account the most strong condemnation of the Jews. Eutropius comes back from Jerusalem, where he too took part in the Pentecostal miracle. 'Burning with zeal in his love of Christ, he had the Jews in his country cut down with the sword, because of the Jews in Jerusalem who had condemned Our Lord to death.'

This chapter, in which the saints Aegidius, Saturnius, Fides (St Foy), Mary Magdalene, Leonard, Fronto, Martin of Tours, Hilarius of Poitiers, John the

Baptist, Eutropius, Roland (the Carolingian, named here as a martyr), Dominic (the road-builder) and others are honoured, closes with a prayer, in which once again strict faith is recommended: God works miracles, and the saints can help men by interceding at God's throne: 'Thanks to their services and prayers all the aforementioned saints and others can intercede for us with our Lord God Jesus Christ, who with the Father and the Holy Spirit lives and reigns on high. For ever and ever. Amen.'

Journey's end

When the pilgrim was a few days away from his journey's end, he came to Triacastela, in Galicia, at the western foot of the Cantabrian mountains. From here he took a piece of limestone with him to Castañola, where there were kilns in which it could be calcined to make the lime needed for St James's cathedral; so the pilgrim would be directly contributing to the building of the church.

Just before entering the holy city the pilgrim would take a cleansing bath in a river at a wood called 'Lavamentula' (literally: wash private parts). The pilgrim's guide relates as follows: 'The crowds of pilgrims who come from France to Santiago, wash not only their private parts here out of love for the Apostle, but also the dirt from their entire body – and while they are doing so they often suffer the misfortune of having their clothes stolen!'

Near the river is the 'Mountain of Joy', from which St James's cathedral could first be seen. The first to climb it became the 'King' of his group of pilgrims. Many families with names such as 'King', 'König' or 'Leroy' are probably descended from pilgrims to Santiago, Rome or Jerusalem or Mont St Michel in Normandy or other places where that particular pilgrim was first to get to the top of the 'Mountain of Joy' (Montjoie).

The author devotes his ninth chapter to the town and to St James's basilica, and the tenth to the giving of offerings. He describes the gates and churches of the town, dedicated to much revered saints: Peter, Michael, Martin, the Holy Trinity (in whose shadow many pilgrims who had died in the town were buried). He directs pilgrims first to a square, a stone's throw wide and, he says, paved and surrounded by arcading, and adorned by a particularly beautiful well which he describes in detail. In this square pilgrims can change money, find lodgings, and also wine in skins, shoes and laces, bags and girdles, herbs and spices, and above all 'small scallop shells, to show that they have been at St James's shrine'. Unlike the palm fronds of pilgrims to Jerusalem, the scallop shells were often kept by pilgrims. On the return journey they could put them 'in their cap' like a badge. They can be found all over Europe. At the end of his life the pilgrim would have his scallop shell buried with him in his grave, in the firm belief that St James the Apostle, whose shrine he had made such an arduous journey to visit, would lead him safely to his eternal home.

The cathedral is described in detail: dimensions, exterior, towers, altars. The decoration of doors, walls, windows and so on was conceived as a kind of 'pictorial Bible'; particularly important passages of the holy story were illustrated and imprinted on the memory not only by the words of preachers but also by visual means. The pilgrim's guide shows that in the Middle Ages people could clearly interpret and draw inspiration from such frequently depicted scenes. So the south portico shows: 'Next, the Virgin Mary, the Mother of God, with her son in Bethlehem; the Three Kings come to visit the Mother and Child; they offer him their three gifts; the star shines above them; finally an angel warns them not to return to Herod.' Then the author turns in moralising tone to a woman shown near the scene of the temptation of Jesus. 'In her hands she holds the head of her lover, whom her own husband has killed, who now forces her to kiss the stinking skull twice a day. How impressive, how wonderful is the way in which justice was done to this woman taken in adultery! Let all be mindful of it!'

Inside the cathedral, the grave of St James the Apostle and the altar dedicated to him naturally received particular attention. The author had measured the latter himself, and enjoins the reader to share his wonder at its magnificence: 'The altarcloth must be nine by twenty-one handsbreadths in size.' Anyone who could not or did not want to make the long pilgrimage himself, had the opportunity to pay his respects to the mighty apostle by sending such a gift as this; and even better, by sending the altarcloth he would himself be present at the altar. This token of physical embodiment was important because it helped to mitigate the inevitability of being forgotten after death. It was for this reason that living and dead were remembered by name during the mass, that pilgrims dedicated candles, that those who had been cured hung up their artificial limbs – or as in St Leonard's basilica, their chains – in churches, as a visible sign of help received, as tokens of thankfulness from those saved and to perpetuate the memory of one-time pilgrims.

The canopy over and lamps in front of the altar were described in detail; the 'nobility' of the basilica, its canons and cardinals was stressed. Santiago vied with Rome in importance at times, as was demonstrated by the setting up of a college of cardinals, and the practice – still current today – of announcing jubilee years.

The author of such a guide would not automatically have thought of the stonemasons who created such a magnificent edifice. But his account is particularly interesting for the general impression which the building made on a visitor in the twelfth century. The interior of the church has the same effect on many visitors today. 'Wonderful things have been done here: the church is large, spacious, light. The proportions are right: breadth, length and height are fitting. The building is more beautiful than one can say; its upper storey is reminiscent of a royal palace. If anyone who is sad should proceed to the choir, he will – walking along the upper galleries – be joyous, and uplifted by the sight of this unusually beautiful house of God.'

Listing the miracles performed, the author both honours the Apostle and promotes pilgrimages to his shrine. 'The sick are healed here, the blind restored to sight, the tongues of the dumb loosened, the deaf given back their hearing, the lame walk again, the possessed are freed from demons, and most important of all, the requests of the faithful are heard, their vows are taken up to heaven, the fetters of sin are unbound, heaven's gates are opened, and the weary are comforted. Great crowds of people from all races and from every direction stream hither together, to honour God with their gifts.'

The author states that the poor who seek help at the hospice, have a right to a tenth part of everything that is laid at the altar of St James's cathedral. If any priest of the church should appropriate these offerings, the sin will stand 'between God and him' for ever. 'All poor pilgrims have the right to full board and lodging for the night following their arrival at the altar of St James – a right bestowed for the love of God and the Apostle.' This friendly welcome is still shown today: pilgrims who come on foot to Santiago have a right to free board at the Parador by the church. The pilgrim's guide also added that the sick must be 'lovingly' cared for until their death or until they had completely recovered their health.

The last chapter is entitled 'How pilgrims to St James's shrine should be received.' Punishments and miraculous vengeance are listed as a warning: those who had refused to give help or shelter had had their bread turned to stone, their roof had fallen in, a thousand lodgings had burnt down. Those on the other hand who received with love and honour pilgrims, whether rich or poor, on their way to or from Santiago, and gave them proper shelter, received not only St James but also Christ himself. With this statement the author was echoing the generally held belief. In 1149, at about the time the pilgrim's guide was written, a certain knight had a vision: Tundal saw a king sitting enthroned at the gates of paradise, probably the Emperor Henry IV, surrounded by the poor people and pilgrims whom the Emperor had helped during his lifetime and who now interceded on his behalf.

The author of the guide continually puts forward his own ideas and opinions, so it is fitting that his work should end not with a plea on behalf of the pilgrims, but with praises for himself and his readers. 'Praise be to him, who wrote it, but also to him, who reads it.'

JOURNEYS ACROSS ASIA

In the mid-thirteenth century Europe was faced with a new threat. Under the leadership of Genghis Khan, the Mongols – or Tartars – had from the beginning of the century founded a great empire in eastern Asia, reaching from China to Russia and Persia; in 1241 they defeated a German-Polish army at Liegnitz, but did not go on to conquer Europe, as a dispute broke out over the successor to the Great Khan Ogotai who had died the same year. In 1251 Mangu Khan, a grandson of Genghis Khan, became Great Khan.

In 1245, only a few years after the catastrophic defeat of the German-Polish army, Pope Innocent IV sent three legations – one of which was Carpini's – to visit the Mongolian ruler. Franciscans and Dominicans were to collect precise information about the much feared and dreaded race, and assess the chances of winning the Mongols over to the Christian faith and turning their expansionary zeal against Islam; then Europe would be spared threats like that of 1241, and further crusades to the Holy Land would become superfluous. The hoped for alliance was not achieved, nor were the Mongols converted to Christianity – and yet the legations were valuable, if only for bringing to Europe for the first time exact information about the countries and people in central and eastern Asia.

From the middle of the thirteenth century there was great curiosity concerning the vast reaches of Asia, about which people had held certain, partly legendary, beliefs, since Alexander's campaigns. To illustrate this lively interest and the eagerness of people to experience the new and foreign, three travellers are included here, who have left us accounts of their journeys. The Franciscan William of Rubruck (born c. 1215/20, died c. 1270) travelled in 1253–55 to the court of the Great Khan at Karakorum; he was only a little over two years on the road, but Marco Polo (1254–1324) and Ibn Battuta (1304–1377/78) were both abroad for several decades. Marco Polo travelled from 1271 to 1295 in the Mongolian empire including China as well as many parts of south and south-east Asia. Battuta, an Islamic scholar (possibly merchant as well) was even longer on the road in Asia, Europe and Africa, from 1325 to 1354. Before describing particular events during their travels, we can compare what they had in common and the differences between them.

Battuta had the initial advantage. He travelled at first exclusively in the Arab-Moslem world. Polo had the advantage of being introduced when he was seventeen by his father and uncle, who had previously lived for a long while among the Mongols, to their strange world and speech. Rubruck had the greatest difficulties to contend with: because of the comparatively short duration of his journey, he had little chance to grow accustomed to the life.

Because of the considerably longer time he was abroad and his greater ability to collect information, Marco Polo has left us a more varied and extensive account than Rubruck. In all their very varied material, there are different points of emphasis. Rubruck is filled with missionary zeal, likes to preach and therefore to know what religious beliefs he is dealing with. Polo also gives much information about religion and cults, but he writes like a merchant, noticing above all crafts, trade and traffic. With Battuta the historical interest is uppermost: he tells us, as in modern guidebooks – with particular emphasis on the Islamic era – the history of towns, and their famous men, buildings and curiosities. Unlike Rubruck, Polo and Battuta were not bound by the vows of chastity and poverty, but devoted to the enjoyment of this world; they tell without embarrassment of the love-life and marriage customs of the people among whom they stayed, and make no attempt to hide their sympathies for the – according to them – free-and-easy sexual attitudes in many places which they visited. Battuta writes about his own experiences with married women and concubines with an openness to which western readers would not have been accustomed.

Different patrons and public inspired the three accounts: for Rubruck it was King Louis IX of France and the superiors of his Order, for Marco Polo all those readers who were curious about these matters and for Battuta the Sultan of Fez. Rubruck wrote his account himself; Marco Polo's adventures were written down by Rustichello, a fellow prisoner in a Genoese gaol, and Battuta's by Ibn Juzayy, a secretary of the Sultan. The writers influenced the form, sometimes even the content (the descriptions of battles in Marco Polo's adventures, for example). Polo addresses a wide audience right from the start: 'Emperor, kings and princes, knights and citizens – and all of you who are curious and anxious to learn about the many races and characteristics of the countries of the world – take this book and have it read to you.' The mode of addressing the reader directly was not just a stylistic means of catching the attention; Marco Polo himself at least saw his book as a travel guide, for the merchants of his home town amongst others. Of Sumatra he says: 'Note well: here too the Pole star cannot be seen'; and similarly he records where the star can be seen again.

All three authors repeatedly stress that they have themselves seen what they describe or have been told it by reliable witnesses; compared with many modern travel accounts they include only a few fairy-tale elements (such as men with dog's heads, for example) which did not mean that their contemporaries believed everything which later research may have proved to be true. Rubruck, Polo and Battuta were driven by a desire for knowledge which was unusual in the Middle Ages. In Polo it was combined with pride and self-confidence: 'Since the creation of our forefather Adam, there have been no Christians, no heathens . . . no single men of any race, who have known and discovered as much and who have seen as many marvels as Master Marco Polo alone.' Battuta considers his role more modestly, if no less firmly: 'I have really – praise be to God – realised my heartfelt desire in this world, which was to travel through the world, and in this respect I have achieved what no one else to my knowledge has done.' With their unquenchable curiosity, the three authors point the way towards the future; but that they also remained children of their own age is clearly shown by the fact that they did not hesitate to visit notable Christian or Moslem holy men and sacred places and to honour them duly in their accounts.

The three travellers were only able to survive because they were strong and adaptable. When Rubruck had to drink horse's milk and Polo got diarrhoea after drinking date-wine, these were only among the minor discomforts with which they had to contend. How small the chances were of travellers returning home safely can be judged not only from the dangers which are described in detail but also from a chance remark of Polo's: of the 600 members of a legation, only 18 survived. A similar, if not quite so great, loss of life was experienced on the first world circumnavigation by Magellan.

Rubruck, Marco Polo and Battuta all had in common a passionate interest in 'others', which was more pronounced than among their contemporaries; Marco Polo was well aware of this. He recounts how in a very short time he became acquainted with the customs, speech and writing of the Tartars; the Great Khan recognised his capabilities and his quickness to adapt to foreign ways. The ruler showed a remarkable lack of prejudice as to culture, language and religion when he entrusted an important mission to a distant province to the barely adult Marco Polo. 'The young man fulfilled his mission with skill and care. It had not escaped his notice that the Great Khan considered envoys, who on their return from foreign lands reported only their mission and related nothing about the country and people, stupid and limited. He had remarked that the leader of the mission was important, but information about the circumstances, events and way of life in the territories travelled through even more important.' Knowing the Great Khan's interest in these matters, Marco took care to observe events and practices carefully as he went along, so that he could report back on them in detail.

It is amazing how many subjects are covered by the three authors, some of them being only recently 'discovered' by the world of science. Obviously the travellers' experience of different worlds sharpened their insights in a way not possible for those authors who never go beyond their own cultural sphere. Here are a few of the subjects which Rubruck, Marco Polo and Battuta deal with, in greater or lesser detail: natural geographical characteristics: climate, mountains, hills, rivers (length, width), seas, flora (including cultivated and edible plants, sowing and reaping times, timber) and fauna (including domestic animals); country and town settlements; trade (markets, ports, goods, merchants); occupations (silk-trade, metalworking, food production, salt-works); mining (precious stones, oil and coal as heating materials); peoples, languages and writing; religions and cults (including magic and devil worship); customs and ways of life (food; dress; ornaments, fashion; houses, building; position of women before, during and after marriage; honouring of the dead; burning of widows); law (and punishment), constitutions, administration, government and the practice of government; money and finance (particularly the Chinese paper money); military matters (weapons, knights, battles); communications (ships, bridges, roads); the educational arts; care of the body and medicinal arts (baths, pharmaceutics, aphrodisiacs) and so on. The authors are continually at a loss for words: the new and unusual is so overpowering and manifold that they cannot express it by words alone. Rubruck says once to the French king how much he regrets having only the medium of language at his disposal: 'The women construct beautiful wagons for themselves, which I could only describe to you by visual means. And I would have painted everything for you, if I could have done so.'

Whereas Rubruck returned to life in his religious Order after carrying out a mission which was limited in both duration and distance, the excitement of discovering foreign lands led Marco Polo and Battuta to undertake further travels. One is occasionally reminded of a Greek historian, Arrian, who tried to express the universal amazement at Alexander the Great's craving for action: 'And he was seized with the longing . . .' Battuta writes at one point: 'I decided to go on a journey to the Maldive Islands, of which I had heard tell.'

The three authors are an inexhaustible source of information not only for historians, but also as to the geography of the countries they visited, for anthropological studies, and for comparing different cultural and religious spheres. A few examples will show the breadth of their interests; first Rubruck: on his outward journey to the court of the Great Khan, he is struck by 'German speaking' Goths in the Crimea, descendants of the people who a thousand years before had travelled through this area. On his return journey, in Asia Minor, only winter and snow prevent him from making a detour to the source of the Euphrates. Marco Polo noticed that in the icy high altitudes of the Pamirs, food when heated did not cook properly. Battuta mentions (copying the classical authors?) as worthy of note that the Nile has most water at the hottest time of year, when many rivers run dry.

Rubruck's and Battuta's accounts show how frequently people of their day travelled, either because they wished to do so or because they were forced to. In the Tartar empire Rubruck met not only an immigrant from Jerusalem, and other envoys from the Pope to Mangu Khan, but also many Russians, Armenians and Georgians deported by the Mongols to central Asia; many of those deported from Hungary in 1243 had only been there a short time or had been captured by the Mongols on their way back: German mountain villagers and metalworkers, a woman from Metz, William, a goldsmith from Paris, a woman who could speak good French and Cumani, an Englishman's son . . . The vow of a Nestorian Christian at the court of the Great Khan also illustrates people's willingness to undertake long journeys: if he was cured from his serious illness, he would travel to the Pope in Rome as a sign of thanksgiving. On his return journey Rubruck met an Armenian who was prepared to continue wandering rather than remain under the Tartar yoke. Battuta's account bears testimony to an equal mobility in the Islamic world: in southern Russia a Jew from Andalusia speaks to him in Arabic; in Bangalore in India he meets a legal scholar from Mogadishu in East Africa, who has been a long while in Mecca and Medina and has travelled through India and China; in China he sees a man from Ceuta in North Africa, whose brother he would later meet on the Niger.

The accounts are also valuable because their authors continually make comparisons – consciously or unconsciously – with their own world. Certain remarks of Rubruck tell us that in the mid-thirteenth century forks were not yet in general use: his hosts offer their table companions mutton, 'on the point of a knife or with a fork made for the purpose, like ours with which we eat pears or other fruit cooked in wine' (so speaks the poor Franciscan monk!) He finds it worthy of note that Mongolian women ride like men – so clearly women in Europe preferred to ride side-saddle. Of washing crockery, hands and hair, he says: 'They never wash their bowls, but when meat is cooked, they rinse the dishes in which they are going to put it with broth from a pot and then pour this back into the pot . . . When they want to wash their hands or hair, they fill their mouth with water and let it pour down slowly over their hands, then damp their hair with it and wash their heads.' Battuta mentions equally casually that in the Maldives they can dispense with costly prisons; criminals are locked in wooden sheds intended for merchants' goods. 'They are put in the stocks, like Christian prisoners in Morocco.'

Together with this open-mindedness about foreign customs however, there are also many hasty and biased conclusions and judgements in their accounts. Marco Polo writes of the inhabitants of 'Fugiu', the capital city of a Chinese province which he had possibly not seen himself but only knew from hearsay: 'The people are heathen and wicked through and through. To steal and do wrong is not regarded as a sin, and these people are the worst scoundrels and robbers on earth.' Battuta, in his account, clearly draws limits: where people are not of his faith, he misses the accepted way of life: 'The country of China, although it contains so much of beauty, didn't appeal to me; on the contrary, I was very worried by the fact that the heathen have the upper hand there. When I left my house, I saw countless dreadful things. That disturbed me so much that I stayed at home and only went out when I was forced to do so. When I saw Moslems in China, I felt as though I were seeing my own kith and kin.'

Faced with the new, the travellers become aware of the strengths and weaknesses of their own cultural spheres. Battuta is as convinced of the superiority of Islam as Rubruck is of Christianity. Marco Polo remarks that the Mongols had taken a Chinese town thanks only to the expertise 'of the Venetians' (a fact not mentioned in Chinese sources). But more important than their self-satisfied expressions of superiority are remarks in which they admit that foreigners may be right, may even excel, and which can therefore lead to a modification of accepted standards. Marco Polo writes of Quilon in south-west India: 'It is all simply different from us, it is more beautiful *and better*.' Rubruck gets involved in arguments between those of different faiths at the court of the Great Khan. In connection with a disputation between Christians, Moslems and Buddhists he repeats words of the Khan which bear upon the assumption of Christianity to be the only true faith – words which might raise doubts, as did the accounts of European travellers at the time of the Age of Enlightenment: 'But as God gave the hand different fingers, so he gave men different ways. God gave you the Holy Word, but you Christians do not follow it . . . But he gave us prophets, and we do what they say, and we live in peace.'

William of Rubruck

The envoy must have 'a good interpreter or rather several, and plenty of money for his journey'. Rubruck ended his report to the French King with these words. He had prepared carefully for his mission to the court of the Great Khan. He had studied the pronouncements of the classical 'authorities' on the countries through which he would travel, and had spoken to men who had visited the area more recently; he had provided himself with presents for the local rulers and for those to whom the legation was directed (not enough, as it turned out); finally he had obtained a letter of recommendation from the King of France, and had this translated into Turkish and Arabic. Despite all this his final sentence hints at dissatisfaction with the outcome of his travels.

Rubruck set out on 7 May 1253 from Constantinople; he was accompanied by another monk, an interpreter, two men to look after the animals, a bearer and a young slave. When he landed in the Crimea on 21 May, he learnt that the news of his coming had preceeded him. The overland journey began at the beginning of June; on about 20 July he crossed the Don, and at the end of July he reached the camp of the regional khan, Sartach. The latter was said in Europe to be a Christian; the French king's letter was therefore handed to him. Sartach did not dare to give the requested permission to the missionaries on his own account, but sent Rubruck on to a superior authority, Baatu. When Rubruck reached him, the same thing happened: Baatu sent him on to the Great Khan. In this way Rubruck got to know a large area of the Mongolian empire, and finally the Great Khan himself. At his court he learnt that the distinctions between a diplomatic and a spying mission were inclined to be blurred here too: he saw how an envoy was instructed to find out as much as he could about the lands through which he travelled, 'the roads, scenery, towns, fortifications, the people and their weapons'.

After he reached Sartach, Rubruck was travelling on the instructions of the Mongolian rulers; he was therefore given valuable free assistance, was able to use the Mongolian post-routes with their staging-posts and had knowledgeable guides and also provisions put at his disposal. On 5 August he crossed the Volga, on 28 September the River Ural; from the second week in August until 16 September he was at Baatu's camp. On 27 December he reached Mangu

Khan's headquarters camp, and was granted his first audience with him on 4 January 1254. In April he travelled with the court to Karakorum (about 219 miles to the west of Ulan-Bator, capital of present-day Mongolia). Here Rubruck found only the palace of the Khan impressive; the actual 'capital' of the Mongolian empire struck him as being about the size of Saint-Denis, in Paris. On 9 July Rubruck left Karakorum for the journey home, at first travelling to the west. From 16 September to 16 October he was at the camp of Baatu. As he hoped to meet the French King in the Holy Land, he travelled on to the south and south-west along the western bank of the Caspian Sea, across the Caucasus and through Asia Minor. Two years after he had left Constantinople he reached Curta (on the Cilician coast) on the Mediterranean on 5 May 1255; after an expedition to Cyprus he went via Antioch and Tripoli to Acre.

The journey to the Great Khan took Rubruck across vast tracts of Asia, over at least 9,000 miles. In summer heat and winter cold he was beset by every kind of hardship – by hunger, thirst and exhaustion, not to mention spiritual weariness. Regarded with suspicion, he and his companions had to make their way in a strange world; they were dependent on unreliable interpreters and untrustworthy local guides, and moreover did not enjoy the protection which official envoys could usually expect. Once when Rubruck showed impatience on the journey out, a Nestorian priest in Sartach's entourage told the messengers from the west that they must be 'very patient and humble'. Rubruck's patience and trust in God were sorely put to the test, as details of his journey show.

On the way to Sartach, Rubruck and his party 'never slept in a house or a tent, but always under the open skies or under our wagons.' Flooded rivers seemed to pose no problems, as their crossing of the Don shows. On the eastern bank the Mongols had imported Russians as ferrymen, to take messengers, merchants and men such as Rubruck and his group across in small craft. 'They put a small barge under every wheel, then roped the barges together and rowed them across.' On the return journey Rubruck saw a pontoon-bridge in the Caucasus, 'which was held together by an iron chain stretched right across the river.' After crossing the Don they were in trouble: the people of the ferry station were supposed to supply Rubruck's party with horses, as the local guides had sent back the draught-cattle which had brought them to the western bank. 'And when we then asked these people for draught-animals, they spoke of a privilege granted them by Baatu, saying that they were only bound to ferry across those who came and went. They even received a large payment from merchants.' After having to wait three days, they finally got some oxen, and later horses; meanwhile they had to go on foot.

On the second Sunday in Advent (13.12) the small caravan came in the late evening to the 'really terrible rocks' of a narrow pass; the guide asked Rubruck to say prayers 'to drive away the evil spirits, which suddenly carry off people in that ravine. And you never know what becomes of them. Sometimes they only take the horse and leave the men behind. Sometimes they rip the intestines out of men's bodies and burn the rest with the horses. And many other things happen there.' Rubruck expresses no doubts about the truth of such tales. He gladly complies with their request. 'We sang "Credo in unum Deum" loudly there, and by God's grace we all got safely through.' And at other junctures the Christians are asked to intercede with their prayers, for the Great Khan – for whom Buddhists and Moslems also prayed – or to get rid of a strong wind, severe cold and deep snow, which were endangering the pack-animals while going over the mountains.

Another plea by the Mongols was also typical of their syncretic attitude to religion, wishing to fuse various elements from different faiths: they asked Rubruck to write a helpful prayer as a safe-conduct, which they could carry on their heads. Rubruck wanted to teach them the Creed and the Lord's Prayer, 'that you may carry them in your hearts, and whereby you will be saved in body and spirit for all eternity'; this first attempt at conversion was obstructed by the interpreter.

The hope of being permanently supplied with provisions for the rest of their journey to the Great Khan as arranged by the Mongols was not fulfilled: Rubruck had to break into their 'iron rations' on the first month of their journey – so using up part of the extra presents. 'We had run out of wine, and the water was so churned up by the horses that it was undrinkable. If we hadn't had biscuit and God's help, we would possibly have died.' They were sometimes given cow's milk in leather bladders, but the delegation had to get used to the food and drink of the Mongols, which meant getting used to mare's milk. Rubruck writes of this liquid: 'The cosmos [mare's milk (*kumiz*)] was quite new to me, as I had never drunk any, and I sweated with horror when I tasted it. But afterwards it seemed to taste quite pleasant, as in fact it is.' Later, at the Great Khan's court, he and his companions were lent a kettle and tripod, so that they could prepare hot dishes for themselves. Their food consisted of rather rotten meat; millet which was cooked in the broth; occasionally there was honey, millet-meed, butter, curdled milk and unleavened bread that was baked over ox or horse dung. These varied foodstuffs soon gave way to a sparser diet: bread cooked in ashes and dough cooked in water with meat broth to drink, 'as we had no other water than that from melted snow or ice, and that was very foul'; his fellow monk was very dispirited by the food.

The Khan heard of the spartan lifestyle of his guests through intermediaries; he had wine, meal and oil sent to them. However that did not help the situation but only made matters worse; a Nestorian monk who was not very friendlily inclined towards Rubruck let it be known all over the camp that there was wine at the western delegation's quarters. Upon which Mongols and Nestorian priests rushed 'shamelessly over to us, like dogs . . . So this wine brought us more trouble than comfort, because we couldn't refuse any of them without causing trouble.' Rubruck made the discovery that it is 'a great sacrifice, to give generously, when one is poor oneself'.

For the journey back he and his companions received a pass, which allowed them to get a sheep every four days.

'It seemed to me, as if I were in another world.' Thus Rubruck describes his impressions on meeting the Tartars. Another world – which meant not only food, clothing, and the unaccustomed habit – for him – of living in tents, which could be carried on carts without being dismantled. Another world – the people above all. Rubruck must have known from his western European homeland how pressing the poor and sick could be. What he saw here, went far beyond anything he had experienced. It was true that he and his companions were rarely robbed directly; but the Tartars begged 'in an importunate and shameless manner for everything they see. And it is no use giving them anything, for they are ungrateful. They consider themselves lords of the world and take it for granted that they will be refused nothing. If one does refuse them and needs their services afterwards, they behave correspondingly badly.' Interpreters, travel guides, local potentates – all made endless demands, either on their own account or on behalf of the rulers to whom they were taking Rubruck; they crowded round, jostling Rubruck and his party, to see what they had with them. Nothing was safe from their 'attentions'; biscuit and wine, vestments and valuable books, liturgical apparatus – they coveted everything. Rubruck had to give them many precious things as 'presents'; he was worried that he would also have to part with a psalter, which the French Queen had given him.

Sometimes it is not clear whether the Mongols are trying to cheat Rubruck and his companions or whether they just have no sense of shame. Rubruck is thoroughly disgusted by them: 'To relieve their needs, they go no farther than one can throw a bean. Chattering right by us, they deposit their filth, and do many other quite disgusting things.'

More serious was the fact that he could not rely on his successive guides or his interpreter. The latter proved incapable of conveying difficult ideas in the Mongol language; when Rubruck tried to preach, the interpreter refused to translate – quite often saying something quite different to that which Rubruck had told him, in fact 'whatever occurred to him. When I realised the danger of speaking through him, I decided it was better to remain silent.' Other travellers had typical interpreter stories to tell, or repeated what they said in good faith, not having recognised them as such. On the return journey, in Asia Minor, Rubruck realised how greatly he was at the mercy of his guide. He did not dare protest that the man was buying far too much food on the way, 'as he could have sold or killed me and our servants, without anyone being able to stop him.'

An earlier official delegation from the French King had come to naught, because it was already known at the court of the Great Khan before their arrival that the King had been captured, and the envoys appeared like supplicants. In spite of his only 'semi-official' status – Rubruck had set out as a missionary but with the King's letter of recommendation – his account gives valuable information about the standing of a member of a foreign legation at the court. Several incidents are combined together below.

He continually had to identify himself, answering the questions 'where are you from' and 'where are you going'. Christians who knew the habits of the Mongols had impressed on him, to take immense care 'never to change the wording'; the information he gave would be noted and sent on ahead, so that if he diverged from this wording at his next audience he would confirm any latent suspicions. In the course of his journey Rubruck carefully studied the protocol practised at the Mongol courts, and questioned other envoys whom he met. He was grateful that at the Great Khan's court envoys could make contact with one another. He learnt that the Mongols took envoys from countries which were not subject to them by long detours to the Great Khan, with the intention of 'making the way appear longer and their empire very great'. At an arrow's length from the Khan's palace, one dismounted; as a gesture of humility Rubruck took off his sandals and went barefoot – to the great surprise of the Mongols, who were used to very different behaviour – Rubruck himself witnessed how the envoy of the Caliph of Baghdad had himself carried to the court in a litter slung between two mules. Before Rubruck could appear before the Khan, he was 'searched everywhere – legs, breast, arms, – to see if we carried knives. They made the interpreter take off his girdle with its dagger and leave it behind in a gatekeeper's hut.' If they wanted to humiliate someone, the body-search would be carried out 'in a rather shameful way', details of which Rubruck however refrains from giving. One approached the Great Khan – as a Nestorian monk was rudely made aware – bareheaded.

Rubruck is a petitioner; so he must wait until he is summoned; 'one doesn't go to the court unbidden'. He may only speak when the ruler has indicated that he may do so, and then only briefly – unlike a true envoy. 'They listen to whatever an envoy wishes to say, and always ask, if he wishes to add anything else', writes Rubruck in the final sentences of his report to the French King.

On his journey out he is led before Baatu. 'So we stood before him for as long as it takes to say a *Miserere mei, Deus*, and everyone remained in complete silence.' Meanwhile Rubruck could study the inside of the tent: throne, men and women, furnishings – near the entrance there was always a bench with mare's milk on it, and here there were great gold and silver jewelled beakers. 'Baatu watched us carefully, and we him . . . At last he permitted me to speak. Our guide then told us, to kneel and speak. I knelt on one knee as one does before a human presence. Then he insisted that I go down on both knees, which I did, as I didn't want to make difficulties over it.' Rubruck worded the beginning of his speech in the form of a prayer, for which one would kneel. He expressed fundamental Christian truths, but was aware that his hearer was not very receptive to the foreign message. Baatu received the words 'whoever does not believe, will be damned' with a calm smile, 'and the other Mongols began to clap, to taunt us; and my interpreter became so terrified that I had to tell him not to be afraid'.

Rubruck had several talks with the Great Khan. It is clear from his account that he succeeded in winning the respect of Mangu Khan by his open, persuasive manner; he expressly justified in a sermon the right of the poor to take food to eat; he testified to the Christian way of peace and to the poverty laid down by his monastic order, and lived accordingly. He gave back valuable presents or immediately gave them to the poor, and he tried to effect reconciliation among the feuding members of different Christian sects at the Great Khan's court.

Like other travellers – Battuta for example – Rubruck experienced the difficulty of not knowing for months, what the Great Khan intended to do with him; to stay or go could only be done with the express permission of the ruler. In a final interview Rubruck hoped to get his agreement to a further journey. After much consideration Mangu Khan left the decision open, but dismissed Rubruck with friendly words and a gesture of peace: ' "You plan a long journey, see that you have provisions, so that you may return strengthened to your homeland." He ordered a drink to be handed to me, and then I went from his sight and appeared no more before him. If I had possessed the power like Moses to perform a miracle, perhaps he would have bowed.'

Marco Polo

Marco Polo's *Il Milione* – a modern mixture of travel guide, fact and fiction – is in three parts. A long introduction tells of the journey of his father and uncle to the court of the Great Khan, of their return journey as the latter's envoys to the Pope, of a more recent expedition to the Mongols, on which they took Marco with them, and of their return after fourteen years. The main part describes the provinces, towns and countryside of the Mongolian empire from west to east, then south-east Asia and India, which Marco Polo got to know on the long journey home. A third part gives information about Russia and other areas. Woven into the account is information which merchants in towns such as Venice, Genoa and Florence would find useful, details about China and India, about travel routes, trading posts and goods on offer, places and people.

Difficulties over status and language, with which Rubruck had had to contend, did not arise for the Polos: they were welcomed as honoured merchants at the court of the Great Khan, who sent messengers to meet them forty days in advance. Marco quickly learnt the Mongol language, won the confidence of the Great Khan and travelled for many years on his behalf throughout the empire. There was no question of him trading himself; but he highlights an interesting detail of ancient trading methods, which could be summed up by saying: rulers do not trade, they merely exchange gifts. On their first journey to the Mongols the elder Polos were honourably received by Barca, an under-khan in present-day southern Russia. 'The two brothers gave him all the treasures they had with them. Barca received them with delight and was extremely pleased with them, and gave them double the value in return.'

There were various points particularly noticed by travellers in the empire. Rubruck, Battuta and Marco Polo all remarked how well the messenger service and transmission of news was organised by the Mongols. Along

Marco Polo setting out from Venice.

important routes, Marco Polo writes, a messenger would find a staging-post with guesthouse every twenty-five to thirty miles (in sparsely populated areas every thirty-five to forty miles). 'In this guesthouse there would be good large beds, with soft silk sheets; every comfort would be offered to high officials.' Even kings were suitably accommodated in such post-houses. Freshly rested and well-equipped horses would be at the disposal of the authorised envoys who travelled through. Marco Polo considered these arrangements appropriate for so great an empire: the central authority had to be quickly informed and able to communicate decisions speedily.

In the Mongolian empire envoys were distinguished by different tokens. Gold tablets stood for special authority and the emperor's protection and guaranteed free escorts and lodging. The Polos were sometimes given such tablets, 'on which was written that they might go everywhere freely in his [the Great Khan's] empire and that everything necessary for the journey and for overnight lodgings must be put at the disposal of themselves and their men.' A tablet with a falcon was the sign of mounted messengers. When they received an order they 'bandaged their bodies, and bound their heads, and rode off at a gallop and rode and rode for twenty-five miles to the first post, where they were given two fresh saddled horses', and so on, without resting, for two hundred and fifty miles a day or in exceptional circumstances three hundred miles. Whether such a feat was physically possible is questionable.

Between the main post-stations provided with horses there were imperial runners situated every three miles, who wore belts with bells on when they ran. The runners covered the three miles 'with the speed of wind'. You could hear them coming a long way off, and the next runner would get ready, take the message and run until he met a third runner after another three miles, and so on. These couriers covered a distance in twenty-four hours which would usually take ten days. Battuta reported that the same happened in India; here the runners were even faster than the mounted messengers, perhaps because they could make their way more easily across trackless country (jungle) or because they also ran at night. If one reckons the daily distance as thirty miles, in a day and night's run they did a speed of about eight miles an hour; this may have been the top speed for the Mongolian empire, but speeds of well over twelve miles an hour are reached today in five-thousand-metre races. The Mongolian relay-runners usually carried news, but sometimes fresh fruit for the Khan as well. They were exempt from taxes – you could say that they paid their dues by running, as many bondmen on the Rhine had to do by undertaking ship's service.

Marco Polo adds, concerning north Russia, that because of the amount of water and marsh there was no question of horses for the express messengers. 'At least forty dogs are kept at every staging-post, powerful animals, almost as large as donkeys.' The Tartars built sledges, which were drawn by six dogs each and could glide over the ice, marshes and mud without getting stuck; such sledges, Polo explains, were used in his homeland in winter when it rained and the roads were miry, to carry hay and straw. 'The Tartar sledges are covered with a bearskin, and the messenger sits on that.' The animals did not even need to be guided, as they knew the way to the next station; here new sledges and fresh animals would be ready waiting; the dogs returned to their home base each time.

In Venice the authorities kept a suspicious eye on the population; in Italian cities in the late Middle Ages strangers were carefully registered. Possibly the Chinese had set an example in this matter – just as Chinese ships with their oars manned by several men may have influenced the development of the Mediterranean galleys. It is clear anyway, that according to Marco Polo, the Chinese habit of keeping an eye on strangers and local inhabitants was 'worth adopting': every citizen put up over the door of his house the names of all those dwelling there, including all slaves and lodgers, and also the number of horses. The names of the dead or newly born were deleted or added. As a result the number of inhabitants in a town could easily be calculated. In Marco Polo's day it was particularly important for European towns to know the number of their inhabitants at times of crisis, for example during a siege, when scarce provisions had to be shared out. Anyone lodging strangers in China, gave written notice of a visitor's name and the date of his arrival; thus the Great Khan knew who had travelled through his territories in the course of a year. Marco Polo's final remark smacks of a more despotic age: 'A clever statesman will know how to use such information.'

Battuta adds to the information about intelligence gathering, control of strangers and levying of dues, details which show that in the highly civilised Islamic states the position fell far short of the ideals set by the Chinese. Battuta praised the China of his day as a country with an unusually high standard of public safety: even if one travelled alone for months one could safely take large sums of money with one. But he had reservations about the strict rules in the Chinese post-houses: the merchant had to give his money to the keeper of the hostelry, who would be responsible for it and buy provisions on behalf of his guest. 'If the latter wants a concubine, he gets him a slave, gives him a room to use with a door leading into the hostel and pays the expenses for both. The female slaves are only a small part of the bill.' The guest can also marry, if he wants to. 'To spend his money on loose living is quite another matter, however – there will be no chance of him being allowed to do that.' Every night all the guests who were staying there were listed by two officials; the list would be sealed and the door locked. At daybreak the officials would reappear, call everyone by name and check the register. Then the travellers would be taken to the next staging-post; there the manager had to check that they had all arrived safely; the guide would be responsible for anyone missing.

Warrants would be put out for criminals, with text *and* picture; anyone resembling the portrait would be taken into custody. Ships were only allowed to leave when archers, slaves and seamen had been listed by name by the authorities; on their return the latter would compare the list with the ship's crew; if the master of the junk could not prove that anyone missing had died, or had fled or was missing for some other good reason, he would be taken into custody. Besides the list of passengers the ship's captain had to give a detailed description of all the goods on board. Then all could go ashore, and customs men would check the declaration. If they found anything that had not been declared, 'the fisc would take possession of the junk and everything in it'. Battuta declares angrily that he has never met such an injustice in any other country, either heathen or Moslem. The worst he has to say on this subject concerns India: there customs offences used to be punished with an elevenfold fine.

Marco Polo and Battuta found many Chinese accomplishments worthy of emulation: travel there was facilitated by means of long, wide stone bridges, paved roads, over which one could ride or walk 'with dry feet, I mean, without getting dirty'; main roads were lined by tall trees which provided shade for the traveller; as the trees could be seen from a long way off they helped travellers find their way. Polo was also much impressed by the public hot baths: 'The people enjoy going there several times a month, for they have a high standard of cleanliness.' In ship's cabins, merchants can 'rest comfortably': according to Battuta there were even ships in China, in which the cabins had their own private lavatories. He praises rulers for having had wells dug in dry areas in India to help the traveller, and for having had hospitals built in Arabic countries. He is aware of the value of places of refuge: hospices in many Arabic lands and, on the Malabar Coast (south-west India), the 'Sanctuary Gate' on the border between states.

Marco Polo and Battuta describe sea raiders and storms at sea from their own experience or from the tales of others. According to both, those sailing across the Indian Ocean would only meet 'humane' pirates, who were 'only' interested in the ship and its cargo. Marco Polo seems almost to have sympathy for the pirates operating from the west coast of India, and sees them rather as partakers in a successful business enterprise than as criminals: they take their families on board, and travel in convoys, one ship behind the other at a distance of about five miles; in this way twenty ships make a chain up to a hundred miles long, and they have control over a wide expanse of sea. If one of the pirates sees a likely prize, they signal from ship to ship with flares and then all descend on it together to overpower their prey. 'Merchants and crew are left unharmed and they call out to them "Go and get more wares! If we are lucky we too will profit from them!" ' Marco Polo probably dealt in pearls and precious stones and knew that these, and also money, could be concealed in clothing when the need arose, in a hem or nailed between the leather soles of shoes; if one thought that one's clothes would also be taken – Battuta once lost everything including his trousers: pearls and gems, clothing and food – gems could be hidden in bodily orifices or swallowed before one was captured. Pirates who worked from Gujarat in north-west India had caught on to this trick and were called 'perfidious' and 'evil' by Marco Polo. Possibly he is speaking from his own bitter experience: merchants who fell into their power were forced to drink a frightful brew of sea water mixed with tamarind pods. 'They vomited at once and regurgitated the entire contents of their stomachs. The pirates collected up the vomit and raked through it for pearls and precious stones.' The Christian Portuguese on their trading, piratical and terrorising sorties in the Indian Ocean were not as 'humane' with their victims as the 'heathen' pirates were according to Polo and Battuta. 'And we burnt the ship and all its people to powder on 1 October [1502] . . . [End of October]: We took the ship and set fire to it and burnt many of the king's subjects.' Such remarks are repeatedly included in the records of an unknown seafarer, who at the beginning of the sixteenth century sailed in a Portuguese ship off the East African and Indian coasts.

Marco Polo was given an almost idyllic description of the Indian solution to shipwrecks. As soon as the wind got dangerously high, ship's passengers put any valuables such as pearls and gemstones, and also clothing and food, in leather bladders taken expressly for the purpose. Then all the bladders were tied together to make a kind of raft. If the ship sank, the crew could hang on to the bladders. 'Sooner or later, after a few days, depending on the current, they would be driven to the shore, even if they were far out at sea, at a distance of two-hundred miles. If they wanted to eat or drink while they were still at sea, they could take food or drink out of the bladders, then blow up the bladders.' So they saved themselves, even if their ship was lost. Several points about this description are open to doubt however: even taking into consideration that the Indian Ocean is warmer than the North Sea, not many shipwrecked mariners would have had the strength to remain in the sea for days; leather bladders eventually let in water, so that they begin to sink. Nevertheless the air-filled bladders perhaps offered more hope to those who were shipwrecked than the boats on European ships, which, even if they were seaworthy, could take only a few people on board.

One of Battuta's experiences was of a hallucination – probably conjured up by a mirage. In the South China Sea the ship's crew suddenly saw themselves threatened by a mountain, which all who knew the area said did not exist there; all they knew was that his 'haven' would immediately destroy the ship and anyone who saw it. The men's reaction was similar to that of the Christian seafarers described by Columbus a hundred and fifty years later. 'Everyone took refuge in humble prayers, and did penance, and the people confessed their sins again and again. We prostrated ourselves before God in prayer, and begged His prophets to intercede for us. The merchants pledged alms, which I entered myself in a register . . . I saw the sailors cry and bid one another farewell.' Battuta ends his description of the mass hallucination with the words: 'But then God granted us a favourable wind, which took us in the other direction away from it [the rock]. We could no longer see it and didn't learn its true shape.'

On another occasion Battuta was in a terrible storm on the Indian Ocean. He saw how a fellow passenger covered his head with his cloak and pretended to be asleep. When the danger had passed, he questioned this pilgrim about his behaviour. 'When the storm broke I kept my eyes open; I wanted to see if the angels who take men's souls had come. As I couldn't see them, I said "Glory be to God. If any of us were going to drown, they would have come to fetch our souls." ' In spite of keeping a careful lookout, the pilgrim saw no angels, 'before God saved us'. During a storm on the Black Sea, Battuta's cabin-mate came below from on deck with the terse bidding, 'I commend you to God.'

Ibn Battuta

A PILGRIMAGE TO MECCA

Very few people in the Middle Ages were as widely travelled as Battuta. He systematically covered the ground between Tangier and Java, Spain and the Niger, southern Russia and Somaliland. Between whiles he made continual pilgrimages to Mecca. As a scholar he was able to profit from the goodwill of influential people in the countries he visited, and bore recommendations from one sultan, holy man or scholar to another. Ibn Juzayy, who wrote down Battuta's memoirs, says of him in the foreword: 'He embraced the world with an enquiring mind, and travelled through its cities with open eyes; he studied the differences between peoples and examined the lives of Arabs and non-Arabs.'

On 13 June 1325 Battuta, then twenty-one years old, set out from Tangier to make the prescribed Moslem pilgrimage to Mecca. On the way he visited ascetics and potentates, saw all the sights worth seeing and seized every opportunity he could to make excursions. He was not at all worried that he had to travel down the Nile again because it was not possible to cross the Red Sea owing to a state of war. He then made a detour from Cairo via Damascus to Mecca. Below are some of his remarks concerning Damietta, caravanserai, the Church of the Holy Sepulchre and the pilgrimage to Mecca.

In western accounts the mistrust of Islamic rulers towards Christian merchants and pilgrims is often stressed. But even professed Moslems had to contend with rigid controls. Battuta writes of Damietta, which lies on an easterly arm of the Nile and was captured by Louis the Pious in 1249/50, and which in Battuta's day was an important marine centre: 'No one who enters the town may subsequently leave it without the governor's permission. Influential people carry with them a pass with a seal affixed, to show to the gatekeeper; others have the seal stamped on their forearm, and must show that.'

For thousands of years the narrow strip of land between Asia and Africa was the carefully guarded doorway to Egypt. On the way from Cairo to Gaza one caravanserai – which were called *funduk* by Battuta (from which the name 'Fondaco dei Tedeschi' in Venice comes), and *khan* – follows another. Single buildings were grouped round a walled courtyard, which was usually square with a single entrance; animals and merchandise were lodged on the ground floor and the travellers slept above. According to Battuta, outside the caravanserai there would be a well, and a shop in which people could buy what they needed for themselves and their animals. One of these caravanserai, Qatiya, also served as a customs and control post; many officials, clerks and notaries were in charge of levying the alms tax due according to the value of goods, a sum which brought the state a considerable income. As Battuta noted, no one could pass this control point between Egypt and Syria or back again without a valid pass; the check served to protect travellers' property and to ward off enemy spies. At nightfall, the sand round the caravanserai was swept clean; if the commandant of the border post found any traces in the sand the next morning, he told Arabs to find whoever had left these tracks; the wrongdoer would be unfailingly caught and punished by the commandant 'after careful consideration'. A similar safety strip is carefully swept clear several times a day on the Egyptian-Israeli border today. Bedouins can tell from any marks on this strip, if an attempt is being made to cross the border illegally.

On his way through Palestine, Battuta also visited many holy places which are common to Jews, Christians and Moslems, for instance Abraham's grave in Hebron. He writes of the Church of the Holy Sepulchre, honoured only by Christians, that the Christians lie when they say it contains the grave of Jesus. He continues fairmindedly however: 'All who come to the Church of the Holy Sepulchre as pilgrims are liable to a tax set up by the Moslems and suffer various indignities most unwillingly.'

In Damascus Battuta joined a caravan going to Mecca; he proudly describes the distinguished people with whom he travelled. As Chaucer shows in his Prologue to *The Canterbury Tales*, one could meet people from all walks of life on a pilgrimage. The pilgrims gathered at a spot about nine miles south of Damascus; they were now under strict discipline and had to obey the 'pilgrimage commander'. This office of 'Amir al-Hajj' was much respected. The commander, after whom the caravan was named each year, had to ensure the safety of the pilgrims from attack on the way to and from Mecca. As Battuta writes, experienced commanders adopted a military-style discipline; Bedouins were given no chance to attack and rob the caravan.

In Basra (about seventy miles south of Damascus) the caravan rested for four days; the pilgrims could provide themselves with travel necessities. And those who had not finished their business in Damascus could catch up with them; the Koran expressly allowed pilgrims to Mecca to undertake business on the way. The route continued in an arc – first to the south and then to the south-east – following the watering places. Battuta recounts episodes from the life of Mohammed in connection with the places he visited, and historical anecdotes up to the time of the crusades; sometimes he strews his text with aphorisms, for instance of the desert south of Ma'an 'Whoever goes there, is lost; whoever returns from there, is reborn.' When the hot simoom (desert wind), which dried up all the water sources, blew, it was said that once all the pilgrims at one place and most of those at another place died painfully of thirst.

A caravan would repeatedly stop for a few days' rest on the way; water containers would be replenished, and the camels would drink their fill, so that men and beasts were ready for the next stage of the journey. The caravan would stop for instance for four nights at Al-Ela (about half-way between Tebuk and Medina). Christian merchants from Syria could travel out as far as this but no farther; pilgrims could get provisions and other things they needed from them; in Al-Ela they could wash their clothes and leave anything behind that was not essential for the last lap of the journey. Battuta said: 'The inhabitants of this village are trustworthy.' He mentions a similar 'depot' mid-way between Mecca and Baghdad; there were clearly more of these useful places than are recorded in the sources, even on the Christian pilgrims' ways.

After a stay of four nights in Medina, a high-spot of the pilgrimage, the caravan went on towards Mecca. The pilgrimage now began in earnest for Battuta, as could be seen from the fact that he changed his clothes. He took off his tailored clothes, bathed, put on the seamless robe of sanctification, intoned the appropriate prayers with words and gestures and dedicated himself to the great pilgrimage; in his exaltation he cried again and again 'Labbaika Allahumma' (O God, I am your servant). After further exhausting days, the caravan finally reached its destination. Battuta describes the famous sights of Mecca: mosques, minarets, cemeteries, the surrounding mountains, the observance of ceremonies and festive seasons, the inhabitants and their good qualities; he records details about Mohammed, scenes from the lives of other holy men, anecdotes from the lives of pilgrims; but above all he concentrates on describing the holy shrines and particularly the Kaaba and the rites and actions of the pilgrims, which we need not go into here.

Battuta does not go back straight away – that would have gone against his declared aim of never travelling over the same ground twice if he could help it – but joins another caravan; the commander had paid for a place in a litter for him as far as Baghdad (over nine hundred miles as the crow flies!). Certain remarks of Battuta's indicate that well-to-do Moslems were travelling with this caravan: a great number of luxury goods were taken with them and every kind of food and fruit; they could even travel in the cool of night, as torches were carried ahead of the camels and litters; and finally several camels were loaded with water containers, provisions, medicaments and other things the poor pilgrims might need, which were not mentioned in connection with the Damascus-Mecca caravan. At every halt hot dishes were prepared for the pilgrims in great brass pans. Bedouins had presented themselves on the way to offer provisions to the travellers. When the caravan finally drew near the Euphrates, the people there hurried forward with meal, bread, dried dates and fruit, 'and the participants congratulated themselves on having arrived safely'.

INDIA

Of Battuta's countless other journeys, his stay in India is particularly interesting. He won the confidence of the Sultan Mohammed, whom he describes as follows: 'This King is of all men the one who most loves to give presents and –

to shed blood. At his door you will always find a poor man who will be richly rewarded or a living man who will be put to death.' Battuta shows that he was well aware of the situation: he describes Mohammed's concern for the poor and homeless as exemplary, but realises that he is paying dearly for the benefits he enjoys at the Sultan's court. He knew that Mohammed did not hesitate to have individuals or whole groups of people tortured and killed. An imprisoned man grew sick, and could not defend himself; 'the rats ate his fingers, and his eyes, and he died.' Detractors were flayed alive as traitors – the skin was cut from their living bodies, stuffed with straw and hung up in public. Battuta does not faint at the sight of such horrors – as he nearly did at the burning of a widow – but looking back he gives many a heavy sigh. 'God have mercy on him!', 'God preserve us from such a death!' Like other distinguished visitors, Battuta has to acknowledge the Sultan's orders in writing, so that he cannot claim ignorance at a later date. He feels Mohammed's displeasure towards himself growing, would like to get away, but – like many another traveller – makes the bitter discovery that his departure is not permitted. Finally to his surprise he is entrusted with the leadership of a delegation to China, which fails, but enables him to be master of his own fate once more.

From among the details of his further travels, it is interesting to compare Battuta's attitude to love and sexual matters with similar utterances by Marco Polo. Both authors and their scribes possess the gift of giving rein to sensual and titillating descriptions of the women of exotic lands, Marco Polo being rather more refined in this matter than Battuta. The Christian Polo draws a discreet veil over his own experiences in the field, but gives an account of a broad spectrum of sexual attitudes, and describes the sexual freedoms of girls and married women as well as the proving of unmarried girls in countries where the virginity of brides was insisted upon. His account of the women of Tibet – a country which he probably did not visit himself – can be taken as an example of the many descriptions of this sort. Girls were pressed upon travellers, who might do with them what they wished, but could not take them away with them. The traveller would leave a keepsake with the young woman with whom he had enjoyed himself all night, 'a piece of jewelry or some other keepsake, so that when she got married in the future she could prove the experience she had. It is usual for these girls to wear more than twenty such ornaments round their necks, to show how many men have already taken their pleasure with them. The woman with the richest necklace is the best and most desired; the Tibetans say she is endowed as no other.' After marriage the wives were held in esteem as elsewhere, no one touched another's wife and unfaithfulness was considered a flagrant sin. Summing up, Polo – who with his editor gladly returns to the subject – says it was worth while describing these marriage customs to his readers, 'and it would not be out of place for a lad of sixteen to twenty to visit the region'. It was at precisely this age that Marco himself visited the court of the Great Khan.

Battuta speaks openly of his love life. One would find it very difficult to know exactly how many women he had during his travels. They included concubines and 'pretty slaves', whom he bought on the way and then lost from sight when he continued on his journey, as he did wives and children; he then writes coolly, that he does not know what has become of this or that person. The women of the Indian race of Malays, he reminisces, are 'exceptionally beautiful and famed for their willingness in love and for the great degree of voluptuousness they awake in one, as are the women of the Mahratta and the Maldives.' Battuta often refers to aphrodisiacs. He was not totally convinced about pills which a fakir had prepared for an Indian sultan. The latter had eaten them, 'to increase his enjoyment in love. Among the ingredients were iron filings. Their effect pleased the sultan; he ate more of them than was necessary and died.' Battuta preferred natural means. He praises the coconut for its strength-giving qualities and 'wonderful' power to increase potency. He notices that the inhabitants of the Maldive Islands feed mainly on coconuts and a certain kind of fish. This gives them 'a striking and unequalled power in the practice of sexual intercourse. The islanders achieve astounding feats. I myself had four legitimate wives in this country, apart from concubines. I was potent for them all every day and besides that spent the whole night with whichever of them whose turn it was; I lived like this for a year and a half.' The relative importance of this statement is clear from the fact that it is included in a passage on 'the trees of the Maldives' and Battuta immediately goes on – the statement about his potency is admittedly included in a digression about coconuts – to discuss oranges, lemons and other delicious crops which flourish on the Maldive Islands.

Rubruck, Marco Polo and Battuta immeasurably enriched westerners' knowledge of Asia. Rubruck had prepared himself for his journey to the court of the Great Khan by studying the classical authors. He checked the statements of Isidore of Seville as he went along – from his own observations and by repeatedly questioning contemporaries who knew the country. Below are three examples of the many results of his research. In his report to the French King he states that the antique 'Seres' is identical with the medieval 'Cathay' (China), that the Caspian Sea is an inland sea and not – as Isidore and others claimed – part of the ocean which the ancients held flowed round the whole inhabited earth. Rubruck also made enquiries about the human monsters described by Isidore. His attitude bears testimony to the weight of tradition that would continue for centuries more to weigh on European explorers (and those who illustrated their accounts); often the statements of eye-witnesses or those who were present carry less weight than the 'authorities'. 'They tell me that such a thing has never been seen, and so we wondered whether it could be true.' Marco Polo had only been able to pick up fragments of scholarly learning before he set out for Asia. But he took a valuable element of the classical–western education with him on his travels: a keen sense of observation and a boundless interest in the widest sense in countries and people. Battuta and Marco Polo describe – the latter more frequently and at greater length than the former – the riches of Asia: it often seems in Marco Polo's writings that jewels and pearls, gold and ivory, precious spices and woods can be got almost effortlessly in the 'wonderland' of India. Marco Polo is distinguished by a great openness to the new and by the occasional wholesale recognition of Asiatic superiority. But there is also another side to him: he writes in connection with the legendary account of a bishop martyred by Moslems: 'It would make mockery of everything that is honourable, if Saracens had power over Christians.'

In the travel accounts of Rubruck, Marco Polo and Battuta a great deal of space is given to the descriptions of dangers: men saw themselves threatened in the countries the three travelled through by sickness and shipwreck, pirates and unpredictable potentates. And yet such accounts had the effect of awakening men's desire for action – their striving for power, by extending their rule over the 'heathen', their striving for possessions as for example by forcing Moslem middlemen out of the spice trade, and their lust for enjoyment. The descriptions which Marco Polo and Battuta gave of the sexual prowess of women in distant lands, were bound to arouse all the more strongly the desires of men whose sexuality had been suppressed by their Christian upbringing.

It was only logical for Columbus to consult Marco Polo's work when preparing for the journey that would lead him to the westerly route to India. The men who, two hundred years after Marco Polo, and a hundred years after Battuta, set out from Europe to 'discover' the world, were also searching for power, material possessions, and pleasure.

EDUCATIONAL JOURNEYS

A 'library visit' to Chartres

'When I left, my abbot gave me only a packhorse. Without any money, or clothes to change into, or any other necessities, I came to Orbais.' The Benedictine monk Richer of Reims, in his history of the West Frankish kingdom, includes the account of a journey which he made in March 991 from Reims to Chartres. Richer had met, one day when he was 'by chance' in the town of Reims, a horseman from Chartres, and, as a chronicler interested in the events of the day, he immediately asked him who he was, in whose service, what he was doing there and from whence he came. The stranger had readily replied that he was the envoy of the churchman Heribrand in Chartres and that he wanted to speak to Richer. The latter told him who he was and led him aside; he read the letter the messenger was carrying, which invited him to go to Chartres; he would be able to read the material he wanted in the cathedral library there.

As a Benedictine Richer had to obey the monastic rule of remaining in one place; as a scholar he wanted to study the writings of Hippocrates of Kos, one of the great medical authorities, whose oath is still taken by doctors today. Many classical texts were only available in a single, jealously guarded copy. Anyone who wanted to read them had to travel to do so, and those who valued the writings of such authors were sometimes rather like those who honoured the saints in that if they felt the original texts (or relics) were not properly revered by their owners, there was a great temptation to take them away with them.

Richer appears to have obtained permission to travel without any difficulty. He had few preparations to make; a boy, who would look after his small amount of luggage, was soon found. But he had to allow at least four days to a week for the journey which today, if there is not too much motorway traffic, can be done in under two hours (140 miles in a direct line).

On the evening of the first day, after a ride of about thirty miles, Richer and his companions enjoyed the hospitality of a friendly Benedictine monastery in Orbais, an island of tranquillity in the wilderness; the fewer commercial lodgings there were, the greater was the warmth of spontaneous welcome, and not only among Benedictines, as Richer's companions soon discovered. The next morning they set out in the direction of Meaux, where there was supposed to be a bridge over the Marne. 'But as I struggled with my two companions along the winding woodland ways, our difficulties increased.' They got lost at crossroads and made a long detour (no one thought of putting up and maintaining waymarks in the almost impenetrable forests). The packhorse got slower and slower, and finally collapsed and died; sixty miles in two days had been too much for it. There was now no animal to carry the baggage; the boy, who had never been on such a long and arduous journey before, could only lie apathetically there after the death of his horse. To add to their misfortunes it was pouring with rain, and night fell. Richer left the boy behind with the luggage, told him what to say to any passers-by who questioned him, and not to go to sleep however tired he was. Thieves and bandits had to be reckoned with; the messenger from Chartres was armed.

Richer rode on with the envoy towards Meaux; their hazardous crossing of the Marne bridge there has already been described (p. 108 above). It was quite dark by the time he had discovered the way to his brother monks. Amidst the warm welcome he did not forget his lad: he sent the messenger, still armed, back with the horses and the man managed to get across the bridge for the second time. After wandering around for a while and calling out repeatedly he found the boy long after midnight; the two decided not to tempt fate for a third time on the bridge. After a whole day without food, they were allowed to sleep in 'a man's hut . . . but were not given anything to eat.'

Richer had a sleepless night worrying about his companions; he was relieved when they both turned up at the monastery in the morning, safe but starving. They and the horses were fed. Richer left the boy, for whom there was no horse, behind at the monastery; then he rode on with the messenger to Chartres; arrived there safely, he sent back the horses and had the boy fetched from Meaux. After his safe arrival, Richer could study the aphorisms of Hippocrates in peace. 'But because I only found medical diagnoses there and was not satisfied with simply learning about the illnesses,' he asked Heribrand, his kind and learned friend, to read a further book with him; for Heribrand knew 'the methods of pharmaceutics, botany and surgery'.

For centuries men like Richer travelled eagerly in search of knowledge and scholarship. They wanted to see manuscripts, listen to teachers, seek advice, get to know foreign lands and places, distant monuments and works of art. The casualness with which such journeys are mentioned, indicates that they were quite usual. In Bede's *Ecclesiastical History* there is repeated mention of this or that learned man going to Rome, or someone travelling through Italy and Gaul to learn and pray, or of another whose bishopric had been plundered by enemies accepting invitations from various places to teach church music. Bede also makes it clear that men were not the only ones to make educational journeys abroad; in his day girls from noble English families were sent to Gaul to be educated. And women were equally sought as oracles by people from far and near; Bede writes of the Abbess Hilda, that the fame of her wisdom was so great that even kings and princes asked for her advice. If it was a case of satisfying scholarly curiosity or finding an answer to life's mysteries, people were prepared to put up with the deprivations and dangers of long journeys.

Wandering scholars

In the early Middle Ages, the foundations of scholarly life were laid at monastery schools; in the ninth to tenth centuries episcopal schools joined them in attracting leading scholars in the west, and in the eleventh century the number of centres of learning visited by wandering scholars increased – there were for example the 'advanced schools' in the shadow of the cathedrals of Chartres and Reims. It is said of Benno of Osnabrück that in 1040 'after the habit of students' (*studentium more*) he travelled around for a while and visited other towns, and also sought to make the acquaintance of influential and noble men there. Such efforts often bore fruit. Benno was successful and was raised to the bishopric of Osnabrück; in the fourteenth, fifteenth and sixteenth centuries there were eight bishops of Passau, four of Meissen and three of Dorpat who were graduates of the University of Bologna.

Universities originally arose from gatherings of students and/or teachers, or grew from existing schools. The name 'university' has nothing to do with education; it means the brotherly meeting of men with similar interests. Besides the *universitas scholarum* there was the *universitas civium*, where citizens of a town could meet, and the brotherhoods of merchants. Unlike the pilgrim groups, the groups of citizens and students were more permanent; if they became institutions they formed a separate element in a society stratified by class, with its hierarchical upper and lower orders; with equality and self-government, they introduced an important new element into the history of Europe. Scholars met – whatever their rank or means – as equals, chose their own rector and enjoyed special privileges, often granted by church and temporal rulers. These rights benefited not only the university as a whole but also gave individual students an enviable status. Enjoying the protection of the Church, they were exempt for up to seven years from local regulations; this privilege of self-jurisdiction was of immense value in a world in which 'short shrift' was often given, as François Villon found in the fourteenth century: sentenced to death several times, he managed to gain a reprieve each time because a longer interval was granted to members of the university between sentence and execution than to ordinary citizens. At the university differences between clerics and laymen were waived; brave new ideas could be brought forth in an atmosphere of relative intellectual freedom. Luther's theses of 1517, igniting a spirit of disputation, form one of the great turning-points between the Middle Ages and the modern era.

Travelling was just as dangerous for students as for the rest of the population. They could seldom obtain concrete and detailed information about their journey, or advance warning of special dangers. As men of good family, enjoying the protection of the Church, students were regarded as subjects for extortion. As they were often still children when they came to a university, they frequently suffered from their own inexperience; for this reason too students often travelled in small groups of two to ten people; those who could afford to do so, would often send a servant or tutor to the place of learning with their son. Begging letters from students were (and are) often exaggerated; they knew that they could wring tears – and further funds – from those at home, if they painted their own situation in the blackest possible terms. But traditional modes of speech, legends and records all give us added clues to the life of wandering scholars.

Haec et plus benedicat Dominus (the Lord bless this and more) was the traditional reply when students on their way to the schools went begging and had the impression that the donor could have given them more. A scene from the legend of St Nicholas tells how the saint brought back to life some students whom a landlord had killed and pickled. The Emperor Frederick Barbarossa spoke with some emotion of students in a document of 1158, of importance for the history of western universities: 'Become homeless because of their love of learning, poor instead of rich, they dispossess themselves of their rights, expose their life to every kind of danger and often suffer – which is very hard to bear – unwarranted bodily injury from the lowest of men.' Barbarossa therefore granted important privileges 'to all scholars who are travelling abroad in the cause of learning . . . through whose knowledge the world will be enlightened and the life of citizens enriched'. They, and their servants, were to be allowed to 'travel unmolested' to the places where scholarly studies were carried on, and to be 'allowed to live there' unharmed; they were not to be punished for the wrongs of a fellow countryman, 'which we have heard, has been done from time to time according to a devious custom'; quarrels with scholars were not to be settled in the ordinary courts, but by their master or the bishop of the town.

If the authorities considered it expedient to interfere with the autonomy of the university, there was a rapid 'exodus': students and teachers preferred to leave rather than give up their – often hard-won – freedoms. It often happened that such exoduses were from the oldest universities – from Oxford to Cambridge, from Paris to Angers, Bologna to Padua and Arezzo. Many groups were decimated by war, disease, lack of funds, or strife between members of a university. Changes and departures by teachers and students were in any case brought about by the great mobility of the population, and the unassumingness of those hungry for education, and were facilitated by the very modest infrastructure of the university establishments. At the beginning of the twelfth century Abelard fell out with his teachers, gathered scholars round him and held lectures in the solitude of his monastery. No special facilities were needed; 'lectures' were even held in Paris in houses on the Seine bridges. On the other hand at well-founded or enlarged and later privileged universities, well-endowed chairs were set up to attract teachers from abroad; Charles IV put the houses of exiled or slain Jews at the disposal of the students of the University of Prague founded by him in 1348. The exodus of teachers and students, as from Prague to Leipzig for example, was also made easier because other towns were glad to have a university if it would bring an increase in status and trade.

A wave of new foundations formed a network of universities throughout Europe in the thirteenth, fourteenth and fifteenth centuries. Just as master builders introduced into their homeland new churches in the 'Gothic' style which they had seen during their student days in the Ile de France, founders of colleges followed the model of the 'old' universities, which they had got to know on their travels or during their studies abroad. Charles IV 'wished the University of Prague to be regulated and run in every respect according to the rule and customs of the University of Paris, at which the King himself had once studied in his youth.'

The more universities were founded (in the Holy Roman Empire in the second half of the fourteenth century for example at Prague, Vienna, Heidelberg and Cologne), the less need there was for students to make long journeys; the founding of colleges was not only a means of furthering the development of a country but also an attempt to dampen the desire to travel (taking money abroad) and to put a brake on undesirable ideas about freedom by influencing the content of studies and the appointment of teachers.

In spite of this, by the end of the Middle Ages thousands of students were on the road. It has been estimated that the number entered as university students increased sixfold between 1400 and 1500 (from about 4,800 to 27,000). Even if only every fourth or fifth scholar changed his place of learning once during the course of his studies, it can be seen that students contributed to the unification of the West. They spread books and new ideas, such as Roman law, throughout the whole of Europe.

Richer, in the tenth century, was far from being the only one with a thirst for knowledge and the desire to get to know the authors of antiquity. The humanists in the later Middle Ages made extensive researches into source material, carried on lengthy 'international' correspondences and made long journeys to further and complete their studies.

Petrarch: a life of wandering

In the mid-fourteenth century, Petrarch, one of the greatest of the humanists, wrote, looking back, that he had 'spent his whole life up to this point in wandering'.

He became acquainted with the dangers of travel at a very early age. As a seven-month-old baby he was carried by a strong young man from Arezzo, from whence his father had been banned and where Petrarch was born, through Tuscany to Pisa: 'The young man carried the child wrapped in linen, hanging from a thorn-stick in his right hand, in order not to harm the small body by holding it.' When the man rode through the Arno, 'he was thrown by his stumbling horse – and was almost drowned himself in the rushing water while trying to save the precious burden entrusted to him.' As a seven-year-old while on a journey from Pisa to Marseilles, Petrarch was nearly killed in a snowstorm.

In August 1333 Petrarch sent his impressions of a journey through France and Germany in a letter to Cardinal Giovanni Colonna. The letter shows that meeting foreign people and seeing foreign places did not necessarily reinforce prejudices and arouse animosity, such as that expressed in the pilgrim's guide to Santiago. In Aachen Petrarch visited the hot baths, as Dürer would do almost two hundred years later. Then he travelled to Cologne, 'famed for its site and its river, famous also for its people'. He cannot conceal his astonishment at the civilised nature of the 'land of barbarians', the beauty of the town, the nobility of the men and the grace of the women.

Petrarch is present at a 'marvellous spectacle' on Midsummer's Day, which he describes enthusiastically to his friend the cardinal. He saw a great crowd of women on the river bank. 'I stood still in my tracks . . . Good God! What figures, what faces, and the way they carried themselves! Anyone might have been consumed with love, who had not come there with a heart already forfeited.' He watched the 'unbelievable proceedings' from an uncrowded vantage point. Many of the women had wreathed themselves with sweet-smelling herbs and pushed back their sleeves above the elbow. 'And thus they washed their white hands and arms in a happy throng in the flowing water and in their foreign tongue murmured entrancingly to one another as they did so.' He reiterates Cicero's discovery 'that all men, when they hear unknown languages, are as if deaf and dumb'. But there was no lack of attentive interpreters to explain the meaning of the rite to him: the women were convinced that by this age-old custom, everything that in the course of the year 'might threaten them would be washed away by this purifying washing in the river on this day, and after that they would meet only with happiness'. Petrarch muses dispassionately, envying such simplicity, 'Oh how happy are you, you dwellers by the Rhine, if this washes away your troubles; neither the Po nor Tiber has ever been able to wash away ours. You send your sorrows over to Britain ferried by the Rhine, and we would gladly send ours over to the Africans and Illyrians. But we have, as all can see, more sluggish rivers.'

Petrarch remembers his friend's request to tell him every detail of what he sees and hears, 'in writing, just as I am accustomed to do by word of mouth'; he was neither to spare his pen nor to strive specially for brevity or elegance of expression. Petrarch agreed; a letter should not glorify the sender but inform the recipient. Despite that he gives only a few glimpses of the further course of his journey. On 29 June he left Cologne, and on 9 August he finished the letter in Lyon. In the Rhineland he had been so laid low by bad sunburn and the dust, that he soon longed for the cool of the Alps. Although there was a war on, he travelled through the 'dark and frightening Ardennes forest', but was lucky; 'God', he quotes an old saying, 'looks after the carefree.'

Three years later Petrarch is writing to another friend, Francesco Dionigi, an Augustinian monk and professor of theology at the Sorbonne in Paris, about climbing Mont Ventoux in Provence. This must be one of the first descriptions in the Middle Ages of the ascent of a mountain for other than purely practical reasons; the reason Petrarch gives for doing so at the beginning of his letter is typical of his enquiring mind and that of his contemporaries – he takes it for granted that the Augustinian monk will also be interested – for many years he has wanted, 'to get to know this unusually high spot on the earth by seeing it with my own eyes'. The desire to prove facts by seeing them for oneself is also typical of the explorers and scientists of the age.

Petrarch's letter is larded with quotations and associations, with reminiscences about the mountain climbers of antiquity and the experiences of others; his description of climbing the mountain is in many places overlaid by meditations on man's journey on earth.

Petrarch had thought for a long time about who to take with him on the perilous ascent. 'One was too dilatory for me, another too indefatigable, this one too slow, that one too quick, another too heavy, or too merry, or too stupid, or cleverer than I liked.' Silence and noisiness, portliness and frailty, a cold indifference and warm enthusiasm cause him to ponder. 'All this, difficult as it is, can be borne with at home . . . but everything will be much more difficult on the way.' He finally decides to invite his younger, only brother, who accepts enthusiastically.

The brothers rest for a day at Malaucène, on the north side of the mountain, from where a road today leads to the summit. On 26 April they climb the 6,271 foot mountain, each accompanied by a servant, 'not without great difficulty. It is a steeply precipitous, almost unclimbable rock mass. However, as the poet rightly said: bold striving conquers all.' On the way they met an ancient shepherd, who tried his best to talk them out of their project: fifty years ago he had himself climbed 'the highest peak in just such a rush of youthful fire'; he had won only disappointment, weariness and clothes torn by the jagged rocks and thorny scrub; he had never heard of anyone else attempting it since. 'As he shouted this at us, our enthusiasm grew all the more fervent.' They left any unnecessary baggage behind with the shepherd. When the latter saw that they paid no attention to his warnings, he pointed out a steep path to the four of them with his finger, 'remembering many things as he did so and still sighing after us, when we had left him'.

At first impetuously, and then more slowly, the four climbed the mountain. The thirty-two-year-old Petrarch soon had to fight against exhaustion. He hopes to find a gentler, easier way to the top than the steep direct route chosen by his brother; he frequently gives in to the temptation to make long, useless detours. 'When the others were already high up, I was wandering through valleys where I couldn't see a more gentle ascent anywhere, but only made the way longer and tired myself out in the useless attempt.' Petrarch summoned up all his strength and caught up with his brother. Looking back, he draws general conclusions from his experience: 'The nature of things is not altered by man's spirit, and it is not possible for any living thing to reach the heights by going downhill.' Laughed at by his brother, he sinks down in a valley and muses on the symbolic meaning of his actions: life lies on a high peak which can only be reached by a narrow path. 'At the summit is the end of all things and the traveller's goal, to which our pilgrimage is directed.' Instead of informing the reader, as he had set out to do, about flora and fauna, rocks and view – Petrarch continues in a moralising vein: 'The way of earthly and base delights is easier, and, at first glance, appears more comfortable.'

Finally they reached the summit; possibly the old shepherd was not the only person Petrarch met on the way, because he writes that 'woodsmen' called the summit the 'little son'. The climbers rested on the plateau at the top. For a moment Petrarch is spellbound by the view; he stands there 'as if intoxicated by the unaccustomed draughts of air and the view all round me'. Seeing clouds beneath him, he is reminded of accounts of the ascent of Mount Athos and Mount Olympus. The Alps, close at hand, wake in him thoughts of the legendary Alpine crossing of Hannibal, 'the savage enemy of the Roman name'. Suddenly he is filled with homesickness; before he can stop this 'unmanly weakness': 'I sighed, I admit it, for the Italian sky, which rose before the mind's eye rather than the eye, and an unbearable, burning longing filled me, to see friends and fatherland again.' From space, he moves on to time: about ten years before he had completed his studies in Bologna. Pondering over these ten years, he forgets where he is.

At last he looks about him and sees for the first time 'what I had come to see'. His companions are eager to make the descent, as the sun is already going down and the shadow of the mountain is growing longer and longer. Petrarch hurriedly tries to make up for lost time. Below him he sees the Rhône (at least thirty miles away), in the distance the sea (sixty miles); he looks in vain for the Pyrenees (over 180 miles). He enjoys the view, then decides to improve their souls; he opens the *Confessions of St Augustine*, which his correspondent had given him in a 'handy-size volume in a tiny format'. Petrarch calls God as witness that it was 'by chance' that he opened the volume at the tenth book; he reads his brother a sharp condemnation of the craving for knowledge, and travel: 'And men go to wonder at the height of mountains and the great waves of the sea and the far flowing rivers and the bounds of the ocean and the stars in their orbits, and pay no attention to themselves.'

He shuts the book, amazed, and angry with himself for still admiring earthly things. He should have learnt long since from the 'heathen' that nothing is worthy of admiration but the spirit, and nothing great compared with its greatness. Petrarch declares that he has seen enough of the mountain; his inner eye turned in on his own soul, he wordlessly makes the descent. He is convinced that what he has read was meant especially for him. Meditating on the words of Augustine and the Apostle Paul, he considers the lack of insight of mortal men, 'so that by paying no attention to their most noble aspects they lose themselves in a multitude of things and interest themselves in empty spectacles and seek without, what they should find within'.

Immersed in such thoughts, without noticing the rocky path, he comes late at night to the humble inn at Malaucène, which they had left before dawn; although he does notice that the moonlit night gave welcome assistance to the tired wanderers. While the servants prepare a meal, he goes to another part of the house to write to his friend, 'in haste and on the spur of the moment'. The example of Augustine leads him to make his own confession: he will hide nothing from his fatherly friend. He begs him to pray for him, that his restless thoughts may at last 'turn to the one true, sure, certain, lasting good'.

BOCCACCIO'S MERCHANT'S JOURNEY

In the 'Decameron', his collection of a hundred stories written in about 1350, Boccaccio gives us an insight into love and marriage in his day, and sheds light on many aspects of the risk-filled life of a merchant. One merchant is badly deceived, another shipwrecked, a third is sold into slavery by pirates; a fourth, having lost everything he possesses, turns to piracy himself, in order to return to the life of a good citizen again when he has 'remade' his fortune. But should the historian take such tales seriously as source material? Can the content of passages of this book be based on fiction? Stories, comedies and novels have, since ancient times, given writers a special freedom to describe in particular the people of the middle and lower classes, and everyday life. Authors of tragedies, to take another literary form, were limited much more stringently by the rules of the genre: tragedies were concerned with men of the upper classes – until the beginning of the nineteenth century, when Schiller wrote a bourgeois tragedy, *Luise Millerin*.

In the second story of the second day Boccaccio describes in realistic terms the adventures of a merchant, whose blue-eyed ingenuousness threatens to be fatal. Scattered throughout the story are references to the everyday concerns of the traveller, among them the constant pleasurable or worrying question of where and how he would spend the next evening and night. Boccaccio gives his heroes a profound trust in God's power and the mediation of the saints. A merchant's piety, and aspects of hospitality are described with many graphic details, which would otherwise have to be pieced together by studying various different sources. I have therefore taken the liberty to quote this tale at length, with a minimum of commentary, and have followed it up with a merchant's advice to his young wife.

The merchant Rinaldo lives in Asti, in northern Italy, about thirty miles east of Turin. He has had to do business in Bologna (about 160 miles from Asti) and wants to return by a less direct route. Accompanied by a single servant, he rides from Ferrara in the direction of Verona; on the way he meets three men, whom he takes to be merchants, and gladly joins up with them.

Boccaccio's remark, that this was 'rash' is justified in one respect: travellers were foolish to put too much trust in total strangers, and if they did join them, were well advised at least to remain circumspect in their conversation with them. On the other hand it was obviously an advantage for single travellers to seek the company of others – for protection and company; pilgrims, merchants and students all did this.

Rinaldo's new companions learn from his conversation that he has money on him, and decide to rob him at the first good opportunity. In order not to arouse his suspicions they behave in a friendly and unassuming way; as they go along they converse with Rinaldo, as much as they can, like polite and well-bred people. One subject leads to another, and soon they are on the subject of 'prayer'. When questioned, as to how he prays, Rinaldo freely admits that he is 'simple and inexperienced in such matters'. When travelling he always says the Lord's Prayer on leaving an inn in the morning, and a Hail Mary for the souls of the parents of St Julian. 'And then I ask God and these saints, to find me a good lodging for the next night. Now I have often in my life been in great danger when travelling, but have always managed to escape and find a lodging with honest people at night. Therefore I am of the firm belief that St Julian, to whom I pray, has asked God to grant me this mercy, and I think I would have a bad day's travel and be unable to find a decent lodging at night, if I didn't say these prayers in the morning.' When questioned, he replies that he has said the same prayers that morning. One of his new companions is determined that Rinaldo shall find no comfort that night. He cheekily says that he has frequently been in those parts, but has never prayed; in spite of that he has always found good accommodation, 'and tonight you will see who finds the best place, you, who have said your prayers, or I, who haven't done so.'

As the travellers are crossing a river, amidst much talk, the three men seize their opportunity: it is a lonely spot and night is falling. They overpower Rinaldo, steal everything but his shirt, take his horse and shout mockingly after him: 'Now go and see whether your Saint Julian will find you a good place tonight.'

Rinaldo sees himself deserted on all sides: his faith in his saintly protector is shaken, not to mention the treachery of his servant, who has cut and run and calmly returns to a near-by fortress-town, without bothering to help his master. The latter searches shivering and with chattering teeth in vain for a roof for the night; a war has recently laid waste the surrounding countryside. He runs barefoot through the snow to the near-by town; when he gets there the gates are already shut for the night and the drawbridges drawn up.

Under the jutting roof of a house, that is built out over the wall, he hopes to find protection from the snow; he gathers some rotting straw together, crouches down on it leaning against a closed door and waits for daybreak. He heaps bitter reproaches on St Julian, who has betrayed his trust.

Boccaccio then gives his tale a surprising twist. He unexpectedly opens the second part of his story with the sentence: 'Saint Julian had not forgotten him however, and was quickly preparing a pleasant night's shelter for him.' In the house under whose roof Rinaldo was crouching, lived a pretty young widow, whom the day before a marquis had arranged to visit that night; he had asked for a bath and a sumptuous supper to be prepared for him that evening. This lover had to cancel his planned visit at short notice; his servant told the lady not to expect him. She disconsolately decides to get into the bath she has prepared for the marquis herself, then to eat the supper and go to bed. The name of the widow is not given; she is portrayed as a model of generous hospitality.

The bath happened to be right next to the door, against which Rinaldo was leaning. The widow hears his tears, feels the door shake and finally sends her maid to see who is there. Shivering and shaking, Rinaldo can hardly utter a coherent word; he begs the maid not to leave him there all night to freeze. Maid and mistress take pity on him and the widow orders that Rinaldo should be brought in. 'The supper is all ready, and there is too much for the two of us to eat, and there is plenty of room to offer him a place.'

It is not a question of obeying a half-remembered Christian commandment to offer shelter to strangers. It is simply a case of feeling a basic sympathy for someone in need of help and protection; and being in the happy position of having plenty to give. When the widow sees the half-frozen Rinaldo, she tells him to get into the bath, 'for it is still warm'. It was a part of hospitality to give a guest water to wash his hands with, and perhaps – as Benedict had ruled – to wash his feet, or prepare a bath for him. In the mid-fourteenth century, people were not too fussy about having clean water when they took a bath; often two people – perhaps of different sexes, and not necessarily married – got into a tub together, were served with food and drink and after feasting for an hour or so indulged in the pleasures of lovemaking. Much recovered after his bath, Rinaldo feels that he has been restored to life. The lady of the house has had some clothes of her late husband's laid out for him, which fit him perfectly. Rinaldo has reason to thank God and St Julian.

Meanwhile the widow has had a large fire lit in the parlour, at which Rinaldo can warm himself before sitting down to eat. He sees at once that his saviour is a lady of rank, greets her respectfully and thanks her for her kindness. The widow greets him friendlily, invites him to sit beside her near the fire and enquires about his misfortunes. She is more worldly-wise than her guest; she believes his story, as she has already heard of his servant's arrival. In a small place news quickly gets around when a stranger rides in.

Hostess and guest wash their hands, then Rinaldo sits down at table as invited. As they eat the widow takes to him more and more – a man in the prime of life, with a fine figure, handsome face and excellent manners. Finally, when they are sitting by the fire once more, she admits openly how much she would like to embrace and kiss Rinaldo – a wish with which her guest gladly complies; 'and after she had held him close and kissed him at least a thousand times and had been kissed by him a thousand times in return, they both stood up and went to her room together, where they lay down without more ado and had full and frequent satisfaction of their desires, before dawn broke.' The widow was following in an ancient tradition, in stretching hospitality to include her bed.

To avoid any gossip, the following morning the widow gave Rinaldo some cast-off clothes, filled his wallet with money, showed him the way to his servant, begged him to keep silent about what had happened and let him out through the same door through which he had come the night before. As soon as the gates were opened, Rinaldo went into the town, as if he had come from a distance. He finds his servant and puts on the clothes which were packed in the saddlebag of the man's horse. Just as he is setting out, the three thieves are

A robber with a cudgel attacks two travelling ladies.

led past, who have been seized on account of another crime. Rinaldo gets his horse, clothes and money back; only a pair of garters are missing, which the miscreants cannot account for.

Boccaccio ends the story thus: 'Full of thanks to God and St Julian, Rinaldo mounted his horse and got home safe and sound. But the three highway robbers were already dangling in the wind the next day on the gallows.'

Certainly, not every merchant who fell among thieves, experienced such a happy ending. The highway robbers had let Rinaldo off lightly; to avoid witnesses they might have killed both him and his servant at once. On the other hand the story shows the concern of the authorities to uphold the law – even after a war, when everything was in disorder. Anyone caught red-handed committing a crime, and highway robbery was a breach of the peace, was given summary justice: he would be strung up the same day or – as here – a day later on the gallows or the nearest tree.

About half a century after Boccaccio, a French citizen drew up some house-rules for his much younger wife. He reckons that she will outlive him; he wants to give her advice which will make her life and that of her future husband easier. As the responsibility for outside business is a man's affair, her husband must 'travel hither and thither, in rain, wind, snow and hail, wet through or parched dry, bathed in sweat, or freezing, ill fed, poorly accommodated, with a cold room and uncomfortable bed.'

A wife should therefore take care that her husband finds at home that which the traveller, according to this comfortable citizen, most misses on the road: his description is like an echo of Boccaccio's tale. Clearly Boccaccio and the Parisian had experienced the same things when travelling and missed the same comforts: clean bedlinen, white bedcaps, good furs as covers, 'pleasant conversation, intimacies, loving services and secrets which I won't mention. And fresh shirts and clothes next day. For in truth, such things keep a man's love alive and make him glad to come home and see his wife again, and keep him away from other women.'

There is nothing in Boccaccio's story to indicate that Rinaldo was married; there was therefore no question of adultery. The Parisian knew well that on long journeys there was a great temptation to seek solace with another woman; it remains questionable whether he always resisted the temptation. At any rate he kept his eyes open when he travelled. His wife should heed the old peasant maxim which tells how three things drive a man from his home: a leaking roof, a smoking chimney and a bickering wife. If she is to live in love and harmony with her next husband, she must always be gentle, charming and obedient, spread a happy atmosphere, and take trouble with his bed, food and drink, hose and shirts. Otherwise there will be recriminations and the quite unjustified complaint that another woman has bewitched her husband: love, care, intimacies, joys and pleasures of every kind – that is the only magic.

The Paris citizen's warnings concern winter particularly: as there are fewer things to do outside than in summer, a man likes to be at home, where he can be sure of a warm fire. The days are short and cold, lights are expensive, smoky and smelly; so people spend longer each day in bed. The well-meaning husband's final plea probably stems from unhappy experiences on the road: 'Take care in winter that he has a good fire that doesn't smoke, and that he can rest in peace and warmly wrapped on your breast, and so do your magic on him. And take care that there are no fleas in your room and in your bed.'

FLAGELLANT MOVEMENTS

In the mid-fourteenth century Europe was devastated by a unique catastrophe: the plague, which had been introduced from the Far East, struck down millions of victims. Many places and regions were spared by the Black Death (or it is not mentioned there in the sources); others lost half or more of their population; sometimes all the inhabitants of a village were said to have died – with the exception of those who laid out the corpses.

People had no resistance to the disease, against which doctors were powerless: there were often only hours between falling sick and dying. Countless numbers fled in mass terror; there were movements such as that of the Flagellants, and massacres of Jews; others awaited the inevitable; in one place there would be frantic enjoyment of the joys of this world, in another the pouring forth of terrified prayers of repentance. In trying to flee, many spread the disease even further. In his introduction to the 'Decameron' Boccaccio gives a realistic description of the plague and a further example of people's reaction to it: in Florence all normal social activity had broken down because of the plague, so a group of young men and women go off to a country house; here they while away the time in safety by telling, often frivolous, stories. Later, outbreaks of the plague caused people to make a journey which they might have planned for a long time: some went on a promised pilgrimage; Dürer probably left Nuremburg in 1505 on the outbreak of the disease, to make his (second) journey to Venice.

In the mid-fourteenth century people still thought there might be a way to avoid the horrors of the pestilence, by propitiating Heaven by prayers, religious services, processions and acts of penance. For centuries there had been men who following Jesus had scourged themselves or let themselves be lashed by others. The later Flagellant movements were different: they were not single individuals but large groups who practised this form of penance, and not in private but publicly, going from place to place.

In the autumn of 1348 Flagellant processions left Austria or Hungary and in 1349 reached Bohemia, Saxony, Franconia; they went from town to town and finally reached the Rhineland; in the Netherlands the movement lasted longer than elsewhere, until the beginning of 1350. The Flagellants were organised as a brotherhood; clerics could become members, but not 'masters', and every brother had to pledge himself for 33½ days. In that way there would be continuity when the processions travelled through the countryside: as they went along one person or another would drop out, and others join the group. The movement was planned to last 33½ years, the number corresponding to the age of Jesus. The Flagellants could not ask for shelter from the inhabitants of the places they passed through, but might accept the offer of a night's hospitality; in order to preserve their economic independence, each 'brother' had to bring with him 4 pence per day. The Flagellants were strictly forbidden to speak to a woman during the time they were with the brotherhood.

The Strasburg chronicler Closener gives a detailed account of the two hundred or so Flagellants, who arrived in his home town on 8 July 1349; in this case the figures are probably reliable. As he is writing after the event, he adopts a critical tone almost straight away; but it is also clear that in the beginning wide circles of people were influenced by the rigorous earnestness of the movement and gave the Flagellants material and spiritual support.

When the Flagellants approached a town or village, they would be greeted by the ringing of bells. Carrying candles and richly decorated banners ahead of them, they marched two by two; they wore cloaks, and hats distinguished by a red cross. In a song they ask Christ for help:

> We do penance on ourselves,
> To please God the more.

After the procession into the church they would all throw themselves down – crosswise, with outstretched hands, 'with a clatter' as the chronicler pointedly remarks. After they had lain there for a while, the leader of the choir would order the Flagellants three times to raise their hands, 'so that God will turn away the Great Death'.

If they now wanted to do penance – 'as they call scourging', Closener writes coolly – they went at least twice a day, in the morning and evening, with bell-ringing and chanting of songs, in pairs outside the town to the 'scourging place': clothed only in a white cloth from waist to ankles, they all lay in a large ring on the ground to confess their sins: if anyone was a 'perjuring wretch', he lay on one side and held three fingers over his head; the adulterer lay on his stomach, and so on; 'so one could easily tell, which sins each of them had committed'. This public admission was regretted by many when their enthusiasm had waned, as they might be pursued by the law. Finally the 'Master' stepped over each member, touching him with the scourge and saying:

> Stand up through the pure martyr's mercy
> And take care to sin no more.

The man would stand up and join the Master, step over those who were still lying, touch them with his scourge and repeat the Master's words. When all had been freed, they stood in a ring again; the choirleaders began a song, which was taken up by all. Meanwhile the brothers went two by two round the ring, scourging themselves with thongs, 'which had knots in them, in which needles were hidden, and beat themselves on the back, so that many bled profusely'.

In the long chant, reproaches are mixed with the hope of mercy: Christ asks the sinner how he will repay the sufferings with which he has been freed; Mary begs her son – parts of the song are taken from the 'Stabat mater' – to have mercy on sinful men. The song deals harshly with those who have broken the commandment to fast on Friday and rest on Sunday, and even more so with liars and perjurers, usurers, pitiless murderers and highway robbers; they are all certain to go to Hell. Between each verse the Flagellants kneel down, throw themselves 'crosswise' on the ground, and stand up again; then the choirleaders continue and tell all to raise their hands heavenwards, so that God will turn away the Great Death.

Now we lift up our arms
So that God will have mercy on us.

After this penance they all get dressed again; then a long missive from Christ supposedly left on an altar in Jerusalem is read out – also reproaching them: accusations are sprinkled like a leitmotif through the letter, that men neither honour the Sabbath nor fast on Friday; because of their wickedness and pride, because of their countless transgressions all imaginable disasters have descended on men: earthquakes, destruction of the crops by beetles, locusts, maggots, mice, hoar-frost, frost, drought, floods; also lightning, war and attacks by the heathen; at the end of these tribulations hunger had forced men to eat dry wood and fircones.

Meanwhile the 'heavenly missive' made bitter reproaches concerning the 'hellish' Jews, because they had not accepted the message of redemption: Closener precedes his account of the Flagellant procession with the brief note that in 1349 all the Jews in Strasburg were burnt, as they had poisoned the wells and other water.

Priests who hesitated to read the 'letter' to the people, and all who refused to believe the message, were threatened with banishment from Heaven; on the other hand he who believed would receive 'many blessings on his house'. Blessings were also promised to those who gladly went to church and gave alms, especially those who copied out 'God's message' and spread it further from town to town, from village to village and from house to house.

After reading the 'Heavenly missive' the penitents scourged themselves again. Finally they went two by two – with candles and banners – and chanting songs into the town again and amidst the ringing of bells into the cathedral; they prostrated themselves crosswise on the ground and then after further prayers and rites went to their lodgings.

The chronicler's attitude to this movement is clear. He freely admits that all were greatly impressed by the Flagellants: the authorities paid them sums from the public purse; never had people repented more sincerely; cries of grief had accompanied the reading of the 'letter', which was universally accepted as true. If churchmen queried its authenticity, questions were put to them in return which went to the very heart of their faith: who had given the seal of approval to the evangelists then? People had at times believed the Flagellants more than the 'preachers'; many laymen, including 'upright' citizens, and numerous 'preachers', if not scholars, had joined the Flagellants. But Closener also writes that 'evil men' had joined the Flagellants and had an influence on them; many had done the 33½ day journey several times over, not out of piety, but because they had developed a taste for idleness: it did not matter where they came from, they were still invited in and offered hospitality. Their claim that they could perform miracles also led to scepticism. The Flagellants wanted to restore a drowned child to life, and carried it round their circle while they performed their rites. Closener says with satisfaction: 'nothing happened however'. He was sorry to see a fragmentation of the accepted social order: women and then even children were caught up in the movement in Strasburg, and travelled through the countryside scourging themselves.

After a while the movement began to die down: the ringing of bells and payments by authorities for the purchase of candles and banners were withdrawn; no one was any longer prepared to offer the Flagellants a roof. Finally there were prohibitions: Flagellants were forbidden to enter Strasburg, and scourging in groups was forbidden in general; 'anyone who wanted to scourge himself, should do it privately in his own house.'

Then the Church authorities stepped forward with their own prohibitions. The Church had many reasons to regard the movement with mistrust: by giving absolution from sins out of their sight the 'Masters' were appropriating an authority which should have been reserved for priests alone. According to the teaching of the Church, revelation was an individual matter; visions and heavenly messages might have meaning for individual believers; they could not be binding for the Church as a whole. In retaliation the Flagellants called the priests who refused to read the 'Heavenly letter' to the people 'the enemies of God'.

The movements of Flagellants were another example of the great mobility of people in the late Middle Ages. Their attempt to turn God's anger away from men was combined with criticism of the Church as an institution and with attitudes critical of society.

TOWARDS THE MODERN ERA

The theme of this book, with all its varied strands, does not easily lend itself to general conclusions. Each viewpoint must be evaluated; 'such and such a thing happened' may have to be qualified with 'but . . .'

Travel in the Middle Ages was not the privilege of a certain class. Rich and poor, churchmen and laity, men and women, young and old were all to be seen travelling along the roads. It is true that in his account of a journey from Reims to Chartres, Richer says that his servant had never travelled so far before; but – especially since the turn of the millennium – a large part of the population were more widely travelled, many people going on a journey several times a year, to a near or distant place of pilgrimage for instance.

People travelled with a clear knowledge of the dangers, which threatened women in particular. Possibly in this respect too, medieval travel was less different from travel in our own day than one might imagine; modern mass tourism has given a new impetus to robbery on the streets and certain forms of piracy.

Together with the many things which facilitated travel, such as the building of bridges and founding of hospices, there were also certain prohibitions in medieval times, as for instance regarding long-distance pilgrimages or study abroad. In the early Middle Ages Boniface pleaded for women to be forbidden to undertake long pilgrimages; at the height of the Middle Ages Peter the Venerable doubted the value of travelling to the Holy Land; at the beginning of the modern era Sebastian Brant considered all those who wanted to explore distant countries to be 'fools'. The great number of rulers and seats of power in Europe led to the juxtaposition of different cultures; under these circumstances no one set of rules could continue for ever – as in a centralised state such as China – so that the individual had greater freedom of movement.

Whether wandering monk or king, merchant or student, the medieval traveller was used to risking his health, possessions, and life, while undertaking hazardous journeys. Travel was so general, that every means of transport was used. Monks travelled from Ireland to Iceland in open boats, and Scandinavians from Norway to America. This shows that it was not the method, but the motive which was the deciding factor. China had ocean-going ships, stern-rudder and compass considerably earlier than Europe, but the will and desire to discover distant countries was less strong. As a result the New World was not discovered from a culturally and technically superior China, resting on its feelings of superiority, but from the more backward Europe.

'Travelling folk', on the road with all their household chattels, ducks, pigs, hens and a pet cat: the woman spins as she goes: a fifteenth-century German woodcut.

Travel did away with social distinctions: all had to suffer equally from heat and vermin, dust and disease – although the well-to-do may have been less prone to many infections because of their better food. Religious faith and pilgrimages to holy shrines were also great levellers – bringing together all classes – in the Islamic world perhaps more than in Christendom. Pilgrims to Mecca – regardless of whether they were white, black or yellow-skinned, whether from Africa or Asia, whether king or beggar, whether speaking the Berber or Malay language – felt united in experiencing an all-enveloping solidarity and in their search for God's mercy. The pilgrimage to Mecca runs like a unifying thread through the Middle Ages, the modern era and the present-day world; it recreates anew each year, despite tensions and rifts, the feelings which the Islamic states have in common, in the face of the world of 'unbelievers'.

Why do you travel, when so much hardship is involved? Many travellers must have found it difficult to answer such questions. Most people saw life as a vale of sorrows, and death as ever present. Someone living in a draughty hut is not likely to be afraid of crossing a river or mountain, but may well find the idea of finding good food in a monastery on the way very tempting. Missionaries, kings, bishops, popes, soldiers, craftsmen, artists, knew or thought they knew why they were on the road. Thousands wanted – in modern terminology – a change of scene, or adventure, or possibly loot. Others used the opportunity of going on a crusade or 'duty journey' to look around them for better living conditions while they were abroad. The farmers, craftsmen, and merchants who emigrated have barely been mentioned. Before they finally left their homeland, many would have undertaken an exploratory journey first, as those wishing to emigrate do today. The German family of the London alderman Arnald Fitzhedmar were certainly not the only ones to decide to remain in England after making a pilgrimage to Canterbury. Northern Spain, which had been depopulated by the wars between Christians and Moslems, was re-settled by Santiago pilgrims. University registers and town archives of medieval cities are full of the names of those who came there to study or do trade, and then stayed on for good in their pleasant new home. That did not mean that their ties with their 'old' homeland were broken. The Reformation quickly took root in Transylvania, because there was a continual coming and going of students and citizens, merchants and monks between Hungary and Germany.

The possibility of travel helped to ease tensions. Even women could drop their work in house and courtyard at short notice once or twice a year to go on a pilgrimage, and get out into the world; in the short term a conflict between father and son might be avoided if the young man went abroad for a year, even if he intended to return home again later; or a younger son might consciously or unconsciously find in travel a long-term solution to inadequate living conditions or the lack of a future inheritance at home. Some went even further in order to escape from difficult conditions. If skilled artisans – craftsmen and miners, merchants and farmers – could not get the conditions they demanded, the most active among them went abroad, legally or illegally. They contributed to the spread of special skills; the standards they demanded were in sharp contrast to the living conditions of those who remained at home, and sometimes to the expectations of those who had summoned them. As they then enjoyed better work conditions than the people of their new (and often of their old) country, conflict could arise. But in general they gradually led to the living conditions of the underprivileged in their new country being improved also.

The results of the exchanges between people of different language, culture and religion are incalculable. Travel can educate, by broadening the horizon, and by doing away with preconceived ideas; it can also strengthen enmity and national prejudice. The sources often tell of the narrow-mindedness, or even hatred, of people who should have known better. Slanders – such as that of the author of the Pilgrim's Guide concerning the supposed unnatural practices of the Navarrese – can be traced back to antiquity and would continue into the modern era. Ill-nature is not a question of education. Possibly it was in fact exceptional when Petrarch described the Rhinelanders so favourably, or Dürer heaped praises on the art of the Mexican Indians which he saw in Brussels in the 1520s. One of the great western theologians, Bishop Otto of Freising, got to know Hungary in 1147, on the Second Crusade; looking back ten years later he described what seemed to him to be the contrast between the country and its inhabitants. The former was pleasing, rich and as beautiful as a heavenly paradise. The inhabitants however were boorish and coarse in their habits and speech, with 'ugly faces, deep-set eyes, stumpy figures, barbaric customs and speech'; one had to blame providence or rather wonder at God's tolerance in giving this beautiful country to such human monsters – for one could hardly call them men.

The stark contrast was so simple and convenient: in the Pilgrim's Guide 'we French' on one side and on the other the Navarrese, Basques, Castilians; as the Middle Ages ran into the modern era, 'we' the Europeans, Christians, Westerners, the good, the civilised, and over there 'the others', the barbarians, the wicked ones . . . Members of a group might arrogantly outlaw or slander one another, but when brought face to face with the non-European world, Europeans became conscious of their common interests and directed their feelings of superiority on non-Europeans – American Indians, Indians, Chinese. People knew little about them and could therefore not be fair to them. The presents for local rulers which Vasco da Gama took on his voyage round the Cape of Good Hope indicated how the ruling class in Portugal regarded Indians; people imagined they could please Indian potentates with trifles, such as those they gave the 'natives' on the southern coasts of Africa.

But here too one must qualify. Blinkered as people were, there ran like a bright thread through the history of Europe an openness to the new which was unusual compared to other cultures. It was like the eagerness of a student who wants to learn and if possible surpass his teacher. There was the initial desire to learn, and the wish to explore unknown countries and get to know other peoples which expressed itself in different ways. A bishop like Bernward of Hildesheim saw to it that he was accompanied on his travels by talented craftsmen, who would study new methods. European artists studied Byzantine and Islamic works of art and attempted to copy eastern artists and architects. The glossary which Breydenbach (a pilgrim from Mainz to the Holy Land in 1483/84) gave with his account of the journey, and Columbus's journal, tell of the desire to get to know the world of 'the others' and their thoughts and culture, by learning their language, and not only in order to gain booty and possessions. In the late Middle Ages foundations for the later 'Oriental Studies' faculties were laid at universities, long before a comparable 'Occidental Studies' faculty was founded in Arab or Chinese universities.

The Reformation brought a halt to travel in one respect: pilgrimages to distant shrines fell off among those of the 'new faith'. But to replace this another type of travel had already begun to emerge even before the Reformation: the same places were often visited on such gentlemanly educational journeys as had been visited by pilgrims, but now the traveller no longer went in search of absolution or the mediation of a saint, but to get to know the works of art which earlier generations had executed to honour such saints. Among those of the 'old faith' pilgrimages suddenly became increasingly important again; people wanted to demonstrate their faith in the mediating role of the saints and in the healing power of good works.

The material gains brought about by travel should not be underestimated: gradually, in a centuries-long process, the new crops from the New World such as maize and potatoes, replaced the old millet-pap; cocoa and pineapples, tomatoes and spices enriched the menu; hammocks made sleeping on board a rocking ship more pleasant for those travelling by sea. From America came tobacco, which with coffee (partially) replaced alcohol. Many European successes in the modern era might arguably be explained not by the fact that men's work capabilities and creative capacity were no longer – as previously – stunted by alcohol, but that they were stimulated by the enjoyment of coffee and tobacco.

Travel by millions of people in medieval times encouraged a unifying process which continues to this day. There were close international links on all sides: that of the nobility, the Church in general and monastic orders in particular, the merchants, pilgrims, Jews, craftsmen and stonemasons, artists, scholars, lawyers, all flourishing through the exchange of visits, letters, ideas, manuscripts, goods, despite any differences of nationality, language or culture. Meetings between monks (as at the general councils of their order) and merchants (at major fairs), journeys by scholars to distant universities, whose diplomas would be recognised throughout western Christendom, ensured that Europe would become more than just a geographical entity. The countries of the west became interlinked, a common European feeling arose. This had a negative effect, when it became an arrogant dismissal of 'the others', and a positive one when it enabled a member of this 'international brotherhood' to feel at home even when he was living in another country. The humanist felt at home when he was with his own kind and his beloved manuscripts and books whether he was in Florence, Paris, Heidelberg or London – which did not necessarily exclude feelings of homesickness in one such as Petrarch.

Thanks also to this immense amount of travel undertaken by millions of people in the Middle Ages, links were forged which have proved stronger than the religious differences of the sixteenth and seventeenth centuries, more enduring than the national boundaries of the nineteenth and twentieth centuries, and more powerful than the 'iron curtain' of our own time.

AFTERWORD TO NORBERT OHLER, *THE MEDIEVAL TRAVELLER*

Translated by Michael M. Metzger

This new edition is dedicated to my wife Annemarie and my sons Michael, Andreas, Christian and Ulrich. In the 1970s and 1980s we covered much of what it is in this book together. Without their ideas, questions, and observations, it is unlikely that I would have grasped as many aspects of the everyday experience of travel in the past.

This book is based on investigations undertaken over many years, associated with fondly-remembered travel experiences. In 1984, I offered a German translation of the *Pilgrims' Guide* to Santiago de Compostela, then little known, to the publisher Artemis & Winkler. Although that volume did not fit their list, they suggested I write a wider-ranging book, with the *Pilgrim's Guide* forming one of the chapters. I agreed, and began to explore, with growing delight, a world that had been largely unknown to me. I studied historical sources and scientific descriptions, analyzed atlases and pictorial evidence, and visited exhibitions and museums. With my wife and sons, on foot or by car, I became familiar with regions and destinations frequented by travellers in the Middle Ages. I then wrote, edited, and added to chapter after chapter of the book. By the spring of 1986, I felt that I had sufficiently covered the most essential aspects of medieval travel. When *Reisen im Mittelalter* (*The Medieval Traveller*) appeared later that year, it was received favourably, and has been reprinted several times since. I attribute its popularity, at least in part, to a widespread and enthusiastic curiosity about the Middle Ages.

There are now numerous studies of medieval travel, transport, and communication. Bookshops stock vast numbers of publications on pilgrimages. Travel in the Middle Ages appears as an important theme in radio and television programs, in documentary and popular films. Much of northern Europe is equipped with the financial means and talented scholars to advance research in this area and its many related fields. Eastern Europe has, for the moment at least, far fewer such resources. Thus, there is a wide gap between the breadth and depth of research in these areas in Europe and, for example, southeast Asia. Perhaps because of this, my book was translated not only into English and Italian, but also into Chinese, Japanese, Polish, and Czech. And in 2004, an enlarged German edition appeared.

I was often asked to lecture and write in greater detail on particular themes in the book; thus, I soon came to be acquainted with source materials that were new to me, and became aware that many more scholarly disciplines had touched upon medieval travel than I had imagined. This Afterword covers the basic sources and assumptions, and presents insights from the 2004 edition; but I also want to focus on the actual experience of travel itself in the Middle Ages.

I will begin by describing various sources that provide investigators with relevant information. Many have only recently been discovered. Further insights have been gained through a more intensive scrutiny of familiar documents. These new facts in turn provoke new questions that remain unanswered, and to which I particularly draw the reader's attention. The Addenda supplement the original English translation, and follow the sequence of its chapter titles and page numbers.

In addition, readers will find excursions into new themes: on 'couriers on special assignments', on how travel was financed, on inns and other accommodation, and on law and navigation. I will pay particular attention to the last, because of its relevance to the British Isles and the English-speaking world.

Evidence for travel in the middle ages: the sources

Research on medieval travel is often enriched and, surprisingly, many questions can be answered when investigators step back and reassess familiar materials (annals, chronicles, travel journals, documents, legal records, archaeological discoveries, and various kinds of pictorial representations). In addition, newly-discovered writings or historical events can further our understanding or confirm earlier hypotheses, providing fresh insights into how medieval travellers actually lived. However, historians need to be acutely aware of how meaningful and authentic any source is. Does a text perhaps only repeat a traditional, commonplace opinion; does it describe something that even then no longer existed? It can be difficult to distinguish in any given source between what was genuinely observed at the time and what was fictional.

Not many of the written sources that touch on the theme of 'travel' are available in modern printed editions; still fewer texts exist in a modern translation. Most sources that have survived remain unpublished – not least because they are so numerous. Given also that they are frequently poorly preserved, difficult to decipher, incomplete, in fragments, and scattered among several archives, the only option available to the investigator is to examine them personally. But analyses of legal texts and records can, for example, reveal how freedom of movement was maintained in certain areas or restored after an interruption. Letters, contracts and accounting ledgers deal with the building and maintenance of roads and bridges. Regulations on transport and the safe conduct of travellers, customs registers, manorial registries, and maps and sketches appended to legal records yield a wealth of names of and information on natural features, towns, roads, and inns, and much else. Manorial registries merit more detailed discussion. Lists of what the estate owners actually received from tenants, arranged according to tenants' names, their particular fields, amounts owed for each, and the names of neighbours, they include references to paths, roads, and streets, often too to shops, inns, and hospitals, enabling us to discover the transport infrastructure of a rural area. In many communities, registers of citizens have survived which indicate the origins of incomers, without whom the towns would literally have died out. These new arrivals were particularly active travellers because they maintained contact for long periods with their home towns.

Occasionally, a little-noted source is 'discovered' and made accessible in a modern, scholarly edition. One example is the *Libro del pellegrino* from the Ospedale di Santa Maria della Scala in Siena, dating from the years 1382–1446. The book lists the names of pilgrims to Rome who deposited there money they planned to withdraw on the way home. If a depositor did not return, the funds were used to benefit the Hospital. In any case, they were to be accounted for scrupulously. To guard against abuses, each depositor was described precisely. Analysis of the *Libro del pellegrino* reveals that men deposited mainly gold coins and women mainly silver, and that, in 1400, a 'Holy Year', 210 men and 36 women did not return to retrieve their money.

The travel journals of pilgrims and others yield a great deal of information, as many of them reflect both common concerns and the concrete details of travel. Remarkably, the journals became ever more exact and reliable over time. Their depictions may well have spurred contemporaries to write about their own travels in increasingly precise detail. Authors learned and frequently discussed former and current place-names, the origins and history of a city or region, significant sites, famous citizens, and the nature of public life, local customs, climate, and topography. They explained why a place was important: this could be owing to its location at a river-crossing, industries such as metal work or textiles, or the residence of a bishop or prince. With the wealth of information they offer, such descriptive works provide valuable information to authors of modern geographical reference works: many modern travel books, used to prepare, conduct and document journeys, draw upon this inheritance. Illustrations in these old travel journals often supplement the reality that the text does not mention. For example, when did four-wheeled carriages acquire a front axle that could be steered? On what is probably the first picture of a traffic accident in European history, we see the vehicle of Pope John XXIII, on the Arlberg Pass bound for the Council of Constance (1414–18), suffer a broken axle. Since the fifteenth century, this event has appeared in many illustrations that are demonstrably intended as antipapal propaganda. Like other Alpine passes, the Arlberg could not then be negotiated with a carriage with two axles, or even with a cart. Travellers had to resort to litters, whether borne by humans, or, more often, by animals.

The task of identifying, cataloguing, and analyzing the large amount of available pictorial material has by no means been accomplished. Countless miniatures in medieval manuscripts, and the designs of tapestries, yield information about travel. From the late fifteenth century on, massive numbers of woodcuts and engravings on steel and copper plates have been produced. Caution is always needed in dealing with these sources. Dürer's floor plan of an inn, discussed further below, is probably more factually correct than the sketch of a hostelry in those racy novellas which describe the twists involved when male and female travellers spend the night in the same room. We must not underestimate, however, how close to reality such illustrations are when they show, for example, that all guests put their clothes and luggage on a bench next to the bed. If each guest had taken his or her possessions to bed, there would not have been so many thefts carried out under cover of darkness. To this day, such conditions in pilgrim and other hostels are still often discussed, and not only in fiction.

The general inaccuracy of historical maps exemplifies how unreliable some sources are in depicting the realities of past times, no matter how convincing they may seem. If we compare them with contemporary written records, the almost inexplicable fact emerges that rulers, even with 'reliable' maps in their hand, had only nebulous ideas about the nature and extent of their territories.

Archaeological discoveries are no less informative than pictures and maps, but often more difficult to evaluate. Archaeologists uncover and determine the function of artefacts relevant to travel, such as horseshoes, wagon tyres, simple boats and stately ships. Experimental archaeology pursues such questions as: how many heavily laden wagons must have travelled a road to have created a rut ten centimetres deep in rocky soil? Aerial photographs make it far clearer how human activity affects the landscape, prior to the industrialization of agriculture; experts can see in such photographs traces of hills and dales that were levelled long ago. We owe much knowledge too to archaeologists working underwater, finding and assessing submerged objects. Such finds are brought to the surface if that is worthwhile. (This can present a problematic situation. Say that amateur divers discover a submerged boat that first estimates suggest dates to the fourteenth century. It is brought to the surface and placed in the storage shed of a research institute. If, however, a new director with other concerns takes charge, there is a chance that the artefact will be neglected, and decay entirely before it can be scientifically analyzed and the findings published.)

Without competent interpretation, any artefact from the past may lead us astray. Old laws, regulations, and other orders may sound reasonable, but the scholar must then ask: how binding were they? How effective? The idea of financing road construction with income from brothels may seem practical, but when and where were roads repaired or bridges built with such funds? Trial records often yield more information than laws. Conflict always provides additional facts about the past; this is particularly true of lawsuits, involving accusers and defendants. Records of the period following the decision in such a case often show that daily life was changed by it.

In summary, then. Research on medieval travel involves analysis of many kinds of written and material evidence, over a number of disciplines. Many aspects of historical inquiry contribute to this endeavour: study of climate, culture, geography, psychology, the military, legal institutions, regional developments, social structure, urban growth, technology, transportation and communication, governance, and economics. We should bear in mind too the geographic aspects of developments in culture, communications, and economics.

International and interdisciplinary co-operation

Co-operation between scholars in different disciplines, using a variety of methodologies, has expanded interest in questions of travel and created new areas of specialization. The purview of the research includes travellers themselves, their motives, their equipment, and much else that was important to them. Questions about paths, roads, and highways are significant, but so are the particular conditions of the places travellers passed through, especially the cities. We learn more about how people travelled by investigating population growth, the expansion of population centres, the function of markets, and use of rudimentary machinery. The founding and growth of new towns intensified travel. Where were they located? What did they offer travellers? Location was significant: after around 1300, towns were founded in places accessible to traffic, on navigable rivers, at fords, harbours, bridges, and other traffic hubs.

Historians of finance, governance, and economics investigate who was responsible for planning, building, and maintaining roads, bridges, and waterways. They look into how inns, hospices, and other accommodations were used, especially in mountainous areas, and into toll and customs stations and other restrictions on travellers. (Even today, passengers on the railroad from Mainz to Koblenz can see the 'Mouse Tower' near Bingen. It is named not for mice (*Maus, Mäuse*), but for the toll levied there (*Maut*), an expense already unpopular in the Middle Ages.)

Sociologists contribute greatly to our understanding, through their insights into how groups and nations co-operated with or opposed each other. They show us the importance of words and gestures in aggravating or resolving a conflict. They introduce to historical thought questions about how those who travelled and those who did not interacted, and the roles played by moods, attitudes, and prejudices. A particular example deserves attention. When a German King travelled to Rome with a military escort, to be crowned Holy Roman Emperor, tensions arose abruptly in the Italian cities where they stopped en route. Sometimes rebellions burst out. Thietmar, Bishop of Merseburg (d. 1018), wrote: 'The climate and the qualities of the people in that land do not accord with our kind. In the Roman lands and in Lombardy, there is much treacherous cunning. Whoever goes there encounters little friendliness. Travellers must pay for every little thing they need and must always beware of trickery; in that country, many die of poisoning.' Imagine the effect of words like Thietmar's on a young warrior going to Italy. Germans followed certain customs, Italians others. In Italy, money then played a far larger economic role than it did in Germany. The summers could become unbearably hot. Food spoiled quickly, with consequent problems for health. If our young man had heard nothing to the contrary, he could easily have regarded the people on the other side of the Alps, who demanded money for everything, with contempt. He would constantly expect to be swindled or poisoned. Tense and insecure, he would probably have acted at least stiffly, if not arrogantly, thus provoking those he encountered. Soon honour would have been called into question: his own, that of the German nation, the King's. A soldier was expected to behave correctly and react appropriately to any occasion. But what *was* appropriate to a particular situation? Officers at all levels needed a high degree of tact if they expected their orders to be carried out.

Studies of microcosms supplement those of macrocosms. We are interested in individual journeys: where, when, why, how did Winfried/Bonifatius travel, or Ibn Battuta, or Marco Polo? We are concerned with the various types of itineraries, with finding out how pilgrims started their journeys to Compostela, whether focusing on all of Germany, or only on Franconia or the Rhineland. Very helpful in this undertaking today are volunteers who dedicate time, effort and money to tracing pilgrims' routes, restoring and marking them, and preparing historical signage and other aids to appreciating their significance. Pilgrims, hikers, and ordinary walkers can thus now journey on the restored pilgrimage routes towards Einsiedeln, Compostela, and Vézelay.

While there is currently great interest in better understanding the phenomena of pilgrimages, other kinds of travellers are also studied. Year after year, for example, aristocrats travelled from southern and western Europe to East Prussia and the Baltic, regarding it as pleasing to God and an act of true knighthood to support the Teutonic Order in its struggle against the heathen Prussians. Much information has been gathered on the travels of students who populated the roads from the thirteenth and fourteenth centuries, in order to become qualified at distant universities for high offices in church and state. At home these young men had been taught to respect authority; university teachers awakened in them the urge to ask questions, to doubt, and to find joy in new knowledge. From which strata of society did these young men, who journeyed from Germany, England, and other lands to Bologna or Paris, come from? Where were the origins of students who matriculated at Montpellier or Oxford? Much information is available about the travels of German journeymen, but only from records begun in the fourteenth century. Why is there so little in earlier documents? Why is it only in the fourteenth century that journeyman bakers, shoemakers, and inn-keepers start to be urgently sought in Rome, Paris, Lyon and elsewhere?

Attention is increasingly paid to 'marginalized' population groups. That is the term used in modern research to characterize those their contemporaries called 'itinerants' (*fahrende Leute*). Poor and almost without any rights, they roamed the countryside as tinkers, tramps, musicians, vagabonds, and gypsies. They sometimes supported themselves with casual labour, sometimes by performing at festivals, but more frequently by begging. Carters too were constantly travelling, but they had a fixed home, while the itinerants were at home only on the roads and streets. Members of the lower classes frequently joined this group, their wanderings often making them rootless. Other travellers generally kept their distance, making contact with them chiefly to ask their help in times of need. Who was to know if they were robbers? Modern research finds it difficult to distinguish between 'innocent' vagrants and robbers, as there is hardly any evidence in writing of the life of this class beyond the many court records. The appearance of such itinerants *en masse* may perhaps be regarded as the symptom of a crisis resulting from an overly rapid increase in population or from a famine.

Scholars often scrutinize a particular country in minute detail. It is not by chance that it was in Switzerland, a small country, that two projects offering a model for other countries were undertaken and successfully completed: the 'Inventory of Historic Routes of Communication in Switzerland' (Inventar Historischer Verkehrswege der Schweiz; 1984–2003) [hereafter IVS], and, after its completion, 'ViaStoria, The Centre for Traffic History' (ViaStoria, Zentrum für Verkehrsgeschichte), located in Berne since 2003. These projects had their origins in a Swiss federal law for the preservation of nature and the national heritage. Together with the 'Inventory of Protected Local Features of Switzerland' (Inventar der Schützenswerten Ortsbilder der Schweiz) [hereafter ISOS] and the 'Federal Inventory of Protected Regions and Natural Features of National Significance' (Bundesinventar der Landschaften und Naturdenkmäler Nationaler Bedeutung) [hereafter BLN], they enjoy a high level of support and respect. The IVS describes the historic communication routes of Switzerland to a level of detail unrivalled anywhere else. This grants us insights into the history of travel that should be instructive for other countries because of the wide variety of Switzerland's surface features: plains, lower mountains, and the Alps. Ever since prehistoric times, routes on both water and land have played a major role there. In addition, Switzerland has always been a major European conduit of communication. Think of the pilgrims to Rome who have passed through Switzerland, especially in 'Holy Years', since 1300.

The IVS was designed to be interdisciplinary: archaeologists, geographers, and historians worked together with specialists in many other fields. Since the IVS' statement of purpose discusses basic assumptions about travel in history in exemplary ways, it is appropriate to quote from it at length:

> The routes in the inventory have been drawn and identified on terrain maps, evaluated on an inventory card, and their various parts, routings, and sectors described. Findings about earth forms are indicated according to the following criteria: Form (hollow-way, cliffside path, causeway, etc.), Surface (paving, gravel, etc.), Adjacent features (walls, trees, rows of trees, fences, etc.), Structures (bridges, tunnels, etc.), Distinctive features (hostelries, wayside crosses, milestones, etc.). Ideally, historical descriptions of these features include analyses of surviving maps, indications of ultimate destinations of the routes, important starting points, intermediate

way stations, and ends of routes, remarks on how old settlements are with possible conclusions about the age of a given route, relevant relations between towns, the development of governmental, economic, strategic and social functions, of judicial institutions, customs fees, tolls and barriers, as well as the means of transport used, the frequency of travel and its volume.

The IVS has generated more than 24,000 descriptions. Studying them increases the reader's awareness of the importance of local and regional transport, whose role down to the present is greater than that of long-distance travel. The project has greatly inspired experimental archaeologists. For example, it is now widely considered that, contrary to earlier ideas (and to the chagrin of the travel industry), only a few of Switzerland's most intensively travelled medieval roads were relics of Roman times. Most were developed much later. Supposedly 'Roman' roads were not built by the Romans, but rather must be seen as 'roads to Rome', generally dating from the Middle Ages.

As these remarks suggest, the purview of the investigations of the IVS transcends common periodic distinctions – antiquity, Middle Ages, the modern period – making more fruitful comparisons possible. For example, one of the roads negotiable by carts had an average gradient of 16.5%. In order to overcome such a slope, not only would more horses have had to be harnessed, but, to pull it upward, a rope would have had to be attached to the cart, then wound by a windlass or, when going downhill, carefully unwound. By the 1760s, this road had been replaced by one with an 11% gradient, which was modernized and improved to 5.3% by 1838. Such engineered roadways could accommodate carriages with two axles and of various widths. Until well into the nineteenth century, most travellers were on foot. In hilly areas, they might have found steps to ease a steep climb; traces of those that remain suggest how vital they were. The way uphill was laborious, becoming dangerous downhill, because a tired traveller on shaky knees might easily lose his balance. Walking these paths, researchers have established what 'steep' might mean in a particular instance. Travellers had to ride pack animals to negotiate an altitude difference of 500 m within 2.5 km, a 20% gradient.

It would be useful to apply the conclusions from such precise sources in other contexts. Such comparisons, however, can be made only with the utmost caution. A fact about navigation on the Rhône in the fourteenth century *might* also apply to conditions on the Rhine at that time, but not necessarily.

Open questions

The more investigators from various fields of study and from many countries co-operate in interdisciplinary research, the more important it is to agree on terminology. Concepts such as communication, migration, mobility, and traffic need to be more sharply defined and differentiated from each other. For European languages, including Greek and Latin, and for non-European languages, the inclusiveness of meanings for frequently-used terms relating to travel should be investigated comparatively. In particular, attention should be paid to words such as boat, bridge, to travel, raft, small boat, cart, path, to journey, ship, stile, street, wagon, to wander, way, and many others.

Travellers in the Middle Ages perceived differences in the level of development in the lands they visited. They noticed that money-economy and commercial hospitality were more developed south of the Alps than in central or northern Europe. Did such differences appear in other aspects of life? Or were such differences more imaginary than real? Encounters between the natives of an area and strangers passing through give rise to further questions. Did they ease relations between peoples, perhaps even improve them? How did the natives perceive travellers? How did the populace of heavily-travelled areas respond, especially in valleys that funnelled traffic to the Alpine passes? Today, for example, on the Camino de Santiago that leads to Compostela, natives sometimes react irritably when strangers time and time again request what may (to them) seem small favours.

Historians are not content with statements such as 'many people were travelling'. However, many aspects of travel research cannot be easily quantified. If a source indicates, for example, that in 1466 130,000 pilgrims' badges were sold at Einsiedeln in Switzerland, it may at first sight seem an impressive figure. But then scepticism arises: how reliable are figures ending in several zeros? Today, we do not readily trust an organization that claims to have brought 40,000 demonstrators to the streets. The figure from Einsiedeln is questionable for other reasons too. It is concerned with the *number* of pilgrims badge sold. Did every pilgrim buy one? Or only every second or third pilgrim? Or did some buy more than one, so that relatives and friends at home could claim to have been pilgrims? Pious fraud (*pia fraus*) had many faces. In short, save for exceptional circumstances, we must content ourselves with less conclusive statements, such as: in a Holy Year, more pilgrims travelled to Rome than at other times; sometimes, the Fair at Nördlingen was less popular than those at Frankfurt, Leipzig, or Lyon; at customs house X, at certain points, more (or less) money was paid in taxes, etc.

Is it true that people considered winter a bad season for travel? Deep snow can cover uneven road surfaces, and sleighs might have had a greater load capacity than carts or wagons. In winter, too, expert guides and draught animals were available and not needed for farming.

There are too few studies of travel in eastern and south-eastern Asia. They would help to verify the claims of Marco Polo and Ibn Battuta and let us draw far more valid conclusions about travel in general. Even in Asia itself, there has been little research done on the history of commerce, despite its great significance and what has been described as an abundance of promising documentary materials.

It is not clear why documents from places where many travellers congregated do not record epidemics more frequently. Was prevention more effective during the Middle Ages than in later times? Pilgrimage centres could not depend on Heaven's mercy alone – even if it was manifested at times. We have a report from the seventh century, written by Bishop Arkulf and Abbot Adomnanus, complaining of the 'revolting excrement' that camels, horses, mules, and oxen, transporting massive numbers of people to Jerusalem, had left in the city. People could barely move without stepping into it and the stench was unbearable. (The document says nothing about human waste.) 'Miraculously', however, during the night following the departure of the animals, torrential rain fell that 'removed the disgusting filth' from the streets and cleansed the city.

What was life like for travellers? Much has yet to be discovered. They had needs beyond food, drink, and shelter for the night. How did they interact with their fellow travellers, with strangers, with natives of the area? How did they deal with boredom? A journey from Spain to East Asia, after all, took at least eight months. How did travellers resolve conflicts within their groups? What were their attitudes toward people, rich and poor, and circumstances, regions and cities, that had been unknown to them? Historians are not content to examine how a document reflects differences between the country a traveller visits and his own; they ask, in addition, what exactly does an author perceive as being different, as strange?

Interest has long been growing in what influenced a traveller to embark on a journey, provoked especially by translations of travel journals. How did people know whether a trip was worthwhile? To what extent were such journals or maps really consulted to prepare for a journey or to better comprehend it afterwards? Or have many documents come down to us merely because they were safely in a library, but never read?

Unanswered questions about medieval travel have caused international disagreements up to the present day. For example, when, in 1992, Spain wished to celebrate the five hundredth anniversary of the voyage of Columbus to the 'New World', there were protests elsewhere that Leif Eriksson, starting from Iceland, and Brendan, sailing from Ireland, had reached America centuries earlier.

ADDENDA

Climate (pp. 5ff)

Between the years 900 and 1300, Europe enjoyed a mild climate favourable to travellers on land and sea. People then, contrary to today, preferred high mountain passes to long, circuitous routes through mountain valleys. Several passes in Switzerland that led from the southern Valais to Italy lay at altitudes up to 3,500 m. At the start of the 'little Ice Age', which lasted in phases until 1860, traffic over many of these routes ceased. Today, however, glaciers are once again melting. Thus, in the torrid summer of 2003, unique objects from the Middle Ages were found in the Bernese Alps. They prove the existence of a previously unknown pass between the cantons Berne and Valais. The 2,756 m high Schnidejoch Pass between Lenk and Sitten was glacier-covered until quite recently; earlier, it would seem that it had been used by travellers for a long time.

MOUNTS, DRAUGHT- AND PACK-ANIMALS (p. 15ff)

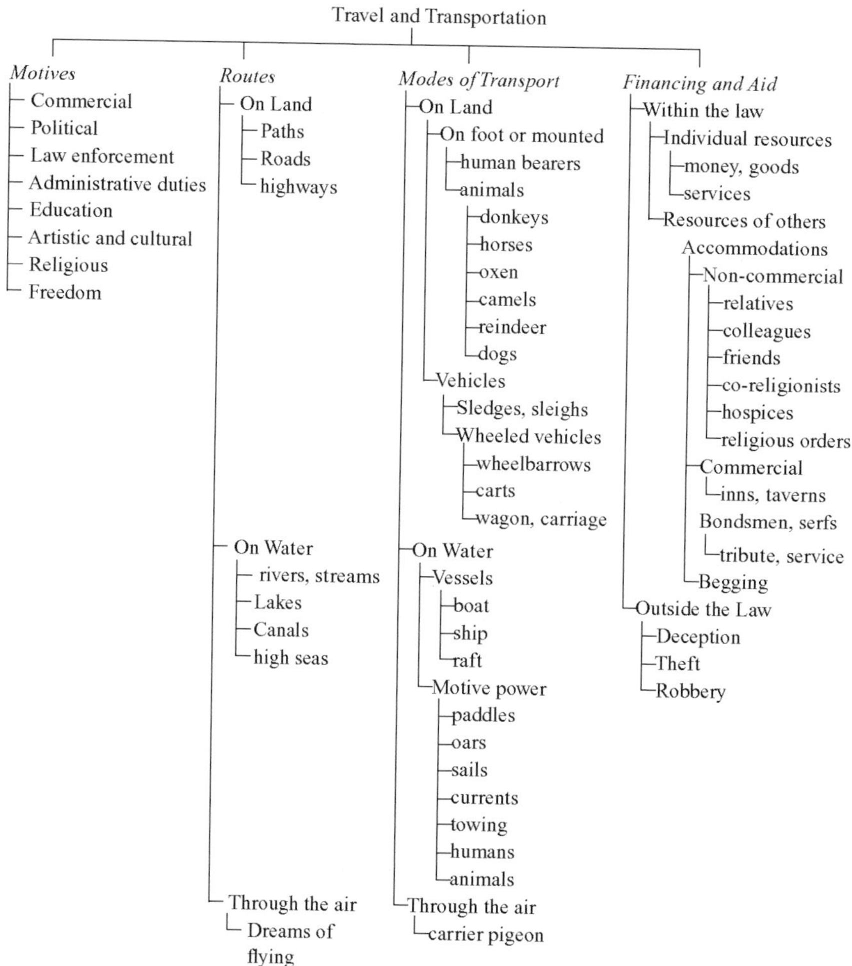

Under the heading 'Means of Transportation', I list pack-animals and mounts, vehicles for land and water, as well as the carrier pigeon. There are two further kinds.

Oxen and Dog

As cities grew, their inhabitants required increasing amounts of meat. Preserving and transporting animal protein was difficult. To solve the problem, oxen were bred in Denmark, Poland, Hungary and other thinly populated areas, and then driven hundreds of miles on 'ox-trails' to major population centres of the day. In the sixteenth century, up to 10,000 oxen per day passed through customs at Rendsburg (Schleswig-Holstein) alone. Shortly before reaching their destination, the animals were fattened on special pastures and only then slaughtered in the city. The traders and drovers of oxen were an important group of travellers.

Dogs probably served as draught-animals for light vehicles in many European countries. Marco Polo reports that in the expanses of Asia, too, they proved to be speedy and capable when yoked to sleds. A famous treatise from the sixteenth century (Georg Agricola: *De re metallica libri* XII, Basel 1556) has illustrations showing dogs at work in mining.

JOURNEYS BY LAND, RIVER AND SEA

Travel on Land (pp. 22ff)

Investigations of medieval land travel have progressed appreciably, thanks both to major research projects and individuals. 'Research on Ancient Routes' seeks to determine which roads were actually used by certain persons and groups. To this end, scholars have already systematically analysed dates and places mentioned in royal decrees of the early and high Middle Ages. This enables them to determine, for example, the two known dates between which a prince travelled from Augsburg to Frankfurt. Given the large number of possible routes, however, we cannot content ourselves with that, but must investigate the whole network of historic places and routes in a context suggested by the IVS (see above).

It has recently been proved that, in Italy, systematic road construction, including surveying and demarcation with stones, began during the twelfth century, some 200 years earlier than in Germany. The journals of Felix Fabri, from the 1480s, reveal that gunpowder was used to blow away rock formations in order to widen the Brenner Pass.

Piety is often mentioned in documents as a motive for building roads and bridges. One patron of such works had his salvation in mind, and the recollection of his sins (*pro dei timore, propter peccata mea* etc.) moved him to his humane acts. Religious hermits not only aided travellers at river crossings and over mountain passes, but also helped to build roads.

Many roadways were constructed of wood and sand, and even if they were not washed away entirely in bad weather, could not be used for some time thereafter. Bricks made for more durable roads, but the cost of their production made them more expensive than quarried stones. From the high Middle Ages, major streets in some cities were paved, but until well into the fifteenth century, if not beyond, many people had to content themselves with stepping-stones set into the 'street' at varying intervals, on which they could make their precarious way when it rained. A traditional tale tells how Saint Elisabeth (d. 1231), balancing on such stepping-stones, was pushed into the mud by a hostile woman and needed to wash her clothing. Travellers hurrying along risked losing their shoes in the mud.

Even experts on medieval travel feel obliged to base their arguments more on probabilities than on certainties. The frequent, widely accepted assertion that a given roadway was 1.7 m wide makes us pause; yet, until a more plausible measure and hypothesis is offered, we can only assume that evenly burdened pack-animals needed that width to use the path safely.

PREPARATIONS: THE STAFF (pp. 29ff)

For travellers on foot, a staff (especially with a metal tip) was indispensable, not least because they could use it to fight off animal or human attackers. They were obliged, however, to respect the laws of the lands they were passing through. The principle that ignorance of the law is no defence against punishment proved to be a misfortune for many. Thomas Platter of Basel was a frequent traveller in the late sixteenth century; he narrowly escaped being condemned to the galleys in Spain because he unknowingly violated a law: 'Non se pue traer baston con hierro' (it is forbidden to carry a staff tipped with iron). In Spain, such staves were evidently considered to be weapons. The prohibition could have been a sign of hostility to foreigners or of bad experiences with aggressive fellow-travellers. The latter possibility is suggested by statements found in other sources, such as: 'I could have defended myself well with my staff.'

Inland waterways (pp. 32ff)

In the course of my research for this book, I discovered that rivers and lakes with a depth of 50 centimetres were considered navigable. For inland lakes, it probably remains a good rule of thumb even today. For moving bodies of water, however, one now relies on figures based on an average flow. For small vessels, 4 cc. per second suffice, while coastal ships require at least 40 cc. per second.

As an additional note, sails, oars, and poles made a more rapid passage downstream possible. They were more important, however, in keeping the boat on its course and preventing a collision with floating tree trunks, running aground on a sandbank, or wrecking the boat on shallows.

I have gathered the following data on the navigability of certain rivers:

River	Length in km	Navigable Length	Navigable from:
Danube	2.860	2.600	Ulm
Elbe/Moldau	1.165	1.000	Melnik or Budweis
Ems	370	224	Greven
Loire	1.002	825	Noirie
Main	495	330	Mouth of Regnitz River
Mosel	514	344	Frouard
Oder	850	750	Ratibor
Po/Tessin	672 (Po)	570	Turin/Pavia
Rhine	1.320	900	Schaffhausen
Rhône/Saône	812	490	Lyon/Chalon
Thames	350	317	Lechlade
Vistula	1.100	800	Cracow (?)
Weser, Werra/Fulda	750	450	Münden

The data under 'Navigable from' is to be used with caution. Larger boats, for example, could navigate the Main only below Miltenberg. On the Rhine, even below Schaffhausen, there were dangerous cataracts, and only daring and experienced sailors challenged their cliffs and rapids. Under such circumstances, ordinary passengers preferred to walk, perhaps on towpaths laid along many rivers. As the towpaths were regarded as part of the waterway, they were King's Roads, accessible to everyone who observed local laws and customs.

The dangers threatening sailors and passengers on the Rhine became part of the legend of the Loreley (which Brentano invented around 1800). The narrows at Bingen were widened with explosives in 1834, though at low tide the shallows are still visible today. Legends of beckoning mermaids or of the frightening mermen of the Elbe, Oder, Danube, or Drave testify to the numbers of crews, passengers, and swimmers that fell victim to the treacherous rapids and reefs of seas, lakes, and rivers every year. In Leipzig, at the juncture of the Pleisse and Weisse Elster, a common legend held that the water 'demanded a human being every year', and that 'a water-nymph pulled men under'. A 'Book of Misfortunes' kept by the Basel boatmen's guild tells of many catastrophes on the Rhine and closes with a prayer: 'May our ever-just God and Father protect us all in his Grace and grant us good fortune and safety in all of our voyages to come. Let his holy angels accompany us as steersmen, in the name of Jesus Christ. Amen.'

Travellers would have informed each other about the best, safest, and least expensive ways to reach a distant destination. In 1599, the pastor Urban Pierius was transferred from Amberg in the Upper Palatinate to Bremen. He asked that his travel and moving expenses be refunded, and his detailed accounts are revealing. He took 42 days to travel 772 km., on both land and water; 11 days were spent on 336 km. of highways and 7 on 436 km. of the Werra and Weser Rivers. His account also reports that his possessions were unloaded by crane from the ship and transferred to wagons. Waiting for transport and for loading and unloading required 24 days, more than half of the total time. Lighter baggage would doubtless have made for better progress, but waiting has always been part of the routine of travel. People had to wait for ferries, guides needed for crossing mountain passes, escorts, repairs to damaged bridges, or the ending of torrential rains or snowstorms.

Ocean navigation (pp. 37ff)

Travel on the Mediterranean was interrupted more frequently and for longer periods than on the North Sea. Geography helps to explain this. The British Isles shield the North Sea from the Atlantic like a gigantic breakwater. It may be even more significant that the North Sea and the Baltic are relatively shallow. In the Baltic the median and maximum depths are 55 metres and 459 metres and in the North Sea 100 metres and 725 metres. Accordingly, the shallows are close to the surface; the Adlergrund in the Baltic is 6 metres below sea level, the Dogger Bank in the North Sea 13 metres. The Mediterranean is quite different. There, depths up 4,000 metres are not uncommon, and up to 5,121 metres have been measured. Thus, during the dreaded winter storms, much higher waves can occur on the Mediterranean than on the North Sea.

Even in calm waters, voyagers were subject to seasickness, and nausea as the ship's food and water often became unfit for consumption. Matters became worse in stormy seas, when cooking was forbidden because of the danger of fire. If there was an epidemic on board, authorities might not let passengers disembark anywhere.

Most travellers were probably so preoccupied with their own problems or so unfeeling that they were blind to the lot of those who had to serve them. From the late Middle Ages, galleys were the preferred mode of transport for large numbers of passengers. While these ships did have sails, in order to move quickly and independently of the wind they were, in addition, powered by rowers. Often these were either slaves or men who had been condemned by a court to labour in the galleys. In the early modern period, such punishments were also decreed for those who had violated a prohibition against undertaking pilgrimages. On the galleys, they had to toil with bare upper bodies so that the whipping they suffered from their overseers was even more painful. If they were chained to their benches, it is unlikely that they could even leave them to answer the call of nature. Their groans, the curses of the overseers, the snapping of the whips, and their stench must have assaulted the ears and noses of the passengers in ways that travellers by land were spared. Passengers paid a high price for travelling so (relatively) effortlessly. Or should we consider that enduring the hardships that sea travel involved was just another variety of the hard work that all travel then required?

Felix Faber, a Dominican monk from Ulm who travelled to the Holy Land in 1480 and 1483, reported on the everyday life of seaborne pilgrims (though of course much of his experience is similar to that found on land travel). He even discusses questions of personal hygiene robustly and frankly. We learn that every pilgrim had a glass or earthenware vessel next to his bed to receive his urine or vomit. As it was cramped and dark on board, and as people moved about constantly, it often happened that some 'clumsy oaf', moved by an urgent need, in passing knocked over one or two of these vessels, causing an unbearable stench. At night, it was difficult to reach the latrines because countless people lay on the deck. On the way to the bow, where latrines were installed on either side of the ship's prow, travellers risked tripping over a sleeper at every step. 'The wakened sleeper curses, the trouble-maker curses back – after all, he hadn't meant to rob the other of his cherished slumber.' In the morning, there could be some ten or more pilgrims waiting for a seat on the latrines. If anyone took too long, the others became angry rather than embarrassed. Whoever was daring and not afraid of heights swung himself over the water on the ship's tackle to do his business. Faber reports that he did that several times despite the danger. In rough seas they risked getting soaked from head to toe. Many, therefore, shed their clothing and ran naked to the bows. Whoever was ashamed to do that squatted at any place, 'which he made filthy, enraging others, leading to blows, and causing even decent people to forget their manners'. Some even defecated into their urinals, which Faber calls revolting, as it poisoned the others; such behaviour could be tolerated only if a person was seriously ill, in which case he should not be scolded. Faber tells of the difficulties that a sick sleeping partner caused him, warning too that one can easily become constipated during sea travel and should make sure to keep regular.

Very few authors were as frank as the Dominican monk in their observations, but thousands must have had comparable experiences. If they do not complain of inconveniences too often, it is because, all in all, the journey was in line with their expectations. The problems they encountered were no worse than what they were accustomed to.

A sea journey was only considered a true 'pilgrimage' with conditions. One had not, after all, travelled on foot like Jesus and his disciples and was bound to a predetermined route, so that it was not possible to honour other saints. Also, no masses were celebrated on board, as the wine, which became Christ's blood, might be spilled on the rolling ship. The risk of this happening inspired the inventiveness of pilgrims sailing towards distant shrines. During the later Middle Ages, chalices came into use whose upper part was mounted in a gimbal, so that the rolling of the ship was neutralized and the wine in the cup was as secure as if it were standing on an even surface.

Even though travel by sea was riskier than by land and pilgrimages by sea were considered less spiritually meritorious, millions of pilgrims journeyed overseas to the Holy Land from the Church's early days. One pious man had to agree to a compromise if he wished to walk in the Redeemer's footsteps. Although his journey to the Holy Land was relatively easy, he encountered genuine hardships in Jerusalem, and carried a cross barefoot to Golgotha, which he then climbed, sliding on his knees under a blazing sun.

PIRATES (pp. 46ff)

When pirates captured a ship, they usually either killed the passengers, or sold the women into harems and the men as slaves. Captives held for ransom were especially badly off. Deprived of enough food, light, fresh air, and exercise, they had to fight off rats and other vermin day and night, with the fear of never emerging alive from their ordeal. Saints like Leonard, who is said to have liberated thousands from such dungeons, were widely honoured. Indeed, still to be seen in the 1980s, in the Church of St Leonard of Noblat, were votive requests like this one: 'Délivrez Papa, 17 oct. 1941, M. T. A. L.' (when speaking to God and the Saints in French at the time, people used the polite forms; the initials might stand for the children's names.) On other votive tablets pilgrims to Noblat during the Second World War plead with St Leonard for the release of their son, husband, or fiancé from German captivity.

Christians held captive in Muslim lands and in danger of renouncing their faith received special kinds of help. If they could not be ransomed, free compatriots volunteered to take their place as slaves. Postulants for the Mercedarian Order ('Ordo Beatae Mariae Virginis de mercede redemptionis captivorum', founded in 1218), in addition to taking vows of poverty, chastity, and obedience, pledged a fourth vow: 'I will be a hostage in the power of the Saracen if that should be necessary for the salvation of believers.' The Trinitarian Order was founded in 1198 for similar purposes. According to reliable reports, Mercedarians and Trinitarians freed 900,000 and 70,000 such prisoners, respectively, from captivity.

Great distress prevailed, even in Christian lands, during outbreaks of coastal banditry. A Spanish galleon, *El Calvador*, part of the Armada, which foundered on the coast of Normandy in 1588 and was plundered by locals, lent its name to the entire coastline, and today the Département Calvados is famous for its apple brandy. Well into the nineteenth century, along the coasts and islands of the North Sea and the Baltic, inhabitants seized the cargoes of stranded ships. 'God bless our shores', a traditional church prayer in some areas, was banned in Mecklenburg as 'barbaric' only in 1777.

A ship could be destroyed by human incompetence as well as by storms and fog at sea. On 25 November 1120 one of the worst maritime catastrophes of the Middle Ages occurred. King Henry I of England and his courtiers departed from the Norman harbour of Barfleur, bound for England. One of the finest ships of the fleet, *Blanche-nef*, famed for its elaborate construction, had the heir to the throne, William, on board. The crew of this ship, apparently drunk, tried to overtake the other ships when leaving the harbour and ran aground upon a reef. The 'White Ship' sank in the waters of the Channel. 300 passengers, among them many barons and nobles of the Anglo-Norman kingdom, and the crown prince, were killed. The catastrophe had far-reaching political-dynastic consequences.

As trade and travel on the North Sea and Baltic increased, coastal towns erected towers visible from afar to show seamen where to enter their harbours and to reflect their civic pride. The tower of St Peter's Church in Rostock, for example, had a height of 132 metres and was visible at a distance of 50 km.

What constituted a harbour at the time? Early in the Middle Ages, sailors dropped anchor at any convenient spot, usually a sheltered bay or the mouth of a river. Ships carried their own gangplanks to facilitate unloading cargo, especially at low tide. If traffic increased over time, wooden posts were rammed into the bottom, joined by planks leading to the shore. Later, costly jetties were built. King Louis IX of France was far more ambitious; wishing to be free of Marseilles, which was not subject to his power, he ordered a new port city, Aigues Mortes, to be designed and built, whence he departed on his Crusade to liberate the Holy Land in 1248.

Harbours, bridges, and fords are points where different kinds of transportation meet. There, passengers had to 'change' and cargoes needed to be unloaded and loaded anew, perhaps from a small boat to a seagoing vessel. Places like Geneva, Constance, and Zurich, where rivers opened into lakes, flourished. Shipwrights, anchor-makers and other artisans in metal crafts, sailmakers, ropers, carters, barrow-drivers, crane-operators, and porters found steady work at such places, as did inn-keepers, cartwrights, shoemakers, tailors and many others.

The important Humanist, Johannes Butzbach (1478–1516), travelled extensively, first as an apprentice tailor and later as a monk. He describes his hometown with affection: 'Miltenberg is the most important harbour town on the Main, as it is from here on that the river is navigable. Goods coming from Frankfurt are loaded from ships onto wagons and those going downriver from wagons onto ships.' Aside from a few industrious traders, most inhabitants were concerned with 'shipping, fishing, freight hauling, farming, and even more, textile production. Because of the lively trade and the many visitors on their way to the Fair in Frankfurt, to Aachen and other places in northern Germany, there are many bakers, butchers, and tavern-keepers there.'

When I wrote this book, I believed that Europeans had not encountered scurvy until the long voyages of Vasco da Gama. In reality, vitamin C deficiency was already creating problems during the Middle Ages, where poor transport made it difficult to provide a diet rich in vitamins. Citrus fruits are generally considered necessary for the prevention and cure of scurvy, but sauerkraut too contains vitamin C, and that was available long before Europeans undertook lengthy sea voyages. Working together, historians, nutritionists, and pharmacologists may well increase our knowledge about plants used in the Middle Ages, whether for food, and spices, or medicinally, which indeed may help us today.

Trade (pp. 59ff)

Traders procured precious merchandise, they knew foreign lands and languages, and could provide information about possible enemies and allies. Rulers therefore offered them protection and special legal status, essentially extraterritorial trading districts in cities, and freedom from onerous taxation, especially in matters of inheritance. Such privileges aroused the hostility of the general population, especially if they abused their rights, sold bad goods, or pretended to be pilgrims to avoid paying certain fees.

COMMUNICATION ON THE WAY (pp. 74ff)

Couriers on special assignments: reconnaissance agents, spies

Toward the end of of the tenth century, Richer, a monk from Reims, tells of a commando operation that his father, Radulf, had carried out in 956. His mission was to win back the fortress town of Mons, then occupied by Reginar II, Count of Hainaut, for the west Frankish crown. Radulf was a *miles*, a knight (though a knightly class did not yet exist). He was considered suitable for this assignment (*idoneus*) because he had reconquered the city of Laon for the west Frankish king Louis IV in 948. Following the king's death, he served his widow Gerberga. Radulf said he was prepared to carry out the new mission, but questioned its feasibility. He sent two men, trained by him personally, to investigate matters in Mons, with precise instructions about what to look for. In Mons, the count's residence was being enlarged, so that there were many workers coming and going through the castle-gate carrying building materials. Dressed to look poor, the two spies took jobs as hod carriers, and observed what was going on for four days. They found out where the countess and her children slept, when and where servants entered and departed, how the household was organized, and from which side the fortress might best be attacked. On Sunday, paid and dismissed, they returned and reported their findings to Radulf. He led a group of armed men to Mons. Guided by the spies to a favourable place, they entered at night and occupied the gates to prevent escape. Radulf overpowered the castle guards and captured the countess and her children; his soldiers plundered the valuables and set fire to the castle. The captives were brought to Queen Gerberga, who stipulated that if Reginar returned the royal properties that he had seized illegally, he could depart in peace with his wife, children, and troops.

It is likely that thousands of such missions were carried out in antiquity and in the Middle Ages, about most of which we hear nothing, although we can determine facts about others. Richer's colourful rendering is certainly exceptional. While even the Bible pays considerable attention to spies, chroniclers provide only sparse details regarding 'couriers on special missions'. Ancient and medieval historians too have only dealt with the topic sparingly.

A few remarks on details from Richer's story that reveal the special nature of such 'reconnoitring': Radulf accomplished his purpose without bloodshed; written messages played no role; loyalty to the commander was essential for success, as were disguises and precisely defined tasks, but also the adaptability of the agents; after all, they were carrying out duties not in keeping with their dignity as warriors.

In every age, those fighting wars or feuds have prized intelligence about their enemies. Radulf prepared for his mission with military espionage, generally thought to be underhand, if not treacherous. Yet our chronicler affirms that patience, mental acuity, and sovereign self-control are entirely in keeping with the ethos of the *miles*. Epics such as the *Chanson de Roland* and *El Cid* do not touch upon espionage, and revel in rash acts of combat; but that does not justify generalizations, even if limited to the later Middle Ages, such as that put forth by Barbara Tuchmann: 'Reconnoitring the region through which one was travelling was not a part of medieval tactics, because it was not part of the tournaments; the battle was everything.'

Medieval vocabulary associated with espionage suggests that it was not despised. Latin sources speak of *explorare* (to explore), and of *speculatores* (seers, scouts), who are also referred to as *nuntii* (couriers), *legatii* (legates), or *relatores* (informants). In German, *Kundschafter* (informant, later spy) became a pejorative only late, supplanted by *Spion* (spy), which perhaps still has disreputable connotations for us today. This word is derived from the Middle High German *spê* (sharp-sighted as a falcon). The noun *Spăhe* was already associated with 'lying in wait', 'eavesdropping', 'covert observation', and 'spying' in military and civil contexts, especially commercial speculation. Other languages adopted *spê*; from the French *espion* came the German *Spion* and English *spy*.

Informants expressly termed 'talented' were often assigned to find out useful military details: entrances and access routes, the size and movements of the enemy army, and other military secrets. An Arab commentator, Al-Kalkashandi (d. 1418), a legal expert and secretary of the Egyptian chancery of the Mamelukes, provides a perspective from the Islamic world. He requires that a spy be, above all, loyal and honest to his employer, and, in addition, intelligent, sharp-witted, and cunning. He must be a seasoned traveller and familiar with the lands to which he is sent, and able to endure great pain, for even under torture he must not divulge what he knows.

Trickery and deception were held to be honourable. To intimidate prospective enemies, a ruler might parade his troops before their emissaries, assuring them that they were seeing only a part of his forces. If the inhabitants of a besieged city were starving, they showed enemy couriers bulging sacks that were really filled with sand covered with a thin layer of flour. Such couriers, however, frequently learned more than their enemies wished, who then did their best to prevent them from passing on their information. Killing a stranger for such reasons was only a last resort. The honourable solution to the problem was simply to prevent a courier from returning to his camp. An excuse was always to hand: flooding, snowdrifts, the danger of attacks by bandits, etc. Emissaries to an enemy camp lived dangerously, especially if they brought unpleasant tidings: a declaration of war, an excommunication, or a writ of interdict. It was no accident that, as many sources confirm, papal legates were always guaranteed safe passage.

METHODS OF SECRET COMMUNICATION

Passing on secret information verbally, as described by Richer, was not just common around the turn of the first millennium. From late antiquity, written communication was infrequent, especially in the secular realm. Aside from a few laypersons (among them women), usually of high status, only clerics and monks could read and write. That does not make it impossible that, during a siege, someone might shoot an arrow with a message attached into the enemy camp. However, secret written messages must have been used more than the sources suggest. Couriers hid them between the wax tablets they carried for making notations, or in their clothes or shoes. Muslim guards could be deceived if notes were hidden between hams. Hiding such messages from unwanted scrutiny was a challenge to the imagination.

In the ancient world, written information could be encrypted, a method used by the Papal Curia, for example. In due course, Italian trading houses all over Europe used this means of discussing confidential matters. Jews were often entrusted with delivering secret messages. They had international connections and their own language and writing system, incomprehensible to most people. While their services as bearers of secrets were in demand, they also suffered the disadvantages of that role. Time and again they were accused of intrigues against Christians. During the Great Plague of the mid-fourteenth century, they were charged with having put foreign poison into wells. Couriers were thought to bear not only secret papers but also highly toxic materials.

MILITARY INFORMERS

In order to procure first-hand information, a commander would despatch informants who spoke the prospective enemy's language. They were to identify potentially threatening people and see to it that they did no harm. *Spectator* (scout, look-out) was therefore also a term to describe those guarding city gates and storehouses. The scouts that Richer described probably passed such guard posts without arousing suspicion. An early medieval Byzantine author describes how camps guarded against spies who had entered unnoticed through the camp-gate. At a pre-arranged signal, all of the soldiers returned to their tents except for a few officers. Whoever then remained outside or tried to enter a strange tent was, at the very least, suspect (Maurikios, *Strategikon*, IX, 5). In 775, Saxon warriors deceived their Frankish enemies in a way that must often have succeeded. When the Franks left camp to find fodder for their animals, the Saxons mingled with them and helped them take it back, where they subsequently carried out a bloodbath.

A commander needed to get timely information from the territory of a likely enemy. Warriors who had hunted since their youth were especially fitted for such tasks, especially if they knew the area from earlier campaigns. This was true of the campaigns of the Franks in the seventh to ninth centuries, as well as for those of the Saracens, Normans, and Hungarians in western, central and southern Europe in the ninth to eleventh centuries, for Germans in the borderlands of the Slavs in the tenth to twelfth centuries, for the Crusaders in the Holy Land between the eleventh and thirteenth centuries, and for the Teutonic Order and European knights on the Baltic during the twelfth to fourteenth centuries. What one side considered trickery or treachery, the other regarded as successful reconnoitring and intelligence activity. Most sources discuss these matters indirectly, if at all.

It was not always possible to guard important military outposts against the enemy. Travellers descending on much-frequented routes from the Alps to the Po valley had to pass through guard posts at narrow defiles as they left the valley. Elite troops using dangerous paths repeatedly bypassed such barriers and attacked the defenders from the rear. Assaulted from both sides, the defenders had to let the enemy army enter.

The Franks conducted pincer offensives against the Saxons and Bavarians in the eighth century, as did the Hungarians against the Saxons in the tenth. In both cases, these operations were made easier because the aggressors had won influential individuals or whole groups in the enemy camp over to their side. In times of internal dissension, that was not so difficult. An order that Charlemagne was moved to issue, forbidding any enemy person to enter the realm in connection with a feud, characterizes such situations. As there was not as yet a firmly established state polity, a ruler could not completely trust his closest relatives or the nobles of his court. Thus, in 954, Liudolf, a son of King Otto I, let the Hungarians penetrate into the Empire as far as the left bank of the Rhine. In the following year, Hungarian emissaries came before him to renew the peace agreement. They were suspected, however, of wishing to assess the level of internal unrest in order to attack once more. This was confirmed when, in August 955, the Battle of the Lechfeld, one of the most significant in European history, was fought near Augsburg.

Before an army went into battle, the commander had to send out scouts to assess how secure the roads were. Other soldiers were to guard the army's flanks and its baggage train. Such simple rules were often ignored, whether because the terrain made reconnaissance difficult, as when the Franks were ambushed in the Pyrenees in 778, inspiring the *Chanson de Roland*, or because the enemy was still believed to be far off, as at the start of the Battle of the Lechfeld, or, as at the

Battle of Otranto against the Muslims in 983, because the Imperial commanders believed they had already carried the day.

Sieges called for special precautions. Individuals or groups in the besieged town were often prepared to co-operate with the attackers. In AD 500, for example, the commander of besieged Vienne on the Rhône drove 'useless eaters' out of the town, one of whom had been in charge of the water supply. As revenge, he led the attackers directly into the city on the aqueduct.

Even if a commander was familiar with a region, uncertainties remained. Where, for example, could a river be forded? Did pathways exist through dense forests or extensive swamps? Local inhabitants had to be relied on, and often enough forced to guide the troops. If they refused, they were maimed or killed. Quite often, 'pathfinders' led the enemy into waterless wastes or ambushes prepared by their own people.

SECRET POLITICAL COMMUNICATIONS

Source documents say nothing even of successful and far-reaching intelligence operations. We may deduce, however, that they did take place. How else could Byzantium have defied Arabs, Avars, Bulgars, Huns, Persians, and others for a thousand years? Its rulers followed the traditions of the empires of antiquity, among which was the art of espionage and counter-intelligence, as well as the ability to procure the information necessary to placate enemies with gifts of gold or to play them off against one another.

The royal courts of the West were clearly quite nonchalant in their dealings with potentially hostile powers. At the Imperial Diet at Paderborn in 777, Charlemagne received Saracen emissaries from Spain. When he was fighting in Spain the following year, the Saxons attacked. Perhaps Charlemagne had meant to impress the Saracens with the idea that Saxony was pacified and part of the Frankish Empire! Now he was tied down at a distant battlefield, and the Saxons were making it clear that they were in no way defeated. Had the Saracens told them that it was worthwhile to arrange an insurrection? They may have had such discussions with the Saxons at the Diet of Paderborn.

The Byzantines systematically screened emissaries from abroad. Readers may recall how Liutprand of Cremona complained about such unaccustomed treatment. At Charlemagne's court and those of his successors, foreign emissaries could mingle freely among themselves and make contact with the nobility. That was not always in the interests of the Empire. At Easter AD 973 in Quedlinburg, in addition to many lords of the Empire and from Poland, legations of Bulgars, Danes, Greeks, Slavs, and Hungarians were also present. In 983, the Slavic tribes between the Elbe and the Oder rose in rebellion against their Saxon-German rulers at the very same time as the armies of the Empire led by Emperor Otto II were fighting the Muslims in southern Italy. Was this a coincidence? In the short term, the freedom of the courts of Charlemagne and Otto the

Great could be damaging; in the longer term, it may well have strengthened the western kingdoms more than the mistrust prevailing at Byzantium.

King Louis IX of France conducted long-range, even intercontinental, intelligence operations. As discussed on p. 204, above, in 1253 he commissioned William of Rubruck to travel thousands of kilometres to the Great Khan of the Mongols to explore possible missionary activities. Great problems might be solved thereby. Could the aggressive potential of the Mongols, who had destroyed a Christian army at Liegnitz in 1241, be redirected? Would a Christian empire of the Mongols not be the ideal ally against the Islamic powers in the Near East? Christian Mongols would help to neutralize Islam as a political and military force permanently, which would make Crusading to liberate the sacred sites in Palestine unnecessary. To his sorrow, Rubruck found that the Mongols were prepared neither to be baptized nor to give up their claim to being destined to rule the world. He understood that they were serious in this, and expressed his respect and admiration for them in his report. He regretted never seeing them in full armour, despite his frequent requests.

Princes found it more important to observe, on a daily basis, the designs of ambitious nobles and neighbouring states than to be informed of distant circumstances. Rulers have always dreamed of placing a dependable spy at the heart of an enemy's territories. It is difficult even now to get indisputable facts about the intrigues of others; it was substantially harder during the Middle Ages. We know this much about a famous instance. During the night of August 7–8, 1472, Philippe de Commynes, the closest adviser and confidant of Duke Charles the Bold, joined forces with King Louis XI of France, the Duke's adversary of many years' standing, to whom Commynes had probably passed on vital information even earlier.

MISSIONARIES EXPLORE FOREIGN LANDS

Christian missionaries, such as Boniface and Rubruck, wanted to carry out the command of Jesus that they travel to all peoples, make all men his disciples, and baptize them (Matthew 28: 19). To fulfil this task, these messengers of faith had to know the lands in which they planned to work. Accordingly, during the course of history, missionaries often functioned as pioneers, combining commitment and self-sacrifice with the desire to learn the language of the 'heathens' they hoped to convert.

Ansgar (d. 865) brought the Christian mission to Denmark and Sweden. With the support of local rulers and the Bishops of Hamburg and Bremen, Ansgar was able to explore a wide area while preaching the faith. Within a few generations, he and his successors appreciably increased what was known and understood about the Baltic regions, Scandinavia, and the North Sea. Archbishop Unni (914–28) was said to have travelled (*penetravit*) to all of the Danish islands. Later authors and modern scientists learned much from the written records of such journeys, including the location of a pirates' lair and how long voyages between Denmark and England took. In other times or places, such information was highly confidential and could cost a person divulging it his head.

Laymen and clerics often acted as couriers, self-appointed or commissioned, transporting precious relics from Rome and elsewhere to their homelands, often under hazardous circumstances. In 827, for example, the remains of Saints Marcellinus and Peter were brought from Rome to Seligenstadt in Hesse, and in 829 those of Mark the Evangelist from Alexandria to Venice. The bones of Bishop Nicholas, who was active in the Near East and buried at Myra, today rest in southern Italy. We must regard as moot the question of whether their transfer to Bari in 1087 met with the approval of all concerned or whether it was outright theft. Substitute-pilgrims, carrying out the religious duties of those who paid them, were also among such travellers.

Even more than members of recognized churches, religious heretics had to depend on secret messengers they could trust. Only through them could they maintain contact with individuals or groups who thought like them; only in this way could they survive the many varieties of persecution. How far they might divulge their identity was a vital question. Should they lie? Or were they obliged to tell the truth even if they would be burned to death? 'Heretics' had to face such questions during the high Middle Ages and even more so after the Reformation. During the twelfth and thirteenth centuries in southern France, the Cathars communicated in a language of their own with special signs and phrases. They often entrusted their messages to shepherds. They also communicated between mountain peaks with shouts or visual signals.

That fanatics can do great harm more easily in a multicultural society than in a more homogeneous one was already evident during the second half of the twelfth century, when the 'Assassins', part of a Muslim sect, gained a certain notoriety. Under the influence of their ideology and of hashish (hence the name), young men murdered prominent persons for political reasons. They may have killed Conrad of Montferrat, King of Jerusalem, in 1192, causing a crisis in western dominance in the Holy Land. Their name, meaning 'murderer', has been adopted into French and English, *assassin* and into Italian, *assassino*.

COMMERCIAL ESPIONAGE

Scouts charged with obtaining tactical information appear in the Biblical narrative of how the Israelites conquered the 'Land of milk and honey'. Moses' instructions to the scouts on assessing the terrain would still be useful today. As he had ordered, the scouts brought back fruits of the land; two men bore a bunch of grapes on a pole into the Israelites' camp to demonstrate its fertility (Numbers 13). As it often appeared in illustrations, this scene might have inspired later leaders to follow Moses' example. Few sources, however, have anything to say about commercial espionage.

Earlier, we touched briefly upon a case of transcontinental commercial spying during the early Middle Ages (p. 63). According to the historian Procopius, the Byzantines at the time of Justinian I (527–65) managed to break a profitable Chinese state monopoly. Justinian had gladly accepted, from a party of monks, silkworm eggs they had hidden in their staves and smuggled out of China, defying possible death sentences, together with instructions on how to care for them and harvest the silk. From then on, silk was also produced in Byzantium, from where its use spread.

I have already mentioned Willibald, a missionary who, in 726, violated an export ban on balsam, an aromatic mixture of resins and oils. If merchants were caught cheating customs officials, they could deem themselves fortunate if they were fined only double the tariff and did not lose their wagons or their ships, their freedom or their lives.

CONCLUSIONS

In the Middle Ages, numerous messengers travelled on special assignments. They provided intelligence on military matters, politics, religion, and trade. Documents tell us more about imaginative efforts to keep valuable goods or information from being purloined than about such secretive undertakings. It is not easy to know how a given chronicler distinguished between obtaining information legitimately, and spying, which intended harm to an opponent by giving one side an unfair advantage.

More significant to future developments was the readiness, palpable in these documents, to encounter other peoples and to gain materially and culturally from these contacts. Strong curiosity was characteristic of many people in the West, with its heritage of Roman Christianity. This probably derived from the pleasure the ancient Greeks took in perceiving the world and gaining knowledge about it, joined with the experiences of early Christian communities. Commanded to preach to all of mankind, disciples were prepared to learn other languages.

There is as much to be said about how newly-found knowledge and technology were transferred as a matter of course between nations, as about covert investigation and spying. People passed along to others insights they had achieved through thinking, speculation, and experimentation, by observing, collecting, and comparing phenomena, and also by finding out what others were doing. The rapid spread of scientific and technical knowledge since the late Middle Ages, including the clock, the printing press, and firearms, reveals that concealment and espionage and the transfer of knowledge and technology did not work against each other, but rather were complementary in their effects.

SUMMIT MEETINGS (pp. 72ff)

'Summit meetings' have even been conducted on the middle of bridges. In addition to those of princes, referred to already, a later such encounter merits attention. It ended badly. During the Hundred Years' War, on 10 September

1419, the Dauphin Charles, later King Charles VII, and Jean 'sans peur', the Duke of Burgundy, agreed to meet on the bridge of Montereau, a small town on the river Seine in northern France. They hoped to set aside their mutual hostility and together fight against their English enemy. In a pavilion erected on the bridge for the meeting, nobles from the Dauphin's entourage killed Duke Jean with axes, just as he was greeting his vassals and kinsmen. It was not spontaneous, but a pre-meditated, cold-blooded act of revenge for a murder that the Duke had ordered to be committed years earlier. Europe was badly shaken by the killing. Currency values crashed in Bruges and Venice. The victim's son, Philippe le bon, swore bloody revenge. He allied himself with the English king, and together the English and Burgundian troops devastated the territories still belonging to the French King. It took the King another decade to become 'master in his own house' once more, thanks to the courageous conduct of Joan of Arc.

HOSPITALITY AND INNS (pp. 79ff)

Recent investigations have shown that fully-developed inns have existed since about 1300. They provided necessary shelter to travellers and played major roles in local trade and communication. Establishing the dates when these facilities arose in particular areas remains quite difficult. Based on a detailed study in Switzerland, it is thought that far more inns existed than previously assumed. Before 1550, for example, there were at least eight inns between Berne and Thun, 40 km distant, not counting those within the towns themselves.

What inns looked like depended on their location, their clientele, and regional surroundings. Disused town- or farmhouses were often made into inns simply by adding more beds. Some houses could harbour 35 persons for the night, and 38 horses. Drinks were available at any inn, and often food and a place to stay the night. Prices varied according to the quality of the lodgings; 'certified' houses charged three times what simpler inns demanded.

Most inns could offer what travellers needed, but they were there mainly to serve the local populace as a communal meeting-place, along with the church; inn-keepers depended on local customers who returned regularly. But of course travellers found inns indispensable. They would meet there people familiar with the locality who could give helpful advice and point out dangers. They could exchange information with other travellers that would help in planning their routes. Ideally, before undertaking a risky venture, they could leave money for safekeeping to be retrieved upon their return. They could stable their horses and, if they meant to travel by water, rent a boat. In harbour towns, voyages were booked at inns; in the mountains the host could give advice about finding reliable guides over the passes, when best to start a journey, and when there was a risk of fog, heavy snow, or avalanches. As guilds of merchants and craftsmen held their meetings and ceremonial feasts at the inn, a traveller on business could get to know his counterparts and learn about local fees and taxes.

Travellers were likely to tell others about positive experiences: 'We recommend the "Three Kings" inn at Chur in every respect!' Travellers to foreign lands preferred to stay at inns operated by former compatriots because it made them feel safer and more at home. If famous guests arrived, distinguished local citizens came to the inn to win their favour, perhaps even supplying the host with wine and fish that they and their visitors might enjoy together. Such meals reinforced ties of common interest and fostered peace.

Probably during his second journey to Italy in 1505–6, Albrecht Dürer drew the floor plan that shows how the rooms on one storey of a sizable inn in northern Italy were arranged and furnished. He points out the *stub* (sitting room), *kamer* (sleeping room), *kuchen* (kitchen), *spiskamer* (pantry), *scheishaus* (latrine), *pett* (bed), *ofen* (oven), *schlot* (chimney), and *fenster* (window). For each of the sitting rooms, Dürer has drawn in three tables, each likely to have accommodated at least four guests; sleeping rooms have between one and four beds. An inn's main buildings and annexes might be arranged around a courtyard (courtyard type), or, just as frequently, under a single roof (block or gatehouse type). Galleries along the exterior of rooms on upper storeys afforded guests individual access to their rooms and a degree of privacy. Some inventories that have survived show that the better inns provided bed linen and, occasionally, mattresses, sheets, blankets, and pillows. The condition of the linen is sometimes also noted, possibly at the insistence of guests who refused to pay for a worn-out sheet. Cups, bowls, and other implements, usually of wood, were counted, making it easier for the host to prevent guests from taking such items away with them.

An inn-keeper was obliged to provide lodging to respectable strangers who requested it, and, if need be, to protect them from unfriendly local inhabitants. Nonetheless, some visitors must have been more welcome, and better treated, than others. Many taverns were considered to be blatantly disreputable, breeding grounds for rebellion and violence, disorder and moral corruption. Like public baths, some were hardly distinguishable from brothels. Many tavern-keepers were accused of fraud or murder. We must take such negative comments with a pinch of salt, however, and remember that sensational, scandalous doings were far more likely to be recorded in the sources on which historians depend than the peaceful everyday life of ordinary people.

Erasmus of Rotterdam (d. 1536) travelled extensively all over Europe and came to know many hostelries that were not to his liking. He demanded that no guest be obliged to use bed-sheets that another had slept in. He abhorred German inns especially. 'The bed-sheets were last laundered perhaps six months ago.' He also has little good to say about the facilities and hospitality in Germany, telling how eighty or ninety sweating, unwashed people were crowded into an unventilated, overheated room: walkers, horsemen, merchants, sailors, carters, peasants, children, women, the sick and the healthy, with dripping clothes hanging near the oven to dry. 'One person is combing his hair, another is wiping off his sweat, a third is polishing his shoes or boots, while yet another one belches the stench of garlic.' He declares himself unwilling to speak of the farts and other evil emanations, 'but how many of these people are secretly ill, and every illness is infectious'. Syphilis, the 'French' or 'Spanish' disease, he said, was widespread. Washing one's hands helped, but one must demand fresh water to rinse the filth off thoroughly.

Erasmus reports that dinner began with a glass of thin, sour wine; bowls of porridge followed, interspersed with soups. Once the guests had eaten their fill of these, roast meats or trout were served, which were passable, except that they were offered sparingly and quickly taken away again. Next came a wine of better quality and a spoiled cheese overrun with maggots. The entire meal was accompanied by a confusing din of voices, noise, and the smutty jokes of paid jesters. At the end, the host, bad-tempered and clothed revoltingly, appeared and divided the entire expense of the dinner by the number of diners. Everyone paid the same amount, regardless of how much he had consumed. No one could retire until the bill had been paid. Whoever objected was rudely told, 'If you don't like it, go and find another place!'

To what degree such complaints were justified is not easily established. In the late sixteenth century, after all, Michel de Montaigne, a demanding traveller, spoke positively of German hostelries. As far as the quality of European inns is concerned, there was probably both a north-south divide and an east-west divide. And Erasmus's criticisms might also be understood as a challenge: try harder, especially in the areas of hygiene and cleanliness!

Simple hostels where penniless pilgrims could count on a bowl of soup and a place to sleep for the price of a 'Thank you' offered aid and comfort. The House Rules of such a hostel at Bruchsal in Baden reveal much about the daily routine of the *ellenden herberg* (hostel for foreigners and the poor) in a middle-sized German town. 'For the sake of God', pilgrims might spend one night free of charge. In the summer they might be admitted two hours before dark, in winter one hour. Swearing, cursing, fighting, quarrelling, complaining, and idle talk were forbidden, as was gambling. Anyone defaming God or disturbing the peace of the house was to be summarily ejected. Before the soup, evidently the only meal, was ladled out, pilgrims were to say five *pater nosters* and five *Ave Marias* devoutly. Furthermore, they were to retire promptly, with men and women in separate rooms, and clothed only in an undershirt. Outer clothes and luggage were to be placed outside the rooms, which were locked from the outside and not opened until morning. Then the pilgrims made their beds. As everything was in an inventory, the host then had to make sure that no sheets or blankets were missing. When this had been done, and all the pilgrims were satisfied that they had all their possessions, the hostel's gate was opened and the pilgrims dismissed. Despite their austere facilities and discipline, we must regard such houses as humane, as they saved many people from exposure and death.

SPEED OF TRAVEL (pp. 97ff)

The speed of travel improved very little until well into the eighteenth century. If 'high level politics' were involved, however, impressive performances could be achieved even in the late Middle Ages. In 1438, couriers brought Albrecht von Habsburg in Wiener Neustadt word, only nine days later, that he had been elected King of the Germans in Frankfurt am Main, 980 kilometres away. The news took far longer to reach the King of Poland, who was not much further away from Frankfurt.

Speed of travel had little effect on the dissemination of ideas and technology. Printing was passed on rapidly from one town to the next during the fifteenth century and granted the West unprecedented advantages over other cultures; but it hardly mattered at all if a master printer needed twenty days to reach Paris from Mainz, or thirty. What mattered was that he would find in Paris, or London, Burgos or Florence, infrastructures similar to those in Mainz: people who took an interest in printing, skilled craftsmen who could quickly construct the machinery needed for printing, and lovers of books living there. The educated wished to read the classical works previously available only as manuscripts in affordable books; others wanted to learn about recent technical developments from printed descriptions and illustrations; others still wished to learn the opinions of reformers in many spheres. Common basic conditions and techniques, among them writing systems, were the result of earlier exchange relationships.

SOVEREIGNTY AND LAW (pp. 102ff)

Travellers were subject to many dangers, but they were protected in various ways too. Wherever possible, they avoided threatening areas. It was advisable to travel in parties of at least three persons; if one was taken ill, the second stayed with him, while the third sought aid. The members of such a group might be bound by an oath to remain loyal to each other until reaching their destination – or until death. Such groups tended to arouse less suspicion.

Travellers also turned to local governments for aid and protection. At the end of the twelfth century, Germans and Swedes asked the Prince of Novgorod for a guarantee of peace and protection by the laws within his domains. They were to be safe from theft or injury, 'unharmed, inviolate by anyone'. As such promises were only as effective as a prince's power and influence prevailed, merchants travelling with precious goods were at greater risk than poorer wayfarers. At certain times, therefore, they joined together in a *hanse* (company) for the journey. Later, this name was adopted by the commercial league of Hanseatic cities. In some cases, such companies travelled with military escorts, so that they would not be helpless in the face of attacks by bandits or marauding knights and soldiers. Such caravans on land were like convoys on the seas. But bandits, too, formed alliances to plunder with greater ease.

In 1269, the Hanseatic merchants in Novgorod were granted permission to take wood as needed to repair their ships and construct buildings: 'When a guest comes to the Neva requiring timbers or masts, he may cut wood on both sides of the river, as far as he wishes.' Such rights aroused the desires of the 'underprivileged', and a process of 'equalization' began. Whenever one party of merchants achieved certain rights, other groups clamoured for similar or better conditions. Privileges earlier enjoyed only by a few developed tortuously, over the centuries, to rights for all citizens.

The limited value of such alliances was well understood. In 1428, Conrad von Weinsberg captured a caravan from Imperial cities in Swabia and Franconia on its way to the Fair at Frankfurt; the cities paid a ransom of 30,000 guilders to free the 150 merchants and their goods. When banditry on the roads and rivers became intolerable, the cities took protective measures. Strasbourg (the leader), Berne, Lucerne, Basel, and Freiburg formed an alliance in 1333 to fight against Walter III von Geroldseck-Tübingen, the most powerful nobleman of the Ortenau region. The league besieged and destroyed Schwanau, his castle on the Rhine, west of Lahr, beheading nearly all of the defenders. Usually, though, merchants preferred to avoid bloodshed, contenting themselves with economic weapons. In their disputes with Bruges and Flanders from 1358–60, the Hanse towns made effective use of boycotts.

The states which emerged during and after the high Middle Ages found it in their humanitarian and commercial interests to foster peace within their lands. Rulers offered travellers escorts of two kinds, both to be paid for. Merchants required the company of armed guards. Individual travellers could obtain letters stating the ruler's guarantee to provide compensation if harm should befall them in his territories. Claims for such compensation could only succeed if the victim could persuade his own government to exert pressure, either on the person harming him or on the prince who had issued the guarantee. Though escorts offered only relative safety, they must have provided a greater sense of justice and tranquility in the land.

Wise rulers advised their own subjects to show goodwill to travellers and worked to their benefit by concluding agreements with other rulers. Even if they could not eliminate troublesome regulations, they worked to limit their worst effects. The unprecedented success of the fairs of Champagne, which contributed decisively to developing European innovations in trade and finances, owed much to the protection that the Count of Champagne offered to merchants at the fair and in their travels to and fro. In Troyes and at other sites, he maintained his own staff of judges, notaries, and market inspectors, as well as armed guards patrolling the roads on foot and on horseback. The merchants' treasures nevertheless lured bandits to attack. If they did, however, they were, as a rule, pursued by the authorities. Most unusually for the time, the Count sued in other territories to procure justice for merchants and money-changers who had been robbed.

In Champagne it was understood that the fairs could only flourish if merchants with their far-flung connections continued to trust that the roads were safe to travel, quashing rumours to the contrary.

MISTRUST TOWARDS TRAVELLERS

It may seem that I have generally depicted restrictions on travel as exceptional, for instance when concerns arose that travellers might pass on infectious diseases. Understandably, however, once they had reached their destinations, travellers had only limited freedom. What was the traveller doing there? Was he a spy? Authorities in the traveller's homeland did not view their subjects' delight in travelling completely favourably. Many travellers had to contend with downright mistrust. In 1416, for example, the King of England forbade people from leaving the country without his express written permission. Each member of a company of travellers had to be named in such a document. When entering another country, travellers of higher rank had to present a letter, a kind of pass, from their king requesting that authorities grant the visitor safe conduct. Only pilgrims could embark with just a blanket 'exit visa'. These regulations were not motivated by vague concerns about disorder and so forth, but rather by the concrete fact that minted currency and precious metals were in short supply and could only be taken out of the country, if at all, in limited quantities. Royal officials at ports were ordered to arrest pilgrims who claimed poverty but actually had valuable coins or precious stones hidden in their belts.

Sovereignty and Law (pp. 102ff)

DEVELOPING INTERNATIONAL 'MARITIME' LAWS

Travellers were far more isolated on the seas than on land. Once they had left a harbour, extraordinary dangers threatened a ship, its passengers, and cargo. If storms and periods of dead calm, mutinies and piracy were to be withstood, matters had to be regulated ahead of time that were dealt with on land case by case.

From the high Middle Ages, customary practices evolved gradually into local rights, were then brought into accord with practices elsewhere, and finally codified. This took place earlier on the shores of the Mediterranean than the Atlantic, the North Sea, or the Baltic. The best-known and most important collection of maritime law documents comes from Barcelona, one of the greatest ports in the western Mediterranean. The *Consolat de Mar*, originally a private compilation of the rules of navigation from the thirteenth and fourteenth centuries, was widely accepted because it dealt with practical, everyday matters. In 1272, a royal maritime court, the *Loge de Mar*, was established, also at Barcelona, in which marine councillors (*consules maris*) were charged with resolving conflicts between ship-owners and pilgrims, merchants and ships' crews. They had to define the rights and duties of shippers, property rights in case of shipwreck, piracy, abandonment, or partial scuttling of a cargo to save lives, the ship itself, or the rest of the cargo.

Major ports were dependent on earnings from maritime commerce and valued their good reputations accordingly. Civic commissions, therefore, supervised ship-owners and captains (*patronus)*, kept registries of ships, inspected vessels and certified their seaworthiness and the adequacy of their outfitting. In the mid-twelfth century, authorities in Arles were concerned that captains of pilgrims' ships should give proper guarantees (*fidejussores bonos et ydoneos)* to their passengers; pilgrims were to be treated fairly (*bona fides)*, and their property protected. A Genoese statute of 1316 demanded guarantees (*ydoneas securitates)* that passengers be carried in safety. To guard against pirates, ships in convoys on long voyages were to sail no further than one mile apart. The owner, often the commander too, of his vessel was legally responsible for the soundness of the ship and its equipment, and for ensuring that his crew were experienced and hardworking sailors who could use weapons if need be, and that the ship's provisions were sufficient for the voyage. In order to prevent mutinies it was stipulated that each sailor should receive a certain number of rusks on a daily basis.

A ship's commander could also act as a proxy for an absent owner, which gave him wide latitude for action. He shared responsibility for the care, equipping, and seaworthiness of the vessel; he hired the crew and determined the route of the voyage. He saw to it that the ship sailed and arrived promptly, without unnecessary detours or stops. Like an inn-keeper, the captain was responsible for keeping the peace on board and for protecting passengers, especially women, from being annoyed or harmed by the crew or other passengers. He could punish violators of the ship's rules by stranding them on shore, having them whipped, or inflicting other bodily harm. He was required to take proper measures if an epidemic broke out. He convened a ship's council if pirates threatened, if cargo was to be jettisoned, or if decisions were needed on similar losses to passengers, to whom he might have to provide compensation. During the late Middle Ages, Venetian ships had two city magistrates on board to resolve disputes.

During the later medieval period the rights and responsibilities of passengers in connection with ship-owners and commanders were written down. Such contracts, often filed in a city's registry and intended to prevent conflicts, reflect the experiences of both partners. They stated that passengers should do nothing to disturb the orderly operation of the ship. Anyone paying little or nothing for the voyage was obliged to do menial tasks on board, such as pumping out the stinking bilge water that collected in the lowest part of the hull. In 1441, Genoa required two merchants to be elected on each ship, who were obliged to attest under oath whether or not the captain had overloaded his ship during the voyage (*onoraverit navem suam ultra debitam portatum*).

When possible, travellers would inspect a ship before signing a contract and negotiate more favourable conditions. In time, all of the important points were codified in a kind of template: time and place of departure; the route; the maximum number of passengers; the minimum space allotted to the passenger, including room for any cages of chickens, etc., he might bring; food and drink on board; the frequency and the ingredients of meals; and the sorts of drinks offered, possibly wine from Malaga 'without cunning or deceit'. The reasons why travellers might go ashore during voyages included the need to purchase medicine and visits to holy places. While passengers were on land, the captain, like an inn-keeper, was to protect their property on board. Care for the sick was also stipulated; they were, if possible, to be given space on deck. If a death occurred, the corpse was not to be cast into the sea, but properly buried at the next opportunity. A captain familiar with conditions in the Holy Land was to share any risks with his passengers, mainly pilgrims, and protect them from attacks by infidels, accompany them to the holy sites, pay any fees and taxes for them, rent donkeys, and so on. He was responsible for finding competent guides for pilgrims planning to visit Mount Sinai and Egypt. A cover-all clause at the end was designed to satisfy even sceptical travellers: if any of the captain's obligations required by law and custom were omitted from the contract, they should nevertheless be considered as included. However, as one might expect, complaints arose constantly, often about food and drink. Whether or not such complaints were compensated on the basis of the guarantee depended on who had the upper hand and had paid sufficient bribes.

No laws could guarantee comfort to travellers or protect them from storms, which threatened even if a captain had agreed to sail along the coast on a voyage from Venice through the Adriatic to the Holy Land. But more specifically-worded contracts helped to bring about more peace on board and an increased sense of security.

TRAVEL IN THE MOUNTAINS

HENRY IV CROSSES THE ALPS (pp. 122ff)

Even into the nineteenth and twentieth centuries, many people travelled on horseback, and would have had a reasonable general knowledge of equestrian skill: they might have known how to cross a river with horses or, in mountainous regions, how to lead horses down steep, snow-covered paths. Such knowledge is useful if we ask ourselves whether Emperor Henry IV's transit of the Alps in winter 1066–67 could have taken place as described by the chronicler Lampert von Hersfeld. Lampert was not an eye-witness, but he presents details surely unlikely to be known in the lowlands. Certainly peasants were helpful to the king. They were familiar with their surroundings, had the necessary technical and logistic skills to deal with them, and possessed the requisite tools and draught-animals. Words like the French *vilain* and English *villain* suggest how peasants were generally looked down upon, but their special knowledge was very much in demand if a king and queen were to be conducted safely across the Alps through the ice and snow.

The Safety of Pilgrims (pp. 191ff)

Very few reports exist of panics or human catastrophes occurring at places frequented by masses of pilgrims or fairgoers. This suggests that local authorities responsible for public well-being were able to cope with problems that increased with the size of the transient population. During the first Holy Year (1300), Rome is said to have managed to accommodate one million pilgrims. Many matters had to be considered well in advance: the provision of massive amounts of food and drink, affordable lodgings and sufficient drinking water, caring for the sick and handicapped, and seeing that bridges and ferries were safe for greatly increased numbers. We learn from Dante that Rome's traffic moved on one-way streets, perhaps inspired by the way in which the movements of masses of pilgrims were regulated in the city's three- and five-aisle basilicas. Local and regional businesses, as well as shops and street-sellers, adapted to seasonal peaks in demand; the late Middle Ages were already acquainted with baking ovens mounted on carts.

Keeping the peace was one of the most important achievements for the sites of pilgrimages, markets and fairs. The interests and sensitivities of thousands of people had to be taken into account; and locals and visitors alike had to be protected against swindlers, thieves, and troublemakers, whether in the streets, at inns, at market-stands, and, last but not least, at sacred sites, where natives of different, often mutually hostile, lands engaged in rivalry for the best place to worship. For example, in Einsiedeln in 1561 agents in disguise were employed to protect pilgrims from being molested.

The high level of travel on pilgrimages had lasting results. Christian and Muslim countries alike exploited the large, religiously motivated gatherings as starting points for trade fairs. Pilgrimages and fairs were usually separate occasions, but, as pilgrims sought out ever more shrines and merchants visited ever more fairs, the network of roads that both groups travelled grew ever denser. That facilitated communications between civil authorities responsible for arranging for pilgrimages and fairs, and also between the organizers of Imperial Diets and church synods, for which arrangements regarding provisioning, accommodation, and security also had to be made. Furthermore, pilgrimages and journeys to trade fairs accelerated the spread of innovations in the areas of law, commerce, and technology. Pilgrims visiting the popular sites of Canterbury and Compostela, which lay some distance from medieval cultural and political centres, helped to link England and Spain more closely with other areas of Europe.

Travelling craftsmen and artists (pp. 221ff)

In the late Middle Ages, artists and craftsmen reached countries on their travels that, from the vantage point of the West, lay 'at the edge of Europe'. Following his conquest of Constantinople in 1453, the Ottoman ruler Mehmet II summoned Italian artists to his court. One fruit of this all too brief cultural opening of the Muslim empire to the West is the portrait of the Sultan painted by the Venetian Gentile Bellini at Istanbul in 1479. The Grand Dukes of Muscovy regarded themselves as the intellectual and spiritual successors to Byzantium, now in Muslim hands. After they had cast off the 'yoke of the Tatars', they recruited skilled architects from Italy and Germany to serve them, a momentous step that is often, unjustly, thought not to have taken place until the time of Peter the Great. The construction of the Church of the Ascension of Mary, 'Uspenskij Sobor', in Moscow, which Ivan III commissioned in 1475 from the great Bolognese architect Aristotele Fioravanti, praised as 'Heaven on Earth' by Josef Volockij, a contemporary theologian, lent new impulses to Russian architecture. The cultural exchange evidently went in both directions: Russians, who had travelled to Jerusalem and the monasteries of the Sinai for centuries, began to appear occasionally as travellers to Europe. The most famous Old Russian travel journal, however, concerns a trip to India, *A Journey over Three Seas*, which Afanasij Nikitin, a merchant of Tver, made in 1466–72.

In eastern Europe, men were also sought who could mine precious metals and jewels, lead, copper, tin, and zinc, from the depths of the earth. The work was extremely difficult and dangerous. Miners were threatened by floods or falling rocks; the shafts were usually so low that they had to work kneeling or lying down; the burning of the lamps they had to carry consumed the oxygen they needed to breathe. Ecclesiastical or secular princes wishing to exploit the mineral resources of the Ore mountains, the Beskydy mountains, or the Carpathians must have made very attractive offers to miners working in the Harz, the Black Forest, and the Vosges mountains. Why else would such experienced workers travel such distances? Why take the risk of starting anew elsewhere? Such miners could improve their status in regard to laws of inheritance, for example. A ruler interested in developing his country offered similar privileges to merchants he wished to attract. The rule of law spread more quickly; often too even local plaintiffs could prevail at trials.

Travel Expenses and Finance

Travellers were responsible for finding any goods and services that they themselves, their companions, mounts and draught-animals would require on the journey. They had to pay for food, drink, and accommodation, and procure suitable clothing, especially shoes, or, at least, new soles, as needed. Cloaks and other garments needed to be cleaned and mended from time to time. Tolls for roads and bridges and fares for ships and ferries were another expense, as were 'gratuities'; if we regard the latter only as bribes, we fail to understand the social and economic context of the time. Money-changers, guides, translators, and armed guards demanded payment, and the certification of documents and the soundness of a traveller's health, possibly several times on the same journey, was not to be had free of charge. Expenses needed to be anticipated for medical care and hygienic measures involving diet, bathing, physicians, and apothecaries; a bone-setter, in cases of a sprained ankle or a broken leg, might even be required. Coachmen, blacksmiths, and cartwrights had to be paid. Travellers were also obliged to provide donations to the monasteries or hospitals they visited, as well as alms for the needy. Expenses for gambling and brothels were also a possibility. Pilgrims could expect to pay a few pence at confession and to buy pilgrims' badges, and if they had pledged to make a pilgrimage, they were obliged to make a votive gift. Travellers often forgot that living was not without expense at home either, and were often indignant about prices they deemed excessively high.

Bridge Tolls

These were sometimes levied according to the traveller's station in life. An archbishop might pay 20 shillings, a bishop 15 (both prelates were likely to be on horseback), a horseman with his mount 2 shillings, and a woman on foot 12 pennies, probably equal to 1 shilling; if she was pregnant, half again was levied for the unborn child, totalling 18 pence or 1½ shillings. These are tentative statements, from conclusions based on a document from fourteenth-century Tuscany. Currency units dating back to Charlemagne's time (one pound equals twenty shillings, one shilling equals twelve pence) were still in use in Great Britain as late as the 1970s, so we can only assume that the system was current in Lucca during the fourteenth century. Certainty is assured only if we compare subtotal and totals with the running entries in the original documents or in critical editions.

In winter, expenses for clothing and accommodations increased markedly, as it was not possible to walk barefoot or sleep outdoors, and horses had to be shod more often. As darkness fell earlier, mountain passes had to be negotiated more quickly, possibly requiring a strong man who knew the way to shovel a path through the snow. Armed escorts were more expensive than in summer. This was the case too in turbulent times, as more bandits were on the roads.

In order not to impose upon strangers, travellers had to take means sufficient to their journeys. Secular and ecclesiastical dignitaries, merchants and craftsmen, townsmen and farmers, all met their needs in their own ways. As is the case today, there was no upper limit to travel costs. When Duke Henry the Lion travelled overland to Jerusalem in 1172 with a large entourage, he could afford to bring his own supplies along, in addition to cash and valuables: cartloads of flour and wine, meat and fish. In 1172, returning from the Crusades, King Richard the Lionheart was taken captive, which obliged his subjects to pay an astronomical ransom for his release.

In the fourteenth century, the costs for a journey from Venice to the Holy Land, arranged to include all necessities and lasting approximately eight to twelve weeks, were estimated to be 25 to 40 guilders. The journal of a trip to the Holy Land from Engelberg, Switzerland in 1519 makes it clear that much more might be spent, in this case 300 guilders, the price at the time of a stately house. The following discussion will deal chiefly with the experiences of Crusaders and pilgrims, because these sorts of travellers have tended to leave better records.

A Crusade or pilgrimage might have been financed in several ways. They presented no difficulties for people with huge amounts of money, but there were not many of those. Crusaders often sold their feudal manors in the hope of gaining an estate of similar value or greater. Godfrey of Bouillon, one of the leaders of the First Crusade (1096–99), even sold his family's ancestral castle! The Landgrave Ludwig of Thuringia, the husband of St Elisabeth, demanded from Emperor Frederick II, as a price for joining the Crusade, a guaranteed compensation of 5,000 marks to cover his expenses, in addition to other favours. Others pawned their possessions, hoping to redeem them after returning home with increased wealth. Ecclesiastical institutions often acted as pawnbrokers in these matters, forgoing interest charges on the loan and granting other special conditions.

Frequently, such loans were made in association with a last will and testament. Church and secular authorities urged pilgrims embarking on long journeys to make wills providing for, among other things, the status and support of a spouse, under-age children, and other relatives. In addition, parties might agree upon how long the former owner of a defaulted estate could take to buy it back.

In France and England, the crown levied a tax of up to 10% of income and movable property on towns and clergy to finance Crusades. As this measure was effective, King Louis IX, the Saint, taxed his entire realm to pay for the first of his Crusades (1248–54). It cost some 1.3 million *livres tournois*, roughly eleven to twelve times the crown's annual income. One might regard these levies as forerunners of today's general taxation, which makes demands of everyone.

Poor people too could go on long journeys, especially pilgrimages. Christ's saying 'I was a stranger and ye took me in' (Matthew 25: 35) lent them support, as did the Church, which was to use a quarter of its receipts to help the poor and strangers, as advised by Pope Gelasius I (d. 496). Companies of better-off travellers often took the hungry and in need under their wing and supplied them with food and drink and a night's lodging, or the fare for passage on a boat. Legends and pilgrimage books cultivated the ideal of the prosperous pilgrim who shares his food with the poor. People then believed that such actions would be rewarded in Heaven.

The material and spiritual infrastructures that gave even poor people opportunities to travel lasted into the modern period. A pitiable appearance and polite behaviour melted people's hearts. If a supplicant was entertaining and reliable, and asked for little, even money might be forthcoming. This is illustrated in the seventeenth century by the pilgrimage that takes the author Grimmelshausen's hero Simplicissimus from Germany, then devastated by the Thirty Years War, to Einsiedeln in Switzerland. Simplicissimus survives by begging, but refuses to take money: 'Pilgrims should have no money.' This results in people giving him far more food, drink, and lodging than he could have afforded with a few coins.

A woodcut by Hans Burgkmair, dating from about 1500, shows four pilgrims resting briefly in a lightly wooded area: two men, a woman and a small child, probably a young family and perhaps the mother's brother. There are several reasons why a child might have been taken along on such travels. He could not be left at home unattended; if he had, by some miracle, escaped a deadly danger, his parents might undertake the pilgrimage to offer thanks. Children can learn and wish to do so. On the road, they would have learned that it was best to pay innkeepers, coachmen, and tax officers in the presence of witnesses. In time they would have learned how to determine directions even if the sun was not shining. They learned to recognize which people, inns, and forests it was better to avoid. They learned new languages far more quickly than adults. An alert young man who had gone on several pilgrimages with his parents might one day be told by them: 'Wilhelm, next spring we want to travel to Rome. We want you to be our guide and translator. We will pay all of your expenses and reward you with a guilder. Wouldn't you like that?' Many a penniless young man might have seen the world under similar circumstances.

Many journeys served several purposes at once, easing the pain of the expenses involved. To take one example, a merchant travelling from Danzig to distant Bari, to offer thanks to St. Nicholas for rescuing him from peril at sea, also had a keen eye for markets and goods. In financing the trip from his savings, he took into account the fact that he would find business opportunities on the way. It was no accident that places like St Denis, Siegburg, and Zurzach were sites for both pilgrimages and trade fairs. To which class of travellers did people then consider their pious, yet commercially energetic, contemporaries to belong? Did they deserve the privileges that were customarily reserved for pilgrims?

Travellers often carried valuables which they gradually sold to pay their expenses. A will from Lübeck, for example, stipulates that an heir should use the proceeds from selling a silver belt to finance a pilgrimage to Santiago. If he thought that he might get a better price on the way, in Antwerp perhaps, he should not sell it before reaching there. Another will stipulated that the deceased's best cloak be sold to pay for a journey to Aachen and Thann in upper Alsace. Valuable rings and a golden chain, carefully hidden, were kept in reserve until needed on the journey.

Precious metals and stones were recognized as tradable goods and as votive gifts. Travellers from the Baltic regions, for example, might bring amber, wax, and valuable furs. Those returning from the Holy Land often brought back spices, which weighed little and increased in price with the distance from where they were purchased. Pilgrims in Venice, the final port of their voyage, bought luxury goods, which they sold on the road or after reaching their homes. Customs regulations also suggest how uncertain the boundary was between piety and commercial interest: only what pilgrims needed for their journey was customs-free. It was assumed that officials were able to estimate pilgrimage costs as well as the value of merchandise.

Trade is not a one-way street. According to legend, the following occurred repeatedly in Jerusalem. Pilgrims from the Rhineland carried medals and rings 'with which they had touched the relics of the Three Kings'. Visitors to the Holy Land from India were convinced that such relics had curative powers. And clearly, such relics were traded in Jerusalem's hostelries. Centuries later, in 1748, a former hermit from Cologne was said to have obtained rosaries and 'Three-Kings-cards' cheaply; the latter were imprinted with a prayer and a picture of the shrine of the revered Three Kings from the Orient, often with only their initials: C(aspar), M(elchior), B(althasar); a 'certificate of authenticity' affirmed that the cards and rosaries had touched the sacred reliquary. Travellers could sell these devotional objects, which became more valuable the further they travelled from Cologne, to cover their expenses. In 1786, J. W. Goethe encountered German pilgrims in northern Italy who presented 'consecrated little cards imprinted with a picture of the three kings and Latin prayers' to a boatman to thank him for transporting them to Venice free of charge.

It is likely that relatives, friends, neighbours, associations, and similar groups joined forces to finance travels more frequently than has been recorded. If someone wished to make a pilgrimage to Jerusalem, 'every brother and sister must give him a penny, and if his goal is Santiago or Rome, a halfpenny'. So it is written in the Statutes of the Guild of Tailors in Lincoln, England, which set down in 1389 what must long have been customary. Such pooling of resources made it possible even for less wealthy men and women to see something of the world. It was assumed that the journey would redound to a pilgrim's state of grace, in which those who had helped him to make it would also share. They supported him materially with money, socially by escorting him to the city gates when he departed and welcoming him with festivities upon his return, and spiritually with their prayers.

Sometimes, an 'employer' paid for a journey. Returning from the New World in 1493, Columbus sailed into a dangerous storm. Surviving it, presumably with the help of God, he had his crew pledge to make votive pilgrimages and to draw lots to determine who should travel to the holy places to represent all of them. Columbus promised to pay the expenses of a simple sailor who had been chosen.

Men and women who undertook pilgrimages for others were compensated according to an empirical scale of value. If someone had pledged to make a pilgrimage, but could not do so, whatever the reason, he could ask for a pious, reliable person to pray for his soul's salvation in his stead at a particular holy site. In the late Middle Ages, many last wills and testaments provided for such commissions. After the testator's death, his executors sent men and women on journeys to distant holy places, where they prayed for the deceased. The substitute was to travel 'in comfort' and not to have to beg. One such will stipulated that the substitute be 'faithfully rewarded, so that he may pray all the more faithfully for my soul'.

In the fifteenth century, a substitute pilgrim was offered between two and ten silver marks to travel from Lübeck to Aachen, and ten to thirty if he went to Rome, increasing to twenty to forty-five marks for offering prayers on behalf of the deceased during the forty days of Lent. For Santiago, ten to twenty marks sufficed, because a sea voyage was cheaper. A pilgrimage that included visits to Thann in Upper Alsace and Einsiedeln in Switzerland was to be had for ten marks, while having prayers offered to St Olaf in Trondheim cost fifteen. A woman assigned to travel to Güstrow in Mecklenburg received ten marks because, going barefoot in a woollen garment, she carried a redoubled penitential burden. From sixty up to one hundred marks were offered for pilgrimages to Jerusalem; if a priest accepted an assignment to pray there, he received 130 marks. A will might stipulate that pilgrims planning to go on their own account be given a partial stipend in return for offering prayers for the deceased at their destinations.

A comparison with actual prices of the time helps us to understand the value of the stipends. Between 1376 and 1450, the Lübeck mark contained sixteen shillings [ß], one shilling twelve pence [d]). A drayhorse cost eight marks, an ox four, a cow twenty-two shillings, twenty eggs 1½d, a pound of butter 4d., 100 kilograms of rye six shillings, a pair of shoes three shillings, a pair of boots elevenshillings. A substitute pilgrim bound from Lübeck to Santiago for the maximum fee of twenty marks was thus receiving the equivalent of five oxen for his pains.

The wealthy could afford to send people to various pilgrimage sites in their names. Queen Margarete of Denmark may have set a record in this regard. In 1411, she made available 2,000 Lübeck marks so that 140 pilgrims could go to forty-four sites in Europe and Palestine. A further donation of 3,000 marks, to enable the needy to visit sacred sites and pray for the queen's salvation, provided for training for impoverished clerics, alms for the needy, pilgrimages at home and abroad, and support for the welfare of pilgrims. From the end of the twelfth century, it was also possible for for someone who had made a pledge to go on a Crusade to fulfil that obligation by supplying a paid substitute; later on, a financial contribution to a Crusader's equipment sufficed.

It was important for well-to-do travellers to have trustworthy companions for aid and protection, as guards, guides, and translators, and as signs of their status. In 1064–65, Abbot Richard of St Vannes undertook a pilgrimage with 700 people, whose expenses he paid. Within such a company, members helped each other; if someone had a mule that could carry other people's luggage too, they would be happy to pay some of his expenses on the road.

In summer, when farmers needed more workers, some travellers might help with harvesting hay or grain for a few days, receiving in return food, drink, lodging, and perhaps a little money. Construction work on roads and bridges probably offered similar opportunities. Aboard ship, stinking water had to be bailed from the bilges by hand or, later, with pumps. If a passenger performed this task diligently, he might avoid paying the fare. Others helped to transport goods. Near their destination, pilgrims to Santiago carried chunks of chalk to kilns; others carried iron and lead to be used in building the basilica. Such services to the Church, rendered free of charge, might well have provided help for the needy at other places too. Some money could be earned by carrying verbal or written messages, although a pilgrim carrying important letters or valuables risked losing his special legal status. As a messenger, he could not claim privileges reserved, often grudgingly, for pilgrims. In 1118, Diego Gelmirez, Bishop of Santiago, is said to have sent couriers carrying 120 ounces (= 3.3 kg) of gold to Rome. To avoid attention, they were to travel through hostile territory dressed as pilgrims. The Bishop was obviously unconcerned that this deception might reflect badly on pilgrims in general.

A miniature from a late-fourteenth-century chronicle from Bologna shows a pilgrim before a papermaker's shop. In addition to describing it, a historian would wish to interpret it as evidence of processes and developments from a distant age. The picture suggests that craftsmen, while on pilgrimages, also learned about new devices and methods from their colleagues in other lands. May we regard the picture as evidence of early industrial espionage? The artist may well have had something quite different in mind. It is quite conceivable that the pilgrim received a little money to ease his journey, in return for which he was asked, as a favour: 'Look out for water wheels and bellows in a certain valley; interesting things are going on there', or: 'Bring me back a strong mare that I can use for my breeding stock.' Mere speculation? Exporting horses was prohibited repeatedly, as no ruler wanted to risk losing the upper hand gained with such an important instrument of warfare.

During the 1260s, Jacobus, a Dominican monk and Bishop of Genoa, recounted with disarming frankness, in one of his Legends, how travel costs might be covered in unconventional ways. Mary, later revered as a saint, tells how she once wished to travel from Egypt to Jerusalem to worship before the Holy Cross. When the boatmen demanded their fare, 'I replied: "I cannot pay it, but take my body as payment." So they took me along, and my body provided for the fare.'

TOWARDS THE MODERN ERA (pp. 240ff)

From the late Middle Ages, more and more roads were paved and terrain surveyed for new ones by competent, certified professionals. People were already using gunpowder to construct and widen them. These new techniques demonstrate that, alongside the general desire to travel, the infrastructure necessary to this was improving rapidly and making it an easier experience. Once streets and plazas were paved, cities were more attractive. As they were cleaner, it was healthier to live there.

Travellers demanded all kinds of goods and services. They fostered the dispersion of goods, such as Peter's pence to Rome, and carried ideas, poetic themes, and artistic motifs (and also, less romantically, germs) everywhere. Thanks to them, services of many different kinds were adapted, and refined, such as the loading and unloading of goods.

I would argue that a pan-European sense of community emerged. It may be visibly expressed in an allegorical image: an allegorical map of Europe (see the illustration below), represented as a ruler and not appearing altogether sympathetic, embraces 'Bvlgaria' and 'Moscovia', both influenced by Byzantium, and more naturally, 'Vngaria', 'Polonia', 'Lithuania', 'Livonia', as well as the lands of middle-, southern, eastern, and western Europe. Could the countless roads and rivers not be seen as nerve pathways and blood vessels of this diverse yet unitary organism? And travellers as the corpuscles and impulses that supply all parts with vital energies and substances?

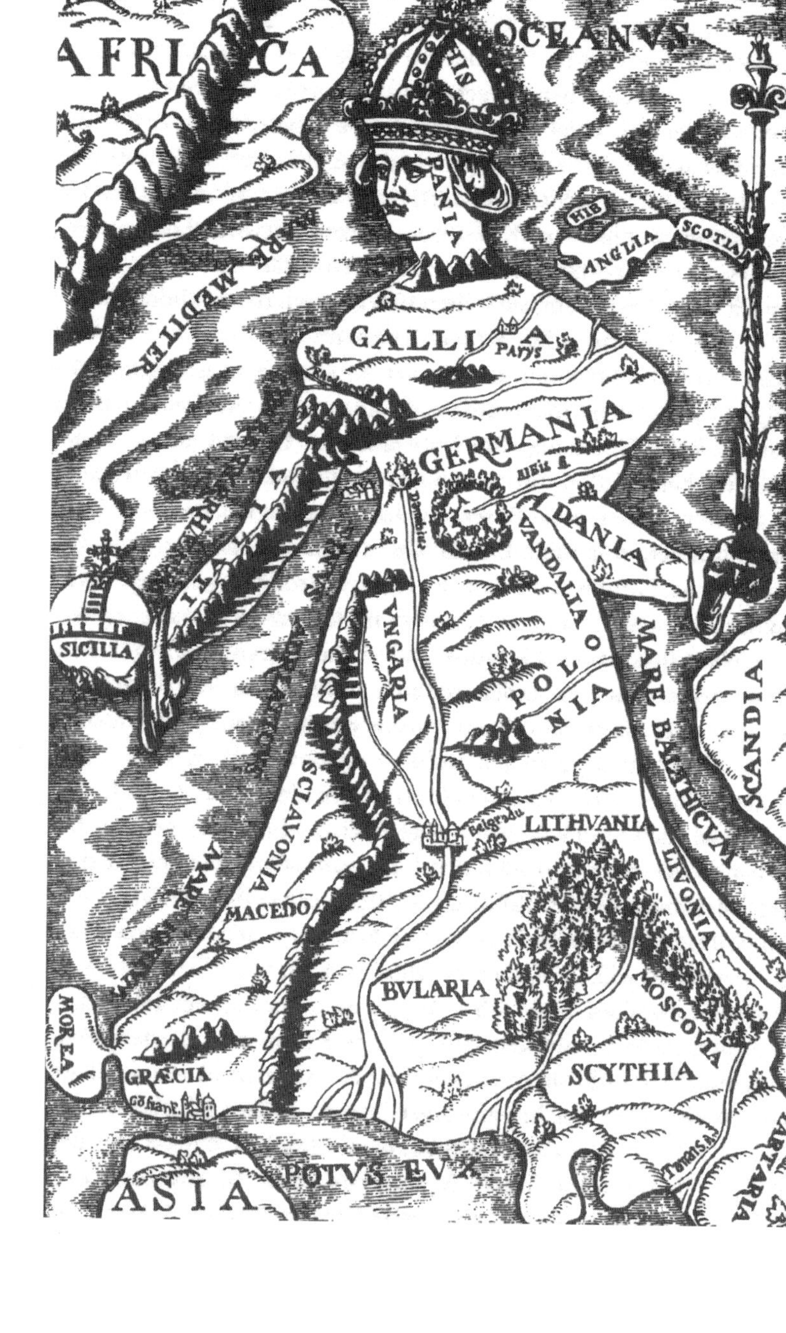
AFRI CA
OCEANVS
HIS
PANIA
MARE MEDITER
HIB
ANGLIA
SCOTIA
GALLI A
Parys
GERMANIA
DANIA
VANDALIA
SICILIA
VNGARIA
POLO NIA
MARE BALTHICVM
SCANDIA
SCLAVONIA
Belgradu
LITHVANIA
LIVONIA
MACEDO
BVLARIA
MOSCOVIA
MOREA
GRÆCIA
SCYTHIA
ASIA
POTVS EVX
TARTARIA

FURTHER READING

Abelard, Peter. *The Letters of Heloise and Abelard.* Edited and translated by Mary M. McLaughlin with Bonnie Wheeler. Basingstoke: Palgrave Macmillan, 2009.

Abulafia, David. *Frederick II: a Medieval Emperor.* Oxford: Oxford University Press, 1992.

Adamson, Melitta Weiss. *Food in Medieval Times.* Westport: Greenwood, 2004.

Anderson, Charles S. *Augsburg Historical Atlas of Christianity in the Middle Ages and Reformation.* Minneapolis: Augsburg, 1967.

The Anglo-Saxon Chronicle. Edited and translated by George N. Garmonsway. London: Dent, 1962.

Bailey, Lisa K., Lindsay Diggelmann, and Kim M. Phillips (eds). *Old Worlds, New Worlds: European Cultural Encounters, c. 1000–c. 1760.* Turnhout: Brepols, 2009.

Barber, Malcolm. *The New Knighthood: a History of the Order of the Temple.* Cambridge: Cambridge University Press, 1994.

Barber, Richard W. *The Penguin Guide to Medieval Europe.* Harmondsworth: Penguin, 1984.

Barbero, Alessandro. *Charlemagne: Father of a Continent.* Berkeley: University of California Press, 2004.

Barnavi, Eli. *A Historical Atlas of the Jewish People: from the Time of the Patriarchs to the Present.* New York: Schocken, 2002.

Bartlett, Robert. *The Making of Europe: Conquest, Colonization, and Cultural Change, 950–1350.* Princeton: Princeton University Press, 1993.

Bassett, Steven (ed.). *Death in Towns: Urban Responses to the Dying and the Dead, 100–1600.* Leicester: Leicester University Press, 1992.

Battuta, Ibn. *Travels in Asia and Africa, 1325–1354.* Edited and translated by Hamilton A. R. Gibb. London: Routledge & Kegan Paul, 1983.

Bede. *The Ecclesiastical History of the English People.* Edited by Bertram Colgrave, translated by R. A. B. Mynors. Oxford: Clarendon Press, 1969.

Bédier, Joseph. *The Romance of Tristan and Iseult.* New York: Pantheon, 1945.

Binski, Paul. *Medieval Death: Ritual and Representation.* Ithaca: Cornell University Press, 1996.

Blondé, B. et al. (eds). *Buyers and Sellers: Retail Circuits and Practices in Mediaeval and Early Modern Europe.* Turnhout: Brepols, 2006.

Boccaccio, Giovanni. *The Decameron.* Edited and translated by G. H. McWilliam. Harmondsworth: Penguin, 1972.

Bork, Robert O. and Andrea Kann (eds). *The Art, Science, and Technology of Medieval Travel.* Aldershot: Ashgate, 2008.

Borst, Arno. *Medieval Worlds: Barbarians, Heretics, and Artists in the Middle Ages.* Chicago: University of Chicago Press, 1992.

Boyer, Marjorie Nice. *Medieval French Bridges: A History.* Cambridge, Mass.: Medieval Academy, 1976.

Braudel, Fernand. *The Perspective of the World.* New York: Harper & Row, 1984.

Brito, Bernardo Gomes de. *The Tragic History of the Sea, 1589–1622.* Edited and translated by Charles R. Boxer. Cambridge: Hakluyt Society, 1959.

Brodman, James. *Charity and Religion in Medieval Europe.* Washington, D.C.: Catholic University of America Press, 2009.

Buisseret, David. *The Oxford Companion to World Exploration.* Oxford: Oxford University Press, 2007.

Byrne, Joseph Patrick. *Daily Life during the Black Death.* Westport: Greenwood, 2006.

The Cambridge History of the Byzantine Empire. Edited by Jonathan Shepard. Cambridge: Cambridge University Press, 2008.

Campbell, Mary B. *The Witness and the Other World: Exotic European Travel Writing, 400–1600.* Ithaca: Cornell University Press, 1988.

Cantor, Norman F. *In the Wake of the Plague: the Black Death and the World it Made.* New York: Free Press, 2001.

Casson, Lionel. *Ships and Seamanship in the Ancient World.* Princeton: Princeton University Press, 1986.

Chaucer, Geoffrey. *The Canterbury Tales.* Edited by Nevill Coghill. Harmondsworth: Penguin, 2003 (revised edn).

Chaunu, Pierre. *European Expansion in the Later Middle Ages.* Amsterdam: North-Holland, 1979.

Chronicles of the Crusades, by Jean de Joinville and Geffroy de Villehardouin. Translated by Caroline Smith. Harmondsworth: Penguin, 2009.

Ciggaar, Krijna N. *Western Travellers to Constantinople: the West and Byzantium, 962–1204.* Leiden: Brill, 1996.

Cipolla, Carlo M. *Before the Industrial Revolution: European Society and Economy, 1000–1700.* New York: Norton, 1980.

Cohen, Mark R. *Under Crescent and Cross: the Jews in the Middle Ages.* Princeton: Princeton University Press, 1994.

Columbus, Christopher. *A Synoptic Edition of the Log of Columbus's First Voyage.* Edited and translated by Francesca Lardicci and Valeria Bertolucci Pizzorusso. Turnhout: Brepols, 1999.

Constable, Olivia Remie. *Housing the Stranger in the Medieval World: Lodging, Trade, and Travel in Late Antiquity and the Middle Ages.* Cambridge: Cambridge University Press, 2003.

Corrêa, Gaspar. *The Three Voyages of Vasco da Gama and his Viceroyalty*. Translated by Henry E. J. Stanley. London: Hakluyt Society, 1869; rptd New York: Franklin, 1963.

Davies, Horton, *Holy Days and Holidays: the Medieval Pilgrimage to Compostela.* Lewisburg, PA: Bucknell University Press, 1982.

Denecke, Dietrich and Gareth Shaw (eds). *Urban Historical Geography: Recent Progress in Britain and Germany.* Cambridge: Cambridge University Press, 1988.

Dietz, Maribel. *Wandering Monks, Virgins, and Pilgrims: Ascetic Travel in the Mediterranean World, AD 300–800.* University Park: Pennsylvania State University Press, 2005.

Dollinger, Philippe. *The German Hansa.* Stanford: Stanford University Press, 1970.

Dürer, Albrecht. *Writings.* Edited and translated by William M. Conway. New York: Philosophical Library, 1958.

Erasmus, Desiderius. *Twenty Select Colloquies of Erasmus, translated out of the Latin by Sir Roger L'Estrange, 1680.* Introduction by Charles Whibley. London: Chapman & Dodd, 1922.

Evans, Gillian R. *Bernard of Clairvaux.* Oxford: Oxford University Press, 2000.

Ferguson, Wallace K. *Europe in Transition, 1300–1520.* Boston: Houghton Mifflin, 1962.

Firebaugh, W. C. *The Inns of the Middle Ages.* Chicago: P. Covici, 1924.

Friedman, John Block and Kristen Mossler Figg (eds). *Trade, Travel, and Exploration in the Middle Ages: an Encyclopedia.* New York: Garland, 2000.

Gerhold, Dorian. *Carriers and Coachmasters: Trade and Travel before the Turnpikes.* Chichester: Phillimore, 2005.

Gies, Frances and Joseph Gies. *Cathedral, Forge, and Waterwheel: Technology and Invention in the Middle Ages.* London: HarperCollins, 1994.

Gimpel, Jean. *The Medieval Machine. The Industrial Revolution of the Middle Ages.* New York: Holt, Rinehart and Winston, 1976.

Graham-Campbell, James. *The Viking World.* London: Frances Lincoln, 2001.

—— and Magdalena Valor. *The Archaeology of Medieval Europe.* Aarhus: Aarhus University Press, 2008.

Harrison, David. *The Bridges of Medieval England: Transport and Society 400–1800.* Oxford: Clarendon, 2004.

Hartmann von Aue. *Arthurian Romances, Tales, and Lyric Poetry.* Translated with a commentary by Frank Tobin, Kim Vivian, and Richard H. Lawson. University Park: Pennsylvania State University Press, 2001.

Haywood, John. *The Penguin Historical Atlas of the Vikings.* Harmondsworth: Penguin, 1995.

Heinzelmann, Martin. *Gregory of Tours: History and Society in the Sixth Century.* Cambridge: Cambridge University Press, 2001.

Henderson, John. *The Renaissance Hospital: Healing the Body and Healing the Soul.* New Haven: Yale University Press, 2006.

Herlihy, David and Samuel Kline Cohn. *The Black Death and the Transformation of the West.* Cambridge: Harvard University Press, 1997.

The History of Doctor Johann Faustus. Edited and translated by H. G. Haile. Urbana: University of Illinois Press, 1965.

Homer. *The Odyssey.* Translated by Robert Fagles. Harmondsworth: Penguin, 2006.

Howard, Donald Roy. *Writers and Pilgrims: Medieval Pilgrimage Narratives and their Posterity.* Berkeley: University of California Press, 1980.

Huffman, Joseph P. *The Social Politics of Medieval Diplomacy: Anglo-German Relations (1066–1307).* Ann Arbor: University of Michigan Press, 2000.

Hull, Caroline S. and Andrew Jotischky. *The Penguin Historical Atlas of the Bible Lands.* Harmondsworth: Penguin, 2009.

Hupchick, Dennis P. and Harold E. Cox. *The Palgrave Concise Historical Atlas of Eastern Europe.* Basingstoke: Palgrave, 2001.

Hutchinson, Gillian. *Medieval Ships and Shipping.* Rutherford: Fairleigh Dickinson UP, 1994.

Jacobus de Voragine. *The Golden Legend.* Translated by Christopher Stace. Harmondsworth: Penguin, 2006

Jotischky, Andrew and Caroline S. Hull. *The Penguin Historical Atlas of the Medieval World.* Harmondsworth: Penguin, 2005.

Kinder, Hermann and Werner Hilgemann. *The Penguin Atlas of World History.* 2 vols, Harmondsworth: Penguin, 2004 (new edn).

King, Russell. *Atlas of Human Migration.* Buffalo: Firefly, 2007.

Komroff, Manuel. *Contemporaries of Marco Polo.* New York: Boni & Liveright, 1928.

Konstam, Angus. *Historical Atlas of the Crusades.* New York: Checkmark, 2002.

——. *Historical Atlas of Exploration: 1492–1600.* New York: Checkmark, 2000.

——. *Historical Atlas of the Viking World.* New York: Checkmark, 2002.

—— and Roger Kean. *Atlas of Medieval Europe.* New York: Checkmark, 2000.

Labarge, Margaret Wade. *Medieval Travellers: the Rich and the Restless.* Norton: New York, 1983.

Le Goff, Jacques. *Time, Work, and Culture in the Middle Ages.* Translated by Arthur Goldhammer. Chicago: Chicago University Press, 1980.

Leighton, Albert C. *Transport and Communication in Early Medieval Europe AD 500–1100.* New York: Barnes & Noble, 1972.

Littell, Franklin H. *Historical Atlas of Christianity.* London: Continuum, 2001.

Logan, F. Donald. *A History of the Church in the Middle Ages.* London: Routledge, 2002.

MacLean, Ian. *Learning and the Market Place: Essays in the History of the Early Modern Book.* Leiden: Brill, 2009.

McCormick, Michael. *Origins of the European Economy: Communications and Commerce, AD 300–900.* Cambridge: Cambridge University Press, 2001.

McEvedy, Colin and David Woodruffe. *The New Penguin Atlas of Medieval History.* Harmondsworth: Penguin, 1992.

McGrail, Seán. *Boats of the World: from the Stone Age to Medieval Times.* Oxford: Oxford University Press, 2004.

Marco Polo. *The Travels of Marco Polo.* Edited and translated by R. E. Latham. Harmondsworth: Penguin, 1958.

Montaigne, Michel de. *The Journal of Montaigne's Travels in Italy by way of Switzerland and Germany in 1580 and 1581.* Edited and translated by W. G. Waters. London: J. Murray, 1903.

Moore, Robert I. *The First European Revolution, c. 970–1215.* Oxford: Blackwell, 2000.

Newton, Arthur Percival, ed. *Travel and Travellers of the Middle Ages.* New York: Knopf, 1926.

The Nibelungenlied: Prose Translation. Translated by A. T. Hatto. Harmondsworth: Penguin, 1965.

Nicolle, David. *Historical Atlas of the Islamic World.* New York: Checkmark, 2003.

The Oxford History of Medieval Europe. Edited by George Holmes. Oxford: Oxford University Press, 1988.

The Oxford Illustrated History of the Crusades. Edited by Jonathan Riley-Smith. Oxford: Oxford University Press, 1995.

Petrarch. *Selections from the Canzoniere and Other Works.* Edited and translated by Mark Musa. Oxford: Oxford University Press, 1985.

Piggott, Stuart. *Wagon, Chariot, and Carriage: Symbol and Status in the History of Transport.* London: Thames & Hudson, 1992.

Platter, Thomas. *Thomas Platter's Travels in England.* Edited and translated by Clare Williams. London: Cape, 1937.

Plutarch. *The Makers of Rome: Nine Lives.* Edited and translated by Ian Scott-Kilvert. Harmondsworth: Penguin, 1965.

Procopius. *History of the Wars, Secret History, and Buildings.* Edited and translated by Averil Cameron. New York: Twayne, 1967.

Pryor, John H. *Commerce, Shipping, and Naval Warfare in the Medieval Mediterranean.* Aldershot: Ashgate, 1987.

Riché, Pierre. *Daily Life in the World of Charlemagne.* Philadelphia: University of Pennsylvania Press, 1978.

Riley-Smith, Louise and Jonathan Riley-Smith. *The Crusades: Idea and Reality 1095–1274.* London: Arnold, 1981.

Roberts, Gail. *Atlas of Discovery.* New York: Crown, 1973.

Rose, Susan. *The Medieval Sea*. London: Hambledon and London, 2007.

The Rule of Saint Benedict. Edited and translated by Francis Aidan Gasquet. New York: Cooper Square, 1966.

Ruysbroeck [Rubruck], Willem van. *The Mission of Friar William of Rubruck: His Journey to the Court of the Great Khan Möngke.* Edited and translated by Peter Jackson with David Morgan. London: Hakluyt Society, 1990.

Smith, Virginia. *Clean: a History of Personal Hygiene and Purity.* Oxford: Oxford University Press, 2007.

Stokstad, Marilyn. *Santiago de Compostela in the Age of the Great Pilgrimages.* Norman: Oklahoma University Press, 1978.

Sumption, Jonathan. *The Age of Pilgrimage: the Medieval Journey to God.* Mahwah: Hidden Spring, 2003.

Tacitus. *Agricola and Germany.* Translated by Anthony Birley. Oxford: Oxford University Press, 1999.

Talbot, Charles H. *The Anglo-Saxon Missionaries in Germany: Being the Lives of SS. Willibrod, Boniface, Sturm, Leoba, and Libuin.* New York: Sheed and Ward, 1954.

Thompson, James W. *Economic and Social History of the Middle Ages, 300–1300.* New York: Ungar, 1959.

——, *Economic and Social History in the Later Middle Ages, 1300–1530.* New York: Ungar, 1960.

Tracy, James D. *The Political Economy of Merchant Empires: State Power and World Trade, 1350–1750.* Cambridge: Cambridge University Press, 1991.

Tuchman, Barbara. *A Distant Mirror: the Calamitous Fourteenth Century.* New York: Knopf, 1978

Ure, John. *Pilgrimage: the Great Adventure of the Middle Ages.* New York: Carroll & Graf, 2008.

Vasco da Gama. *Em Nome de Deus: the Journal of the First Voyage of Vasco da Gama to India, 1497–1499.* Translated and edited by Glenn J. Ames. Leiden: Brill, 2009.

Verlinden, Charles. *The Beginnings of Modern Colonization.* Ithaca: Cornell University Press, 1970.

Villard de Honnecourt. *The Sketchbook of Villard de Honnecourt.* Bloomington: Indiana University Press, 1959.

Vince, John N. T. *An Illustrated History of Carts and Wagons.* Bourne End: Spurbooks, 1975.

Waddell, Helen. *The Wandering Scholars.* London: Constable, 1966.

Warner, David A. *Ottonian Germany: the Chronicon of Thietmar of Merseburg.* Manchester: Manchester University Press, 2000.

Webb, Diana. *Medieval European Pilgrimage, c. 700-c. 1500.* Basingstoke: Palgrave Macmillan, 2002.

——, *Pilgrimage in Medieval England*. London: Hambledon and London, 2001.

Wilson, David M. *The Bayeux Tapestry*: *the Complete Tapestry in Colour.* London: Thames & Hudson, 1985.

Woolgar, C. M., D. Serjeantson, and T. Waldron (eds). *Food in Medieval England: Diet and Nutrition*. Oxford: Oxford University Press, 2006.

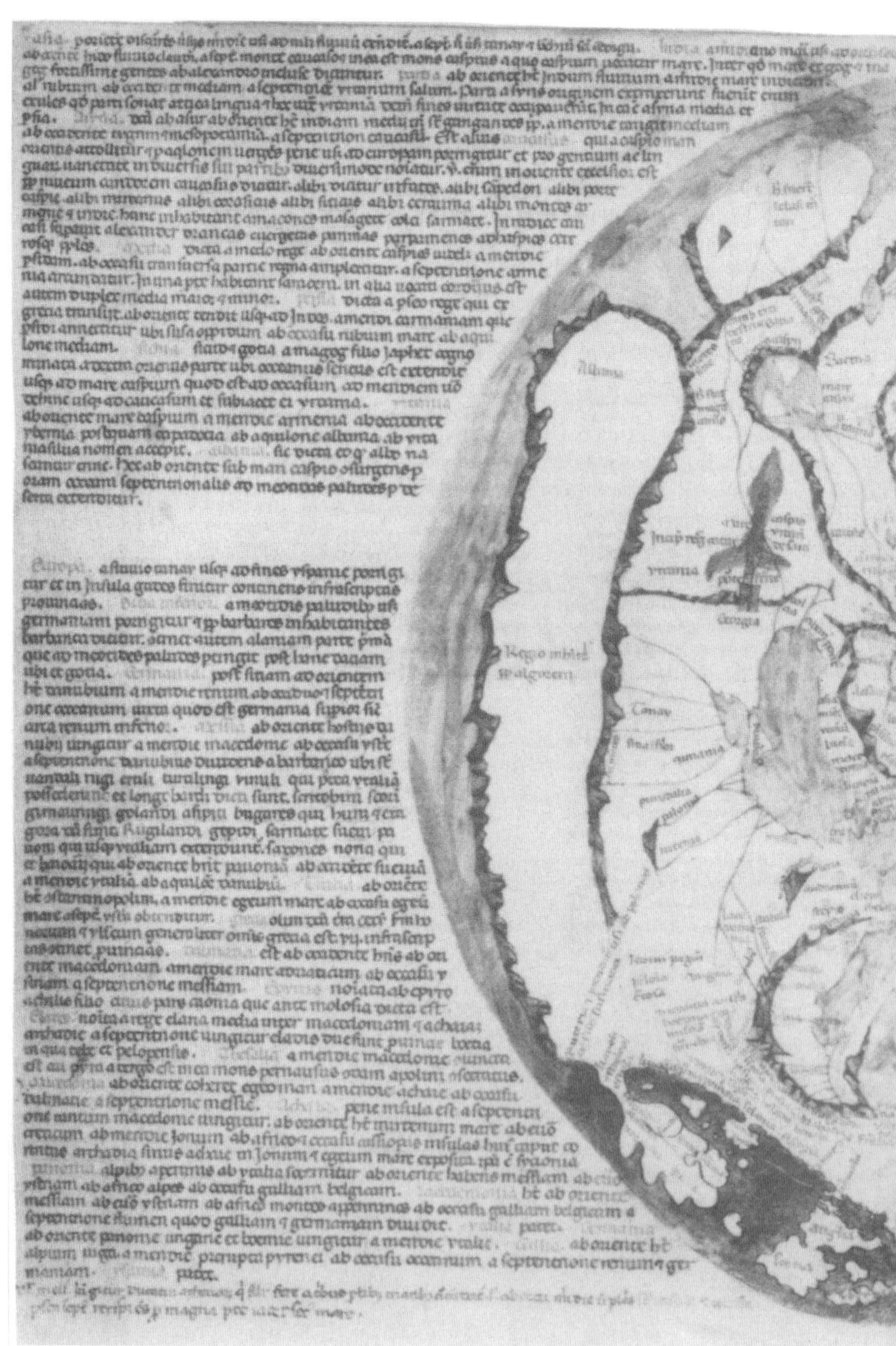

A twelfth-century world map with a detailed description: as was usual, Europe is at the foot, and Jerusalem in the centre.

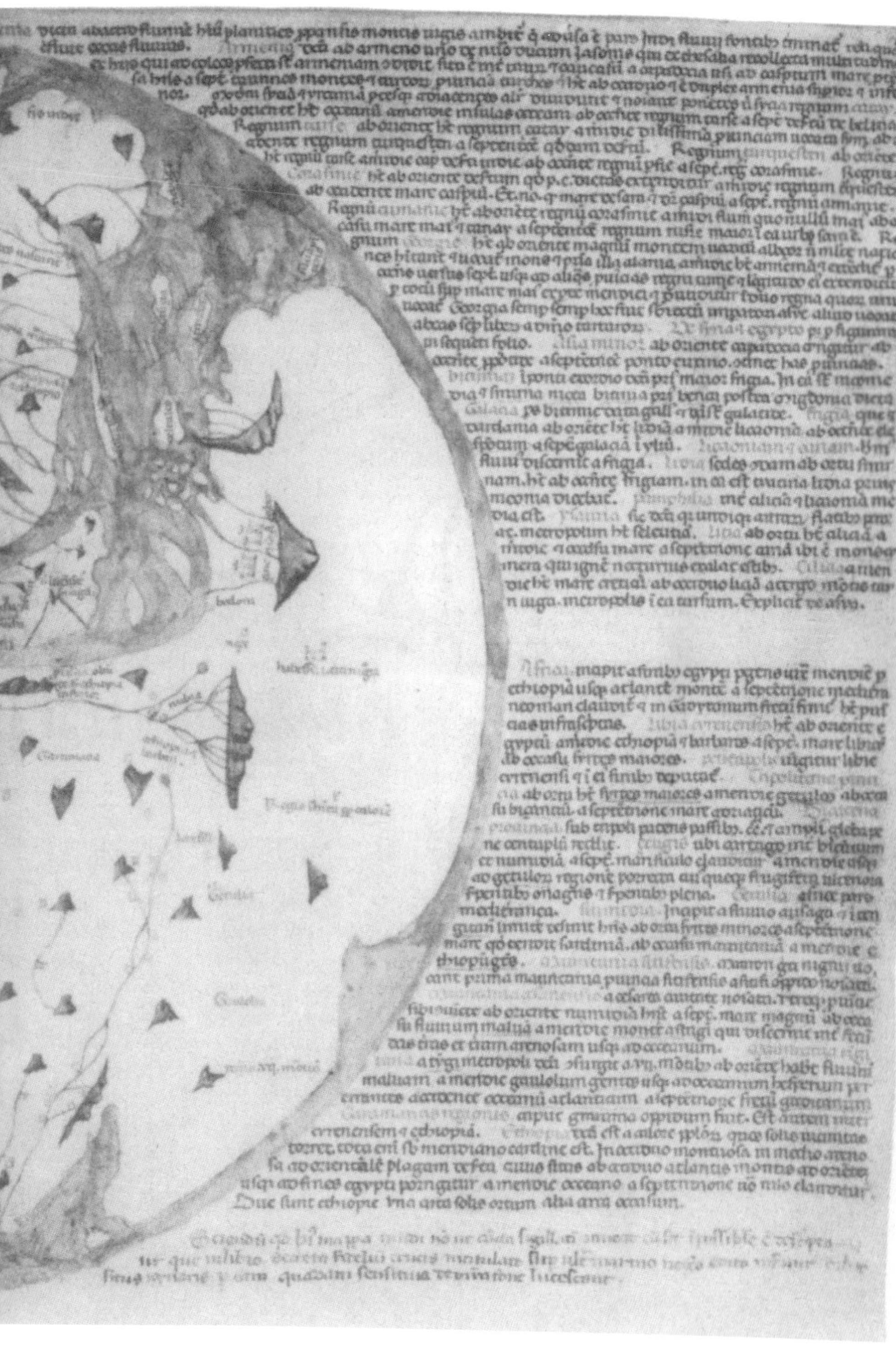